Turfgrasses

Their Management and Use in the Southern Zone

SECOND EDITION

By Richard L. Duble

TEXAS A&M UNIVERSITY PRESS

College Station

The information given herein is for educational purposes only. Reference to commercial products or trade names is made with the understanding that no discrimination is intended and no endorsement by the author or publisher is implied. Products mentioned are not recommended at the exclusion of other products. For all products, follow label directions.

Library of Congress Cataloging-in-Publication Data

Duble, Richard L.
    Turfgrasss: their management and use in the southern zone /
Richard L. Duble.—2nd ed.
      p.   cm.
    Rev. ed. of: Southern turfgrasses. 1989.
    Includes bibliographical references (p.   ) and index.
    ISBN 1-58544-161-9 (pbk.)
    1. Turfgrasses—Southern States.   2. Turf management—
Southern States.   I. Duble, Richard L. Southern turfgrasses.
II. Title.
SB433.D833   1996
635.9'642'0975—dc20   95-39690
                                               CIP

CONTENTS

TABLES

ACKNOWLEDGMENTS

The author wishes to thank the people who contributed so much to the completion of this book. Without their support and encouragment, *Turfgrasses: Their Management and Use in the Southern Zone* would remain on my list of "things to do."

First, thanks to my wife, Shirley, who encouraged and tolerated me throughout the writing of this manuscript. Her understanding and support made this book possible. Thanks to my mentor, graduate advisor, faculty colleague, and friend, Dr. Ethan Holt, who has advised and supported me thoughout my career. He is responsible for all of my professional accomplishments. Also, thanks to Missy Vajdak, who helped prepare all the text, graphs, charts, and tables used throughout the book. Finally, thanks to Janice Drees of the Fuller Corporation for the beautiful drawings that help illustrate the text.

Turfgrasses

Contributions of Turfgrasses

1

Turfgrasses affect the lives of all people living in the United States today. But in the southern states, where turfgrasses grow year-round, their impact on people's lives is great.

A nationwide Harris poll published in *Life* magazine showed that most Americans wished to be surrounded by green grass and trees (Hooper 1970). Indeed, turfgrasses and trees are major considerations when selecting a homesite, a fact which explains why so many residential developments begin with a golf course. A director of the National Apartment Association echoed this preference by stating that even among renters a green lawn was a contributing factor in their choice of apartment complexes or condominiums (Kaplan 1989). Whether the effect of green grass is real or imagined, a vista of manicured turfgrass stimulates people's enthusiasm, accents their awareness to their surroundings, and renews their vitality. Likewise, psychologists and physicians have demonstrated that people feel better and recover faster when placed in an environment with green grass and trees (Ulrich 1986).

Contributions of Turfgrasses

Turfgrass may be defined as a grass cover established on a site to prevent erosion and maintain visibility (a roadside); to reduce dust, glare, and surface temperatures (a lawn or park); to beautify the surroundings (a lawn); and to provide a playing surface for sports and recreation (athletic fields and golf courses). The contributions of turfgrasses to erosion control on roadsides, lawns, and playgrounds can be measured in thousands of acres of land saved each year or in millions of dollars saved by the public or the taxpayer. Without a grass cover, thousands of acres of roadsides, ditch banks, mine spoils, dump grounds, and other sites would be lost to erosion. And without some degree of maintenance, such as mowing, fertilization, and weed and brush control, those areas would quickly become overgrown with undesirable vegetation. As an example, the U.S. Corps of Engineers spends millions of dollars each year removing brush and silt from clogged ditches and waterways and restoring eroded ditch banks. Without question, turfgrasses on these sites save taxpayers many times the cost of grass establishment and maintenance.

Turfgrasses contribute significantly to our physical environment (Beard and Green 1994). During World War II considerable research was conducted on ground covers around airfields to reduce dust which interfered with equipment and safety. Turfgrasses were found to be the most effective ground cover for reducing dust around these facilities. Even in an arid environment where water is precious, turfgrasses are the most popular and effective ground cover to reduce blowing dust around homes and buildings.

To appreciate turfgrasses' role in reducing glare, noise, and temperature, one only needs to walk through a city where concrete is the dominant ground cover. Temperatures are usually 5 to 8 degrees higher in cities than in rural surroundings where trees and turfgrasses cover most of the surface. In southern climates, where utility bills are highest during summer months, a few degrees difference in temperatures around homes translates into millions of dollars saved by homeowners. Turfgrasses also make a difference in temperature on athletic fields. Temperatures on artificial turf approach 140 degrees on summer days compared to 85 degrees on a natural grass turf. As a result, many artificial turf fields in the South are being converted to grass, and nearly all teams practice on grass fields during summer months.

The aesthetic contribution of turfgrasses is more obvious and, perhaps, best exemplified by the millions of manicured lawns in residential neighborhoods. A beautiful lawn is the singular most important feature in a home landscape. If that were not the case, Americans would not spend over 25 billion dollars and 6 billion hours maintaining lawns. In support of these expenditures, real estate agents have shown that beautiful landscapes increase the value of homes beyond their cost of establishment and maintenance.

Turfgrasses not only beautify home landscapes, but parks, schools, churches, office buildings, roadsides, and many other sites are enhanced by turfgrasses. A dense, green turfgrass accents other landscape features and structures as no other ground cover can. A green, manicured lawn is the most enjoyable part of the home landscape. Southwestern author J. Frank Dobie once wrote, "The sight of a turf, whether of shortgrass carpeting the earth or tall grass waving in the wind, restores my soul. A valley of green grass is beautiful in the way that mountains, seas, and stars are beautiful" (Dobie 1972).

Turfgrasses, of course, are the most important feature on golf courses, athletic fields, and other sports fields requiring a resilient playing surface. In all cases the quality of the golf course or sports field is judged primarily by the density, texture, color, and uniformity of the turfgrass. In addition to the aesthetic qualities turfgrasses contribute, player safety is greatly improved by the resiliency of natural grass fields. Also, the cost of establishing and maintaining turfgrass is much less than that of synthetic turf.

Thus, turfgrasses contribute to our southern lifestyle through improved environmental conditions, safer athletic fields and playgrounds, improved mental attitudes, and more beautiful settings for homes, parks, roads, and other facilities. In densely populated urban centers where 80 percent of the South's population lives, turfgrasses make significant contributions to the physical well-being and mental attitudes of its people.

Scope of the Turfgrass Industry in the South

In terms of dollars, jobs, and acres of land, turfgrass is big business. Americans spent over 45 billion dollars in 1993 maintaining lawns, golf courses, parks, roadsides, and other turfgrass areas (Beard and Green 1994). Turf maintenance costs are projected to approach 90 billion dollars by the year 2000. The South accounts for about 30 percent of the dollars spent on turfgrass maintenance. In 1993 over 1 million people were employed in the turfgrass industry. By comparison, that number exceeds employment by the entire petrochemical industry in the United States. Job opportunities in the turfgrass industry encompass all levels of skills including labor, supervisory, management, technical, sales, and professional. Projections suggest that the industry will continue to grow in value and in jobs during the remainder of the twentieth century.

Some components of the turfgrass industry will show significant increases over the next decade. Professional lawns and grounds maintenance will continue to grow in jobs and dollar value. By 1994 professional lawn service exceeded 5.5 billion dollars in maintenance contracts, a fivefold increase since 1978.

The profile of the labor force in the turfgrass industry has also changed significantly over the last twenty years. Women have replaced men in many turf maintenance jobs, such as equipment operators, groundskeepers, and supervisors. The educational level of the labor force has increased as technicians replaced laborers in an effort to improve efficiency. And the professional level of the industry has increased sharply through organization, training, and greater educational opportunities.

Turfgrass is maintained on 35 million acres in the United States, 10 million of which are in the southern states. Roadsides account for nearly one-third of the acreage in turfgrass, but only 3 percent of the dollars spent on turfgrass maintenance. Total acreage of turfgrass will show little change during the latter part of the twentieth century. As the acreage of lawns, parks, golf courses, and other facilities increase, the acreage of maintained turfgrass on highway rights-of-way will decrease. For example, the Alabama Highway Department maintained 124,000 acres of right-of-way in 1979, but the acreage was less than 100,000 by 1985. Other southern states, such as Texas, have reduced the level of maintenance to keep costs down through the promotion of wildflowers along Texas roadsides.

Acreage in individual home lawns, which accounts for the largest acreage of intensively maintained turfgrass, continues to increase due to new construction and to the benefits of a beautiful lawn. Golf courses, commercial grounds, parks, and other intensively maintained turfgrass areas show similar increases because of a greater demand for recreation and greenbelt areas in population centers and because of the growth of those population centers in southern states (table 1-1).

Table 1-1. Turfgrass Maintenance Costs in U.S. in 1995

Turfgrass Areas	Dollars (billions)	Acres (millions)
Home lawns	30.0	6.5
Golf courses	6.0	1.5
Sod production	2.0	1.0
Commercial and public grounds	5.0	8.0
Roadsides	0.5	10.0
Cemeteries	0.5	0.5
Other	1.0	2.5
Total	45.0	30.0

Challenges of the Future

The turfgrass industry has grown from 4 billion dollars in 1974 to 45 billion dollars in 1994. Projections are that it will double again by the year 2000. All such growth industries face challenges with regard to labor, government regulation, technology, and leadership. In addition, the turfgrass industry will be challenged by problems relating to energy, water, and the environment. How the industry approaches these challenges will determine how intact it survives the twentieth century.

WATER. Water, like energy and labor, is a limited resource of vital concern to the turfgrass industry. Water shortages have plagued the turfgrass industry in some areas of the country for years. Severe water shortages affected turfgrass maintenance on the West Coast in the late seventies and the early nineties and in the Southeast in the late 1980s. Projections suggest that water supplies for turfgrass will become even more critical by the end of this century.

Water conservation has been on the minds of turfgrass managers, researchers, and manufacturers for years. Improved irrigation equipment, better management practices, and drought-tolerant turfgrasses have increased water use efficiency and promoted water conservation. But conservation is only part of the solution to the water problem.

Alternative water sources must be explored if the turfgrass industry is to grow. Greater use of effluent water is essential. Industrial waste water, cooling plant water with its accumulated salts, sewage effluent, and other secondary water sources must be utilized.

ENERGY. Increased costs and decreasing availability of energy sources affect most phases of turf maintenance including mowing, water, fertilization, pest management, and clipping disposal. The effect of fuel shortages and prices on turf maintenance was dramatized in the late 1970s throughout the U.S. Other serious shortages can be expected in the future.

The turfgrass industry can survive these temporary shortages without serious consequences. But the attitude and policy changes created by fuel shortages and price increases could have serious implications for the turfgrass industry. For example, the no-mow policy many highway departments initiated during the 1973 energy crisis has not changed appreciably. The low priority with respect to fuel allocations given turf maintenance operations will hurt the industry if fuel rationing plans are adopted. And, the minimum maintenance concept, popular for lawns, golf courses, and landscaped areas in general, is a result of the energy problem. This concept gains impetus each time there is a fuel shortage or significant price increase. These policy and attitude changes produced by the energy crisis of the seventies will continue to impact the turfgrass industry into the twenty-first century.

LABOR. The major resource of the turfgrass industry is labor. Approximately one million people are employed in the turfgrass industry in the U.S. Perhaps more so than any other, labor, too, is a limited resource. The turfgrass industry requires all levels of labor from the worker in the field, to the research scientists, to the business manager. As in other industries, skilled labor is the backbone of the turfgrass industry.

During the last decade of the twentieth century the labor pool formerly available to the turfgrass industry has been depleted by higher-paying industries and government programs. The quality of labor available to the turfgrass industry has reached a critical level. Positions formerly occupied by experienced or trained personnel are being filled today by unskilled and inexperienced labor. For example, a golf course might pay a skilled equipment operator $10 per hour; whereas, the same operator could make $15 or more per hour in construction or other heavy industry. As an alternative, less skilled employees are hired at lower wages to do the same work.

Employment of women as equipment operators, groundskeepers, and supervisors has helped fill the vacancies created by men leaving for jobs in other industries. Also, greater educational opportunities in turfgrass and better training programs for new employees will continue to increase the skills of the labor force.

GOVERNMENT. More and more, governmental laws and regulations dictate what can and cannot be done in all phases of our industry—employment, wages, safety, health, and the environment. The solution to the problem of governmental involvement is perhaps the most difficult task facing the turfgrass industry. As long as turfgrass is a stepchild of agriculture, as long as the industry remains unorganized, and as long as the value of turfgrass remains unknown, the industry will be subject to the whims of politicians.

Greater visibility of turfgrass, as a valuable and useful commodity, is essential to influence legislation on matters of vital concern to the industry such as water restrictions, safety regulations, employment practices, and environmental concerns. Acceptance of turfgrass as a first-class member of the agricultural community is also important to entitle the industry to the exemptions, allocations, and services given other agricultural programs.

ENVIRONMENT. The contributions turfgrass makes towards environmental improvement have been mentioned, and, overall, turfgrasses have a positive impact on environmental quality (Beard and Green 1994). But there are environmental concerns with regard to turfgrass that must be faced. In 1993 some 73 million pounds of pesticides (Aspelin 1994) and 500 million pounds of fertilizer nutrients were applied to lawns and gardens in the United States. Even when properly applied, some of these pesticides and nutrients are lost from the target area by runoff and leaching, thus contributing to pollution of groundwater, creeks, and streams. Misuse of these materials, particularly by homeowners, produces even greater damage to the environment.

Government agencies continue to place more and more restrictions on the use of pesticides that are important to turfgrass maintenance. They are looking more closely at the affect of fertilizer nutrients, particularly nitrogen, on water resources in urban areas. Intensively maintained turfgrass areas, such as lawns and golf courses, are being affected by restrictions on the use of fertilizers and pesticides. The industry must continue to support research to provide answers to questions being raised and to provide solutions to our environmental problems.

LEADERSHIP. Leadership in the turfgrass industry has been provided by major manufacturers and distributors of turfgrass equipment and supplies, by such turfgrass associations and organizations as the Golf Course Superintendents Association of America and the U.S. Golf Association Green Section, and by universities through research and education programs in turfgrass. If the industry is to protect itself against unfair restrictions and excessive government regulation, strong and viable leadership on a national level will be required.

TECHNOLOGY. As the technology available to the turfgrass industry becomes more complex, the skill of the operator and supervisor must also increase. One challenge the turfgrass industry faces in this area is competing with higher-paying industries for skilled labor. Computer-controlled irrigation systems, hydraulic mowing equipment, timed-release fertilizers, pesticides, and other technological advancements require skilled operators and supervisors for turfgrass maintenance operations. As skilled labor becomes increasingly difficult to employ and retain, the turfgrass industry will become more dependent on technology to take up the slack.

More efficient mowing and irrigation equipment has done much to reduce our dependence on labor during the last decade. Perhaps even greater improvements will be made in the future. Research will produce turfgrasses with lower maintenance requirements for use on home lawns and other low traffic areas. Growth retardants which offer greater potential to reduce turf maintenance requirements will become available, and more effective pest management programs, including biological controls and resistance varieties of turfgrass, will be developed to reduce our dependence on pesticides.

2

The Turfgrass Plant

The grass family (*Gramineae*) includes over 5,000 species of plants, but only about 40 species are suited for turf use. Of the 40 species of turfgrasses, only 10 species are in common use in the southern region of the United States. The characteristic that distinguishes turfgrasses from the other grass species is the ability of turfgrasses to persist under regular mowing.

The grass family is characterized by plants with distichous (two-ranked) leaves, parallel veins, hollow, cylindrical or flattened stems with conspicuous nodes, and a fibrous, multibranched root system. The grass leaf, the food manufacturing site of the plant, consists of four parts: the blade, the sheath, the collar, and the ligule. Some grass leaves also possess a structure called the auricle. The structure, shape, and arrangement of these vegetative characters are useful for identifying the turfgrasses.

The Grass Leaf

The basic structural unit of the grass plant is called the phytomer. A complete phytomer consists of a leaf blade and leaf sheath attached on a section of stem, an internode. At the base of the internode is a node where a shoot bud (tiller) arises and adventitious roots develop. The grass plant is made up of phytomers stacked together alternately, one with the leaf to the right, the next with the leaf to the left, and so on. This two-ranked arrangement of leaves distinguishes grasses from other plants. Each complete phytomer contains all functional units of the grass plant. The root takes up water and minerals, the leaf manufactures food from carbon dioxide and water, the stem stores food reserves for growth, and the bud is capable of reproduction.

Nearly all grass leaves are separated by a collar into a well-defined basal sheath that tightly encompasses the stem for most of its length and a usually flattened leaf blade. The sheath is attached to the stem just beneath the node. The sheath usually has free margins, but in a few grasses the margins are fused at the base. The leaf blade is usually flat and elongated. Some grasses, such as Saint Augustine grass, have a petiole-like constriction at the base of the blade just above the sheath. All grass blades have entire margins, but some have fine epidermal hairs projecting from the margins. In most grasses a membranous or hairlike appendage or rim, the ligule, is present on the inner surface between the sheath and the blade. Membranous projections called auricles may be present on both margins at the apex of the sheath or the base of the blade.

Growth, or expansion, of the leaf results from cell division and cell elongation from meristematic tissue at the base of the sheath and at the base of the blade.

In contrast to large plants, such as trees, the grass plant is infinitely more efficient. The root hairs of grasses, which take up water and nutrients, are separated from their site of use, the leaves, by only a few inches. In larger plants the leaf must produce food to nourish a large transport system, the stem, or trunk. Also, in larger plants water and minerals must move several feet from the root to the leaf, and food for root growth must move all the way back down the stem.

In terms of growth, a grass plant may double in size in only a few days; whereas, a tree may require several years. A single grass plant is capable of producing several thousand daughter plants, or tillers, in one year. These daughter plants, or tillers, develop between the leaf sheath and the stem, or the main axis of the shoot. Initial appearance of tillers is determined by the age of the parent shoot, temperature, day length, and other factors (Taylor and Templeton 1966). In warm-season turfgrasses tillering is common between spring and late fall. In the cool-season turfgrasses tillering occurs from fall through spring. In a turf tillering may be stimulated by mowing, irrigation, and fertilization (Youngner and McKell 1972).

The Grass Stem

The grass stem is made up of a series of nodes and internodes. The internode is usually cylindrical and hollow, while the node is always solid. The stem may be erect, decumbent, or creeping. It may also be simple or freely branching. A branch, or tiller, is borne only at the node in the axile of the sheath. Some grasses have a stem that grows along the surface of the ground and produces roots and shoots (tillers) at the node. Such stems are called stolons. Saint Augustine grass is an example of a stoloniferous grass.

In some grasses, underground stems, called rhizomes, spread horizontally and produce new shoots and roots at the nodes. Kentucky bluegrass is an example of a rhizomatous grass. Still other grasses spread by both stolons

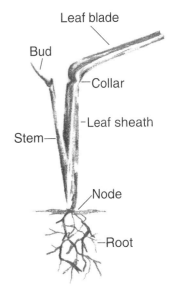

Grass phytomer

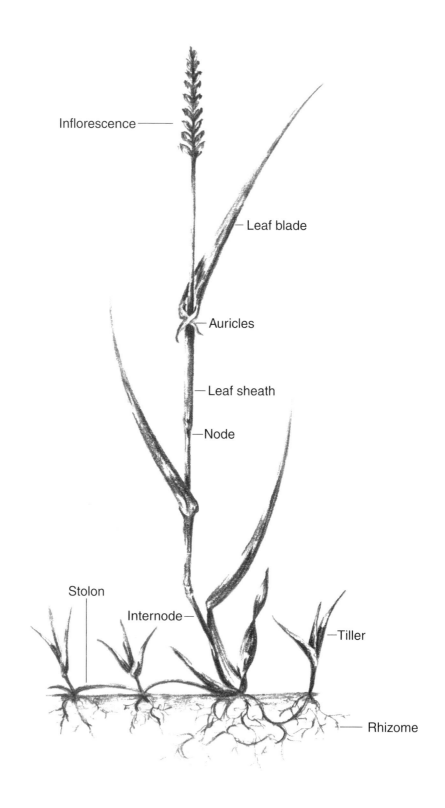

Inflorescence

Leaf blade

Auricles

Leaf sheath

Node

Stolon

Internode

Tiller

Rhizome

Grass stem

and rhizomes. Bermudagrass and zoysia are examples of the latter type.

Growth of the stem results from cell division and cell elongation at the apical meristem and at intercalary meristems at the base of the internodes.

The Root System

The root system of a turfgrass is typically multibranching and fibrous in nature. Growth of roots results from cell division and cell elongation in meristematic tissue just behind the root tip. Roots of turfgrasses are the major sites of mineral (nutrient) and water uptake. Roots of turfgrasses are not major sites for storage of food reserves (carbohydrates).

The major portion of the root system of turfgrasses mowed at less than 2 inches in height is in the upper 4 inches of the soil. The size, depth, and distribution of the root system varies considerably among species and cultivars (Burton 1943). Most warm-season grasses have larger and more extensive root systems than the cool-season grasses. Bermudagrass, Saint Augustine, and centipedegrass (warm-season grasses) roots have been observed at depths of 6 feet. In contrast, ryegrass and bentgrass (cool-season grasses), maintained as turf, seldom develop roots below 1 foot in depth.

Longevity of turfgrass roots varies with species from less than 6 months to almost 2 years. Longevity also depends on the season of the year when roots are produced. Generally, roots produced in the fall and winter live longer than those produced in the spring or summer. Root death and replacement is a continuing process in most grasses. However, there are specific times of the year when peak root loss and root initiation occur (DiPaola, Beard, and Brausand 1982). In cool-season grasses root loss is at a peak during midsummer heat stress periods, and root initiation peaks in the fall. In warm-season grasses root loss peaks during late winter and spring, and root initiation peaks in spring and early summer.

In grasses the primary root develops from the embryo of the grass seed and functions for 6 to 8 weeks. It serves as the complete root system for the grass seedling. Secondary (adventitious) roots originate from the lower nodes of the stem within 2 to 3 weeks after germination and eventually replace the primary root. In turfgrasses having a bunch-type (noncreeping) growth habit (ryegrass), the adventitious roots originate from the basal nodes of the main axis and from tillers near the ground level. In turfgrasses with a creeping-type growth habit, adventitious roots may also develop from the nodes of stolons and rhizomes.

Adventitious roots exhibit a high degree of branching; branches of the third order are commonly being produced. Considerable variation occurs among species in their degree of branching. In turf competition among plants can significantly reduce the amount of branching displayed by a plant root system.

The size and strength of roots declines progressively from the main root to the lowest order of branches—the lowest order being composed of young, actively absorbing tissue. In a turf the ability of a grass plant to compete with other plants for water and nutrients depends to a great extent on the degree of branching.

Along the epidermal cells of grass roots, the cell wall is pushed out at its weakest point and continues to elongate in a new direction to form a long, narrow projection, the root hair. Root hairs are produced in the region just beyond that of cell elongation in the root apex.

Root hairs are particularly well developed in turfgrasses and tend to be persistent. In warm-season grasses the root hairs persist for several years and are found over the entire length of the root. The persistence of root hairs contributes greatly to the ability of roots to take up nutrients and water.

The actual distribution of grass roots throughout the soil profile is influenced by many environmental and cultural factors (Burton, DaVane, and Carter 1954). Requirements for a deep, extensive root system include a healthy, actively growing turfgrass growing in a soil with adequate moisture, aeration, and nutrition.

The Inflorescence

The inflorescence, the grass flower, consists of a series of spikelets arranged in various patterns along a main axis or stem. Based on the arrangement of the spikelets, grass inflorescences are classified as spikes, racemes, and panicles. In a spike inflorescence all spikelets are attached sessile (without a stalk) on the main axis. Zoysia grass has a spike-like inflorescence. In a raceme inflorescence all spikelets are borne on individual stalks (pedicels) directly along the main axis. Bermudagrass, bahiagrass, and other *Paspalum* species have a raceme inflorescence. In a panicle inflorescence spikelets are attached by

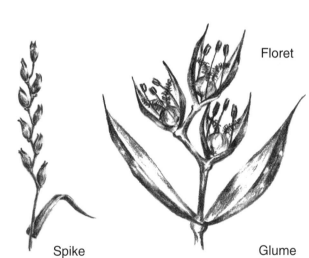

Raceme   Panicle   Spike   Floret

Glume

Inflorescence types

Spikelet

branches to the main axis. Some panicles are little-branched (closed panicle) and some are multibranched (open panicle). The inflorescence of Kentucky bluegrass is an example of an open panicle.

The individual spikelet usually consists of a short axis, the rachilla, bearing two glumes at the basal node and one or more florets. Each floret consists of two bracts, the lemma (lower bract) and the palea (upper bract), which enclose a flower.

The typical grass flower has three stamens (male structure) and a pistil (female structure). A pistil consists of two stigmas attached to a single ovary. After pollination the ovary develops into a caryopsis, the grass seed.

3 Growth and Development of Turfgrasses

The grass flower (inflorescence) may seem inconspicuous, but empires and civilizations have depended on the fruit of this plant.

The Grass Seed

The transfer of pollen from the anther to the stigma of the grass flower (pollination) with the help of wind, water, insects, or humans initiates the formation of a seed. Soon after pollination the pollen germinates and grows down through the style into the ovary, where fertilization occurs. This fertilized egg begins a series of cell divisions and forms a mass of cells that develops into the embryo of the grass seed. Apparently unorganized in the early stages of development, the embryo of a mature seed shows a well-defined shoot and primary root. This embryo develops into a mature turfgrass plant after germination. Along with the development of the embryo from the fertilized egg, the starchy endosperm fills the space between the embryo and the seed coat. The endosperm remains as a mass of food-containing cells in the mature grass seed that ultimately is used by the germinating seed for growth.

While the embryo and endosperm are developing, a hard, more or less impervious, seed coat develops around the embryo and endosperm. Thus, after repeated cell divisions the fertilized egg develops into a young plant which, with its protective coat and its stored food, is called a seed.

SEED GERMINATION

After maturation the seed enters into a resting, or dormant, period during which growth and development of the embryo are at a standstill. Resumption of these activities is called germination. For the resumption of growth and development to take place, the following environmental conditions must occur: (1) a sufficient supply of water, (2) a favorable temperature, and (3) an adequate supply of oxygen. A fourth requirement, light, is essential for some grass seeds. (Kentucky bluegrass and crabgrass are examples.) If any one of these environmental conditions is not favorable, the seed will not germinate.

Water plays several important roles in the germination of seeds. Water absorbed, or imbibed, by the seed usually softens the seed coat and causes the embryo and endosperm to swell. This swelling ruptures the seed coat and activates enzymes to begin the process of cell enlargement and cell division. Water also facilitates the movement of oxygen into the seed. Dry cell walls in the seed coat are almost impermeable to oxygen. As the seed takes up water, the oxygen supply to the embryo increases and respiration—the conversion of stored food reserves to energy—increases rapidly. Water also makes possible the transfer of soluble food from the endosperm of the seed to the growing points of the embryo—the shoot and root. If the availability of water to the seed is interrupted after these processes have begun, death of the seedling may occur as the processes of plant growth are not reversible. Thus, grass seed must be kept in a moist environment during the germination process or until the seedling can extract water from the soil. Drilling grass seed into the soil, covering seed with a mulch, or topdressing with soil provide methods of maintaining a moist environment around the seed.

Temperature is another factor that influences seed germination. Minimum, maximum, and optimum temperatures exist for the germination of seed of each grass species. These cardinal temperatures may vary among species and among varieties within a species. The seed of most cool-season grasses will germinate rapidly at air temperatures between 60° and 85° F. The seed of warm-season grasses require higher temperatures for germination, 70° to 95° F (Weinbrenn 1948). Alternating temperatures are beneficial to the germination of grass seeds and may be a requirement in some species. Alternating temperatures between 60° and 85° F favors the germination of creeping bentgrass, ryegrass, and tall fescue. But alternating temperatures between 70° and 95° F favor germination of bermudagrass and buffalograss. Germination of freshly harvested seed of some species is increased by 8 weeks of prechilling at 38° F. Examples of the latter include creeping bentgrass and buffalograsses.

Oxygen is essential during germination because the rate of respiration, a process with a high oxygen demand, increases rapidly in germinating seeds. The need for adequate soil aeration during germination and succeeding plant growth is well recognized. Compacted soil conditions or excessively wet soil conditions will reduce seed germination by excluding oxygen.

Light exposure promotes the germination of some grass seeds. Freshly harvested seed are more likely to benefit from light exposure than older seeds. The germination of crabgrass seed is stimulated by light exposure. Thus, a complete turf cover maintained during the germination period of annual weeds such as crabgrass helps to reduce weed seed germination.

SEED VITALITY

Seed vitality refers to the seed's capacity to germinate and produce a seedling capable of developing into a healthy plant. Several factors, including the vigor of the parent plant, environmental conditions to which seeds are exposed while developing, maturity of the seed, and environmental conditions under which seed are stored, influence seed vitality (Youngner 1969).

Environmental conditions (temperature and humidity) during the period of seed maturation influence seed vitality. Grass seeds develop best under dry atmospheric conditions. High humidity during seed maturation results in poor seed vitality. Excessively high summer temperatures or low autumn temperatures may also damage partially matured seed.

Seed harvested prior to maturity also have poor seed vitality. Immature seed may germinate but may not tolerate unfavorable conditions during the seedling stage. Immature seed also lose their vitality faster than do mature seed.

Seed vitality is gradually lost during storage since vital processes (respiration, enzyme synthesis, etc.) continue even under ideal storage conditions. Seedling emergence may be 20 to 50 percent lower than expected based on germination tests if seed have been stored for a year or more. Such seed may lack the vigor or energy to emerge from the soil when planted at a depth of only one-eighth inch under optimum conditions. Seed should be stored in cool, dry environments to minimize this decline in seed vitality. Favorable storage conditions for most grass seed include a relative humidity below 20 percent and a temperature below 80° F. With respect to the length of time seed can be safely stored, seed may be classified as short-lived, intermediate, or long-lived. Bermudagrass seed is short-lived, ryegrass and fescue seed are intermediate, and bentgrass and buffalograss seed are long-lived.

SEED DORMANCY

Some seed fail to germinate even when placed under favorable environmental conditions. A hard, impermeable seed coat may impede the absorption of water and delay germination even when seed are placed in a moist environment. This hard, impermeable seed coat is commonly found in seed of legumes such as crownvetch, bluebonnets, and clovers. This type of dormancy can be overcome by mechanical or chemical seed scarification. Unhulled bermudagrass and buffalograss seed are also examples of this type of dormancy. With these grasses removal of the hull or bur, respectively, will greatly increase germination.

Freshly harvested seed are frequently dormant. Although such seed may appear mature, they must undergo a period of postharvest ripening. Exposure to low temperatures will generally overcome this type of dormancy.

Dormancy may also be attributed to the presence of inhibitory substances in the seed or seed coat. Such substances must be removed by leaching before the seed will germinate. In some grass species dormancy may last only a few weeks, while in others it may last from one to three years. Such is the case in buffalograss and some bentgrasses. In the case of buffalograss, the inhibitor is found in the bur surrounding the seed. Removal of the bur increases the germination of buffalograss seed.

GRASS SEEDLINGS

When placed in a favorable environment the seed imbibes moisture and swells. The primary root is the first embryo structure to emerge from the seed coat (Bonnett 1961). Very soon after the emergence of the primary root several branch roots appear. In the grass seed the growing point of the shoot and the first young leaves are enclosed by the leaf sheath (coleoptile). Shortly after emergence from the seed coat the tip of the sheath is broken, and the first foliage leaf emerges. It is from this first leaf node that the first secondary roots arise. Clusters of secondary roots arise at the basal nodes which are separated by very short internodes and serve both as feeders and as mechanical support. The growth rate of a grass seedling follows a distinct pattern from the time of germination to maturity. The typical growth pattern involves relatively slow initial and terminal growth rates and an extended intermediate period of rapid growth.

SEEDLING VIGOR

Grasses that have a rapid germination rate, fast rate of root and shoot growth, a robust growth habit, or resistance to environmental stresses are referred to as having a high degree of seedling vigor. Thus, success in seedling establishment may be enhanced by providing favorable environmental conditions and selecting grasses that have high seedling vigor.

The size and weight of the embryo and endosperm are important factors in determining the vigor of a grass seedling. Weak parent plants often produce seeds which are deficient in stored food materials (endosperm) and which contain abnormally small embryos. Such seed produce less vigorous seedlings than those produced from normal seed. Considerable variation also exists in the size of seeds produced from the same plant or variety. Generally, the larger seed will establish a turf faster than the smaller seed. Within species seed weight is of greater importance to seedling vigor than between species seed weight. Perhaps seed weight or seed count, expressed in seeds per gram, should be required information on the seed label.

Seeds which germinate rapidly have an advantage in terms of competition for water, light, oxygen, and nutrients. Rapid germination is often a characteristic of weedy grasses that invade turf when a short period of favorable conditions occur. Species that germinate rapidly demonstrate the same competitive advantage beyond the seedling stage, thus sustaining a vigorous growth habit. Seedlings that develop rapidly have an obvi-

Primary root

Coleoptile

Branch roots

Grass seedlings

ous advantage over seedlings that are slow to produce leaves. Likewise, early development of a root system capable of taking up water and nutrients gives seedlings a decided advantage. The ryegrasses are an excellent example of this type of seedling vigor and explains their use in seed mixtures as a nurse grass or a temporary grass.

Resistance to environmental stresses such as low or high temperatures, drought, and diseases gives some seedlings a critical advantage during turf establishment. In most turf situations these conditions can be modified by mulching, frequent irrigation, or seed treatment to give less vigorous seedlings an opportunity to become established. Timely fertilization is another way to increase seedling vigor and improve turf establishment. Small, frequent applications of soluble fertilizers or the use of organic or slow-release fertilizers are recommended during the critical establishment period. During this period small amounts of fertilizer may promote seedling development, but excess fertilizer, particularly if water becomes limited, can cause dehydration and inhibit seedling development and reduce seedling survival.

High seeding rates can be used in turfgrass establishment as a means of overcoming low seedling vigor. Where high seeding rates are used, the most vigorous seedlings, those capable of obtaining water, nutrients, etc., are more likely to survive. Likewise, those resistant or more tolerant to environmental stress (temperature extremes, drought, diseases, salt, etc.) are more likely to survive and develop.

SUCCESSFUL SEEDLING ESTABLISHMENT

Proper seedbed preparation to provide favorable physical conditions (aeration) and adequate nutrient availability is essential to successful seedling establishment. Organic matter, lime, fertilizer, and other soil amendments may be needed to modify natural soil conditions prior to seeding.

Planting dates should correspond to the period of favorable temperatures for seed germination. Cool-season grasses should be planted in late summer (first choice) or spring (second choice). Warm-season grasses should be planted in late spring or early summer (first choice) or early fall (second choice). Dormant-season plantings of either cool- or warm-season grasses are sometimes successful. Success from dormant-season planting is enhanced if the seed being planted has a hard seed coat or a germination inhibitor.

Seed quality in terms of germination percentage, purity, and weed content can also influence seedling establishment. Germination percentage and purity are used to help determine seeding rates, and weed content identifies potential problems. All of these traits (germination percentage, purity, and weed content) are described on the seed tag on every bag or lot of seed.

Seeding rates are more critical for grasses with a bunch-type growth habit than for those with a creeping habit of growth. Most turfgrasses are seeded at rates that apply between ten and fifteen seeds per square inch. Lower seeding rates require much longer to provide a dense, uniform turf. Excessively high seeding rates produce weak, spindly seedlings that are highly susceptible to environmental stresses. Ultimately the more vigorous seedlings dominate the stand and crowd out the weaker ones. Although high seeding rates produce a rapid cover, the establishment of a healthy turf is faster when optimum seeding rates are used. Excessive seeding rates are used to provide a rapid, temporary winter cover on bermudagrass golf greens where a mature turf is not the goal.

Seedling vigor is a major factor in the successful establishment of turfgrasses. Seeds which germinate rapidly and have a rapid shoot and root growth rate have a decided advantage over less vigorous seedlings. Likewise, resistance to environmental stresses gives some seedlings a critical advantage during turf establishment.

Mulching with straw, hay, wood fiber, or other materials helps to maintain favorable temperature and moisture for germination and seedling establishment.

Postgermination management practices including watering, fertilization, mowing, and pest control determine the ultimate success of turfgrass establishment. Each species or mixture must be managed according to the requirements of the particular grass or grasses.

Grass Leaves

Leaf color, density, and texture are criteria by which people judge turfgrass quality. All of these are characteristics of grass leaves; however, they differ among grass species according to the cultural practices of the turf manager. Color, density, and texture of grass leaves change dramatically in response to changes in temperature, moisture, and day length. The skill of the turfgrass manager to adjust his cultural practices (watering, mowing, fertilization, etc.) to satisfy environmental conditions determines the color, density, and texture of the turfgrass. To make the correct adjustments in his cultural practices, the turfgrass manager must understand the dynamics of the growth of grass leaves and their response to environmental changes and management.

Although one grass variety may respond favorably to close mowing and high fertilization, another may deteriorate very rapidly. Likewise, grass species and varieties differ dramatically in their response to changes in temperature. Some grasses remain green year-round, while others turn straw-colored after frost.

Factors that influence the growth of grass leaves are dynamic. Environment and management change constantly to alter the growth of grass leaves. And predicting the response to these changes requires some understanding of the growth of grass leaves.

GROWTH OF LEAVES

Grass leaves initiate from the apical meristem of a seedling, shoot, or tiller which is situated near the soil level in turfgrasses. The apical meristem elongates above that level only when seedheads develop. However, in a heavily thatched turf many of the apical meristems are situated in the thatch layer.

Although in a healthy turf the source of new leaves, the apical meristem, is somewhat protected from the mower and from extreme environmental changes, in a heavily thatched turf or in a weak, thin turf, the apical meristem is exposed to removal by a mower (scalping) or to extreme environmental changes (heat, cold, drought). Also, the meristems of grasses with a high ratio of reproductive to vegetative shoots, such as tall fescue, are more susceptible to removal by mowing.

In grasses new leaves develop from the base of the meristem toward the shoot apex (Sharman 1945). As a result, the emerging leaves enclose the apical meristem and provide additional protection against environmental changes. Thus, the apical meristem of turfgrasses is well protected against the environment and removal or injury by mowers.

The rate of appearance of leaves on a tiller or shoot is primarily dependent on grass species and temperature (Cooper 1958). However, defoliation (mowing), fertilization, and light intensity have some effect on the rate of leaf appearance (Cooper and Tainton 1968). The average rate of appearance of leaves for perennial ryegrass is about one leaf in 7 days. This interval may range from 14 days in midwinter to 5 days in late spring. The optimum temperature for leaf appearance for perennial ryegrass is about 75° F. Tall fescue has a longer interval between leaf appearance. In tall fescue the interval varies between 50 days in midwinter, 20 days in spring and fall, and 10 to 15 days in summer. Thus, the potential for leaf replacement (regrowth) is much greater for ryegrass than tall fescue.

For a particular grass species and environment, the number of visible actively growing leaves is constant (Evans 1940). For perennial turfgrasses the number may range from 3 to 7 leaves, depending on species and environment. Since the rate of leaf appearance and the number of visible leaves are constants for a specific grass and environment, the life span of a grass leaf must also be constant. The length of life of a fully expanded grass leaf may range from 20 to 40 days, with 30 days being average (Anslow 1965; Taylor and Templeton 1966). Again, species and temperature are the main factors that determine the life span of a grass leaf.

Mowing height and frequency (Booysen, Tainton, and Scott 1963) and nitrogen fertilization can influence the rate of leaf appearance. Uncut grass has the highest rate of leaf appearance until the upper leaves begin to shade the lower leaves. Thus, mowing at moderate heights sustains the rate of leaf appearance in turfgrass. As mowing height is reduced from 3 inches to less than 1 inch, the rate of leaf appearance is slowed. Mowing frequency has

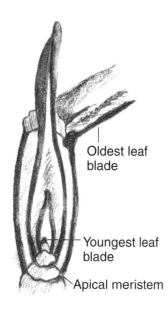

Oldest leaf blade

Youngest leaf blade

Apical meristem

Grass leaf

little effect on leaf appearance in turf growing in full sun. But in shade, frequent mowing slows the rate of leaf appearance.

In contrast, nitrogen fertilization has little effect on leaf appearance in shade. But in full sun, higher nitrogen levels increase the rate of leaf appearance. In summary, management practices that increase leaf area, or increase the flow of assimilates (carbohydrates) to the meristematic tissues, increase the rate of leaf appearance.

Growth characteristics such as leaf appearance and leaf longevity help explain the difference in regrowth potential between grasses. Tall fescue with a slow rate of leaf appearance requires longer to recover from injury or wear than ryegrass, which has a faster rate of leaf appearance.

Leaf expansion or leaf growth, in contrast to leaf appearance, is more responsive to management and environmental changes. The grass leaf is separated into two segments by the collar: the upper part, or the leaf blade, and the lower leaf sheath that encircles the shoot or stem (in stoloniferous grasses). The leaf matures from the tip of the blade downward, the sheath being the last to mature. As the leaf develops, the blade continues to expand until it emerges from the encircling leaf sheath. After it is completely emerged, the leaf blade does not expand further (Esau 1943). Even partial defoliation of a fully emerged leaf blade fails to stimulate additional expansion of the leaf blade. Additional leaf growth must come from the next leaf that has not fully emerged from the sheath.

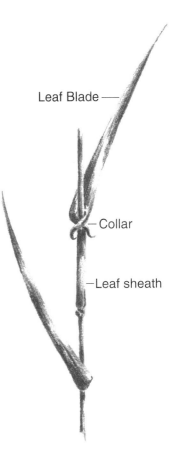

Leaf Blade

Collar

Leaf sheath

Grass leaf

RESIDUAL LEAF AREA—A MEASURE OF TURF QUALITY

During the early stages of leaf expansion, assimilates (carbohydrates) are translocated into the new leaf. When the leaf blade is fully expanded, assimilates are moved out of the new leaf into the roots and growing point of the grass plant. During the latter part of the life of a leaf, it contributes little to other parts of the plant. Thus, leaves contribute to the growth of the entire plant for only about one-half of their life span. Where leaves are frequently removed by mowing, such as intensively managed turf, the grass has little opportunity to accumulate carbohydrates. Under these conditions, maintenance of a high residual leaf area—the green leaf surface that remains after mowing—is essential to the vigor of a turf. Residual leaf area is a better measure of turf quality than leaf growth, or yield.

Leaf expansion is responsive to the environment and to management. Temperature, moisture, light, and day length influence the rate of leaf expansion and the ultimate size the leaf will attain. Leaves that develop under environmental stress are smaller than leaves developed under favorable conditions. Likewise, leaves that develop during late spring and summer are usually larger than those produced in early spring and fall. Leaves developed under shade, or low light intensity, are significantly longer and narrower than those produced in full sun.

Management, including mowing height, mowing frequency, fertilization, and irrigation, also influences leaf expansion. High nitrogen, frequent irrigation, high mowing heights, and infrequent mowing favor leaf expansion. However, leaf expansion, or leaf yield, has little value for turf; residual leaf area is much more important. Moderate nitrogen levels, frequent mowing (Hall 1995), and optimum mowing heights help maintain a high residual leaf area.

During periods of rapid leaf appearance and expansion, turf management practices should favor the maintenance of a high residual leaf area. If leaf area is maintained, regrowth from new leaves and tillers will also be maintained. Where residual leaf area is reduced by excess nitrogen, frequent irrigation, and infrequent mowing, regrowth will be significantly retarded. Under these conditions grasses use reserve carbohydrates for new leaf growth. Thus, tillering and turf density decline. If these conditions continue, carbohydrate reserves are depleted and turf quality deteriorates rapidly.

Regrowth in frequently mowed turf results from expansion of partially emerged leaves, emergence of new leaves, and emergence of new tillers. The latter occurs only when leaf area is maintained or when carbohydrate reserves are adequate. Expansion of partially emerged leaves and emergence of new leaves are favored by a high residual leaf area. Under conditions of frequent mowing, moderate nitrogen fertilization helps maintain a high residual leaf area; but low nitrogen levels retard leaf growth, and excessive nitrogen levels stimulate leaf growth at the expense of reserve carbohydrates.

MOWING INTERACTIONS

Much has been written about the effect of mowing height on leaf growth and turf quality (Beard 1973; Turgeon 1980; Hyder 1972). Grasses with a prostrate growth habit, such as bentgrass and bermudagrass, maintain a high residual leaf area at close mowing heights. These grasses produce higher quality turf when mowed shorter than one inch. Also, leaf area and tillering are promoted by close mowing; while carbohydrate reserves and root development are not significantly reduced by close mowing in these grasses. Such grasses are capable of maintaining a high residual leaf area when mowed at greater heights, but the turf becomes quite stemmy. At greater mowing heights the dense leaf cover shades lower leaves and results in a spindly turf that is susceptible to scalping and wear.

Grasses with a more erect growth habit, such as tall fescue, maintain a higher leaf residual when mowed higher than one inch. Such grasses have sufficient light penetration to maintain the lower leaves at greater mowing heights. Higher mowing heights also favor tiller production and root development in these grasses. When these grasses are mowed short, leaf area, tiller production, carbohydrate reserves, and root growth are significantly reduced.

Nitrogen and light intensity interact with mowing height to affect leaf appearance. In shade, nitrogen rate has little effect on the rate of leaf appear-

Grass tiller

ance. But in full sun, high nitrogen rates increase the rate significantly.

Mowing height and mowing frequency also interact to affect leaf growth. When mowed daily, mowing height (within limits) has little effect on leaf growth rate. But when mowed weekly, higher mowing height favors leaf growth.

LEAF GROWTH AND THATCH

The relationship between leaf residues (clippings) and thatch accumulation has been debated for some time. Current research suggests that leaf clippings from frequently mowed turf do not contribute significantly to thatch. When mowed at regular and frequent intervals leaf clippings consist of short segments of succulent leaf blades that decompose rapidly. However, when turf is mowed infrequently or when turf is fertilized excessively, leaf residues are produced faster than soil microbes can decompose them. Under these conditions leaf clippings can contribute to thatch accumulation.

Two management factors—mowing frequency and nitrogen fertilization rate—determine the contribution leaf residues make to thatch accumulation. Infrequent mowing results in an abundance of leaf clippings being left on the turf to decompose. Infrequent mowing also produces more mature leaf clippings which do not break down as rapidly. The quantity and maturity of clippings resulting from infrequent mowing leads to their accumulation in the thatch layer.

High nitrogen fertilization rates also produce excess leaf clippings that accumulate more rapidly than they can decompose (Meinhold et al. 1973). These residues accumulate in the turf and contribute to the formation of a thatch layer. Frequent mowing and moderate nitrogen fertilization rates reduce the quantity and maturity of leaf residues and allow clipping decomposition to keep up with clipping production.

Tillering—The Source of New Growth

In grasses the increase in plant size, commonly referred to as growth, results primarily from tillering—the development of buds in the axil of leaves into branch shoots, or tillers. The production and development of tillers determines not only the thickness of the turf but also the recuperative potential of the turf after mowing or injury. Tillering has been shown to vary between grass species and to be affected by season, defoliation, fertility, moisture, competition, temperature, light, and other factors. Those factors which can be controlled can be used to the advantage of the turf manager. Those factors that cannot be controlled—day length, temperature, and light—must be considered when selecting a grass variety and planning a turf maintenance program.

SEEDLING GROWH

Grass seedlings emerge as a single shoot (main stem) that consists of a shoot apex, a very short stem, and leaves arising at the nodes. In the axil of each leaf, buds are produced which under favorable conditions develop into branch shoots, or tillers. The shoot apices of grasses, like other plants, produce a substance called auxin, a growth hormone that inhibits development of the axillary buds. This control over the development of axillary buds is called apical dominance (Leopold 1949). Temperature, day length, and other environmental factors have more influence over apical dominance than cultural practices. Where mowing removes the shoot apex, apical dominance is destroyed. But in most turfgrasses the shoot apex remains near the soil level below the blade of the mower. In stoloniferous grasses removal of the terminal shoot apex by mowing increases the development of lateral shoots along the stolon.

A seedling produces its first tiller only after a certain minimum number of fully developed leaves are visible. In some grasses as many as five leaves are normally visible before the first tiller appears. Tillers produced on the main stem are called primary tillers, shoots produced by them are called secondary tillers, and so on to denote successive orders of tillers. In the early stages of growth, the rate of tiller production is linear, but as growth continues in the new shoots, the increase in numbers of tillers becomes exponential. In annual grasses tiller production ceases about 70 to 100 days after planting although the density of the turf continues to increase. This increase in density after cessation of tillering is due to an increase in leaf number and leaf size.

New tillers grow upwards within the sheath of the subtending leaf or horizontally through the base of the leaf sheath. The former type of tillering produces a tuft- or bunch-type growth habit (ryegrass and annual bluegrass). The latter types give rise to a creeping or spreading growth habit (bentgrass and bermudagrass).

After its appearance the tiller normally develops its own root system, although it remains attached to the parent shoot. Initially, the tiller is depen-

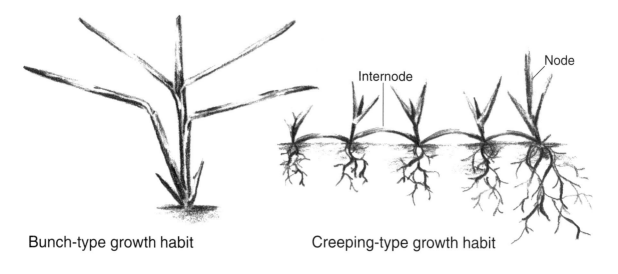

Bunch-type growth habit   Creeping-type growth habit

dent on the rest of the plant for water, minerals, and carbohydrates. As the tiller matures it becomes less dependent on the parent shoot.

In a newly seeded turf, assuming that water, nutrients, and environmental conditions are favorable for growth, the growth rate of the young seedlings will be near maximum during the early stages of growth. During this period the tillering rate will be high because of availability of sunlight, water, and nutrients to the individual seedlings. As the number of tillers increases, they begin to compete for available light, water, and nutrients. As a result, the rate of tiller production and growth decreases.

Mowing a seedling turf reduces the competition for available light and helps sustain the rate of tillering. In the case of stoloniferous grasses (bentgrass, bermudagrass, and others), where the shoot apex of tillers (stolons) is removed by mowing, tillering is promoted by the elimination of apical dominance.

CYCLIC GROWTH OF TILLERS

The life cycle, or longevity, of tillers varies considerably with grass species, time of origin, and environment. Tillers may have an annual life cycle—that is, they originate, flower, and die in the same year. Annual ryegrass and annual bluegrass typify the annual life cycle. However, perennial grasses may also have tillers that are annual in nature. Tillers that originate in the spring usually have an annual life cycle.

Other tillers may have a life cycle that extends beyond the year in which they originated. Such tillers enable grasses to be perennial in nature. Kentucky bluegrass, bentgrass, and bermudagrass have tillers that survive from one year to the next. In these grasses, tillers produced in the fall usually dominate the stand the following spring and account for the perennial nature of the grass.

In most perennial grasses the tiller is the organ of perennation. Although tillers may be produced in any month of the year, their life span is normally limited to no more than a year. In late spring or summer, depending on grass species, the shoot apex may change to a reproductive state, produce an inflorescence, and terminate further tiller formation. Not all tillers produce inflorescences. Some die during the year without ever changing to a reproductive state. Others remain vegetative even though environmental conditions favor flowering. These are the tillers that enable the grass to survive from one year to the next. Tillers produced in the fall usually make a major contribution to the turf the following spring; however, most of these die during the following summer. Meanwhile, new tillers arise in the spring and early summer and the cycle is repeated. New tillers completely replace those produced the preceding year.

A number of perennial grasses have a dormant period during the summer, even though they may be supplied with adequate water. During this dormant period very few tillers are produced. Tall fescue and bentgrass have a semidormant period during the summer months when few tillers are produced regardless of cultural practices.

TILLERING RESPONSE TO MOWING

The tillering characteristics of a turfgrass determine to a large extent its response to mowing. Grasses that produce stolons respond quite differently than grasses that spread by rhizomes or tillers. For example, close mowing of perennial ryegrass, bluegrass, or tall fescue decreases tillering and slows the rate of spread of these grasses (Youngner, Nudge, and Ackerson 1976). However, close mowing of creeping bentgrass, bermudagrass, and other stoloniferous grasses may increase tillering and the rate of spread.

In the former type grasses close mowing severely reduces residual leaf area (the amount of leaf area remaining after mowing) and, as a result, reduces the photosynthetic capacity of the shoot. Thus, development of new tillers is delayed in favor of leaf growth. In stoloniferous grasses close mowing removes some shoot apices in addition to the leaves; thus, apical dominance is destroyed and axillary buds develop. If mowing is not close enough to remove some of the shoot apices, it will not increase tillering.

After mowing, regrowth arises from expansion of leaves on active tillers and from growth of previously dormant or inactive axillary buds. Expansion of leaves on active tillers provides rapid regrowth, but regrowth from previously inactive buds is quite slow. In fact, the utilization of carbohydrates by the grass for leaf expansion and production after close mowing further delays the development of new tillers (Hyder 1972).

The rate of growth (leaf and tiller production) after mowing is highly dependent on the level of carbohydrates in the leaves, stem, and crown of the tiller (Ward and Blazer 1961). Carbohydrate reserves in a tiller are consumed for several days after mowing to produce new leaf growth. Thus, the overall carbohydrate level in the tillers is reduced for several days following mowing. When carbohydrate reserves are high initially, the rate of regrowth after mowing is greater than when reserves are low. Also, the residual leaf area influences the rate of regrowth. The greater the residual leaf area, the faster will be the rate of production of carbohydrates and new tillers. Consequently, the height and frequency of mowing should be scheduled, within the limits of turf use requirements, to maintain a high residual leaf area. A golf green provides an excellent example of the importance of residual leaf area.

The close, frequent mowing schedule used on golf greens is not as detrimental to tiller development as close, infrequent mowing. The frequent mowing schedule maintains a high leaf residual, which allows the grass to maintain a high rate of carbohydrate synthesis and tiller production. Although the grass maintained under close, frequent mowing has a low level of reserve carbohydrate, the rate of production of carbohydrates is reduced only slightly because of the high leaf residual.

The response of grasses to mowing may be significantly altered by environmental factors such as temperature, fertility, light, and moisture.

ENVIRONMENTAL FACTORS
AFFECT TILLER DEVELOPMENT

Within the limits of a grass species or variety, the development of a tiller is responsive to external factors (Sharman 1945). Also the response of a tiller to one external factor, such as fertility, is conditioned by the level of the other factors. In other words, external factors such as temperature, light, fertility, and moisture interact to produce the tillering response.

TEMPERATURE. In most cool-season grasses, such as Kentucky bluegrass, tall fescue, ryegrass, and bentgrass, cool temperatures (50° to 60° F) favor tillering. But in warm-season grasses, such as bermudagrass, higher temperatures (80° to 90° F) promote tillering. Kentucky bluegrass produces more tillers and fewer rhizomes when exposed to low temperatures. But there is an interaction between low temperature and photoperiod (day length) with respect to tiller production. With an 8-hour photoperiod, plants exposed to low temperatures produce fewer tillers than those not exposed to low temperatures. But as the photoperiod increases above 8 hours, cold-treated plants produce more tillers than those not exposed to low temperatures.

Temperature also influences the growth habit of grass tillers. Low temperatures favor a prostrate (horizontal) growth habit, while tillers grown above optimum temperature have a more upright growth habit.

Another important effect of temperature is that of vernalization—changing of a vegetative tiller to a flowering tiller by exposure to low temperatures (40° to 50° F). Kentucky bluegrass, for example, must be exposed to low temperatures before vegetative tillers can be induced to flower. Most cool-

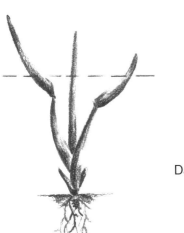

Day 1

Day 3

Day 5

Regrowth after mowing

season perennial grasses respond to vernalization. Annual grasses, such as annual bluegrass and annual ryegrass, show only a minimal response to vernalization; while the warm-season turfgrasses do not have a vernalization requirement.

LIGHT. Two aspects of light, intensity and duration (photoperiod), influence tiller production and development in grasses (Moser, Anderson, and Miller 1968). Tiller production in turfgrasses declines continuously as light is reduced from 100 percent of full sunlight. Even shade-tolerant grasses produce fewer tillers in moderate shade than in full sunlight. Shade from trees or structures is not the only shade that affects tillering. The reduction of light reaching the lower leaves and stems of a turf as a result of light interception by the upper leaves may also reduce tillering. Reduced tillering observed in tall fescue mowed at taller heights may be partially due to the shading of the lower leaves and stems. Tall fescue mowed at shorter heights, or where individual plants are spaced father apart to allow greater light interception by lower leaves, produces significantly more tillers.

In most cool-season grasses and in some warm-season grasses, increasing light duration decreases tiller production. Photoperiod also influences the growth habit of grasses. Saint Augustine grass and Kentucky bluegrass, for example, have an upright habit under long days and a prostrate habit under short days. As previously discussed, the photoperiod also affects the development of the grass inflorescence (flower).

It is important that the turf manager recognize the interrelationships between external factors and tillering. For example, nitrogen fertilization is known to increase tillering in grasses, but where light intensities are low there is no measurable response to nitrogen. Likewise, grass varieties interact with light intensity to produce differences in tillering. Varietal differences with respect to tillering may be small in full sunlight, but at low light intensities these differences may be much greater.

FERTILITY. Nitrogen (N) is the most important mineral nutrient in relation to tillering in grasses. However, phosphorus (P) and potassium (K) also affect tiller production. At low levels of N variations in P and K levels have less effect on tillering than where N levels are adequate.

One of the main effects of N is on the duration of tillering. Grasses that are adequately fertilized with N continue to produce tillers long after those that are not adequately supplied with N. Where nutrients are repeatedly supplied to the grass, the rate of tillering remains nearly constant if other factors are favorable. Late season fertilization of Kentucky bluegrass with N decreases rhizome development and increases tillering. In warm-season grasses, late-season N applications increase tillering and rhizome development.

Nitrogen appears to interact with light intensity to affect tillering. At low light levels N has little influence on tiller numbers, but in full sunlight N promotes tiller development. Nitrogen also interacts with mowing to affect tillering. At low N levels mowing severely retards tillering, but at high N levels the effect of mowing on tiller numbers is greatly reduced.

MOISTURE. The extent to which drought depresses tillering is often demonstrated. Tillering decreases as soil moisture decreases from field capacity to the permanent wilting percentage. Although drought stress always suppresses tillering, some stimulation occurs immediately following rainfall or watering.

In some grasses, soil moisture determines whether a bud develops into a tiller or a rhizome. Under dry soil conditions a bud that would normally develop into a rhizome may develop into a tiller.

MANAGE TURF TO PROMOTE TILLERING

To maintain a dense, vigorous turf, grass varieties and cultural practices should be selected to promote a high rate of tillering. Initially, the grass varieties selected for a particular site must be adapted to the local environment. For example, bluegrasses should not be planted in shaded areas, tall fescue should not be planted where the mowing heights will be below 1 inch, and hybrid bermudagrasses should not be used where mowing heights will be above 2 inches. These are only a few examples to illustrate the importance of selecting a grass variety that will respond to proper management.

Within the limits of the turf use requirements, mowing height and frequency should be adjusted to maintain a high residual leaf area. A golf course putting green best exemplifies the value of this practice. Grasses used on greens are adapted to low cutting heights, and the frequent mowing schedule helps maintain a high residual leaf area. The high residual leaf area maintains a high rate of carbohydrate synthesis which promotes tiller development. Common bermudagrass mowed at a height of 1 inch at 5-day intervals would maintain a high residual leaf area. But when mowed at the same height at 2-week intervals, bermudagrass would have a much lower residual leaf area. As a result, carbohydrate synthesis would be reduced and reserve carbohydrates would be used for leaf growth instead of tiller production.

Fertilization and irrigation practices can also help maintain tiller production. Fertilization programs for high maintenance turf should provide adequate, but not excessive, levels of nutrients available to the grass at all times to promote high tillering rates. For low maintenance turf, fertilization programs should include timely applications of nutrients to correspond to periods that favor tillering and carbohydrate accumulation instead of leaf growth. Traditional fertilization programs schedule applications to correspond to periods favorable to leaf growth.

Irrigation schedules should be programmed to maintain moisture in the root zone immediately following defoliation. In turf that is mowed frequently, a light frequent irrigation schedule would be required. In turf that is mowed infrequently, irrigation should be scheduled as far apart as possible without placing the grass under severe moisture stress; but irrigations should be timed to provide moisture immediately after mowing.

Knowledge of the natural pattern of tiller development in grasses and of the response of the tiller to environmental factors can help the turf manager maintain a healthy, vigorous turf. Nearly every practice the turf manager uses to maintain a turf affects tillering. Knowledge of what the effect might be gives the turf manager the upper hand in the struggle with nature.

Grass Roots

In an introduction to a classic article on root growth by turfgrass researchers Eliot Roberts and John Bredakis (1960), Gene Nutter stated, "As the roots go, so goes the grass." Research conducted since that article was published has generally supported that statement. Yet there are those who doubt the importance of a well-developed root system to a high quality turf. In 1925 O. B. Fitts concluded a study on root growth in fine turfgrasses with the statement, "Treat the grass surface and forget all about root growth." Observation of the roots on a bentgrass golf green in the summer might raise some question about the importance of a strong root system. Many beautiful bentgrass greens have a very weak root system in midsummer.

Although there is some controversy about the significance of roots to the quality of putting green turf, there can be little doubt of the importance of roots to a healthy turf. Perhaps a closer look at the evidence would clarify the importance of grass roots and determine turf management methods that can help promote a healthy root system.

THE GRASS ROOT SYSTEM

The primary roots of grasses are produced at the nodes or crowns of tillers, stolons, and rhizomes. They are white, small in diameter, fibrous, and greatly branched. Roots produced in spring and fall are usually larger than those produced during the hot summer months. Each tiller, stolon, or rhizome of a grass plant is capable of producing its own root system and, to some extent, acts as an independent plant.

The main roots of grasses exhibit a high degree of branching, but considerable variation exists among species (Burton, DaVane, and Carter 1954). Within a turf, competition among plants (tillers) reduces the amount of branching. The size and strength of roots decline progressively from the main roots to the lowest order of branches. The branch roots are composed of young, active tissue with a tremendous capacity to absorb water and nutrients. To a large extent, the ability of a grass (tiller) to compete and its value as a turfgrass depends on the degree of branching.

The root hairs of grasses are almost microscopic in size but contribute greatly to the absorptive potential of the root system. The root hairs are quite persistent and may be found over the entire length of the grass root. Root hair formation is largely influenced by environmental conditions and calcium availability.

To give some idea of the magnitude of the grass root system, Dittmer (1938) showed that Kentucky bluegrass per cubic inch of soil had 2,000 roots, 1 million root hairs and a combined root length of over 4,000 feet. Dittmer also reported a single winter rye plant had 13,800,000 roots with a total length of over 387 miles, root hairs over 14 billion with total length of over 6,600 miles. These plants were grown free of competition.

The depth to which grass roots penetrate increases rapidly during seedling growth or following transplanting sod. Shortly thereafter the rate of penetration decreases. The maximum depth of penetration is usually reached during the first year. Grass roots are not equally distributed throughout the whole depth of penetration but are concentrated in the upper six inches of the soil profile. The actual distribution is, however, influenced by environmental and cultural factors as well as by grass species.

ROOT GROWTH PATTERNS

From the time a seed, rhizome, stolon, or tiller initiates a root, the root develops slowly at first, goes through a period of rapid growth, matures, and then dies. The life span of turfgrass roots depends on grass species, time of year initiated, and environmental conditions. The longevity of roots may vary from less than 6 months for some grasses to almost 2 years for others. Kentucky bluegrass and bermudagrass retain a major portion of a functioning root system for more than a year, and are perennial rooting-type grasses. In contrast, perennial ryegrass, fescue, and bentgrass replace most of their root systems each year and are considered annual in nature with respect to roots.

Root death and replacement is a continuous process in some grasses, while in others it occurs at a specific time of the year (Stuckey 1941; Weaver and Zink 1946). In cool-season grasses root death and deterioration is extensive during the midsummer stress period, while root initiation is minimal during this time. Creeping bentgrass root initiation ceases at soil temperatures above 75° F, and the maturation rate of existing roots increases. Root growth of warm-season turfgrasses such as bermudagrass, Saint Augustine, and zoysia is most vigorous during the spring and summer, occurs to a lesser extent in the fall, and ceases during the winter dormant period (DiPaola, Beard, and Brausand 1982). Root growth, however, does occur at temperatures below those at which shoot growth ceases.

As grass roots mature they change in color from white to brown, decrease in diameter, and become less active in absorbing water and nutrients. Environmental stresses, such as drought, extremely high or low temperatures, im-

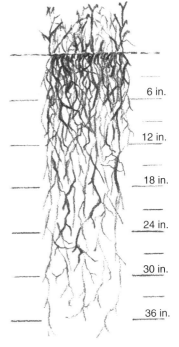

6 in.

12 in.

18 in.

24 in.

30 in.

36 in.

Grass roots

proper mowing, or herbicides, can produce the same changes in root appearance and activity.

The root system serves the plant by providing anchorage, absorbing water and nutrients, and also providing storage sites for carbohydrates (energy reserves). Cool-season grasses accumulate carbohydrates in the fall and spring. During the hot summer months or when vegetative growth is excessive, these stored carbohydrates are utilized by the plant for shoot growth. They may also be utilized for regrowth under close defoliation or when the grass is recovering from injury (mowing, traffic, drought, insect, or disease damage).

Warm-season grasses accumulate carbohydrates during the late spring, summer, and fall when conditions are favorable for growth. In both types of grasses these reserve carbohydrates help the turf tolerate environmental and cultural stresses.

MOWING AFFECTS ROOT GROWTH

The rooting depth of cool-season grasses is greatly reduced by mowing (Krans and Beard 1985), but root distribution of warm-season turfgrasses is only slightly affected by mowing (Hall 1995). Mowing height has a greater effect on root growth than mowing frequency. Kentucky bluegrass mowed at ½-inch height had as much root activity in the surface 6 inches as that mowed at 1 ½ inches. But, root activity in the 6- to 12-inch soil depth is severely restricted by close mowing. Mowing frequency, even at the shorter mowing heights, does not overcome the effect of mowing height on root activity (Hall 1995). In fact, root activity is reduced when turf is mowed more frequently. Research with bluegrass showed that roots increased from 12 percent of the plant weight to 18 percent when mowing frequency was reduced from 5 to 1 time per week at a height of 1 inch. A similar response to mowing frequency was demonstrated with bentgrass. In both grasses a reduction in turf vigor corresponded to the reduction in root growth. Frequent defoliation was also found to deplete carbohydrate reserves in the root system.

Warm-season turfgrasses respond quite differently to mowing. Bermudagrass mowed 3 times per week at a height of ½ inch maintained as much root growth as that mowed weekly at 1 ½ inches (Weinmann and Goldsmith 1948). The low, frequent mowing schedule in this study was maintained for a 2-year period. In addition to maintaining the same level of root production, the carbohydrate reserves in the root system were the same for the low, frequent mowing schedule as for the higher and less frequent mowing schedules.

The ability of bermudagrass to maintain a vigorous root system under close and frequent mowing is to a large extent due to its prostrate growth habit. Even with close, frequent mowing an adequate portion of green foliage remains to prevent a depletion of carbohydrate reserves. Creeping

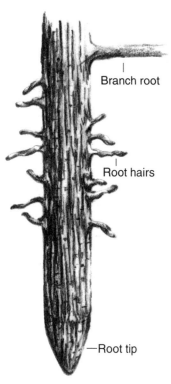

Branch root

Root hairs

Root tip

Grass root

bentgrass, which also has a prostrate growth habit, shows a similar response to mowing. Madison, Paul, and Davis (1974) at the University of California demonstrated that the root system of creeping bentgrass is not adversely affected by close mowing.

Support for the hypothesis that the prostrate growth habit of these grasses accounts for their resistance to close mowing was obtained by complete defoliation of turfs for a sustained period. When bermudagrass turfs were completely defoliated at weekly intervals for 6 months, 97 percent of the carbohydrate reserves in the root system were depleted. With normal close mowing, however, carbohydrates actually accumulated. Apparently, with both bermudagrass and bentgrass sufficient green foliage remains after mowing to maintain photosynthetic activity and prevent severe carbohydrate depletion.

NITROGEN AFFECTS ROOT GROWTH

As with mowing, the effects of N on root development are quite different between warm-season and cool-season grasses. Generally, root development in Kentucky bluegrass, fescue, and bentgrass decreases with increasing N rates. However, the timing of N applications greatly affects the response of the roots to N. Fall and winter applications of N have been shown to increase root growth in these cool-season turfgrasses (Powell, Blaser, and Schmidt 1967a; Hanson and Juska 1961); whereas, spring and summer applications of N reduce root growth. This interaction of N with season can be attributed to the growth pattern of the grasses. Applications of N in the fall and winter, when temperatures do not favor top growth, promote carbohydrate accumulation. Since the roots grow at lower temperatures than shoots, the carbohydrates are utilized for root growth. Spring applications of N, when temperatures favor shoot growth, stimulate the utilization of carbohydrate reserves by shoots. Frequent removal of leaves by mowing further stimulates the utilization of carbohydrate reserves for regrowth. Since the shoots have priority over the roots for carbohydrate reserves, the root system is the first to suffer.

Fall and winter applications of N to bluegrass or bentgrass turf does not eliminate the need for N at other periods of the year. Low rates of N that do not stimulate excess top growth can be made in the spring without reducing the root system. Also, research has demonstrated that the application of iron with N in the fall, winter, and spring increased bentgrass turf quality without decreasing root growth.

In contrast to the cool-season grasses, the roots of warm-season grasses increase in weight and depth with increasing N applications up to a level when N becomes excessive. However, just as with cool-season grasses the root-shoot ratio of warm-season grasses is greatly reduced by N applications; not because of reduced root growth, but because of increased top growth.

AERATION ESSENTIAL FOR ROOT GROWTH

Compacted soils and poorly drained sites restrict the movement of oxygen into the soil and of carbon dioxide out of the soil. Both of these conditions are highly unfavorable for the growth of grass roots. Letey at the University of California at Davis demonstrated the importance of soil oxygen to the growth of Kentucky bluegrass roots (Letey et al. 1966). When oxygen was provided to the root zone, root penetration increased to a depth of 18 inches. He also demonstrated that bluegrass mowed at a 1-inch height required 5 percent oxygen in the root zone for maximum root growth, while bluegrass mowed at 2 inches required only 2 percent oxygen. In other words, as mowing height decreases, root zone aeration becomes more important.

Perhaps more important than oxygen concentration is the rate of movement of oxygen into the root zone, the oxygen diffusion rate (ODR). Turf areas that receive heavy traffic are subject to surface compaction, a condition that greatly decreases the ODR of the soil. Letey measured the ODRs of numerous golf greens and reported that turf quality and ODR could be significantly increased by mechanical aeration and topdressing.

Research has demonstrated that annual bluegrass, bentgrass, and goosegrass are much more tolerant to poor aeration than Kentucky bluegrass and bermudagrass. While the depth of rooting of Kentucky bluegrass and bermudagrass is greatly reduced under conditions of low oxygen supply, bentgrass root weight is only slightly affected. Roots produced under low oxygen conditions are much thicker and have fewer lateral branches.

Working with common bermudagrass, Letey showed a definite improvement in the depth of rooting with increased soil aeration. He found that amendments such as peat, redwood bark, and calcined clay improved aeration of compacted soils and increased rooting depth of bermudagrass.

FREQUENT IRRIGATION PRODUCES SHALLOW-ROOTED TURF

Irrigation practices that maintain moisture only in the surface few inches of soil produce shallow-rooted grass. Madison at the University of California at Davis demonstrated that light, daily irrigation decreased root growth and was in fact deleterious to bentgrass turf (Madison 1971). The combination of frequent irrigation, close mowing, and high fertility further reduced root growth. This combination utilizes reserve carbohydrates for regrowth at the expense of the root system. Less frequent irrigation favored carbohydrate accumulation and root growth. Irrigation schedules that provide adequate water at a single setting to maintain a turf for several days produce deeper rooted and more drought tolerant turf than more frequent irrigation schedules.

However, some soils may require frequent irrigation to overcome environmental stresses for short periods of time. Coarse textured soils have a very low water holding capacity and may require frequent irrigation to maintain turf quality during dry months. But, even under those conditions, irrigations should be spaced as far apart as possible without seriously affecting turf quality.

HERBICIDES AFFECT ROOT DEPTH

Preemerge herbicides such as calcium arsenate, bensulide, benefin, oxadiazon, oryzalin, pendimethalin, prodiamine, siduron, DCPA, and others may inhibit the roots of grasses to some extent. A healthy turf that is properly maintained may not show any damage from these herbicides. But the same treatment may severely damage a turf under stress conditions such as drought, temperature extremes, or traffic. The rate of recovery of turf from injury may also be decreased because of a stunted root system caused by preemergence herbicides.

MANAGE TURF TO PROMOTE ROOT GROWTH

Whether you are concerned with lawns, golf courses, athletic fields, or sod production, the development of a vigorous turf requires a strong root system. Without question a high quality turf can be maintained where the root system is weak, but the intensity of maintenance required is much greater.

Grass species, environmental conditions, and cultural practices interact to determine the extent of rooting for a particular turf. Cool-season grasses should not be stimulated with nitrogen during late spring and summer. These grasses should be mowed as high and as infrequently as practical for a particular use.

Warm-season turfgrasses can be fertilized throughout the growing season without reducing root growth. These grasses can also be mowed closer than most cool-season grasses without affecting root growth.

Root growth of all turfgrasses responds to aeration where oxygen is restricted to the root zone by compaction, poor drainage, or excessive thatch. Likewise, irrigation practices that provide water on a thorough and infrequent basis promote deep rooting of turfgrasses.

4 Southern Turfgrasses

A variety of turfgrasses thrive in the Southern zone of the United States. The species described here represent the most prevalent and suitable for this area. They are listed in order of their importance within the two major groups of warm-season and cool-season grasses.

Bermudagrass—The Turfgrass of the South

ORIGIN AND DISTRIBUTION

Bermudagrass (*Cynodon* spp.) is a major turf species for lawns, parks, golf courses, sports fields, and general utility turfs in Australia, Africa, India, South America, and the southern region of the United States. It is found in over one hundred counties throughout the tropical and subtropical areas of the world (Juska and Hanson 1964). Common bermudagrass, *C. dactylon,* naturalized throughout the warmer regions of the United States, was introduced into this country during the colonial period from Africa or India. The earliest introductions are not recorded, but bermudagrass is listed as one of the principal grasses in the southern states in Mease's *Geological Account of the United States* published in 1807.

The genus *Cynodon* comprises nine species with *C. dactylon* being the most widespread (Harlan et al. 1970). The fact that *C. dactylon* is a tetraploid with broad genetic variability serves to explain its widespread distribution. Other *Cynodon* species have a more limited natural distribution and are often restricted to one particular habitat. *C. dactylon* is highly fertile, whereas the diploid species such as *C. transvaalensis* rarely produces viable seed.

C. dactylon (L.) Pers. is commonly called bermudagrass in many areas of the world. But it is also known by numerous other names including Kweekgras (South Africa), couch grass (Australia and Africa), devil's grass (India), and gramillia (Argentina). The variety of names given this species attests to its wide distribution and to the fact that it is the object of abuse and scorn.

In addition to being a widely used species for forage and turf, *C. dactylon* is a serious weed in many crops. Being a vigorous, stoloniferous grass, it rapidly invades crops in high rainfall or irrigated areas. *C. dactylon* is ranked among the three most troublesome weeds in sugarcane, cotton, corn, and vineyards in many countries. It is a difficult weed to eradicate because of its seed production and deep rhizomes.

In the United States the distribution of bermudagrass extends from New Jersey and Maryland, southward to Florida, and westward to Kansas and Texas. Under irrigation its distribution extends westward to southern New Mexico, Arizona, and to most major valleys in California. The development of more cold tolerant turf-type varieties of bermudagrass such as U-3 and Midiron has increased interest in the species near its northern limits. Low

Bermudagrass

winter temperature is the factor that limits the northward distribution of bermudagrass.

DESCRIPTION OF SPECIES

Bermudagrass (*C. dactylon* [L.] Pers.) is a highly variable, sod-forming perennial that spreads by stolons, rhizomes, and seed. Stolons of bermudagrass readily root at the nodes. Lateral buds develop at the nodes to produce erect or ascending stems that reach 5 to 40 cm (rarely over 90 cm) in height. In most *Cynodon* spp., leaves are borne on stems with long internodes alternating with one or more very short internodes. This characteristic gives the impression that the species has multiple-leaved nodes. Leaf sheaths are compressed to round, loose, split, smooth, sparsely hairy, up to 15 cm long, shorter than internodes, and with a tuft of hairs 2 to 5 mm long. Auricles are absent. Collar is continuous, narrow, glabrous, and hairy on margins. Leaf blades are 2 to 16 cm long, 1.5 to 5 mm wide, smooth to sparsely pubescent, folded, or loosely rolled in the bud, and sharply pointed. The inflorescence consists of 3 to 7 spikes in a single whorl in a fingerlike arrangement and 3 to 10 cm long. In robust forms there may be up to 10 spikes, sometimes in two whorls. Spikelets are 2 to 3 mm long, in 2 rows tightly appressed to one side of the rachis; glumes are ¼ to ½ the length of the spikelet; lemma is boot-shaped, acute with fringe of hairs on the keel, and longer than the glume; seed is 1.5 mm long, oval, straw to red-colored, and free within the lemma and palea.

Bermudagrass has a fibrous, perennial root system with vigorous, deep rhizomes. Roots are produced at the nodes after new leaves or tillers are produced during the growing season and after new shoots are produced in the spring. Mature roots are yellow to brown while new roots are white. Mature roots deteriorate throughout the growing season, and new roots are produced continuously. Root production and dieback has been reported to be particularly high in the spring at the onset of shoot production.

Giant bermudagrass is a naturalized form of *C. dactylon* found in the southwestern United States. This highly fertile rhizomatous form may be distinguished from common bermudagrass by its height, growth rate, lack of pubescence, and seed characteristics. At maturity the upright stems of giant bermudagrass may be over 2 feet while the upright growth of common bermudagrass will vary from 12 to 18 inches. Seed of giant bermudagrass are 50 percent larger than common bermudagrass seed. Giant seed tends to be rougher, less lustrous, and generally has surface striations parallel to the long axis. In the unhulled state, there is usually a hook-shaped structure at the apex of giant seed. Giant bermudagrass seedlings are approximately twice as tall as common seedlings two weeks after emergence. Giant bermudagrass has much less cold hardiness than common bermudagrass.

In the southeastern United States, giant bermudagrass is an undesirable contaminant when found in lots of common bermudagrass seed because it does not persist and has a faster vertical growth than common.

African bermudagrass (*C. transvaalensis*), or Floridagrass in South Africa, is a fine-textured turfgrass, easily identified by its yellowish-green color, erect linear leaves, slender (often red) stolons, and abundant but generally sterile seedheads. Rarely found outside of cultivation except in the southwestern Transvaal and the northern part of the central Cape Providence of South Africa, the species is rather sterile when self-pollinated but crosses readily with different collections of *C. transvaalensis* and *C. dactylon*. Many of the improved turf-type bermudagrasses have *C. transvaalensis* in their parentage including Bayshore (Gene Tift), Sunturf, Tiffine, Tifgreen, Tifdwarf, Tifway, and Santa Ana.

Magennis bermudagrass (*C. magennisii*) is a natural hybrid between *C. dactylon* and *C. transvaalensis* that resembles *C. transvaalensis* very closely in growth form and leaf characteristics. *C. magennisii* does not produce viable seed. It forms a fine-textured, low-growing, dense turf with very short rhizomes. *Magennisii* was introduced into the U.S. in 1949 from South Africa and released in 1956 as Sunturf bermudagrass. Once established, it requires careful management to maintain good quality turf. It is a popular lawn grass in South Africa and the southwestern United States.

Bradley bermudagrass (*C. bradleyi*) is a medium, fine-textured, low-growing species that forms a rather dense sod. It was a widely used lawn grass in South Africa in the mid-1900s, but its popularity declined due to its susceptibility to insects and nematodes. It is distinguished from other turf-type bermudagrasses by the absence of rhizomes and dense pubescence on both leaf surfaces.

ADAPTATION AND USE

Bermudagrass is a warm-season perennial species adapted to tropical and subtropical climates. It grows best under extended periods of high temperatures, mild winters, and moderate to high rainfall. Temperature is the main environmental factor that limits its adaptability to tropical and subtropical areas of the world. The northern limits of bermudagrass extend into the transitional zone of the United States, where low temperatures seldom drop below 10° F. In general, temperatures below 30° F kill the leaves and stems of bermudagrass. Research has demonstrated that bermudagrass will continue to grow with night temperatures as low as 34° F if day temperatures are near 70° F. However, when average temperatures drop below 50° F growth stops and the grass begins to discolor. At the onset of low temperatures in the fall and winter, bermudagrass begins to discolor, protein fractions change in composition, and reserve carbohydrates increase in the stems and rhizomes. After the first killing frost, leaves and stems of bermudagrass remain dormant until average daily temperatures rise above 50° F for several days. The roots and rhizomes of bermudagrass continue to grow several weeks after the leaves and stems stop growth.

In warm frost-free climates bermudagrass remains green throughout the year, but growth is significantly reduced at the onset of cool nights. The species makes the best growth where average daily temperatures are above 75° F. Optimum daytime temperature for bermudagrass is between 95° and 100° F.

Soil temperature, as influenced by air temperature, is also important to the growth and development of bermudagrass turf. Soil temperatures above 65° F are required for significant growth of rhizomes, roots, and stolons. Optimum soil temperature for root growth is around 80° F.

Bermudagrass has a high light requirement and does not grow well under low light (shaded) conditions. The duration of the light period (day length) also influences growth and development of bermudagrass. Both increased light intensity and day length increase rhizome, stolon, and leaf growth in bermudagrass. At low light intensities (less than 60 percent full sunlight), bermudagrass develops narrow, elongated leaves; thin upright stems; elongated internodes; and weak rhizomes. Consequently, bermudagrass develops a very sparse turf under moderately shaded conditions.

Bermudagrass is found in tropical and subtropical climates with 25 to 100 inches of annual rainfall, but it also survives in arid climates along waterways and in irrigated areas. Where annual rainfall is below 20 inches per year, bermudagrass requires irrigation to survive. Bermudagrass develops into a semidormant state during very dry conditions but has the capability of surviving extreme droughts. Rhizomes of bermudagrass can lose 50 percent or more of their weight and still recover when favorable moisture develops. Generally, common bermudagrass, or tetraploids of *C. dactylon,* has the deepest root and rhizome penetration and can better withstand prolonged drought periods.

Common bermudagrass also has the characteristic of producing seedheads under stress conditions such as drought. Thus, the seeds provide another method by which the species can survive extreme drought. Some natural biotypes of *C. dactylon* produce numerous seeds. The seeds are very small with about 2 million seeds per pound.

Bermudagrass grows well on a wide variety of soils from heavy clays to deep sands provided fertility is not limiting. It tolerates both acid and alkaline soil conditions and is highly tolerant to saline conditions. Bermudagrass survives some flooding but does best on well drained sites. Although it may persist under low fertility, bermudagrass has a high nitrogen requirement for good quality turf.

Bermudagrass has numerous turf uses. It has been suggested that if ever a plant deserved a monument for its service to mankind, it was bermudagrass for what it has done to prevent soil erosion; to stabilize ditch banks, roadsides, and airfields; to beautify landscapes; and to provide a smooth, resilient playing surface for sports fields and playgrounds. Bermudagrass also provides hay and pasture for livestock throughout the tropical and subtropical areas of the world.

Turf uses of common bermudagrass include lawns, parks, playgrounds, sports fields, golf course fairways, roadsides, cemeteries, and other general purpose turf. Hybrid bermudagrass and selections of common bermudagrass are used for special purposes such as golf greens, bowling greens, tennis courts, sports fields, and lawns.

Bermudagrass is well suited to high traffic areas, such as golf courses, sports fields, and playgrounds. A dense bermudagrass turf tolerates moderate wear and compaction and recovers rapidly from wear injury. In full sunlight it makes a good lawngrass because it responds well to management. Under moderate fertilization, frequent mowing, and adequate moisture bermudagrass forms a dense, fine textured turf. In low maintenance areas, such as roadsides, dam sites, ditch banks, and airfields, bermudagrass stabilizes the soil and provides a low growing ground cover. Where rainfall is adequate, bermudagrass provides a low maintenance turf for these sites. The only situation where bermudagrass cannot be used is in moderate to heavily shaded sites.

VARIETIES

Selections of superior strains of common bermudagrass, natural hybrids between *C. dactylon* and *C. transvaalensis*, and crosses resulting from grass breeding programs have been released by state universities, the Crop Research Division of the USDA, and the U.S. Golf Association Green Section (Juska and Hanson 1964; Youngner and McKell 1972). All of the hybrid bermudagrasses are sterile and must be propagated by sprigs or sod. Some selections from *C. dactylon* produce viable seed. Nu-Mex Sahara, Sonesta, Cheyenne, and Guymon bermudagrass are improved seeded varieties of bermudagrass. Brief descriptions of the major turf-type bermudagrass varieties follow (table 4-1):

1. Hall's Selection (*C. dactylon* selection). Collection from a golf green of Germistown Golf Course in South Africa in 1933 by T. D. Hall. Similar to common bermudagrass except that Hall's Selection is slower growing and rarely sets seed. Hall's Selection forms a dark green, dense, and wear-resistant sod. It is a popular lawngrass in South Africa.

2. Uganda (*C. transvaalensis*). Very fine-leaved, low-growing variety of African bermudagrass. Leaf blades are not more than 15 mm wide; stolons very slender and tend to develop a reddish-purple cast after the first cool nights in the fall. Uganda tends to develop thatch unless carefully managed. It is used for golf greens and tennis courts in South Africa and South America and for lawns in the southwestern U.S.

Table 4-1. Descriptions of Major Turf-Type Bermudagrasses

Variety	Texture	Density	Color	Uses	Remarks
C. dactylon					
Common	Coarse	Medium	Light green	Lawns, fairways, sports fields, and utility turf	Abundant seed head production
U-3	Coarse	Medium	Light green	Same as common	More cold hardy than common
Tiflawn	Coarse	Dense	Dark green	Lawns and sports fields	Fast spreading
Texturf-10	Coarse	Dense	Dark green	Lawns and sports fields	Few seed heads
Tufcote	Coarse	Dense	Dark green	Lawns and sports fields	Cold hardy
Ormond	Medium	Medium	Blue green	Lawns and fairways	Poor cold hardiness
C. dactylon and *C. transvaalensis*					
Tiffine	Very fine	Dense	Light green	Fairways	
Tifgreen	Fine	Very dense	Light green	Golf greens and fairways	
Tifgreen II	Fine	Very dense	Light green	Golf greens and fairways	More tolerant to nematodes
Tifway	Fine	Very dense	Dark green	Lawns, fairways, and sports fields	
Tifway II	Fine	Very dense	Dark green	Lawns, fairways, and sports fields	More cold hardy and earlier spring recovery
Tifdwarf	Fine	Very dense	Dark green	Golf greens	Very slow to spread
Santa Ana	Medium	Very dense	Blue green	Lawns, fairways, and sports fields	Superior salt tolerance
Pee Dee	Fine	Very dense	Dark green	Golf greens	Very fast spreading
Midway	Medium	Dense	Dark green	Lawns, fairways, and sports fields	Superior cold hardiness
Midiron	Medium	Dense	Dark green	Lawns, fairways, and sports fields	Superior cold hardiness
C. magennisii					
Sunturf	Fine	Dense	Dark green	Lawns	Very few seed heads

3. Bayshore (Gene Tift) (*C. dactylon* and *C. transvaalensis*). Selected at Bayshore Golf Club in Miami Beach, Florida. Very fine-textured, light green natural hybrid between *C. dactylon* and *C. transvaalensis*. Popular on golf courses for greens and fairways from Florida to Texas during the 1950s and early 1960s. Gradually replaced by superior varieties, such as Tifgreen and Tifway.

4. Royal Cape (*C. dactylon*). A selection from *C. dactylon* on the Royal Cape Golf Club in Mowbray, South Africa, in about 1930. It very closely resembles Hall's Selection except that Royal Cape is finer textured and faster

spreading. Royal Cape was introduced into the country in 1959 and released by the USDA and the California Agricultural Experiment Station in 1960 for use along the lower Colorado River Basin. Royal Cape is widely used in South Africa for home lawns and sports fields. It is prized in that country for its fine texture, wear tolerance, and good spring and late fall color.

5. U-3 (*C. dactylon*). Selected from Savannah Golf Club near Savannah, Georgia, in 1936 from a series of fine-strain selections. Selected because of its cold hardiness, fine texture, rapid spread, and durability under a wide range of soil and climatic conditions. The selection was released in 1957 by the Crops Research Division, ARS, USDA, and the U.S. Golf Association Green Section. Adapted for use on lawns, golf courses, and sports fields.

6. Tiffine (*C. dactylon* and *C. transvaalensis*). Selected from East Lakes Golf Course, Atlanta, Georgia, for its very fine texture. Released by the Georgia Agricultural Experiment Station and the Crops Research Division, ARS, USDA, in 1953. Tiffine has a light green color and very fine texture. Recommended for golf course fairways and greens prior to the release of Tifgreen in 1956.

7. Sunturf (*C. magennisii*). Originated in South Africa as a natural hybrid between *C. dactylon* and *C. transvaalensis* and introduced into the U.S. in 1949. Released cooperatively by Alabama, Arkansas, Oklahoma, and South Carolina agricultural experiment stations in 1956. Dark green, fine textured, low-growing variety that forms a very dense turf. Widely used for lawns in the southwestern U.S.

8. Tiflawn (*Cynodon* spp.). A hybrid between two selections from a pasture breeding program at the Georgia Coastal Plains Experiment Station at Tifton. Released in 1952 by Georgia Agricultural Experiment Station and the Crops Research Division, ARS, USDA. A medium-textured, very fast-spreading, wear-resistant variety that forms a dense, weed-free turf. Particularly well suited for lawns and sports fields in the southeastern U.S.

9. Tifgreen (*C. dactylon* and *C. transvaalensis*). A hybrid between a fine-textured selection of *C. dactylon* from the Charlotte Country Club, Charlotte, North Carolina, and *C. transvaalensis*. Released in 1956 by Georgia Agricultural Experiment Station and Crop Research Division, ARS, USDA. Tifgreen is a low-growing, rapid-spreading variety that develops a dense, weed-resistant turf. Its density, fine texture, and soft leaves make Tifgreen an excellent turf for golf greens. Also, it tolerates overseeding with winter grasses better than most bermudagrass varieties. Tifgreen is highly susceptible to injury by ground pearls in the southwestern U.S. and is severely discolored by air pollution in areas where this is a problem. It is also highly susceptible to spring dead spot in the Transition Zone of the U.S., which includes Oklahoma, Arkansas, Missouri, Tennessee, Kentucky, Virginia, and northern parts of North Carolina, Georgia, Alabama, Mississippi, and Texas—that is, the region between north and south where temperatures are too cold in winter

for bermudagrass and too hot and humid in summer months for Kentucky bluegrass. Tifgreen is recommended for golf greens and fairways, tennis courts, bowling greens, and fine lawns with a high level of maintenance.

10. Texturf-10 (*C. dactylon*). Selected from common bermudagrass fairway at the Corsicana Country Club in Corsicana, Texas, for its medium texture, dark green color, sparse seedheads, and dense turf. It also has good wear tolerance and late fall color retention and makes earlier spring recovery than common bermudagrass. Texturf-10 was released by the Texas Agricultural Experiment Station in 1957. It is recommended for sports fields, playgrounds, and lawns. Texturf-10 is sensitive to chlorinated hydrocarbon insecticides, turning a straw color several days after an application of these materials. The grass recovers in 7 to 10 days with no permanent damage.

11. Tifway (*C. dactylon* and *C. transvaalensis*). A chance hybrid that appeared in a lot of seed of *C. transvaalensis* from Johannesburg, South Africa, in 1954. It is very similar to Tifgreen except for its greater stiffness of leaf blades and darker green color. Released by the Georgia Agricultural Experiment Station and Crops Research Division, ARS, USDA, in 1960. Recommended for golf course tees and fairways, home lawns, sports fields, and tennis courts. An improved selection of Tifway, Tifway II, was recently released for its superior cold tolerance.

12. Tufcote (*C. dactylon*). Selection of *C. dactylon* from South Africa introduced in U.S. in 1942. Medium-textured variety with stiff leaves, rapid spread, and few seedheads. Released by the Maryland Agricultural Experiment Station and Crops Research Division, ARS, USDA, in 1962 under the name of Tuffy. Renamed Tufcote in 1963. Release was based on superior cold tolerance and wear resistance. Recommended for use on lawns and sports fields.

13. Santa Ana (*C. dactylon* and *C. transvaalensis*). A selection from *C. dactylon* (Royal Cape) obtained from South Africa in 1954. The initial selection was made at UCLA in 1956 for its deep blue-green color, medium-fine texture, and good fall color retention. Santa Ana was found to have good salt tolerance and a high degree of tolerance to smog, which frequently discolored Tifway and Tifgreen varieties. Released by the California Agricultural Experiment Station in 1966, Santa Ana is recommended for golf courses, sports fields, playgrounds, and lawns. Careful management is required to prevent thatch accumulation.

14. Ormond (*C. dactylon*). Selected from a fairway at Ellinor Village Country Club, Ormond Beach, Florida, for attractive blue-green color, vigor, and prostrate growth habit. It has a medium texture and tolerance to leaf disease but lacks cold tolerance. Released by Florida Agricultural Experiment Station in 1962. Well adapted in Florida for use on lawns, golf courses, playgrounds, and sports fields.

15. Midway (*C. dactylon* and *C. transvaalensis*). A medium-textured lawn

grass that produces relatively few seedheads. Released by the Kansas Agricultural Experiment Station in 1965 for its superior cold tolerance in Kansas. Recommended for lawns, golf courses, and sports fields in the upper South.

16. Tifdwarf (*C. dactylon* and *C. transvaalensis*). A selection from Tifgreen golf greens in Sea Island, Georgia, and Florence, South Carolina, where both greens were planted with Tifgreen obtained from the Georgia Coastal Plain Experiment Station at Tifton. Evidence indicates that Tifdwarf is a vegetative mutant that occurred in Tifgreen at Tifton before the first planting stock was sent out for testing. Tifdwarf resembles Tifgreen except that its leaves and internodes are significantly shorter than those of Tifgreen, and it has a darker green color. Tifdwarf turns a reddish-purple color after the first cool temperatures in the fall. High rates of nitrogen in the fall will reduce the degree of discoloration. Tifdwarf is slower to recover than Tifgreen when both are planted on 12-inch center. Released by the Georgia Agricultural Experiment Station, Tifton, and Crop Research Division, ARS, USDA, in 1965 for its superior putting quality. Tifdwarf is recommended for golf greens, tennis courts, and bowling greens.

17. Pee Dee (*C. dactylon* and *C. transvaalensis*). A selection from an early South Carolina planting of Tifgreen. Like Tifdwarf, Pee Dee is believed to be a mutation from Tifgreen. Pee Dee is a dark green, very fine-textured (dwarf), fast-spreading variety. Unlike Tifdwarf, Pee Dee is faster spreading than Tifgreen when planted on equal spacings. Released by the South Carolina Agricultural Experiment Station, Clemson, in 1968. Recommended for golf greens in the southeastern United States.

PROPAGATION

Common bermudagrass (*C. dactylon* [L.] Pers.) is the only widely used turf-type bermudagrass variety that can be established from seed. Nu-Mex Sahara, Sonesta, Cheyenne, and Guymon are new seeded varieties that have had limited use in the southwestern U.S. All hybrid bermudagrasses are sterile and must be propagated vegetatively by stolons, rhizomes, or sod.

Bermudagrass seed is generally available from two types—common and giant. Both are grown in the western U.S. where much of the common bermudagrass seed is produced. Giant bermudagrass is a vigorous, open, upright, type adapted for pasture and hay. Giant bermudagrass is very undesirable in a common bermudagrass turf, although it generally does not persist beyond the first growing season. It is frequently a weed in seed fields of common bermudagrass. As a result, some lots of common bermudagrass seed sold for turf use have giant mixed with common. Purchasing and using only certified bermudagrass seed will prevent this problem.

Bermudagrass seed should be planted at a rate of ½ to 1 pound of seed per 1,000 square feet. Spring and summer plantings should utilize hulled bermudagrass seed for faster germination. Late fall and winter plantings should be with unhulled bermudagrass seed to delay germination of a significant amount of the seed until more favorable conditions occur in the spring. Unhulled bermudagrass seed might be planted together with annual ryegrass in the fall to provide temporary cover and protection from soil erosion during winter months. Annual ryegrass will delay the development of a bermudagrass turf, but it may be needed for cover and protection.

When planting in the fall and winter on areas subject to severe erosion, wheat or rye can be drilled with unhulled bermudagrass seed. The wheat or rye will establish quickly and provide some cover during winter months. The small grains also provide less competition than ryegrass to seedling bermudagrass in late spring.

Bermudagrass sprigs or stolons for planting should be freshly harvested and protected from desiccation by wind and sun. Also, they should not be subject to excessive heating which occurs when moist planting material is tightly packed or covered for several days. Sprigs are usually distinguished from stolons in that sprigs consist of stolons with roots and rhizomes; whereas stolons consist of above ground parts only. Sprigs are produced by shredding harvested sod or by sprig harvesters. Stolons are generally harvested with a vertical mower or a flail mower set close to the ground. Sprigs will tolerate slightly more environmental stress during planting and establishment because of the energy reserves in the roots and rhizomes.

Sprigs or stolons should be planted at 5 to 15 bushels per 1,000 square feet, depending on the rate of cover required. Higher planting rates up to 25 or more bushels per 1,000 square feet will provide a faster grass cover. A minimum planting rate should be 2 to 3 bushels per 1,000 square feet, or 100 bushels per acre. Sprigs or stolons should be broadcast on a clean seedbed and pressed into moist soil with a roller or covered lightly with soil or mulch. Moist conditions must be maintained for 2 to 3 weeks after planting to obtain a good cover.

Seed or sprigs should not be planted before soil temperature is above 65° F. Planting too early may retard development of a turf and extend the critical establishment period several weeks. Soil temperatures of 68° F to 75° F are ideal for germination and rapid development of bermudagrass.

Fertilizer, as determined by a soil test, should be incorporated into the soil during seedbed preparation. Nitrogen fertilizer can be applied to the soil surface immediately prior to planting or at the time of planting at a rate of 1 pound per 1,000 square feet, or 40 to 50 pounds per acre. Nitrogen should be applied 3 to 4 week intervals until a cover is obtained.

Mowing should begin several weeks after planting to control weed growth and promote spreading of bermudagrass. If additional weed control is needed selective postemergence herbicides can be applied at 3 to 4 weeks after planting. Weed control will greatly enhance bermudagrass growth and coverage.

However, preemergence herbicides should not be applied to bermudagrass turf during the first growing season.

MANAGEMENT

Bermudagrasses, in general, are drought tolerant; that is, they survive dry soil conditions longer than most turfgrasses. However, drought tolerance in bermudagrass is based on their ability to become semidormant during severe droughts and to recover from stolons and rhizomes when moisture becomes available. The grass does not provide a desirable turf under drought conditions.

Bermudagrass does respond readily to irrigation. In general, water requirements of bermudagrass depend on turf use and climatic factors, such as temperature, wind, humidity, and light intensity. Water requirements increase with increasing levels of maintenance (golf green > bowling green > fairway > sports field > lawn > roadside), higher temperatures, higher wind speed, lower humidity, longer day lengths, and greater light intensity. Of course, the longer the growing season the greater the water requirement for the year. Water use rates may range from less than 2 mm per day to 1 cm per day depending on these environmental conditions.

The frequency of irrigation required to maintain growth is dependent on water use rate and soil type. Clay soils, for example, hold more water than sandy soils and, consequently, they require less frequent irrigations. The depth of the root zone also influences the frequency of irrigations. Bermudagrass roots can grow to a depth of 6 feet or more depending on soil profile characteristics. However, the majority of the root system, 80 percent or more, is found in the top 4 inches of soil. Where roots extend several feet into the soil, thorough and infrequent irrigations produce the most drought-tolerant turf. Light, frequent irrigations such as practiced on golf greens produces shallow-rooted grass that shows drought stress very rapidly.

Bermudagrass does not tolerate poorly drained sites. On compacted sites and heavy clay soils, irrigation must be closely controlled to avoid water-logged conditions. Hard, compacted sites can often be improved with respect to water penetration by core aeration and topdressing with sand or a porous aggregate material. The presence of a heavy thatch layer will also interfere with water penetration. Thatch removal by vertical mowing and core aeration also improves water penetration and reduces the frequency of irrigation required.

Mowing requirements for bermudagrass turf are dependent on variety, use, and the level of maintenance. Common bermudagrass and other medium-textured varieties produce dense, wear-tolerant turf when mowed at heights between ½ and 1 inch, the lower heights being good for golf and sports turf and the tall heights for lawns. At mowing heights above 1 inch, bermudagrass develops turf with an acceptable appearance but with poor wear tolerance. For lawns, roadsides, cemeteries, and other low traffic areas, taller mowing heights can be used. Fine-textured hybrid bermudagrasses, such as Tifgreen, Tifdwarf, and Pee Dee should be mowed at a height of ½ inch or less. Taller mowing heights with these grasses produce puffy, stemmy turf that is easily scalped during mowing.

As a general recommendation to maintain good turf density and color, no more than 40 percent of the leaf tissue should be removed at any mowing. Thus, the shorter the mowing height, the more frequent the turf must be mowed. Golf greens mowed at ³⁄₁₆-inch or less are mowed daily, sports fields mowed at ½ inch are mowed at 3-day intervals and lawns mowed at 1 to 1 ½ inches, at 5- to 7-day intervals.

Reel mowers produce the best cut on bermudagrass turf. However, the speed of the reels and the number of blades per cutting reel determine the smoothness of cut. Common bermudagrass mowed at 1 inch or higher can be cut with a reel with 5 or 6 blades. Common and hybrid bermudagrasses mowed at ½ to 1 inch should be cut with a reel containing 7 blades. At heights below ½ inch, 9 to 11 blades per reel are required for a smooth cut.

Bermudagrasses have a relatively high fertilizer requirement to maintain a high level of turf quality. The amount and frequency of fertilizer required depends on the desired appearance and growth rate of the turf, length of growing season, soil type, bermudagrass variety, and the use of the turf. Where high quality is of critical importance and the turf is mowed frequently, 0.5 pound of nitrogen per 1,000 square feet per week may be applied during the growing season. The lowest rate of nitrogen that can be applied and still maintain acceptable bermudagrass turf for lawns and golf fairways is about 0.5 pound of nitrogen per 1,000 square feet per month.

Soil types also influence fertilizer needs. Sandy soils require light but frequent applications of nitrogen because of low nitrogen retention. Sandy soils are also typically low in other nutrients, such as phosphorus and potassium, and these nutrients must also be provided through fertilization. Soil tests are required to determine phosphorus, potassium, calcium, and other nutrient deficiencies. Potassium is particularly important because of its contribution to root growth, environmental stress tolerance (heat, cold, and drought), and wear tolerance. Potassium has also been found to reduce susceptibility of bermudagrass to leaf spot diseases.

Bermudagrass tolerates a wide range in soil reaction but performs best between pH 6.5 and 8.0. At pH levels below 6.5, limestone should be added according to soil test recommendations.

Bermudagrass varieties also differ slightly in nitrogen requirements. Common bermudagrass and selections from common generally have a lower nitrogen requirement than the hybrid bermudagrasses. Tifgreen may have the highest requirement for nitrogen to maintain a dark green color and keep seed production to a minimum. Tifway bermudagrass, which has an inherent dark green color, requires less nitrogen than Tifgreen. Excessive nitrogen fertilization, beyond that required to maintain color and vigor, leads to increased mowing, irrigation, thatch control, and pest problems, all of which result in higher maintenance costs.

Turf use has a significant effect on the amount of fertilizer required. Golf greens, bowling greens, and tennis courts have a very high nitrogen requirement; golf course fairways, sports fields, and lawns, an intermediate requirement; and roadsides, airfields, and other low maintenance areas, a low nitrogen requirement.

Hybrid bermudagrasses require regular cultivation practices—vertical mowing, aeration, and topdressing—to maintain high quality turf. Bermudagrass golf greens may require weekly vertical mowing and monthly topdressing under heavy use conditions. Fairways, sports fields, and lawns may need these cultural operations on an annual basis. Without cultivation bermudagrass turf tends to develop thatch, grain, and spongy conditions that result in scalping and a nonuniform appearance.

Common bermudagrass and selections from common need less cultivation to prevent these conditions. However, under heavy use common bermudagrass needs regular aeration and topdressing to prevent compaction and maintain turf vigor.

PEST PROBLEMS

Bermudagrass tolerates a wide range of environmental conditions and survives in nature where fertility and rainfall are adequate and winter temperatures are not too low. Bermudagrass does have numerous pest problems, however, which tend to increase with higher levels of management. High nitrogen fertilization rates, close mowing, and frequent irrigation tend to increase the susceptibility of bermudagrass to insects and diseases.

Serious insect pests that feed on the foliage of bermudagrass include armyworms, cutworms, sod webworms, bermudagrass mites, and Rhodesgrass scale (mealybug). The latter two insects cause damage by sucking juices from the stems and stunting normal growth of the grass. White grubs can severely damage bermudagrass by feeding on grass roots. Nuisance-type insects found on bermudagrass include chiggers, ants, and ticks.

Insect control on bermudagrass should include cultural, biological, and chemical methods. Under good management bermudagrass can tolerate low populations of most of these insects. Where insect populations are high enough to cause significant damage, biological and chemical methods may be required. Some species of white grub can be controlled with milky spore disease, a biological control that effectively controls white grub populations of the Japanese beetle. *Baccilus thuringensis* is a biological control for armyworms, cutworms, and sod webworms. And *Neodusmetia sangwai,* a fly-like parasite, has effectively eliminated the Rhodesgrass mealybug in Texas (Dean et al. 1979). Where these biological controls are not effective, chemicals can be used together with these cultural and biological controls to reduce insect populations to an acceptable level.

Several serious disease organisms and nematodes also attack bermudagrass turf. Dollar spot, spring dead spot, leaf spot, brownpatch, and *Pythium* are all fungus diseases that attack bermudagrass turf. Several species of nematodes also cause significant damage to bermudagrass turf.

As in the case of insects, cultural and chemical methods may be required to control disease and nematode problems. High nitrogen fertilization rates should be avoided during peak periods of disease attacks. Thatch should be controlled through proper mowing and cultivation. And water should be applied properly to avoid severe drought stress or waterlogged conditions which increase the susceptibility of grass to some diseases.

Where cultural practices do not adequately control turf diseases, fungicides are available for control. In some intensive maintenance situations, preventive applications of fungicides provide the best means of disease control.

Weeds are also serious pests in bermudagrass turf. Vigorous, healthy turf

Saint Augustine

properly maintained provides the best means of weed control in bermudagrass turf. But, where turf thins due to environmental stress, pest problems or poor management, weeds rapidly invade bermudagrass.

Broadleaved weeds, including clover, chickweed, dandelion, henbit, dichondra, and others, can be controlled with the hormone-type herbicides such as 2,4-D, MCPP, and dicamba. Grassy weeds, including crabgrass and dallisgrass, can be controlled with several applications of MSMA in spring or early summer. Annual grasses, including crabgrass and annual bluegrass, can be controlled with preemergence herbicides. However, all of these herbicides must be used together with good management to effectively reduce weed populations.

Saint Augustine Grass

ORIGIN AND DISTRIBUTION

Saint Augustine grass is a widely used lawn grass along the Gulf Coast in the United States, in southern Mexico, throughout the Caribbean region, South America, South Africa, Western Africa, Australia, the South Pacific, and the Hawaiian Islands (Sauer 1972). The species is primarily of tropical origin and is native to sandy beach ridges, fringes of swamps and lagoons, salty and fresh water marshes, and limestone shorelines. Saint Augustine grass gradually moved inland to naturally open areas, such as stream banks, lakeshores, and other moist sites. It tolerates a wide range in soil types but does not withstand waterlogged or droughty sites.

In the United States Saint Augustine grass is found from the Carolinas to Florida and westward along the Gulf Coast to Texas and in southern and central California. Because of its lack of winter hardiness, Saint Augustine grass is restricted to areas with mild winter temperatures. Like bermudagrass, Saint Augustine thrives in high temperatures, but the growth of Saint Augustine is better than that of bermudagrass in cool, coastal climates.

Saint Augustine grass is native to the Gulf of Mexico region, the West Indies and Western Africa (Sauer 1972). For as long as there have been records, Saint Augustine grass has been reported as a seashore pioneer along the Atlantic coasts of Africa and the Americas. Prior to 1800 the species was reported in Uruguay, Brazil, Nigeria, Sierra Leone, the West Indies, Bermuda, and South Carolina. In the Pacific records are not nearly as old, but it was reported in Kauai prior to 1800. By 1840 Saint Augustine grass had also been collected from Australia and New Zealand.

Several variants or strains of Saint Augustine grass have been reported. The normal strain in early records has a white stigma color and was found to be a fertile diploid with eighteen chromosomes. A sterile triploid variant with purple-colored stigmas was first collected around the Cape of Good Hope in 1791 (Sauer 1972). By 1900 it was being used for lawns in Natal and has since been planted in Rhodesia, the Congo, Senegal, Australia, and

Southern California. In Florida it has been planted for lawns since the 1890s.

Saint Augustine grass was moved inland from coastal regions by humans for use in pastures and lawns. Its requirements, other than mild winter temperatures, include moist and somewhat fertile soils. Saint Augustine grass will not survive in dry inland areas without supplemental irrigation. It is not as drought tolerant or cold tolerant as bermudagrass; consequently, its inland movement has been restricted to states and countries bordering coastal zones.

This species is called Saint Augustine grass and sometimes carpetgrass in the southeastern United States and in California, crabgrass in Bermuda and the West Indies, gramillon in Argentina, wiregrass in Saint Helena, and buffalograss in Australia and the South Pacific.

DESCRIPTION OF SPECIES

Saint Augustine grass, *Stenotaphrum secundatum* (Walt.) Kuntze, is a perennial robust grass widely used for pastures and lawns. In the warmer climates of the tropics and subtropics it rivals bermudagrass in importance.

Saint Augustine grass is a coarse-textured, stoloniferous species that roots at the nodes. Unlike bermudagrass, Saint Augustine grass does not have rhizomes. Its stems (stolons) and overlapping leaf sheaths are generally compressed; leaf blades generally folded, abruptly contracted at the base, rounded at the tip, and smooth; ligule is reduced to a short fringe of hairs; collar is petioled; and the sheath greatly compressed and ciliate along the margins. Inflorescences are mostly terminal, some also axillary; spike-like (corky) racemes and spikelets embedded in main axis; each raceme bearing one to three spikelets; spikelets lanceolate or ovate, awnless and sessile; glumes membranous, the lower glume less than half as long as spikelet; lower floret staminate, upper floret complete and caryopsis ovate to oblong, 2.0 to 3.0 mm long, often failing to mature.

ADAPTATION AND USE

Saint Augustine grass is adapted to moist, coastal areas with mild winter temperatures. It is known to be tolerant of high summer temperatures and retains its color at temperatures as much as ten degrees lower than those which discolor bermudagrass.

Saint Augustine grass tolerates moderate shade, being as good or better than other warm-season grasses for shaded sites. However, under densely shaded conditions, Saint Augustine grass develops thin, spindly turf.

As long as fertility and drainage are adequate, Saint Augustine grass tolerates a wide range of soil types. Saint Augustine grass grows satisfactorily at a pH range from 6.0 to 8.5 but develops a chlorotic appearance in highly alkaline soils (above pH 7.8). It does not tolerate compacted or waterlogged soil conditions. Saint Augustine grass is highly tolerant of soil salinity, producing satisfactory growth at salt levels as high as 16 millimhos (mmhos).

Seed are embedded in seed stalk.

Bermudagrass will tolerate only slightly higher salt levels.

Saint Augustine grass is used primarily for lawns as it does not tolerate traffic as well as some other warm-season species. It produces satisfactory turf at moderate levels of maintenance, effectively competes with weeds and other grasses, and has only a few serious pests.

In moist, warm climates Saint Augustine grass maintains a satisfactory turf cover with only occasional mowing. In drier climates (below 30 inches annual rainfall) it survives with supplemental irrigation. At higher maintenance levels, Saint Augustine grass produces a thick, lush, dark green turf that is highly preferred by homeowners.

Petioled leaf blade and compressed leaf sheath are characteristic of species.

VARIETIES

Since Saint Augustine grass has been propagated vegetatively for two hundred years, only a few strains or varieties have been commercially propagated. The common strain, a fertile diploid with a white stigma color, is native to the Gulf–Caribbean–West African region (Sauer 1972). This species may have crossed with another species of *Stenotaphrum* to produce the sterile triploid strain originally reported in South Africa (Sauer 1971). This triploid, distinguished from the common strain by its purple stigma color, has been found in Australia, New Zealand, and in the Pacific Islands. It has been planted in Florida since the 1890s and in California since 1920.

Several selections from Florida were made available prior to 1960 (Wilson 1961). Floratine, a purple stigma type, was released by the Florida Agricultural Experiment Station in 1959. Floratine was released for its somewhat finer texture and darker green color than the typical purple stigma-type strain found in Florida prior to that time. It also retains its dark green color long into the fall and was reported to tolerate closer mowing than other Saint Augustine grass selections.

Prior to Floratine, Bitter Blue was selected as an improvement over coarser textured types of Saint Augustine grass used in Florida for lawns. Both of these selections, Floratine and Bitter Blue, are similar to the coarse textured triploid types reported in Florida prior to 1900.

Floratam Saint Augustine grass was released by the Florida and Texas Agricultural Experiment Stations in 1972 as a Saint Augustine Decline (SAD) virus-resistant (Toler 1972) and chinch bug–tolerant selection. Like other Florida types, Floratam is a vigorous, coarse-textured Saint Augustine grass variety. Floratam has a purple stigma color and is sterile. Stolons of Floratam are large, purplish-red in color, with internodes averaging three inches in length. Leaf blades are wider and longer than common Saint Augustine grass. The morphological characteristics of Floratam are similar to those of Roselawn Saint Augustine grass, which is used as a pasture grass on muck soils in South Florida.

Floratam is not as cold tolerant as the common type found in Texas. Its use should be restricted to South Florida, South Texas, and the coastal zones of other southern states. Floratam also lacks the degree of shade tolerance that other Saint Augustine grass varieties possess. Floralawn and FX-10 Saint Augustine grass have been released by the Florida Agricultural Experiment Station as improvements over Floratam. Both are similar in texture and habit to Floratam but have superior tolerance to chinch bugs and drought.

Seville Saint Augustine grass was released by the O. M. Scott and Sons Company in 1980 as a SAD-resistant and chinch bug–tolerant variety. Seville is much finer textured than Floratam, but it too lacks the necessary cold tolerance to extend its area of adaptation beyond the southern boundaries of the Gulf Coast.

Raleigh Saint Augustine grass was released by the North Carolina Experiment Station in 1980 as a cold-tolerant, SAD-resistant strain. Raleigh is finer textured than Floratam and develops a dense turf much like the Texas common strain of Saint Augustine grass. Raleigh is also more shade tolerant than Floratam. But, unlike Floratam, Raleigh is not resistant to lawn chinch bugs.

A strain of Saint Augustine grass grown and produced commercially in Texas since 1920 is called Texas common. Texas common is typical of the white stigma type reported by Sauer (1972). Texas common was found to be a fertile diploid with eighteen chromosomes. Seedling progeny from this white stigma type show wide variations in morphological characters. However, since the strain has been propagated vegetatively for over one hundred years, only a few variations in the grass have been produced. Natural variants of the common strain are found throughout the state. It is assumed that these variants were developed from seed produced by the common strains of Saint Augustine grass.

Dwarf and variegated types of Saint Augustine grass have also been selected from seed produced by Texas common. However, these strains are more ornamental and novelty grasses than turfgrasses. One of the dwarf types (patented in the U.S. as Garret's 141) has been evaluated for its seed production potential. However, Garret's 141 and its progeny lack the cold tolerance necessary to extend its area of adaptation beyond Southern Florida and South Texas in the United States.

PROPAGATION

As long as Saint Augustine grass has been cultivated, it has been propagated by vegetative means—stolons, plugs, or sod. Only recently has the seed production potential of Saint Augustine grass been realized, but, as yet, significant use has not been made of that potential.

As reported by Long and Bashaw at Texas A&M in 1961 only a few strains of Saint Augustine grass are fertile. The common strain of Saint Augustine found in Texas is generally fertile; whereas, the strains used in Florida since before 1900 were found to be sterile.

Saint Augustine grass is readily established from sod since the species is vigorous and spreads rapidly by creeping stolons. Sod plugs or stolons planted on 1- to 2-foot spacings can be expected to cover in one growing season. In commercial Saint Augustine grass production 300 to 500 square yards of sod are cut into plugs and planted per acre. In small lawn plantings, 2- to 4-square inch sod plugs are planted on 1- to 2-foot spacings. Saint Augustine can be successfully established from plugs anytime during the growing season if water is available.

Unlike bermudagrass, Saint Augustine grass is not effectively propagated from stolons. Saint Augustine grass stolons are much more prone to desiccation than bermudagrass. Also, bermudagrass roots much faster and has a faster growth rate than Saint Augustine grass. As a result, Saint Augustine grass is not successfully established by hydromulching or broadcasting stolons.

Some Saint Augustine grass strains can be established from seed by planting at 1/3 to 1/2 pound of PLS per 1,000 square feet. The rate of establishment from seed planted at that rate would be about the same as for 2-inch sod plugs planted on 1-foot spacings. A seeded Saint Augustine grass lawn should be kept moist for several weeks after planting to obtain a satisfactory stand of grass. Only after the seedlings have begun to spread can the grass tolerate dry conditions. Saint Augustine should be seeded in late spring to early summer. Fertilization during the establishment period (first 3 months after planting) is critical to developing a complete cover of Saint Augustine grass. A starter fertilizer (one high in phosphorus) or a balanced, complete fertilizer should be applied at planting time. Subsequent applications of nitrogen at

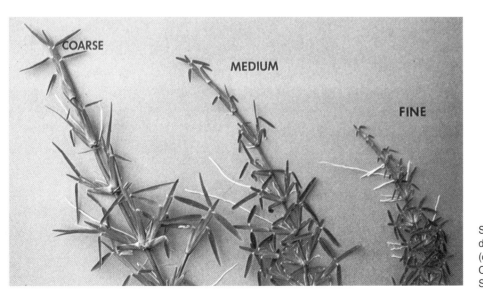

Saint Augustine varieties differ in texture: Floralawn (coarse), Raleigh and Common (medium), and Seville (fine).

monthly intervals at a rate of 1 pound per 1,000 square feet will promote rapid spread of Saint Augustine plugs.

Annual weeds such as crabgrass, spurge, and purslane can be controlled with preemerge herbicides such as atrazine and dacthal; however, weekly mowing will keep these weeds from crowding out the Saint Augustine during the first summer. These annuals will die during the fall, and a preemerge could be applied the following spring. Perennial weeds such as dallisgrass should be controlled by spot treatment with products such as glyphosate (Roundup). If these practices are followed, a weed-free Saint Augustine grass lawn will develop by the second year after planting.

MANAGEMENT

After establishment the success of Saint Augustine as a lawn grass depends largely on management. Mowing, fertilization, and supplemental watering are required to maintain a dense, green, weed-free turf of Saint Augustine grass. In coastal areas where rainfall is adequate, Saint Augustine grass will survive with little care. In inland areas, where rainfall is less dependable, close management of water is required to maintain a satisfactory lawn with Saint Augustine grass.

The growth rate of Saint Augustine grass is dependent on temperature, moisture availability, and nutrient availability. Any one of these factors can limit the rate of growth of this species. In the spring with mild daytime temperatures and cool night temperatures, Saint Augustine grass greens-up, but makes little growth. As day and night temperatures increase during late spring and summer, the growth rate increases. Thus, an established turf of Saint Augustine grass may require mowing every two weeks in early spring and as often as every five days by late spring if nitrogen fertilizer is applied.

During the fall, as temperatures cool, Saint Augustine grass maintains its dark green color, but its growth rate declines sharply. Mowing frequency may be reduced to twice monthly during late fall.

Mowing heights may range from 1 to 3 inches depending on the frequency of mowing and the degree of shade present. At mowing heights below 2 inches, Saint Augustine grass should be mowed every 5 days during late spring and summer. At a 2- to 3-inch mowing height, a 7-day mowing schedule is adequate. Above 3 inches, Saint Augustine grass should be mowed at 10- to 14-day intervals. In moderate to dense shade, Saint Augustine grass should be mowed at about 3 inches at 7-day intervals.

During the fall, mowing height should be raised about ½ inch to increase total leaf area of the turf. The increased leaf area will help the grass accumulate energy reserves to get through the winter. The greater leaf area will also help prevent weed invasion during the dormant season.

Saint Augustine grass is responsive to nitrogen fertilizer in terms of color and growth rate. On sandy soils Saint Augustine grass requires about 0.5

pound of nitrogen per 1,000 square feet per month during the growing season to maintain satisfactory color and density. At rates above 1 pound per 1,000 square feet, Saint Augustine grass produces lush growth that is highly susceptible to insects and diseases. On heavier textured soils 1 pound of nitrogen every 60 days is adequate to maintain good color and growth. Thatch accumulation is also a problem when nitrogen fertilization exceeds the required rate.

Late fall fertilization of Saint Augustine grass helps maintain color and density of the lawn into the winter and promotes early recovery of the grass in the spring. Thus, to extend the length of time a Saint Augustine lawn is attractive, the lawn should receive about 1 pound of nitrogen every 60 days from early spring through late fall.

Saint Augustine is sensitive to iron deficiency and readily develops chlorotic symptoms in alkaline or iron-deficient soils. This deficiency can be corrected with applications or iron sulfate or iron chelate.

Potassium requirements for Saint Augustine grass are about the same as for other grasses. About half as much potassium as nitrogen is required to maintain growth. Potassium has been shown to increase root growth, cold tolerance, and drought tolerance in Saint Augustine grass.

Phosphorous requirements for established Saint Augustine grass are very low and generally met from the soil. Occasional applications of a phosphorous fertilizer material may be required. Newly planted Saint Augustine grass will respond to phosphorous fertilizers in terms of an increased rate of spread.

PEST MANAGEMENT

Several insect pests cause serious damage to Saint Augustine grass lawns. The southern lawn chinch bug is the most serious pest on Saint Augustine grass in Florida where the insect is active most of the year. In other states it ranks among the most serious pests along with SAD, brownpatch, and white grub.

The chinch bug damages Saint Augustine grass by feeding on the stems at the base of the leaf sheath. Populations of chinch bugs may reach several hundred per square foot with damage usually apparent at twenty to thirty chinch bugs per square foot. Initial injury symptoms from chinch bugs resemble drought stress—stunted, chlorotic spots in open (full sun) areas of the lawn. As feeding continues, irregular areas of dead grass develop in the lawn.

Timely applications of insecticides will control chinch bugs. One or two treatments are required during the growing season in most areas, but as many as three or more treatments may be required in some areas of Florida. Floratam, Floralawn, and FX-10 Saint Augustine grass are resistant to the southern lawn chinch bug and are widely used in Florida and South Texas where the grasses are adapted. In Florida damage to Floratam has been observed in lawns infested with chinch bugs.

White grubs are also a serious pest on Saint Augustine grass lawns. The grubs are the larvae of the May beetle or the southern masked chafer and develop in late summer and fall just below the soil surface. The grubs feed on roots of Saint Augustine grass and cause significant losses of turf during some years. Damage usually appears the following spring as dead areas of grass that can be easily lifted from the lawn.

Grub control is difficult since the larvae are often quite large when detected and feed below the soil surface. Also, for insecticides to be effective, they must be drenched into the soil where the insects feed. Since some insecticides are tightly bound to the thatch layer of Saint Augustine grass, drenching the material into the soil is difficult.

Timely and proper application of an insecticide is the only method of controlling white grubs. Since they are only an occasional problem, inspection of the turf in midsummer is required for effective control. Biological control with milky spore disease has not been effective against these species of white grub.

Sod webworms, armyworms, and cutworms can also feed on Saint Augustine grass leaves and can cause damage when infestations are heavy. Evidence of heavy feeding by these insects includes a skeletonized appearance of leaf blade, silk-like webs visible in early morning (webs cover earthen tunnel in the thatch layer of turf), or defoliation of lawn in irregular patches. All of the leaf-feeding insects can be easily controlled by insecticides or biological worm control (*Bacillus* spp.).

Ground pearls, subterranean scale insects that feed on roots of grasses, can also cause damage to Saint Augustine grass lawns. The scale insects attach themselves to grass roots and secrete a wax-like shell around their bodies that resembles a pearl. As the immature scale inside the pearl grows larger, the pearl also increases in size. The pearl may reach ⅛ inch in diameter and can be found attached to grass roots in the top several inches of soil.

Ground pearl damage becomes evident in spring and summer, particularly during dry periods, as small irregular areas of unthrifty or dead grass. Insecticide treatment should be made in May or early June when the insect is in the crawler stage. Consecutive treatments for two or more years may be required for effective control.

DISEASES

Saint Augustine grass is susceptible to a number of turfgrass diseases including brownpatch, take-all patch, SAD, gray leaf spot, *Helminthosporium*, *Pythium*, rust, downy mildew, and others. All of these diseases, except SAD, are caused by fungi and can be controlled by good management and fungicides. SAD is a virus disease for which there is no chemical control. Only resistant varieties of Saint Augustine grass are effective against this disease. Floratam, Seville, Raleigh, and several experimental varieties have shown good resistance to the SAD virus.

Brownpatch, take-all patch, and gray leaf spot are the most serious diseases caused by fungi attacking Saint Augustine grass. Although these diseases rarely kill Saint Augustine, they severely weaken and thin the grass to the degree that the lawn is unsightly. Preventative applications of fungicides are most effective against these diseases.

WEEDS

A healthy Saint Augustine grass lawn effectively crowds out most weeds. But Saint Augustine grass that is not properly maintained or is weakened by insects or disease can be invaded by grassy and broadleaved weeds. Cool-season weeds such as henbit, chickweed, and clover are a serious problem in dormant Saint Augustine grass. These weeds can be controlled by hormone-type herbicides in early spring.

Annual grassy weeds such as annual bluegrass and crabgrass are best controlled by timely applications of preemergence herbicides. Perennial grasses such as dallisgrass and bermudagrass are difficult to control in Saint Augustine grass turf. Nonselective products can be applied as directed sprays to these weeds to obtain control.

Zoysiagrasses

ORIGIN AND DISTRIBUTION

Zoysiagrasses are warm-season grasses native to China, Japan, and other parts of Southeast Asia. The species was named to commemorate an eighteenth century Austrian botanist, Karl von Zois. In 1912 *Zoysia matrella* was introduced into the United States from Manila by a USDA botanist, C. V. Piper (Childers and White 1947). Because of its origin the grass was commonly called Manila grass.

Piper described the grass as abundant on or near the seashore in the Philippine Islands. According to Piper's notes, it made a beautiful lawn when closely clipped. He suggested that the grass had unusual promise as a lawn grass along the Gulf Coast and Atlantic coast of Florida.

Zoysia japonica, sometimes called Japanese lawn grass or Korean lawn grass, is a coarser textured, but more cold-hardy species than Z. *matrella*. Z. *japonica* was introduced into the United States in 1895 from the Manchurian Province of China. In the United States Z. *japonica* could be expected to do very well as far north as Maryland. It is a seeded variety of *Zoysia*.

The third species of *Zoysia* used for turf is called Korean velvet grass, or Mascarene grass, Z. *tenuifolia*. It is a very fine-textured species but is the least cold tolerant of the three species. Z. *tenuifolia* is native to the Far East and was introduced in the U.S. from the Mascarene Islands. In the U.S. it is used in southern California as a low growing ground cover (Youngner 1980).

DESCRIPTION OF SPECIES

Zoysiagrasses are sod-forming perennial species that possess both stolons and rhizomes. The grasses turn brown after the first hard frost and are among the first warm-season grasses to green-up in the spring. The species vary from extremely fine-textured to coarse-textured types, and the leaf blades are very stiff due to a high silica content.

Leaves are rolled in the bud shoot. Leaf blades are smooth with occasional hairs near the base, margins are smooth, and blades are sharply pointed. Ligule is a fringe of hairs. Auricles are absent. Leaf sheath is round to slightly flattened, split, glabrous, but with a tuft of hair at the throat. Inflorescence is a short, terminal spikelike raceme with spikelets on short appressed pedicels.

ADAPTATION AND USE

A highly versatile specie, zoysiagrass makes an ideal lawn grass in some situations and can be used on golf courses, parks, and sports fields. Zoysiagrasses can be grown in all kinds of soils ranging from sands to clays and both acid and alkaline in reaction. In the United States zoysiagrasses are adapted along the Atlantic coast from Florida to Connecticut and along the Gulf Coast to

Zoysiagrass

Texas. They are also adapted throughout the Transition Zone of the U.S. and in California.

In the southern U.S. the zoysiagrasses grow well in moderately shaded locations. In cooler climates, they do not perform as well under shade as some other species.

Zoysia has good drought tolerance. Although it does turn straw-colored under severe drought conditions, it has the capacity to respond to subsequent irrigation or rainfall. Its water requirements are similar to those of bermudagrass. The leaf blades of zoysia are among the first to roll under drought conditions, thus it tends to conserve moisture more effectively than other species. Zoysia also has a deep root system allowing it to extract water more effectively from greater soil depths.

Zoysia is nearly as salt tolerant as bermudagrass. It is widely grown along sandy seashores where drainage is adequate. Zoysia does not tolerate poorly drained soils whether they are saline or otherwise.

Zoysiagrasses are among the most wear-tolerant turfgrasses. However, their slow rate of growth gives them very poor recuperative potential. Therefore, they perform satisfactorily on lawns, golf course fairways, and baseball fields. But they are not recommended for football or soccer fields, where traffic is concentrated in certain areas of the field. If the grass is completely worn in those areas, zoysia is very slow to fill in the damaged areas.

VARIETIES

There are three principal species of zoysia used for turf: *Zoysia japonica*, *Z. matrella*, and *Z. tenuifolia*. These species are differentiated by texture, cold tolerance and aggressiveness.

Z. japonica, often called Korean or Japanese lawngrass, was introduced into

Relative growth of Emerald zoysia *(left)* and Tifway bermudagrass *(right)* four weeks after clipping to one-inch height

the U.S. in 1895 (Hanson, Juska, and Burton 1969). *Z. japonica* is more cold tolerant than the other species, but it is also the most coarse textured of the three species. *Z. japonica* is the only zoysia specie that can be established from seed.

Meyer zoysia is an improved strain of *Z. japonica*. It was selected from a population of plants grown from seed by the USDA in 1941 (Grau and Radko 1951). It was evaluated by the USDA, USGA, and state universities and released jointly by the USDA and USGA in 1951. The selection was named in honor of Frank N. Meyer, a plant explorer for the USDA who made the first collection of zoysia seed in Korea in 1905.

Meyer was selected primarily for its texture, color, and vigor compared to other zoysia selections. Meyer is slow to become established and must be propagated by sod or sprigs. Once established it develops a very dense turf, demonstrates good cold tolerance, and grows well in partial shade. Meyer is best adapted to the Transition Zone where summers are too hot and humid for cool-season grasses and winters too cold for bermudagrass.

Belair and El Toro are new releases of *Z. japonica* from USDA and the University of California, respectively. Both are coarser textured, but faster spreading varieties, than Meyer.

Z. matrella was introduced into the United States in 1912 from Manila. It is chiefly a tropical and subtropical grass but can be grown as far north as Connecticut in the U.S. *Z. matrella* grows well in moderate shade and forms a thick mat in full sun. The leaf blades of *Z. matrella* are narrow, sharply pointed, and wiry. In tropical climates the grass remains green year-round. But in cooler climates it turns brown after several hard frosts and remains brown until late spring. *Z. matrella* must be propagated from sprigs and is quite slow to become established.

Z. tenuifolia is the finest textured, least winter hardy of the zoysiagrasses. It has very fine, short, wiry leaf blades and forms a dense, fluffy turf. It is extremely slow to spread and is most often used as a ground cover.

Emerald zoysia is a hybrid between *Z. japonica* and *Z. tenuifolia* released by USDA and the Georgia Agricultural Experiment Station in 1955 (Forbes, Robinson, and Latham 1955). Emerald combines the fine texture of *Z. tenuifolia* with the cold tolerance and faster rate of spread of *Z. japonica*. Emerald is similar to *Z. matrella* in appearance and habit.

PROPAGATION

Zoysiagrasses can be established from seed, sprigs, or sod. *Zoysia japonica* is the only species that can be established from seed.

Meyer and Emerald zoysia, Manila grass, and *Z. tenuifolia* must be propagated vegetatively from sprigs, plugs, or sod. The slow rate of spread of zoysia makes seedbed preparation and planting techniques very important to successful establishment of a zoysia turf.

The seedbed should be finely pulverized, smooth, firm, and weed-free prior to planting. Zoysia sod may be shredded or torn apart to provide sprigs, or it may be cut into 2-inch sod plugs for planting. A sprig should consist of a section of stem or rhizome with 2 or more nodes. Leaves do not need to be present.

Sprigs should be planted no more than 2 inches apart in rows spaced 6 inches apart, or broadcast over an area at a rate of 10 bushels per 1,000 square feet. If planted in rows it is important that the sprigs not be completely covered with soil. At least one node should be above soil level. If sprigs are broadcast over the surface, they should be rolled to ensure good soil contact. Freshly sprigged zoysia must be kept moist for several weeks after planting. And special attention should be given to weed control, since zoysia is much less aggressive than bermudagrass and some of the common turf weeds.

A newly planted zoysia turf should be fertilized with a 1-2-1 or similar fertilizer at a rate of 1 pound of nitrogen per 1,000 square feet of area at the time of planting. Monthly applications of nitrogen at $\frac{1}{2}$ to 1 pound per 1,000 square feet will promote the spread of zoysia.

Sprigging is the least expensive method of planting zoysia and usually gives a faster rate of cover than plugging. However, keeping the soil moist during the establishment period is most critical with sprigs. Small plantings of zoysia sprigs can be covered with a clear polyethylene tarp to maintain adequate moisture and increase soil temperature in the early spring. The cover can be left in place for several weeks, or until temperatures get too hot. The plastic cover can increase the rate of spread of zoysia and reduce the time required to obtain a complete cover. The best time for planting zoysia is late spring and early summer.

MANAGEMENT

Zoysiagrasses grow from early spring through late fall when moisture and temperature requirements are met. Although zoysia is considered to be a drought-tolerant species, it ceases growth and begins to discolor during extended dry periods. To maintain growth zoysia requires 1 to 1 $\frac{1}{2}$ inches of water per week during midsummer, although it can survive on less than 1 inch of water per week. Water should be applied 2 to 3 times per week depending on temperatures and soil conditions. Sandy soils require more frequent irrigations than heavier clay soils, and, as temperatures increase, irrigation frequency must increase. During prolonged droughts, when it is impractical to water enough to maintain growth, weekly applications of as little as $\frac{1}{2}$ inch of water are adequate to keep the grass alive. Also, during dry winter months, zoysia requires occasional irrigation to prevent desiccation and serious loss of stand even though the grass may be dormant.

Zoysia requires a moderate level of nitrogen fertilizer to maintain a dense turf. In lawn situations 2 applications of nitrogen during the growing season will maintain turf density and color. Each application should provide about

1 pound of nitrogen per 1,000 square feet of area. Applications should be made in late spring and early fall. In areas where zoysia remains green year-round, applications of soluble nitrogen fertilizers will help maintain a green color during the cool season. Where zoysia goes dormant during the winter, discontinue fertilization until spring.

Close, frequent mowing produces the finest zoysia turf. But most people compromise some quality for less frequent mowing. On golf courses and sports fields, zoysia should be mowed at a ½- to 1-inch height every 3 to 5 days. On lawns growing in full sun, zoysia may be mowed at a height of 1 to 2 inches every 5 to 7 days. Less frequent mowing at these recommended heights results in scalping and generally poor quality turf.

In shaded sites zoysia should be mowed slightly higher than recommended for lawns in full sun. Mowing frequency should not change for shaded sites even though the mowing height is slightly increased.

Zoysia lawns tend to build up a thatch layer, a layer of undecomposed organic residues just above the soil surface. Proper mowing is essential to prevent the accumulation of thatch in zoysia turf. Frequent mowing at recommended heights and clipping removal help prevent thatch accumulation. Avoiding excessive applications of nitrogen fertilizer also helps prevent thatch accumulation.

Occasionally, thatch removal by mechanical means is required to prevent serious deterioration of zoysia turf. Vertical mowers or flail mowers may be used to remove excess thatch from zoysia turf. Thatch removal should be done well before fall to allow ample time for regrowth. Scalping the lawn in early spring to remove accumulated growth will also help prevent thatch accumulation.

PEST MANAGEMENT

Zoysiagrasses are relatively free of serious pest problems. Brownpatch, rust, and leaf spot diseases can cause problems in zoysia turf, but the grass usually recovers when environmental conditions change. In intensively maintained areas, fungicides may be needed to prevent these diseases. In the fall applications of Banner, Daconil, or Bayleton are required to prevent rust on zoysia lawns.

White grubs are the major insect attacking zoysia turf. Monitoring the soil underlying the turf during summer and fall is the most effective way of preventing grub damage. When populations of grubs exceed four to five per square foot of turf, treatment with insecticides is recommended.

Centipedegrass

ORIGIN AND DISTRIBUTION

Centipedegrass is native to China and Southeast Asia. It was first introduced into the United States in 1916 from seed collected by Frank N. Meyer in

South China (Burton 1951). Centipedegrass has since become widely grown in the southeastern United States from South Carolina to Florida and westward along the Gulf Coast states to Texas.

Its popularity as a lawn grass stems from its adaptation to low fertility conditions and its low maintenance requirements (Nutter 1955). Where centipedegrass is adapted and properly managed, it has few serious pest problems. It is particularly well adapted to the sandy, acid soils of the southeastern United States. Its westward movement is somewhat limited by severe iron deficiencies that develop in the alkaline soils of the arid regions. And its northward movement is restricted by low temperatures. Centipedegrass is slightly more cold tolerant than Saint Augustine grass, but extended periods of 5° F or less can kill centipedegrass.

Centipedegrass can be found throughout the West Indies, South America, and along some areas of the west coast of Africa. It can be successfully grown in any of the areas where Saint Augustine grass is adapted.

DESCRIPTION OF SPECIES
Centipedegrass, *Eremochloa ophiuroides* (Munro) Hack, is a coarse-textured perennial grass that spreads by stolons. Stolons have a creeping growth habit

Centipedegrass

with rather short upright stems that resemble a centipede—thus, its name. Centipedegrass produces seed and is readily propagated by seed. It has a yellow-green color and is particularly sensitive to iron deficiency (Carrow, Johnson, and Landry 1988).

Centipedegrass forms a dense turf and has a relatively slow rate of growth. It requires less mowing than bermuda or Saint Augustine grasses and is often called lazy man's grass. Centipede remains green throughout the year in mild climates, but leaves and young stolons are killed by a hard frost. It does not have a true dormant state and resumes growth whenever temperatures are favorable. Thus, centipedegrass is susceptible to damage from late-season freezes.

The stolons of centipedegrass are slender, branching, rooting at the nodes, and terminating in a slender flowering stem. Leaf blades are commonly 15 to 30 mm long, 2 to 4 mm wide, flat, lanceolate, rounded at the base, petioled, sparsely ciliate (more numerous along the margins and at the base of the flowering stem); sheaths are overlapping, pubescent at the throat, compressed; ligule a ciliate membrane; and collar is pubescent. The inflorescence is a spike-like raceme, 3 to 5 inches long, purplish in color, somewhat flattened; spikelets in two rows, alternate, one sessile and perfect, the other pediced with a very small rudimentary spikelet. Sessile spikelets are 3.0 to 3.5 mm long. Oblong glumes are about equal. Caryopsis is about 2 mm long and narrowly elliptic.

ADAPTATION AND USE
Centipedegrass is best adapted to sandy, acid soils where annual rainfall is in excess of 40 inches. It tolerates very low soil fertility levels and thrives on moderately fertile soils. Fertilization rates should not exceed 1 pound of nitrogen per 1,000 square feet per year on heavy soils or 2 pounds of nitrogen on sandy soils.

Centipedegrass is moderately shade tolerant but grows best in full sunlight. It is not as salt tolerant as Saint Augustine or bermudagrass. Centipede thrives on moderately acid soils, pH 5 to 6. Above pH 7 iron becomes a limiting factor and supplemental applications of iron may be required.

Centipedegrass does not enter a true dormant state during winter months and is severely injured by intermittent cold and warm periods during spring. Hard freezes kill the leaves and young stolons of centipedegrass, but the grass resumes growth as soon as temperatures are favorable. When this cycle occurs several times during the winter months, the grass is depleted of energy reserves and is susceptible to extreme winterkill. Thus, its adaptation is limited to areas with mild winter temperatures.

Centipedegrass is used primarily for lawns, parks, golf course roughs, and utility turf. Like Saint Augustine grass, centipede does not tolerate heavy traffic and is not suited for sports fields. Centipedegrass is ideally suited for roadside rights-of-way and other low maintenance turf areas, but it can become a nuisance in adjoining pasture and crop land.

VARIETIES

A number of centipedegrass selections have been made, but none have found prominent use in turf. Common centipedegrass produced from seed of early introductions has been about the only available source. In 1965 Oklahoma State University released Oklawn centipedegrass as an improved variety with superior drought and cold tolerance. Likewise, the University of Tennessee developed Tennessee Hardy as a variety with superior cold tolerance. Neither of these has been extensively used since they must be propagated vegetatively. In 1983 Auburn University released AU Centennial centipedegrass as a semidwarf variety (Dickens and Pedersen 1985). AU Centennial has shorter internodes than other varieties and makes a denser, lower growing sod. Shorter seedheads also improve the appearance of AU Centennial centipedegrass.

PROPAGATION

Centipedegrass can be established from sod, sprigs, or seed. Success with seeded plantings is highly dependent on good seedbed preparation. The soil should be disked or rototilled, pulverized with a rotovator or rake, leveled, and firmed with a roller. Seed should be broadcast with a seeder or by hand. To aid uniform distributions of seed, ⅓ pound of seed should be uniformly mixed with about a gallon of fine sand and evenly distributed over 1,000 square feet of lawn area. For large plantings using a grass drill the sand is not necessary.

After seeding, the site should be firmed with a roller and watered frequently. The seedbed should be kept moist, but not wet, for 14 to 21 days after planting. If the area is too large to keep watered, the site should not be planted until soil moisture is adequate. A complete fertilizer should be applied at the time of planting at a rate of 1 pound of nitrogen per 1,000 square feet. Seeded plantings properly managed will provide a complete cover in about 3 months.

Centipedegrass sprigs or sod plugs can be planted in rows about 1 foot apart or on 1-foot spacings. Sprigs require almost the same amount of care as seeds for the first 2 weeks after planting. Sod plugs require much less attention after planting but must be watered regularly for the first several weeks. Sod plugs and sprigs require much more labor to plant than seed. As with seed, with proper care a complete cover can be obtained from plugs or sprigs in about 3 months.

MANAGEMENT

Centipedegrass is a low-maintenance grass. In general, annual fertilization, regular mowing, and irrigation as needed to prevent severe wilting will meet the requirements for a satisfactory centipedegrass lawn. Too often homeowners try to encourage centipedegrass with nitrogen to enhance color and growth. Excessive nitrogen fertilization may enhance color and stimulate growth, but it also leads to thatchy conditions which subject the grass to severe winterkill.

Annual applications of nitrogen in the spring or early summer at a rate of 1 pound per 1,000 square feet are recommended. A fall application of nitrogen at ½ to 1 pound per 1,000 square feet is optional.

Centipedegrass is naturally shallow rooted, and water management is critical on heavy textured soils during summer months. Water should be applied when centipedegrass shows signs of water stress—wilted and discolored turf. Light, frequent applications of water should be avoided since it promotes shallow rooting. Thoroughly wetting the soil 4 to 6 inches deep only when the grass shows signs of moisture stress is the proper procedure for watering centipede lawns. Sandy soils require more frequent applications of water, but the soil should be wet 6 to 8 inches deep after each irrigation. Centipedegrass should also be watered during dry winter months to avoid desiccation. Excessive nitrogen fertilization and improper watering account for many of the problems homeowners have with centipedegrass lawns.

On sandy soils and on soils low in potassium, spring and fall applications of potassium help to promote root development and to reduce winterkill in centipedegrass. Potassium can be applied with nitrogen in a complete fertilizer such as 3-1-2 or 2-1-2 ratio. Avoid continuous use of a high phosphorous fertilizer since it contributes to iron deficiencies in centipedegrass.

When centipedegrass develops chlorotic conditions, applications of iron sulfate or iron chelate may correct the condition temporarily. Monthly applications of iron at ½ to ¾ ounce per 1,000 square feet may be required to maintain a green color. If nitrogen is applied with iron, only ¼ pound of N per 1,000 square feet should be used. If soil pH is above 6.5 on a sandy soil or 7.2 on a heavy soil, elemental sulfur may be needed to lower pH and increase iron availability. Soil test information should be considered to determine the amount of sulfur to apply.

WEED CONTROL

Weed control improves the appearance and reduces the mowing needs of centipedegrass lawns. Winter weeds are particularly unsightly since they contrast so sharply with the dormant grass. Hormone-type herbicides such as 2,4-D and MCPP can be used to control most broadleaved weeds including clover, chickweed, dandelion, and thistle. Herbicides should be applied in the fall or winter before these weeds mature.

Crabgrass and other summer annuals are most effectively controlled with preemerge herbicides applied in early spring before the weeds emerge. Products containing benefin, DCPA or atrazine can be effectively used for crabgrass control when applied according to label instructions.

Buffalograss

ORIGIN AND DISTRIBUTION

Native lawns in the central United States, from Texas to North Dakota, often display the fine, curly, blue-green leaves of buffalograss, curly mesquite, grama, and needlegrasses. Of these, buffalograss produces the most uniform and attractive turf.

Buffalograss, *Buchloe dactyloides*, is a perennial grass native to the Great Plains, from Montana to Mexico. It is commonly found on clay and clay loam soils in areas of less than thirty inches of rainfall but is rarely found on sandy soils or in high rainfall areas. It is one of the grasses that supported the great herds of buffalo that roamed the Great Plains. Buffalograss also provided the sod from which early settlers built their houses.

Buffalograss is, perhaps, our only truly native turfgrass. Its tolerance to prolonged droughts and to extreme temperatures, together with its seed producing characteristics, enables buffalograss to survive extreme environmental conditions. Overgrazing and, in the case of turf, overuse or excessive traffic are the pressures that lead to the deterioration of a stand of buffalograss.

Buffalograss spreads by surface runners, or stolons, and seed. It forms a fine-textured, relatively thin turf with a soft blue-green color. It does not possess underground stems or rhizomes. Buffalograss is also destroyed quite readily by cultivation. For these reasons, it can be readily removed from flower beds and gardens.

DESCRIPTION OF SPECIES

Buffalograss is a low-growing, commonly only 6 to 8 inches high, warm-season perennial grass. Individual leaf blades may reach 18 to 20 inches in length, but they fall over and give the turf a short appearance. Buffalograss has a stoloniferous growth habit, fine-bladed leaves, and both staminate and pistillate flowers. Staminate (male) plants have 2 to 3 flaglike, one-sided spikes on a seed stalk 6 to 8 inches high. Spikelets, usually 10, are 4 mm long in 2 rows on one side of the rachis.

Pistillate (female) plants appear very different from the staminate plants. Pistillate spikelets are in a short spike, or head, and included in the inflated sheaths of the upper leaves. The thickened rachis is woody and surrounded by the outer glumes. The glumes together with the lemma and palea form a burlike enclosure for the mature seed.

Both male and female plants have stolons from several inches to several feet in length, internodes two to three inches long, and nodes with tufts of short leaves. Plants often take root at the node and produce new shoots. Each plant propagates vegetatively its own kind, and only rarely are both male and female flowers produced on the same plant. Commonly each kind of plant is found in patches some distance apart.

As buffalograss and curly mesquite are both low-growing, stoloniferous grasses with curly leaves, some difficulty may be encountered in distinguishing them. If the grasses are not in flower, they can be identified by their nodes and internodes. Nodes of buffalograss are smooth, and those of curly mesquite are villous. Also, the internodes of buffalograss are quite short (less than three inches) while those of curly mesquite are quite long.

The production and utilization of buffalograss is hampered by poor germination of the seed, or bur. It has been suggested that poor germination is the result of the mechanical restraint imposed on the embryo by the tough enclosing outer glumes. The fact that seed extracted from the bur readily germinate is cited as evidence of inhibitor substances in the glumes that delay germination of the seed.

ADAPTATION AND USE

Although buffalograss is prevalent throughout the Great Plains, in Texas buffalograss is commonly found from the south-central region, westward to El Paso and north to the High Plains and Rolling Plains. It favors the heavy clay soils in moderate to low rainfall areas. Buffalograss is rare in the sandy soils of east Texas and the high rainfall areas of southeast Texas.

When buffalograss is planted in high rainfall areas or when it is irrigated and fertilized, bermudagrass and other weedy grasses invade a stand of buffalograss. Buffalograss is best adapted to low rainfall areas (15 to 25 inches annually) or areas that receive thorough, but infrequent, irrigation.

Buffalograss is not adapted to shaded sites or to sites that receive heavy traffic. Also, under intensive management bermudagrass and other more aggressive grasses tend to replace buffalograss in the lawn.

Buffalograss, male plant

Roadsides, school grounds, parks, open lawn areas, golf course roughs, and cemeteries are good sites for buffalograss in the central and western Great Plains. Buffalograss is particularly well suited for sites to be planted to bluebonnets and other wildflowers, since it produces a relatively open, thin turf and requires little mowing. It is the ideal grass for those wanting a native landscape.

PROPAGATION

Buffalograss can be established from seed (burs) or sod (Frolik and Keim 1940). Buffalograss established from seed develops into patches of male and female plants, with the male plants producing the seed stalks that may appear unsightly in lawns. When planting buffalograss vegetatively, female plants are generally selected, since they do not produce the taller seed stalks. Prairie buffalograss is a female plant selection released by the Texas Agricultural Experiment Station in 1990. It produces a more dense and uniform turf than common types.

Another female selection, 609 buffalograss, was released by the Nebraska Agricultural Experiment Station in 1991. The 609 variety is a darker green and more dense variety than Prairie. Both Prairie and 609 buffalograss must be established from sod or sod plugs.

When planting seed, seed treatment, seeding rate, and date of seeding are

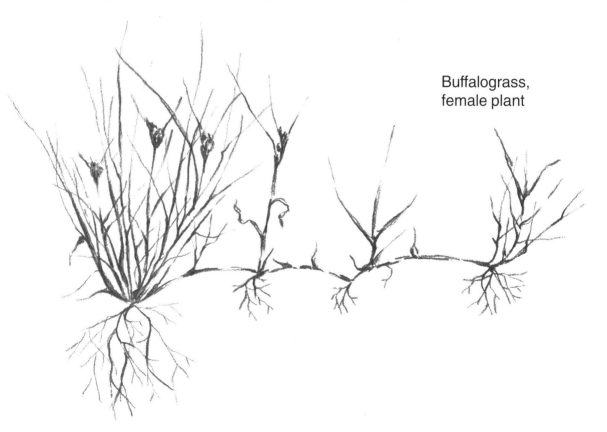

Buffalograss,
female plant

important considerations. Treated seed, seed chilled at 5 to 10 degrees for 6 to 8 weeks, or treated chemically to break dormancy, have a much higher germination rate (80–90 percent) than untreated seed (20 percent). For spring and summer plantings, treated seed should be used.

May is the best month to plant treated buffalograss seed, as temperatures are favorable and moisture is generally adequate. With irrigation the planting date can be extended into July and August.

Fall plantings of untreated buffalograss seed are also successful, but maximum germination does not occur until the following spring.

Treated seed planted in May will germinate in 7 to 10 days if moisture is adequate. Without irrigation the seed will remain dormant until moisture is favorable. Seed planted in dry conditions without irrigation should be drilled ¼ to ½ inch into a well prepared seedbed. Seed broadcast on the surface may germinate when little or no subsurface moisture is present to sustain the young seedlings.

Seeding rates may range from less than 0.5 pound of seed per 1,000 square feet to 4 to 6 pounds, depending on the method of planting and the time available to obtain a cover. Seeding rates are generally much higher for broadcast seeding on the soil surface than for that drilled in rows into the seedbed. Buffalograss seed drilled in rows at 10 to 20 pounds per acre will produce a complete cover in one growing season with favorable moisture conditions. With no irrigation, broadcast seeding rates of 1 to 2 pounds per 1,000 square feet may require several seasons to develop a complete cover. In contrast, broadcast seeding rates of 4 to 6 pounds per 1,000 square feet will cover in several months with adequate moisture.

Fall plantings using untreated seed should be at rates of 2 to 4 pounds per 1,000 square feet of lawn or turf area. Significant germination should not be expected until the following spring or summer when moisture is favorable.

Buffalograss can be established from pieces of sod or sod plugs not less than 2 inches square. These should be planted on a well prepared seedbed in

Female plant *(left),* male plant *(right),* bur or seed *(inset)*

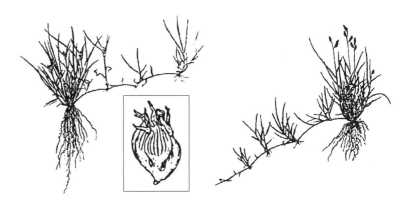

Female plant *(left)*,
male plant *(right)*

about 18-inch rows. Plants can be spaced anywhere from 6 inches to 2 feet apart, depending on how quickly a complete cover is desired. The closer they are spaced, the sooner the ground will be covered. In digging up material for planting, care should be taken to keep the roots moist as the plants die very quickly when the roots get dry. When planting dig a hole deep enough to set the plants in so that the grass is above ground level. If the sod is covered with soil, the grass will die. Planting is best done in moist soil or where irrigation is available. The grass should be planted in early fall, spring, or early summer, when moisture is favorable. Plants should be well watered after planting and as needed for several weeks, thereafter.

MANAGEMENT

Buffalograss is only recommended for low-maintenance, low-use turfgrass areas. It does not persist where use is intensive. Consequently, only minimum maintenance practices are required to keep a buffalograss turf.

Mowing height and frequency depend on the use of the site. In lawns buffalograss can be mowed at heights of 2 to 3 inches. At the shorter heights weekly mowing produces the best quality lawn.

On irrigated golf course fairways, buffalograss is mowed twice weekly at ¾ inch. Without irrigation it is mowed only as needed at a 1-inch height. In rough areas on golf courses, buffalograss is mowed only as needed at heights between 3 and 4 inches.

Buffalograss does not need fertilization, but it will respond to light applications of nitrogen. Nitrogen fertilization should not exceed 2 pounds of nitrogen per 1,000 square feet per year. If bermudagrass is undesirable in the lawn, avoid nitrogen fertilization.

With irrigation buffalograss will remain green throughout the spring and summer. One inch of water per week is adequate to maintain a green buffalograss turf. Without irrigation buffalograss will turn become straw-colored and dormant during the dry summer months. As with fertilization, excessive water promotes bermudagrass encroachment.

Bahiagrass

ORIGIN AND DISTRIBUTION

Bahiagrass is native to South America and the West Indies. It was introduced into the United States as a forage grass in 1913 by the Florida Agricultural Experiment Station (Scott 1920). As a lawngrass bahia has a coarse texture, open growth habit, and produces abundant seed stalks 1 to 3 feet tall.

Bahiagrass has long been used for roadside turf throughout the southeastern states. Bahiagrass is readily established from seed and produces a complete cover on low fertility soils found on roadsides throughout the region. In the 1970s bahiagrass became popular in Florida as a lawn grass because it could be established from seed, had few pest problems, good drought tolerance, and was considered low maintenance.

DESCRIPTION OF SPECIES

Bahiagrass (*Paspalum notatum*) is perhaps best characterized by comparatively short, stout, almost woody, rhizomes and stolons. The rhizomes

Bahiagrass

and stolons are covered with persistent bases of old leaf sheath, giving them a woody appearance. Leaf blades are long, pointed at the tip, folded at the base and commonly ciliate toward the base. The ligule is membranous, very short, with a dense row of hairs in back. Seed stalks terminate in 2, rarely 3, rather long, ascending racemes. Spikelets are solitary, about 3 mm long, ovate, and green. Seeds are about 3 mm long, 2 mm wide, oval, with a very convex back.

ADAPTATION AND USE

Bahiagrass is well adapted to the high rainfall area of the southeastern states (Hoveland 1961). It performs better than bermudagrass on wet, poorly drained soils and on low fertility soils. Bahiagrass survives limited drought but makes very little growth when moisture is lacking.

Cold tolerance limits the northern boundaries of bahiagrass to the lower and midsouthern states. Bahia will remain green longer into the fall and recover earlier in the spring than most warm-season grasses. The Wilmington variety of bahiagrass is considered most cold tolerant.

Bahiagrass is well adapted for roadsides in the southeastern states and is widely used for that purpose. Unfortunately, it does not stay in its place, and the seed from bahiagrass invades pastures, lawns, parks, golf courses, and other fine turf areas.

As a lawn grass, bahia is considered low maintenance with respect to watering and fertilization. However, the prolific production of seed stalk by bahiagrass keeps the mowing requirement high for home lawns. Bahia lawns in the southeastern states are also vulnerable to mole crickets and are extensively damaged by this insect.

PROPAGATION

Bahiagrass can be propagated from seed or sod. As for any turfgrass installation, seedbed preparation is critical to successful establishment. The finished seedbed (for seed or sod) should be smooth, free of debris and vegetation, firm, gently sloping away from buildings, walks, drives, etc., and free of depressions or areas that hold water. Thorough irrigation prior to planting will help settle loose soil and identify any low areas that might require filling.

When sodding bahiagrass, use good quality, weed-free sod. Lay sod blocks side by side so that an instant lawn is produced. Water immediately after laying sod and roll the sod the next day to smooth and firm the new lawn. Fertilize the newly sodded lawn about two weeks after planting.

Establishing a bahiagrass turf from seed is less expensive but much slower than with sod. Early spring is the best time to seed bahiagrass, but it can be seeded anytime through October. Since a high percentage of bahiagrass seed is hard seed (dormant), seeding rates for lawns are usually much higher than for pastures or roadsides. For a rapid cover plant 3 to 5 pounds of bahiagrass seed per 1,000 square feet of lawn area. Seed should be lightly raked into the soil or planted with a seed drill about ¼-inch deep.

Light, daily watering, will be needed for 2 to 3 weeks to ensure good germination. About 2 weeks after seeding, fertilize the lawn with a complete fertilizer such as 12-12-12 at a rate of 1 pound of nitrogen per 1,000 square feet of lawn. Monthly applications of fertilizer until the lawn is covered will speed the rate of establishment. Begin mowing the lawn about a month after seeding.

MANAGEMENT

As with any turfgrass, mowing practices determine the density, texture, color, and overall appearance of a bahiagrass turf. On roadsides where bahiagrass is mowed only 3 or 4 times per year at a height of 4 or more inches, seed stalks are the most noticeable feature.

In contrast, bahiagrass mowed at 5-day intervals at a height of 2 inches would be quite dense, medium textured, and have few seed stalks. At weekly mowing intervals, seed stalks detract from the appearance of the lawn. During summer a sharp mower blade is required to prevent leaf tip shredding which causes an unsightly lawn.

Although bahiagrass is considered drought tolerant, it requires occasional watering to maintain color and density during droughty periods (Burton, Prine, and Jackson 1957). When watering is required, apply ½ to 1 inch of water per application, depending on soil type and soil depth. On slowly permeable soils, ½ inch of water may be all that can be applied at one time. On deep sandy soils, 1 inch of water can be applied. Avoid light, daily applications of water.

Bahiagrass lawns that are mowed weekly need at least one application of fertilizer per year. An early summer application of a complete fertilizer such as 15-5-10 at 10 pounds per 1,000 square feet will produce a satisfactory lawn. Repeating that application in September will produce a denser, greener, and more weed-free lawn through the fall and early spring. On alkaline soils (from pH 7.2 to 8.5) foliar applications of iron sulfate or iron chelate will produce a greener lawn.

Weed control in bahiagrass turf is best accomplished with preemerge herbicides. Early spring and late summer applications of preemerge herbicides will control most annual grassy weeds. Products containing 2,4-D and other similar herbicides can be used to control broadleaved weeds in bahiagrass.

Mole crickets are a serious problem in bahiagrass turf in southeastern states. Baits applied late in the day are most effective for mole cricket control from July through September. Spray or granular applications of approved insecticides are also effective during the same period.

Carpetgrass

ORIGIN AND DISTRIBUTION

From the sandy soils of East Texas, to Florida and north to Virginia, from Alabama to Arkansas, carpetgrass is found in fields, woods, along roadsides, pastures, and lawns. Also known as flatgrass, Louisianagrass, and as *petit gazon* by the Creoles of Louisiana, carpetgrass is native to the Gulf Coast states and other tropical climates. It is a creeping, perennial grass that can be recognized by the blunt rounded tips of its leaves, flat stolons, and a tall seed stalk with two branches at the apex. It forms a dense mat and will crowd out most other species.

DESCRIPTION OF SPECIES

Carpetgrass (*Axonopus affinis*) is a creeping, stoloniferous, perennial, warm-season grass. It is characterized by flat, two-edged runners or stolons; by wide leaves with blunt, rounded tips; and by long, slender seed stalks that terminate with two branches, very similar to crabgrass. Stolons are flat, widely branched, and root at each node.

Leaf sheaths are strongly compressed with fine hairs along the outer margin and densely pubescent around the nodes. The ligule is very short with a fringe of short hairs. The leaf blade is wide, flat, broadly rounded at the base, blunt at the tip, and often fringed with hairs.

The seed stalk is tall, slender, and often drooping. It branches at the apex into 2 slender, 1-sided spikes, sometimes with a third spike below. Spikelets are oblong, acute, 2 to 25 mm long, pale green or tinged with purple, solitary on alternate sides of the rachis and forming 2 rows. The lower glume is absent, the upper as long as the spikelet. The anthers are yellowish white or slightly tinged with purple. Seed are yellowish brown and about 1.25 mm long.

ADAPTATION AND USE

Carpetgrass is best adapted to the middle and lower southern states. It has about the same cold hardiness as centipedegrass and is well adapted to moist, sandy soils. It thrives in areas too wet for bermudagrass and tolerates more shade than bermudagrass.

The ability of carpetgrass to thrive under low fertility makes it suitable for use on low-maintenance areas such as parks, roadsides, airports, and golf course roughs. Its most objectionable characteristic, frequent and prolonged production of seed stalks, limits its use on lawns. Frequent mowing with a rotary mower is required to maintain a nice-looking carpetgrass lawn.

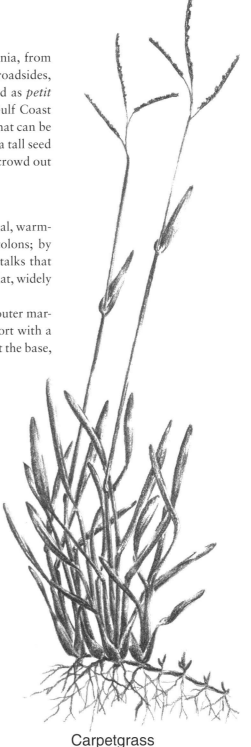

Carpetgrass

PROPAGATION

Carpetgrass, like all small seeded grasses, requires a loose, smooth, and firm seedbed. In heavier soils disking or rototilling, dragging, and rolling may be necessary to develop a good seedbed.

Carpetgrass can be established from seed or sprigs. Seeding is often easier and less expensive. For a quick cover broadcast 2 pounds of carpetgrass seed per 1,000 square feet of lawn. Rake the lawn lightly after seeding to help cover the seed. A grass drill can also be used effectively for planting carpetgrass seed. For large plantings, where a quick cover is not critical, plant 15 to 20 pounds of carpetgrass seed per acre. Again, a grass drill is the most effective means of seeding carpetgrass.

Seed carpetgrass after the last expected frost in the spring. Mid-April to May are ideal months for seeding carpetgrass. Do not seed after September 15.

Keep the soil moist, but not wet, for about 2 weeks after seeding. Continue light, frequent watering until the seedlings are rooted and beginning to spread. After the lawn is established, usually 8 to 10 weeks after seeding, water only as needed to prevent severe drought stress.

Carpetgrass does well on acid soils and on soils with a low fertility. However, establishment is hastened by light applications of a complete fertilizer. Apply a complete fertilizer at 1 pound of nitrogen per 1,000 square feet at planting time and at monthly intervals thereafter until the lawn is covered with carpetgrass. Lime is not necessary unless the soil pH is below 5.0.

MANAGEMENT

Carpetgrass lawns need frequent mowing during summer months to keep the seed stalks cut. During the growing season new seedstalks are produced about every 5 days. If allowed to grow, the seedstalks grow to about 12 inches tall and produce an unsightly lawn.

Carpetgrass should be mowed to a height of ¾ inch to 2 inches, depending on its use. The grass will tolerate the shorter mowing heights for use on golf course fairways with a 5-day mowing schedule. Where mowing is less frequent, the taller mowing height produces the best results. A rotary or flail mower is necessary to remove the tall seed stalks that develop with less frequent mowing.

Carpetgrass will thrive on moderately acid, low-fertility soils. Under these conditions, it will crowd out bermudagrass. On roadsides, golf course roughs, parks, and other low-maintenance sites, carpetgrass will survive without fertilization. But on more frequently mowed sites such as lawns, fairways, etc., occasional applications of nitrogen are needed. Late spring and early fall applications of nitrogen at 30 to 40 pounds per acre (1 pound per 1000 square feet) are adequate to meet nitrogen requirements. Soil test recommendations relative to phosphorus and potassium should be followed.

Carpetgrass is not as drought tolerant as bermudagrass. On droughty soils or during periods of drought stress, occasional watering is needed to maintain carpetgrass. On moist sites where bermudagrass is not adapted, carpetgrass will thrive without supplemental water.

PEST MANAGEMENT

Carpetgrass is susceptible to common soilborne diseases, such as brownpatch and *Pythium,* and to most leaf spot diseases, but rarely do these diseases justify fungicide applications on carpetgrass. The grass usually recovers with little injury when environmental conditions change. The exception in the fall might be brownpatch, which can produce unsightly turf for several months.

White grub and, in the southeastern states, mole crickets can cause serious injury to carpetgrass turf. Again, where infestations of these insects can cause a problem, insecticides are available to control them effectively.

When weeds are a problem in carpetgrass turf, the hormone-type herbicides can be used for broadleaved weed control. Also, most preemerge herbicides are safe on carpetgrass and can be used for crabgrass control.

Seashore Paspalum

ORIGIN AND DISTRIBUTION

Seashore paspalum (*Paspalum vaginatum* Swartz) is native to tropical and subtropical regions of North and South America and Africa. In the United

Seashore paspalum

States seashore paspalum is found along coastal regions from Texas to Florida and North Carolina. The species is also abundant in South Africa, Australia, and the Pacific Rim countries (Liu et al. 1994).

Seashore paspalum is a warm-season perennial grass that spreads by rhizomes and stolons. The stolons and leaves of seashore paspalum are slightly coarser than those of common bermudagrass. However, when mowed regularly at heights of 1 ½ inches or less, the grass produces a dense turf. Adalayd (also called Excalibre) is a selection of seashore paspalum found in Australia by Hugh Whiting during the 1970s. Adalayd has a blue-green color and texture similar to that of Kentucky bluegrass.

One of the outstanding characteristics of seashore paspalum is its tolerance to saline soils. It is reported to tolerate brackish sites much better than bermudagrass. Along the Texas coast the species is often the only grass found growing around brackish ponds and estuaries. The species grows abundantly on coastal dune sites where it provides erosion control (Craig 1974).

Perhaps the most extensive planting of Adalayd (Excalibre) in Texas is on the King's Crossing golf course in Corpus Christi. The entire golf course, except for the putting greens, was sprigged with seashore paspalum. Tees, fairways, and roughs at King's Crossing are covered with the grass. After playing the golf course, one cannot help but be impressed with the appearance and playability of the grass. Perhaps most striking is the uniformity of the turf and the complete absence of other grass species, which reflects the competitiveness of seashore paspalum and its salt tolerance relative to other species. Even many of the live oak trees planted on the site are drying as a result of the salt content of the soil and irrigation water. The only bermudagrass found on the golf course is on the greens constructed of sand with underlying tile drains.

Seashore paspalum is found growing along the edge of the water on several of King's Crossing holes—water that often contained 4,000 or more ppm salts. It is also the only grass species found growing in saline outcroppings of soil along roughs and ditch banks. Its salt tolerance appears to be great.

The quality of the turf is also very good. It is evident that the grass produces the finest turf at mowing heights below 1 inch. Tees mowed at ⅜ inch are more dense and finer textured that fairways mowed at ¾ inch. And the fairways are more dense than roughs mowed at 1½ inches. Studies conducted by Texas A&M University at College Station also suggest that the grass develops higher shoot densities at lower mowing heights (Sifers, Beard, and Hall 1990).

Several years ago, I observed native stands of seashore paspalum on golf greens in Argentina mowed twice daily at ⅛ inch. Under that mowing regime seashore paspalum produced as fine a putting surface as Tifdwarf bermudagrass. But more important, the grass completely crowded out stands of hybrid bermudagrass that had been sprigged on greens. The native species of seashore paspalum on the putting greens in Argentina appeared to be finer textured than Adalayd. However, that may have just been a response to the close, frequent mowing regime.

Fertilizer requirements of seashore paspalum are less than those for bermudagrass. At low annual rates of nitrogen application, seashore paspalum maintains density better than bermudagrass. Research at the University of California showed that seashore paspalum responded to nitrogen fertilizer by increased growth and a darker green color up to about 8 pounds of nitrogen per 1,000 square feet per year. However, above 4 pounds of nitrogen per year, scalping became a problem on seashore paspalum. Scalping is particularly a problem following summer applications of nitrogen. Most of the nitrogen fertilizer should be applied in the spring and fall with emphasis on fall fertilization. A suggested nitrogen fertilization schedule for seashore paspalum on lawns, athletic fields, and golf course fairways where clippings are not removed would be 1 pound in March, ½ pound in May and July, and 1 pound in October.

Research information on shade tolerance, cold tolerance, and drought tolerance of seashore paspalum is limited. But observations indicate the species does not tolerate prolonged freezing conditions as well as bermudagrass. Seashore paspalum thrives in moist sites. It tolerates wet conditions much better than bermudagrass. And, although it survives prolonged dry periods, it shows moisture stress before bermudagrass.

Kentucky Bluegrass

ORIGIN AND DISTRIBUTION

Kentucky bluegrass is native to practically all of Europe, northern Asia, and the mountains of Algeria and Morocco. Although the species is spread over all of the cool, humid parts of the United States, it is not native to North America. Apparently the early colonists brought seed of Kentucky bluegrass to this country in mixtures with other grasses.

In the southern United States, Kentucky bluegrass is limited to the Transition Zone from North Carolina, through much of Tennessee, and northern Arkansas to the panhandle of Texas and Oklahoma. In the western states, Kentucky bluegrass is grown with irrigation.

DESCRIPTION OF SPECIES

Kentucky bluegrass (*Poa pratensis*) grows 18 to 24 inches tall and is readily identified by its boat-shaped leaf tip. It spreads by rhizomes and tillers and forms a dense sod. New shoots (rhizomes and tillers) are produced primarily in the spring and late summer. Most shoots produced in the spring remain vegetative. Shoots produced in late summer often terminate in an inflorescence the following spring. The lifetime of a Kentucky bluegrass shoot that terminates in an inflorescence ends soon after the seeds mature. During late spring and summer, the shoots of Kentucky bluegrass grow in an erect, or upright, position; whereas, in early spring and fall they become more decumbent. This pattern of growth is a response to day length rather than temperature (Evans 1949). During long days shoots grow upright, during short days they become decumbent. Day length also influences the number of shoots that develop. Significantly more shoots are produced during the short days of early spring than during long summer days.

The length of time between the appearance of new leaves on Kentucky bluegrass ranges from about 10 days in the spring to 22 days in the summer and fall (Evans 1949). During winter months few new leaves are produced on Kentucky bluegrass in northern climates. In the Transition Zone new leaves and shoots are produced year-round.

Kentucky bluegrass

Leaf blades of Kentucky bluegrass remain green for 12 to 15 days during the growing season, and the typical shoot has 3 to 4 green leaves at any one time. In comparison, bermudagrass typically has 5 to 7 green leaves per shoot, and new leaves appear at 7- to 10-day intervals during the growing season.

Leaf blades on Kentucky bluegrass are about 4 to 5 inches in length during late spring and summer. Those that appear in late summer and fall become progressively shorter (Stuckey 1942). Leaves appearing in spring and early summer are also quite erect; whereas, leaf blades become more decumbent in late summer and fall. Both of these traits, leaf length and leaf angle, are also typical of warm-season grasses. Leaf length responds to day length and peaks in summer, then becomes progressively shorter in late summer and fall.

In Kentucky bluegrass some shoots turn downward and develop into rhizomes beneath the soil. These rhizomes appear from the axils of leaves, the base of which may be above or just below the surface of the soil. Most rhizomes, however, develop beneath the soil surface as branch shoots of other rhizomes. Rhizomes may branch several times during the year.

Rhizomes of Kentucky bluegrass develop most frequently in early summer as leaf growth begins to decline. During this season, high nitrogen fertilization and close mowing retard the development of rhizomes. Factors which favor photosynthesis, such as long days, high temperatures, and high light intensities, promote rhizome development. Likewise, factors that promote leaf growth, such as high nitrogen fertilization, retard rhizome development in Kentucky bluegrass.

When environmental conditions are favorable, spring and early summer, the growing point at the tip of rhizomes usually turns upward and continues growth as an aboveground shoot. The lifetime of individual rhizomes commonly extends through two growing seasons. The total lifetime of a rhizome and its terminal shoot is usually less than two years.

Carbohydrate accumulation in rhizomes peaks in late fall when aboveground growth of Kentucky bluegrass slows. As temperatures become favorable for growth in the spring, these carbohydrate reserves become available for development of new shoot growth. Factors that reduce carbohydrate accumulation in the fall include high nitrogen fertilization and close mowing.

Roots of Kentucky bluegrass develop from the underground nodes of rhizomes and from the basal nodes of aboveground shoots, the crown. Roots also develop at the terminal nodes of rhizomes that emerge above the soil as shoots.

Root growth is greatest in fall and spring and slows dramatically in summer (Stuckey 1941). Root growth of Kentucky bluegrass peaks at soil temperatures of 60° F and declines sharply as temperatures rise above 70° F. Root growth practically ceases at temperatures above 80° F.

High nitrogen fertilization and close frequent mowing greatly decrease root growth in Kentucky bluegrass (Harrison 1934).

VARIETIES

Nearly 100 cultivars (varieties) of Kentucky bluegrass have been developed during the past 25 years. Some varieties tolerate southern climates better than others (Adelphi, Baron, Fylking, Glade, Vantage, Victa, and Warrens A-34), some have moderate shade tolerance (Bristol, Glade, Nugget, and Touchdown), and some tolerate closer mowing (Adelphi, Bristol, Ram I, and Touchdown). Select a blend of about 3 varieties for planting in the Transition Zone to increase your opportunity for success. Many of these grasses differ in their degree of susceptibility to leaf spot diseases and *Fusarium* blight, both being troublesome in the Transition Zone. A blend of several varieties will usually appear superior to a single variety since all varieties are usually not affected by adverse conditions at the same time or to the same degree.

PROPAGATION

Where bluegrass is established from seed, plant 2 to 3 pounds per 1,000 square feet of lawn. Lower seeding rates require longer to develop a cover, particularly where seed are broadcast over the soil surface. When seed are drilled into the top ¼ inch of soil, lower seeding rates can be used. Kentucky bluegrass can be seeded year-round, but best results are obtained in the spring and fall. New seedings require light and daily watering for the first 2 weeks. After seedling emergence watering frequency can be reduced.

MANAGEMENT

Begin mowing young seedling grass when it grows above a 2-inch cutting height. Either rotary or reel-type mowers may be used, but blades must be sharp and reels properly adjusted to prevent pulling up young seedlings. The initial cutting should be at a 2-inch height. Subsequent mowings should be frequent enough so that no more than one-third of the leaf is removed at each mowing. At a 2-inch mowing height the grass needs mowing before it reaches 3 inches. Weekly mowing is usually satisfactory at the 2-inch mowing height. At lower mowing heights more frequent mowing is required. Some of the improved bluegrass varieties such as Fylking, Ram I, and Touchdown tolerate mowing heights below 1 inch. However, weaker stands of Kentucky bluegrass result when mowing height is below 1 inch. Also, at mowing heights below 1 inch annual bluegrass and crabgrass invade a bluegrass turf. At mowing heights above 1½ inches, weeds are much less of a problem.

Compared to the warm-season grasses, Kentucky bluegrass has a high water requirement. As much as 1½ inches of water per week are needed to keep bluegrass green and growing during summer months in the Transition Zone. Ideally, this amount of water would be applied in one day to wet the entire root zone of the turf. However, the effective root zone is often too shallow to hold that amount of water. No less than ½ inch of water should be applied on any single day to promote deeper rooting of the bluegrass turf.

When bluegrass is allowed to go dormant during drought periods, as little as ½ inch of water every 2 to 3 weeks will keep the crown of the grass alive. Then, after rainfall or significant irrigation the grass will quickly recover. The drought resistance of Kentucky bluegrass is generally underestimated. Bluegrass can survive several months without significant rainfall or irrigation.

Nitrogen requirements of Kentucky bluegrass are much higher during the establishment year than during subsequent years. The grass will respond to 4 to 5 pounds of nitrogen per 1,000 square feet the first year; whereas, 2 to 3 pounds are adequate for maintenance after the first year (Callahan 1977; Kneebone 1979). During summer months Kentucky bluegrass will burn if too much soluble nitrogen is applied at one time or if it is not watered immediately after application. No more than ½ pound of soluble nitrogen per 1,000 square feet should be applied in one application. Slow-release nitrogen sources can be applied in larger amounts and less frequently.

In alkaline soils Kentucky bluegrass often develops iron chlorosis, a yellowing between the veins of young actively growing leaves. Color can be quickly restored with a foliar application of ferrous sulfate at 2 ounces per 1,000 square feet or another iron source at recommended rates. Iron chlorosis is aggravated by high levels of phosphorus in the soil. Where iron chlorosis is a problem, phosphorous fertilization should be kept to a minimum.

PEST MANAGEMENT

Annual bluegrass (*P. annua*), crabgrass, dandelions and clover are major weed problems in Kentucky bluegrass turf. The annual grasses can be effectively controlled with timely applications of preemerge herbicides. The broadleaved weeds are effectively controlled with hormone-type herbicides.

Insects, including white grubs, billbugs, and sod webworms, can destroy plantings of bluegrass. Insect populations should be monitored so that timely insecticide applications can be made. Pest management in this manner is much more cost effective than either routine insecticide applications or replanting large areas of bluegrass turf.

Major diseases of bluegrass turf in the Transition Zone include *Fusarium*, *Helminthosporium* leaf spot diseases, rust, and powdery mildew. Selecting blends of Kentucky bluegrass with different degrees of resistance to these diseases is one means of control. Overseeding bluegrass turf with perennial ryegrass or planting mixtures of bluegrass and ryegrass provides a good suppression of *Fusarium* blight, a disease which causes a bleaching of leaves and severe rotting of roots (Gibeault et al. 1980).

Tall Fescue

ORIGIN AND DISTRIBUTION

Tall fescue was introduced into the United States from Europe in the early 1800s. The grass can be found growing in low, damp pastures and wet meadowlands throughout Europe, North Africa, and North America.

In the United States tall fescue is found from the Pacific Northwest to the southern states in low-lying pastures. Although it grows best in moist environments, tall fescue has good drought tolerance and will survive during dry periods in a dormant state. Tall fescue is adapted to a wide range of soils, but does best on clay soils high in organic matter. Tall fescue is well adapted to the Transition Zone of the United States where summers are too hot and humid for cool-season grasses and winters too cold for warm-season grasses. In the South tall fescue is best adapted to those states in the Transition Zone—Oklahoma, Arkansas, Missouri, Tennessee, Kentucky, Virginia, and northern parts of North Carolina, Georgia, Alabama, Mississippi, and Texas.

DESCRIPTION OF SPECIES

The fescues (*Festuca* spp.) compose a large genus of about 100 species of grasses. Tall fescue (*F. arundinacea*) is a deep-rooted, cool-season perennial

Tall fescue

grass. The plant produces vigorous growth in the spring and fall, and its extensive root system helps it withstand drought conditions. Tall fescue does produce short rhizomes but has a bunch-type growth habit; it spreads primarily by erect tillers. Individual tillers, or stems, terminate in an inflorescence, reach 3 to 4 feet in height, and have broad, dark green basal leaves. Leaf blades are glossy on the underside and serrated on the margins. The leaf sheath is smooth and the ligule is a short membrane. The inflorescence is a compact panicle, 3 to 4 inches long, with lanceolate spikelets ½ inch or more long. The grass flowers in the spring and seed mature in early summer. Seed are 4 to 7 mm long, elliptic and awned.

ADAPTATION AND USE

Tall fescue is adapted to a wide range of soil and climatic conditions but performs best on well drained clay soils in the Transition Zone. Tall fescue demonstrates good shade tolerance in the southern region and remains green year-round under irrigated conditions.

Mowing height requirements for tall fescue limits its use to lawns, parks, golf course roughs, and other areas mowed at a height of 1½ inches or more. Tall fescue should not be used where mowing heights are below 1½ inches during summer months. Although its wear tolerance is considered good for cool-season grasses, it is not nearly as wear tolerant as bermudagrass. Thus, it has limited use on golf courses and sports fields in the South.

The improved turf-type tall fescues are finding widespread acceptance as lawn grasses in the Transition Zone. And in the southern region under moderately shaded conditions, tall fescue is gaining in popularity. With proper management tall fescue can survive in shaded sites that warm-season grasses cannot tolerate. Also, the improved tall fescues retain color during the winter months and provide a year-round green lawn.

VARIETIES

Kentucky-31 and Alta are the two oldest varieties of tall fescue in use today. Alta was selected from a stand of tall fescue in Oregon in 1923, and K-31 is an increase from tall fescue found in 1931 on a Kentucky farm where it had been growing for fifty years. Both of these grasses are coarse textured and produce a rather weak turf. They have been widely used as pasture grasses in the Transition Zone. Kenwell, Kenhy, Fawn, and Goar were later releases but possessed similar turf characteristics. In the 1970s tall fescues were being developed specifically for turfgrasses, and varieties such as Rebel, Olympic, Houndog, Falcon, and Adventure were released. Newer releases include Crossfire, Jaguar, Shortstop, Olympic II, Rebel II, Winchester, Bonanza, and Bonsai. These new turf-type tall fescues are finer textured and produce a denser turf than older pasture-type varieties. They also provide year-round green color for lawns.

PROPAGATION

A well prepared seedbed is essential for establishing tall fescue. A starter fertilizer should be worked into the seedbed prior to planting. The soil should be rototilled to a depth of 3 to 4 inches and firmed with a roller prior to seeding. The site must be well-drained, so attention should be given to final grading of the site. Bermudagrass and some annual grasses are particularly troublesome in tall fescue turf. Steps should be taken prior to planting to eliminate these undesirable grasses. Tupersan can be used at the time of seeding to control crabgrass while nonselective materials such as glyphosate (Roundup) can be used to control bermudagrass prior to planting tall fescue.

The new turf-type fescues should be planted at 6 to 8 pounds seed per 1,000 square feet with a hydroseeder or mechanical seeder. Uniform distribution of seed is essential to develop a complete cover. Tall fescue is a bunch-type grass and is very slow to fill in spaces between plants. Germination of seed and survival of seedlings are improved when seed are lightly covered with soil and the seedbed firmed. Some planters perform both of these operations. When seed is broadcast on the soil surface, rake the seed into the soil or cover lightly with topsoil or mulch.

Early fall is the optimum time to establish tall fescue from either seed or sod. Spring plantings of tall fescue may be successful, but the risk of losing immature plants to summer heat and drought stress is greater. Spring plantings of tall fescue are also more susceptible to *Fusarium* blight and other seedling diseases.

After seeding keep the seedbed moist for 10 to 14 days to obtain maximum germination. Then, gradually reduce the frequency of watering. Begin mowing at a height of 2 inches when the grass reaches a height of 3 inches. Mow often enough so that the grass does not exceed the 3-inch height.

Approximately 1 month after planting tall fescue, apply a complete fertilizer at the rate of 1 pound of nitrogen per 1,000 square feet. Tupersan can be used for preemerge control of crabgrass and other annual grasses in newly seeded and established tall fescue.

MANAGEMENT

Although tall fescue tolerates low fertility, it responds to fertilization, particularly nitrogen. About 3 pounds of actual nitrogen per 1,000 square feet per year are adequate for tall fescue. Apply a complete fertilizer according to soil test recommendations in the fall (September) and late spring (May) at a rate of 1 pound of actual nitrogen per 1,000 square feet. Apply nitrogen alone at the same rate in February when the grass is actively growing. A summer application of ½ pound of actual nitrogen per 1,000 square feet may improve the color of the lawn. However, avoid overstimulation of the turf in summer months from excessive fertilization as this only adds to heat and drought stress problems. In shaded lawns, avoid summer applications of nitrogen.

Mow tall fescue at 2 inches during the fall and spring, raise to 3 inches in heavy shade and during the heat of the summer months. The improved turf-type varieties of tall fescue can be mowed at a height of 1 ½ inches during spring and fall and 2 inches during summer months. Use a sharp rotary or reel mower and remove only one third of the leaf material per mowing. During peak spring and fall growth periods, this requires mowing at 5-day intervals. If the lawn is mowed at the proper height and frequency, it is not necessary to remove grass clippings.

Proper watering is very important to the survival of tall fescue. Do not apply supplemental irrigation until the grass shows signs of needing water (wilting or rolling leaves). Then, apply enough water to wet the soil to a depth of 4 to 6 inches. If runoff occurs before the soil is moistened to a sufficient depth, turn the sprinkler off and allow the water to percolate into the soil. Then, recycle the sprinkler at a later time. Repeat this cycle until the soil is sufficiently moistened. Tall fescue requires frequent watering during summer months, which is one of the disadvantages to growing tall fescue in the southern region.

Tall fescue is fairly tolerant to most turfgrass diseases. However, *Fusarium* blight can cause extensive damage to young fescue lawns, particularly those planted in the spring. As the lawn matures, it appears less susceptible to attack by *Fusarium* blight. Leaf spot (*Helminthosporium*) and brownpatch (*Rhizoctonia*) can cause problems on older fescue lawns. Once the disease is properly identified, treat the lawn with recommended fungicides.

Major insect problems include armyworms, cutworms, and white grubs. White grubs have been particularly damaging to tall fescue lawns. If white grubs are found in populations of 3 or more per square foot, treat with recommended products.

Many tall fescue lawns become thin after hot, dry summer conditions. A thinned tall fescue lawn forms clumps and becomes unsightly. To prevent this from occurring, it is usually necessary to overseed fescue lawns in the fall. Mow the lawn at a height of 1½ inches before broadcasting seed. Rake the lawn to remove grass clippings and other debris. Apply starter fertilizer and seed at 2 to 3 pounds per 1,000 square feet. These steps are usually adequate to rejuvenate the lawn. After seeding keep the soil moist for 2 weeks.

Ryegrasses

ORIGIN AND DISTRIBUTION

Worldwide there are about a dozen species of ryegrass, including both annual and perennial plants. In the United States only two species are used as turfgrasses—Italian ryegrass and perennial ryegrass. The species is native to Europe and Asia and was introduced into the United States at an early date.

Ryegrasses are widely distributed throughout the United States. In the South annual ryegrass appears each fall from natural reseeding. In the Transition Zone perennial ryegrass is used in mixtures with bluegrass for lawns and sports fields. Ryegrasses are widely used as a temporary turfgrass throughout the southern region for overseeding dormant warm-season grasses.

DESCRIPTION OF SPECIES

The ryegrasses (*Lolium* spp.) have a bunch-type growth habit and spread by profuse tillers. The tillers (stems) are erect and reach 1 to 2 feet in length. The leaves are rather succulent, dark green, and glossy on the underside. The leaf sheath is about as long as the internode, and auricles are clawlike, unusually clasping the sheath; the ligule is membranous.

The species is easily distinguished by the position of the multiflowered spikelets, edgewise to the rachis, and the absence of the first glume except in

Ryegrass

the terminal spikelet. The inflorescence is a long, slender spike (usually 6 to 10 inches long) with 15 to 30 solitary spikelets.

Mature ryegrass seed (florets) are 5 to 7 mm long, lanceolate, and with or without awns. Italian ryegrass (*L. multiflorum*) is rarely awnless; perennial ryegrass (*L. perenne*) is awnless. Unlike most grasses, the rachilla segment on the basal floret is long and stout. Seeds of ryegrass are very similar to those of tall fescue. However, in ryegrass the rachilla segment has parallel sides, and the apex is not expanded (knobbed). In tall fescue the rachilla segment is tapered at the base, and the apex is expanded into a disk, or knob.

The ryegrasses flower in early spring and seed mature in early summer. The annual species is a prolific seed producer. Natural reseedings develop each fall where the grass is managed to produce seed. It is common on roadsides each fall and winter from Texas to Florida.

ADAPTATION AND USE
Ryegrasses are best adapted to moist, cool environments where temperatures are not extreme in the winter or summer. Many European countries have climates ideally suited to the ryegrasses. In the United States the northeastern and northwestern states are well suited to ryegrass. In the Transition Zone perennial ryegrass may provide a permanent turfgrass. But in the southern states both species serve as cool-season annuals.

The perennial species, *L. perenne,* is more cold tolerant than Italian ryegrass. However, both species are killed by extreme winter temperatures.

Ryegrasses are adapted to a wide range of soil conditions but favor moist, well-drained, fertile soils. The ryegrasses possess little drought tolerance and must be irrigated during dry periods to ensure survival. Shade tolerance of the ryegrasses is good in southern climates where shade conditions eliminate the extreme heat during summer. Perennial ryegrass often survives the hot, dry summers of the South in moderately shaded sites.

Both species of ryegrass are used for temporary grass cover during the fall and winter months in the South. Their quick establishment from seed (rapid germination and rapid seedling growth) makes them ideal for protection against erosion on newly prepared sites in the fall. They are also used to provide temporary green color during winter months when bermudagrass is dormant.

The ryegrasses have become very popular for overseeding sports fields, golf courses, and lawns during winter months. The improved turf-type perennial ryegrasses have greater cold tolerance, wear tolerance, disease resistance, and persistence than the older types. New varieties also have better turf characteristics—finer texture, greater density, darker color, and better mowing qualities.

In the Transition Zone perennial ryegrasses may be used as permanent turfgrasses on golf courses, sports fields, and, in mixtures with bluegrass, on lawns.

VARIETIES

At lease fifty improved ryegrass varieties have been developed over the past twenty years. Most improvements have been in perennial ryegrass, although intermediate crosses have been made with Italian ryegrass. Improvements in turf quality have been in the area of density, texture, and color (Pennfine, Manhattan, and Derby); mowing quality (Palmer, Manhattan II, Delray, and Loretta); heat tolerance (Derby, Birdie, Palmer, Citation, and Dasher); cold tolerance (Eton, Goalie, NK-200, and Norlea); disease resistance (Manhattan II, Palmer, Prelude, and Delray); insect resistance (Repell); and drought tolerance (Palmer and Prelude).

PROPAGATION

In California and many states where bluegrass sod is produced, ryegrass is often overseeded to form a mixture with bluegrass. This bluegrass-ryegrass sod is commonly used on sports fields and golf courses. In the southern states ryegrasses are established from seed. Ryegrasses are noted for their fast establishment rate and are primarily used for temporary cover in the South. Although ryegrass establishes quickly, it spreads slowly. Thus, relatively high seeding rates are used for turf. On golf courses and sports fields where a fast, uniform cover is required, seeding rates of 25 to 40 pounds of ryegrass seed per 1,000 square feet are commonly used. At these seeding rates a complete turf cover can be expected in 20 days.

On bermudagrass lawns where color is more important than density, ryegrass may be seeded at 5 to 7 pounds per 1,000 square feet. In these overseeding situations, ryegrass seed are broadcast over the surface of a closely mowed bermudagrass turf.

Seeding dates are very important when overseeding a bermudagrass turf. If overseeding is done too early, bermudagrass competes with the ryegrass seedlings and establishment may be poor. If overseeding is delayed, then cold temperatures may delay germination. The recommended seeding date is 2 to 4 weeks before the average first frost date, or when soil temperatures at the 4-inch depth reach 72° F.

In prepared seedbeds ryegrass can be planted 8 to 10 weeks before the average first frost date, and seeding rates can be reduced in prepared seedbeds to 3 to 5 pounds per 1,000 square feet. Keep the seedbed moist for 10 to 14 days after planting to obtain maximum germination. After 2 weeks reduce watering frequency to an as-needed basis.

To promote seedling growth fertilize the seedbed prior to planting and at 3-week intervals after planting. Use a starter fertilizer prior to planting at a rate of ½ pound of nitrogen per 1,000 square feet. Follow up with soluble nitrogen fertilizers applied at 3-week intervals at ½ pound nitrogen per 1,000 square feet until the desired cover develops.

Use fungicide-treated seed to control seedling diseases such as damping-off caused by *Pythium.* To provide additional protection during the seedling stage, apply broad-spectrum fungicides at 7- to 10-day intervals after planting.

MANAGEMENT

Of all turfgrasses used in the South, ryegrass probably has the highest maintenance requirement. Mowing, watering, fertilization, and pest management needs of ryegrass are higher than for any southern turfgrass. Ryegrass has a rapid growth rate in the spring and requires twice weekly mowing at the taller heights—above 1 inch; mowing at 2- to 3-day intervals at heights between ½ and 1 inch and daily mowing at heights below ½ inch.

Ryegrass is the least drought tolerant of the southern turfgrasses and needs frequent watering in the spring and early summer. In many golf course situations, daily watering is not unusual on ryegrass greens and fairways. Even on lawns ryegrass is the first grass to show symptoms of drought stress.

The nitrogen requirement of ryegrass is relatively high during the growing season—about ½ pound per 1,000 square feet per month from February through May. On golf greens mowed daily with clippings removed, about 1 pound of nitrogen per month is needed in the spring. On alkaline soils where iron might be limited, monthly applications of iron greatly improve the color of ryegrass.

Insects and diseases are serious pests to ryegrass. In the fall, during establishment of ryegrass, seedling diseases caused by *Pythium, Rhizoctonia,* and *Fusarium* are problems. Leaf spot, dollar spot, and rust are potential problems in the spring. Regular preventive applications of fungicides are needed on quality ryegrass turf such as found on golf courses and sports fields.

Insects, particularly sod webworms and cutworms, are a nuisance on ryegrass. The dark green color of the grass attracts the moths that lay the eggs of these insects. Often, several applications of insecticide or biological worm control are needed during the spring and fall to control these insects on ryegrass.

Bentgrass

ORIGIN AND DISTRIBUTION

Bentgrass (*Agrostis*) is a large genus with over 100 species, but only about 4 are used for turfgrass in the United States. None of these 4 are well adapted to southern climates. The only use of this species in the South is for golf course putting greens where environments are closely managed.

Throughout the New England states and the Pacific Northwest, where climatic conditions are ideal for bentgrass, the species is used for lawns, sports fields, and golf courses. In Europe and parts of Asia the grass is native and commonly found on lawns, pastures, and sport fields.

Of the four species used for turf creeping bentgrass is the one most commonly used on southern golf greens. The species was introduced into the United States from Europe during the Colonial Period.

DESCRIPTION OF SPECIES

Creeping bentgrass (*A. palustris*) is a perennial cool-season grass that forms a dense mat. The grass spreads by profuse creeping stolons and possesses rather vigorous, shallow roots. Stems (stolons) are decumbent (creeping) and slender and produce long narrow leaves. Leaf blades are smooth on the upper surface and ridged on the underside, 1 to 3 mm wide and bluish green in appearance. The ligule is long, membranous, finely toothed, or entire and rounded; auricles are absent.

The species is characterized by single flowered spikelets in a compact

Bentgrass

panicle. The panicle in flower is purple to bronze in appearance. Seeds of creeping bentgrass are too small to be identified without magnification. Seeds are ovate, less than 1 mm long, usually awnless with an occasional short, straight awn and silvery in appearance.

ADAPTATION AND USE

Creeping bentgrass is adapted to cool, humid environments such as those found in the northeastern United States. Cool nighttime temperatures are particularly advantageous to bentgrass. In the South high daytime temperatures together with warm nighttime temperatures create highly adverse conditions for bentgrass. During summer months in the South, carbohydrate reserves are depleted in bentgrass, and the turf becomes susceptible to any additional stress—drought, traffic, shade, insects, or disease.

As a result, the only use of bentgrass in the South is for golf greens where small acreage allows for very intense management. In the South bentgrass is best adapted to the Transition Zone where cooler temperatures prevail. But even in this area, special attention needs to be given to soil preparation, water management, air circulation, shade, exposure, and other factors.

VARIETIES

Presently, only the seeded varieties of bentgrass are used in the South—Seaside, Penncross, Emerald, Pennlinks, and Penneagle. A number of vegetatively propagated strains of bentgrass are used in the northern states, but they have found very limited use in the South. These include Cohansey (C-7), Toronto (C-15), Congressional (C-19), Nimisilla, and some local strains propagated on individual sites.

Seaside creeping bentgrass is the oldest seeded variety in use today. It is an extremely variable grass that develops into patches of individual strains with different colors, textures, and densities. The seed supply for Seaside is harvested from natural stands indigenous to the coastal regions of Washington and Oregon.

Penncross is a more uniform variety with superior turf quality, disease tolerance, and wear tolerance. Where play is heavy, Penncross is probably the better choice. Penncross was released by Pennsylvania State University in 1954. Seeds are harvested from crosses of three vegetatively propagated strains.

Emerald, Pennlinks, and Penneagle are newer varieties of bentgrass that have seen only limited use in the South. More recently, SR 1020, Crenshaw, and Cato varieties have been released for use on southern golf courses.

PROPAGATION

In the case of bentgrass, particular attention needs to be given to seedbed preparation. Well-drained soil mixtures are essential for growing bentgrass in the South. Highly permeable mixtures of sand and organic amendments placed over a drainage system are commonly used for bentgrass green construction.

Seeding rates for bentgrass golf greens vary from 1 to 2 pounds per 1,000 square feet. If mulch is applied over the seed, about 50 pounds mulch per 1,000 square feet are used. Light, frequent watering is necessary on these highly permeable green's mixtures to keep the seedbed moist. The mulch may reduce the frequency of watering from 5 to 7 times per day to 2 to 3 times per day. Under ideal conditions germination may begin 5 days after seeding.

Frequent fertilization is also helpful to establish a cover of bentgrass on these sand mixtures. A starter fertilizer might be applied before seeding and 1 month later. Soluble nitrogen fertilizers can be applied at light rates at 10-day intervals after seeding until a complete cover develops.

Early fall is the best time to seed bentgrass in the South. Spring planting dates do not allow adequate growing time for plants to mature prior to summer stress.

MANAGEMENT

Intensive management and frequent observation are keys to the success of bentgrass golf greens in the South. Watering, fertilization, mowing, cultivation, and pests must be closely managed to keep bentgrass greens during summer months.

Water must be closely managed to meet the moisture needs of the grass but not exclude oxygen from the soil. Water also serves to moderate the temperature during heat stress periods. Watering schedules and rates must be based on water use rates (evapotranspiration) and the water holding capacity of the soil. During summer months watering practices may determine success or failure with bentgrass. Well-drained greens (permeable soil mixtures and good surface runoff) and well designed irrigation systems give the turf manager an edge on bentgrass greens. At times little or no irrigation may be needed; at other times, very light applications of water (misting) may be needed to cool the turf by evaporation from the leaf surface.

The turf manager must closely manage the water needs of bentgrass during heat stress periods. Excess water, or saturated soils, can be as damaging as insufficient water during heat stress. The successful turf manager matches irrigation rates to water use rates (evapotranspiration) and uses a misting system to cool the turf during midday stress.

Fertilization practices are also critical on bentgrass greens. The successful manager plans fertilizer applications to promote growth without depleting carbohydrate reserves. During cool periods such as fall and early spring, fertilizer promotes stolon and leaf growth as well as carbohydrate storage in stolons. However, late spring and summer applications of fertilizer promote leaf and stolon growth at the expense of carbohydrate reserves. Thus, very little fertilizer should be used between June and September on bentgrass greens. Perhaps monthly applications of nitrogen at ½ pound per 1,000 square feet can be made from October to May and ¼ pound per 1,000 square feet from June to September, for a total of about 5 pounds of nitrogen per 1,000 square feet per year.

In addition to nitrogen, potassium, phosphorus, and iron are required on most golf greens. Soil and plant tissue analyses will alert the turf manager to specific needs of bentgrass for these nutrients. On an annual basis, 1 to 2 pounds of phosphorus, 4 to 5 pounds of potassium, and several foliar applications of iron are generally needed. But soil and tissue samples will indicate specific nutrient needs.

Mowing heights of ³⁄₁₆ inch or less are common on bentgrass greens. But during summer stress periods, raising the height to ¼ inch helps the bentgrass survive heat stress and tolerate wear.

The use of walking greens mowers in place of riding mowers also helps keep bentgrass greens through the summer. If riding mowers are used, turns should be made off of the putting surface.

Cultivation practices, including aeration, vertical mowing, and topdressing, need to be done during the fall and spring on bentgrass greens to avoid added stress during the summer. All of these cultivation practices help the turf manager control thatch, graininess, and compaction on bentgrass greens.

To effectively control insect and disease problems, frequent surveillance is essential. Sod webworms, cutworms, mole crickets, and white grubs need to be treated as soon as the insects are found. In the case of sod webworms, as many as four or five generations may occur in a single year.

Effective disease control requires preventative applications of fungicides for dollar spot, brownpatch, and other disease problems. Turf managers must be alert for development of diseases during warm, moist conditions.

5 Specifications for Turfgrass Establishment

Turfgrass has become increasingly important in today's society as people's needs increase for recreation, comfort, and conservation (Beard and Green 1994). Turfgrasses enhance the appearance and utility of lawns, parks, golf courses, and other greenbelt areas in and around urban centers. They improve the environment of urban centers by reducing erosion, temperatures, noise, dust, and glare. And turfgrasses improve the safety of sports fields and playgrounds by adding resiliency to the playing surface.

A lawn, the single most important feature of a well-landscaped home, is often the first improvement a homeowner plans when moving into a new home. Although a lawn adds to the beauty of a home, its primary purpose is functional rather than aesthetic. The lawn prevents soil erosion, reduces run-off, lowers temperatures around the home, and reduces dust and glare. In addition, it provides an attractive, inexpensive, and nonabrasive surface for recreation.

Successful establishment of a turfgrass on a lawn, park, golf course, or other site involves four critical steps: (1) proper site preparation, (2) selection of an adapted turfgrass, (3) planting the turfgrass, and (4) postplanting care and maintenance.

Site Preparation

Proper site preparation is essential to the successful establishment of a turfgrass. As the foundation is the strength of a building, the seedbed is the support for a turfgrass. The seedbed refers to the several surface inches of soil that are tilled and, perhaps, modified prior to planting. Poor seedbed conditions, like a faulty foundation, result in long-term maintenance problems for the turf manager. Water management is also complicated by poor seedbed preparation. And sites with severe slopes, shallow topsoil, or compacted soils need modifying or amending before a turfgrass is planted to make water management more efficient.

SITE CLEARING. The first step to prepare a site for planting is to remove all debris—construction residues, rocks, tree stumps, undesirable grasses, and weeds. Construction crews often leave lumber, concrete, and other building materials that get buried during construction. Removal of these residues creates a more desirable and uniform seedbed for planting. Common problems found at new homesites include concrete layers where cement was mixed and became covered with topsoil, buried bricks and lumber, and pockets of sand where mortar was mixed. All of these problems create unfavorable conditions for turfgrasses and usually result in dry spots that are difficult to maintain.

Remove rocks from the upper 2 inches of soil to provide a uniform soil medium for grass root development. Where large deposits of rocks are found, the entire deposit of material may need to be removed or covered with topsoil. For large sites, such as golf courses and sports fields, rock-picking machines are available to remove rocks from the surface prior to planting.

Tree stumps and other organic debris should be removed rather than covered with topsoil. Decaying organic residues frequently result in the appearance of so-called fairy rings, with the accompanying mushrooms and puffballs. Buried stumps and logs eventually result in depressions as the wood decays. Although it is common practice when clearing large sites to bury tree stumps and large branches, it creates problems for the turf manager for years to come.

The presence on the site of undesirable grasses and weeds can lead to serious weed problems for the turf manager. In a hybrid bermudagrass lawn, fairway, or sports field, common bermudagrass would present problems for the turf manager. Bahiagrass, dallisgrass, and other perennial grasses also present problems for the turf manager since they cannot be selectively removed from some turfgrasses. Nutgrass, grassburs, and other weeds present similar problems. These all need to be eliminated prior to planting the turfgrass.

The most effective, although most costly, method of weed control is sterilizing with methyl bromide, vapam, or a similar product. These products, when properly applied, will effectively control most weeds and grasses. Critical planting sites, such as golf greens, sod farms, highly visible lawn areas, and sports fields, may require sterilization to eliminate these undesirable plants.

On other areas, nonselective herbicides such as glyphosate (Roundup) may be used to control weeds and grasses. However, plants must be actively growing at the time of application for these products to be effective.

Many annual weeds can be controlled by cultivating (disking or rototilling) the site immediately prior to planting. Other more difficult to control weeds may be controlled by repeated cultivations during dry conditions.

In general, preemerge herbicides should not be used prior to planting the site with a desirable turfgrass. These products may injure the newly planted grasses.

CULTIVATION. Construction sites for homes, commercial developments, golf courses, and sports fields often become compacted as a result of equipment operated on the site, deliveries to the site, and cleanup operations after construction is complete. To alleviate compaction and to create more uniform and more favorable soil conditions, cultivation is necessary. Large sites can be cultivated with tractor-drawn equipment such as a chisel plow, subsoiler, or disk plow, while small areas can be cultivated with a hand-operated rototiller.

If the soil needs to be disturbed more than 4 inches deep, a chisel, disk, or plow can be used. Use of a breaking plow or subsoiler will loosen the soil 6 to 12 inches deep. Such an operation will break up a plow pan or clay pan several inches below the surface.

A plowed soil, or an undisturbed soil, can be further broken up with a disk and harrow. Disking a site in several directions will loosen the upper 4 inches and destroy most of the vegetation. Disking during summer months is most effective for vegetation control. Harrowing or dragging a chain or heavy mat will pulverize and smooth the soil surface after disking. All of these cultivation operations should be done when the soil is moist, but not wet. Cultivating wet soil destroys soil structure and produces large clods, but dry soils become very hard and resist cultivation.

Small lawn sites can be effectively cultivated with a hand-operated rototiller. By operating the rototiller in several directions, the upper 4 inches of soil can be pulverized and uniformly mixed. The rototiller is also used to incorporate organic material and soil amendments into the soil.

SOIL MODIFICATION. Some sites would benefit from soil modification prior to planting grass. Extremely acid sites need limestone incorporated in the upper 4 to 6 inches at 2 to 4 tons per acre depending on soil test recommendations. Alkaline, high pH, sites may benefit from sulfur and/or gypsum. Most sites would benefit from organic matter incorporated in the upper 4 inches of soil.

In each case, the material to be incorporated can be spread on the surface and rototilled into the soil. Thorough mixing is essential to avoid leaving pockets of the amendment throughout the soil. It is possible to create a potting soil mixture with the existing soil, organic material, and whatever amendments may be recommended. Flower beds and gardens often receive this type of preparation. However, turfgrass sites rarely receive the attention and expense of intensive soil modification. Golf greens are the exception, as they are intensively modified with sand, organic matter, and other amendments.

Soil modification with amendments such as sulfur and limestone should be based on soil test recommendations. The use of organic materials will be based more on their availability and cost than on need. All soils, except some of the organic soils found in the southeast, would benefit from organic materials such as peat, composted bark, sawdust, or rice hulls. These organic materials improve soil aeration, increase nutrient content, and promote microbial activity, all of which aid in the establishment of grass.

Aggregate materials such as Turface, Greenschoice (SoilPro), and Isolite also improve the physical characteristics of soils. When incorporated at 10 to 15 percent (by volume) in the top 4 to 6 inches of the seedbed these materials increase aeration and drainage and reduce compaction. In sandy soils these aggregate materials also increase water and nutrient retention.

GRADING. Drainage is the single most critical factor in the establishment and maintenance of turfgrasses. Grasses thrive on well-drained sites; but perish on poorly drained sites.

When developing a site, it is often necessary to cut high areas and fill low areas to establish the desired grade. This on-site contouring is referred to as rough grading. Rough grading is usually done with a dozer on large sites or a tractor and blade on small sites. When rough grading a site, surface drainage must be uppermost in mind. Moving water away from buildings, sidewalks, driveways, traffic areas on golf courses and playing fields, and other critical areas should be the main object of the rough-grading operation.

If deep cuts are necessary on a site, steps need to be taken to replace some topsoil on the cut area. If large areas are excavated for a building site, the topsoil should be removed and stored separately from the subsoil. Then, as the site is being graded, the subsoil can be spread first and covered with the original topsoil.

If possible, avoid steep slopes on grass areas because establishment of grass is difficult and soil erosion is likely. Gentle slopes, with water moving away from critical areas, are ideal on grassy sites. An ideal slope on grass areas is 1.0 to 2.0 percent with 0.5 percent slope being minimum. Where severe slopes cannot be avoided, construct retaining walls to limit the severity of the slope.

If topsoil is to be added to the site, grade stakes are needed following rough grading to establish a uniform depth of topsoil. At least 4 inches of topsoil are needed for grass areas and 6 to 8 inches would be desirable. When topsoil is in place and any necessary amendments are added the finish grading, or fine grading, needs to be done. Fine grading smooths and firms the topsoil in preparation for planting the site. Fine grading can be done by hand on small sites or by a box blade or grader on larger sites. When the final contours are established, the site can be dragged with a heavy steel mat or carpet drag to smooth the surface. Rolling may be necessary to firm the soil if there is not time to let rainfall settle the site. Final grading should be done after the site has been rolled or settled by rainfall or irrigation.

Constructing the Golf Green

There is still much disagreement on the method of constructing the putting green (Hummel 1993). The USGA Green Section method of putting green construction (USGA Staff 1993) is the most popular method in use. But few architects understand the importance of closely following the specifications for a USGA golf green. Consequently, changes or modifications are often made in USGA specifications to reduce the cost of construction or to utilize less expensive materials. As a result, only a few golf greens are actually built according to USGA Green Section specifications. Subsurface tile drains covered with a 4-inch blanket of pea gravel, a 2-inch sand layer, and a 12- to 14-inch layer of seedbed, mixed off-site to specifications developed from laboratory analyses, constitute a USGA golf green. In many cases the 2-inch sand layer and the off-site mixing are omitted to reduce the cost of construction. In some cases, the 2-inch sand layer is not essential. But on-site mixing *always* leads to problems.

The PURR-WICK System of putting green construction developed at Purdue University provides another method of construction (Ralston and Daniel 1973). The PURR-WICK System consists of a plastic barrier, tile drains, and a compacted sand with the top 2 inches modified with peat and calcined clay aggregates. When properly designed and installed, the PURR-WICK System has provided consistent and very good putting greens. But the PURR-WICK System also has some limitation with respect to availability and uniformity of suitable sands, design, and construction.

The fine sand greens being constructed in the West provide still another method of putting green construction (Davis 1973). Fine- to medium-textured sands are consistent and playability is very good. However, where sands are not uniform or depth is not consistent, play is not uniform and problems develop.

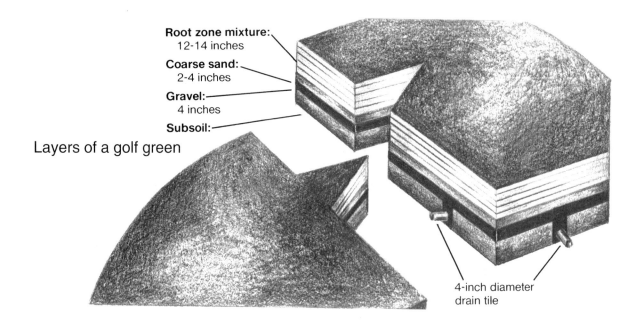

Root zone mixture:
12-14 inches

Coarse sand:
2-4 inches

Gravel:
4 inches

Subsoil:

Layers of a golf green

4-inch diameter
drain tile

All of these methods of greens construction have merit. Some concepts are common to all of these methods. Surface, internal, and subsurface drainage are absolutely necessary for properly built golf greens. All methods provide for the removal of excess water. Compacted sand provides an ideal base for heavily used turf facilities, such as golf greens. All of the modern methods of green construction utilize high percentages of sand in the topmix.

Early specifications for golf green construction recommended about 30 percent sand in the topmix (Roser 1931). By the late 1950s the USGA Green Section was recommending 50 to 60 percent sand in the topmix. Today, 80 to 100 percent sand is used for the topmix of golf greens with excellent results. Also, all of these methods of construction provide some means of retaining moisture in the root zone—the USGA method utilizes a perched water table, PURR-WICK utilizes a plastic barrier, and the fine-sand method utilizes a deep root zone.

These common traits—drainage, compacted sand topmix, and moisture retention—are requirements for well-built golf greens. When specifications meeting these requirements are followed, consistent and satisfactory golf greens can be produced. When the requirements are not met, no level of maintenance will produce consistently good golf greens. The golf club, not the architect or contractor, always suffers the consequences of poorly constructed greens, translating into increased maintenance costs and poor playing conditions.

SURFACE, INTERNAL, AND SUBSURFACE DRAINAGE

Removal of excess water after rain or irrigation is important to the playability of the golf course, growth of the grass on the putting green, and disease control. Wet, waterlogged golf greens are not fun to play. In addition, they result in very shallow rooted grasses which are subject to thinning under traffic, drought, heat, or cold stress. Also, these wet areas develop heavy infestations of algae and are subject to sudden disease outbreaks. Weeds present another problem on poorly drained golf greens. As if these problems were not enough, poor spring transition is common on such greens. Adequate drainage does not solve all of these problems, but is an essential component of their solution. Several aspects of drainage must be considered to remove excess water from the green.

Surface drainage is necessary to prevent the accumulation of water at various sites on and around the greens. Where internal drainage is slow, the importance of surface drainage is accentuated. Water must be carried off and away from the putting surface—preferably to both sides of the center line of the green. Good design followed by proper construction will guarantee adequate surface drainage.

Internal drainage is a function of soil types or soil mixtures. Natural soils typically have very slow percolation rates after being subjected to compac-

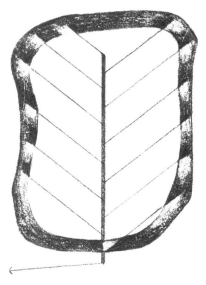

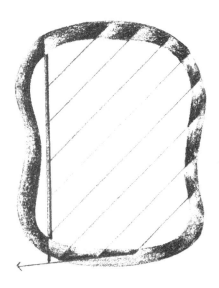

The two most commonly used drainage patterns for putting greens. Four-inch diameter tile is spaced at 15- to 20-foot intervals, depending on slope. Approximately 100 linear feet of tile is required for every 1,000 square feet of putting surface to be drained. Normally, the collar is 3 to 5 feet in width.

tion. Consequently, topmixes for golf greens are modified by adding sand, organic matter, or calcined clay aggregates. As traffic has increased on golf courses over the past twenty-five years, higher percentages of sand have been used in topmixes. The USGA Green Section specifications suggest a percolation rate between 6 and 12 inches per hour for putting green soil mixes. With 70 to 80 percent sand mixes, these percolation rates are easily achieved. Where initial percolation rates are 6 to 12 inches per hour and greens are properly maintained, the golf club can expect the greens to have satisfactory internal drainage twenty or more years after construction.

With good internal drainage golf greens are playable soon after a rain or irrigation, oxygen is moved well into the root zone, and salts can be readily leached from the root zone. Also where greens have good internal drainage, excess water is readily moved to the subsurface drains and carried away from the golf green.

Subsurface drain lines are needed where the subsoil percolation rate is significantly lower than that of the green's topmix. Main drain lines should be embedded 6 to 8 inches in the subsoil along the natural drainage way of the subgrade. Laterals may come off of the main line in a gridiron or herringbone pattern. The main lines should be 4-inch diameter perforated plastic drain tile. Laterals may be 2-inch diameter perforated plastic tile and should be spaced 10 to 15 feet apart, depending on the slope of the subgrade and length of the lateral—the greater the slope and the shorter the laterals, the farther apart the laterals can be spaced. Solid drain tile should be used off of the putting surface to carry the water away from the green. The discharge site for the drain lines must be adequate to handle the drainage water under wet conditions. Sumps are almost always adequate in wet weather. Outlets should be provided to handle excess water when sumps are saturated.

Where surface, internal, and subsurface drainage is adequate, many of the problems associated with greens maintenance can be avoided. Also, well drained golf greens always play consistently and uniformly.

COMPACTED SAND TOPMIXES

The composition of the topmix has been the subject of much research over the past twenty years (Bingaman and Kohnke 1970; Brown and Duble 1975; Davis et al. 1970; Waddington 1974). Resilience, permeability, water retention, and uniformity are the most important traits of the topmix. Without traffic, which is so concentrated on golf greens, a fertile loam soil would prove ideal. But with the level of traffic (compaction) greens receive, soils do not hold up for the expected duration of a golf green.

Soil structure deteriorates under constant pressure, and soil greens quickly become waterlogged. Traffic on wet soils further deteriorates soil structure, and greens quickly become very hard and impermeable to water.

Consequently, artificial soil mixes are recommended for new golf greens. Sands modified with organic amendments, calcined clay aggregates, or other materials have replaced soils as the medium for growing fine turf on greens. Compacted sands retain the traits needed for heavily used greens—resilience, permeability, moisture retention, and uniformity. Laboratory analysis of the topmix is required to assure adequate permeability, moisture retention, and resiliency.

Two characteristics of sands are critical to their use in topmixes—texture and particle size distribution (table 5-1). Both of these characteristics can be determined through a sand sieve analysis. Medium- to medium-fine textured sands (0.2 mm to 0.5 mm diameter) with narrow particle size distribution are best suited for golf green mixes. Coarse-textured sands produce hard and droughty golf greens. Very fine-textured sands also produce hard greens that retain excess water. At least 60 percent of the sand particles should fall between 0.2 and 1.0 mm in diameter. Less than 10 percent of the particles should be finer than 0.1 mm and less than 10 percent greater than 1.0 mm. Some natural sand deposits and many commercially screened sands fall within these ranges.

Ideally, sands may be amended with organic matter and calcined clay aggregates to improve resiliency and moisture retention of the topmix. Organic amendments should be highly decomposed, finely divided, and rich in organic content. Peat, composted gin trash or rice hulls, decomposed bark, and various other organic materials have performed very well as organic amendments to sand.

Calcined clay aggregates such as Turface and Greenschoice have been shown to increase nutrients and moisture retention of sands (Hansen 1962; Johns 1976). The calcined aggregates also help maintain oxygen in the root zone of the grasses.

These materials should be mixed off-site with a large front-end loader or rotovator and moved to the green. In most cases, only the top 6 inches of the topmix need to be amended. The other 6 to 8 inches may be straight sand. Where finer sands are used in the topmix, the depth of the topmix must be 14 inches or more.

MOISTURE RETENTION IN THE ROOT ZONE

The USGA method of greens construction utilizes a perched water table above the gravel blanket to increase moisture retention in the root zone. Without the perched water table, USGA greens would be quite droughty. Therefore, it is very important to maintain a distinct boundary between the gravel layer and the topmix. The two layers must not be mixed or blended together during construction. The boundary is critical to the concept of the USGA method of greens construction.

The PURR-WICK System utilizes a plastic barrier to maintain moisture

Table 5-1. Sand Sizes for Golf Courses

	Sand Particle Size Classification Table			
	ASTM* Mesh	*Diameter (mm)*	*Sieve Opening (in inches)*	
	4	4.76	0.187	
	5	4.00	0.157	
	6	3.36	0.132	
	7	2.83	0.111	
	8	2.38	0.0937	
	9	2.00	0.0787	
	10	1.68	0.0661	
	12	1.41	0.0555	
	14	1.19	0.0469	
Range for Bunker Use	16	1.00	0.0394	Coarse
	20	.84	0.0331	
	24	.71	0.0278	
	28	.59	0.0234	
	32	.50	0.0197	
	35	.42	0.0165	Ideally, minimum of 75% medium sand
	42	.35	0.0139	
	48	.30	0.0117	Medium
	60	.25	0.0098	
	65	.21	0.0083	
	80	.18	0.0070	
	100	.15	0.0059	Fine
	115	.13	0.0049	
	150	.11	0.0041	
	170	.09	0.0035	
	200	.07	0.0029	
	250	.06	0.0025	
	270	.05	0.0021	
	325	.04	0.0017	

(Range for Soil Mixes: 35–150)

*American Standard for Testing Materials

in the root zone. The barrier is critical to the PURR-WICK concept, and care must be taken not to puncture the plastic barrier during construction.

The fine-sand method of greens construction utilizes amendments, organic matter, or calcined clay aggregates, to increase moisture in the root zone. The fine-sand method provides less opportunity for error than either of the other methods with respect to moisture retention.

STEPS TO A BETTER GOLF GREEN
First, select a qualified course architect to design the green. Location, size, shape, contours, bunkering, and surface drainage should all be considered in relation to the direction and severity of the shot to be played.

Second, develop specifications relative to the composition of the topmix and the characteristics of the profile—USGA, PURR-WICK, or fine-sand method.

Third, find an experienced contractor to construct the green according to the design and specifications developed.

Fourth, assign responsibility to someone—the golf course superintendent, another club official, or an outside agent—to inspect the construction operation. This person must have the authority to accept or reject each phase of the construction process—subsurface drainage, composition, and mixing of the topmix and construction. The architect must approve or disapprove the final construction relative to his design. Corrections must be made as discrepancies are found.

Fifth, final acceptance is the responsibility of the club and should have the approval of the architect, contractor, and superintendent.

Turfgrass Root Zones

Turfgrasses are grown on many types of substrates—gravel, sand, silt, clay, organic, or a combination of these components. These components form a matrix, or root zone, that is characterized by specific physical, chemical, and biological properties. These properties of the root zone determine the quality of turf that can be produced under different environment, management, and use conditions.

For example, a fine bermudagrass turf can be maintained on a golf green or sports field if the root zone is well drained. A poorly drained root zone leads to failure because of shallow rooting, compaction, wear, and slow recovery. Likewise, buffalograss performs poorly on sandy root zones, centipedegrass does poorly on alkaline root zones, and ryegrass performs poorly on saline sites—all properties of specific types of root zones.

In addition to the quality of turf, the level of inputs—time and money—required to maintain turfgrasses on different root zones may be equally important. A well-drained root zone on a football field or golf green needs fewer inputs than a poorly drained root zone.

The durability and persistence of turfgrasses are also influenced by the characteristics of the root zone. For example, wear injury is much greater on a compacted, wet root zone than on a loose, well-drained root zone. And some grasses are not persistent on sandy, alkaline, or saline root zones.

Thus, root zones not only affect the quality of turf produced, but also affect the durability, persistence, and level of maintenance required.

ROOT ZONE CHARACTERISTICS. The solid components of a root zone largely determine its physical, chemical, and biological characteristics. The solid components of a root zone include minerals (gravel or coarse aggregates, sand, silt, and clay) and organic matter. The relative proportion of these components, the uniformity of their distribution, and their depth de-

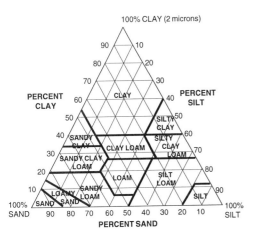

100% CLAY (2 microns)

PERCENT CLAY

PERCENT SILT

100% SAND

PERCENT SAND

100% SILT

USDA soil textural triangle (See *USDA Soil Classification Survey*, 1962. Supplement to USDA Handbook No. 18, pp. 173–88)

termine the physical, chemical, and biological characteristics of a root zone. Physical properties of a root zone include texture, porosity, structure, and bulk density. The texture of a root zone is determined by the relative particle size distribution of mineral components (sand, silt, and clay). Texture can be identified on the soil textural triangle by plotting its percentage of sand, silt, and clay. For a soil to be described as sandy it must have at least 50 percent of its mineral particles in the sand designation (above 0.05 mm in diameter). Likewise, a soil with 50 percent or more of its particles in the clay designation (less than 0.002 mm in diameter) is described as a clay soil. Soils with a wide distribution of particle sizes are usually described as loams (table 5-2).

Soil texture is important because it influences the surface area, the porosity, and the density of a turfgrass root zone. The surface areas of the various particles in a root zone affect the chemical, biological, and physical activity of the root zone. Fine-textured particles, such as silt and clay, contribute great surface area to a root zone. For example, a volume of clay particles has at least 50 times the surface area of the same volume of sand particles. Consequently, clay particles increase the chemical activity of a root zone by providing more sites for holding and exchanging plant nutrients. Clay particles are also important cementing agents in a root zone that contribute to the aggregation of soil particles into structural units or aggregates. Aggregation of soil particles into larger units increases the large pore spaces that allow for the movement of air and water in and out of the root zone. Organic matter is another important cementing agent in the root zone.

Texture also determines the porosity and the size distribution of pore space

Table 5-2. Particle Size Designations

Textural Name	Tyler Scale ASTM*	U.S. No. NBS**	SIEVE OPENING	
			mm	inches
Gravel	4 mesh	No. 4	4.76	0.1870
Fine gravel	9 mesh	No. 10	2.00	0.0787
Very coarse sand	16 mesh	No. 18	1.00	0.0394
Coarse sand	32 mesh	No. 35	0.50	0.0197
Medium sand	60 mesh	No. 60	0.25	0.0098
Fine sand	150 mesh	No. 140	0.105	0.0041
Very fine sand	270 mesh	No. 270	0.053	0.0021
Silt			0.002	0.00008
Clay			<0.002	

*American Standard for Testing Materials
**National Bureau of Standards

in a root zone. Coarse-textured root zones (sands) have limited pore space with large pores making up most of the space. Fine-textured soils (clay loam, silt loam, clay) have greater total pore space and small pores are dominant. Water occupies the smaller (capillary) pores. Consequently, fine-textured soils hold more water than coarse-textured soils.

Bulk density, the weight of a given volume, is another physical characteristic of a turfgrass root zone. Hard, compacted root zones have relatively high bulk densities, above 1.6 grams per cubic centimeter; whereas, well-aggregated soils and root zones high in organic matter have bulk densities between 1.45 and 1.6. Root zones with excessive organic matter are characterized by spongy, waterlogged conditions during wet weather. Such root zones are not well suited for golf courses and sports fields.

Just as the texture of a soil is critical to its use for turfgrass root zones, the depth of the soil is equally critical. An ideal soil for a turfgrass root zone that is only a few inches deep would be difficult to manage. Likewise, a clay layer several inches below the surface of a sandy loam would create problems for turf management. Thus, abrupt changes in soil texture and soil aggregation (structure) in the top several feet of the root zone profile critically influence the management of turf.

An ideal profile for a turfgrass root zone would be several feet of a well-drained subsoil. Such profiles are rare for turfgrass managers. Much more common are shallow topsoils or layered profiles with poorly drained subsoils—conditions that restrict water movement and limit aeration to the few inches near the surface. Waterlogged, compacted, and anaerobic conditions develop on these profiles that make turf management precarious.

Surface conditions that appear ideal can be deceiving. The depth and uni-

Texture affects water retention and movement in soils.

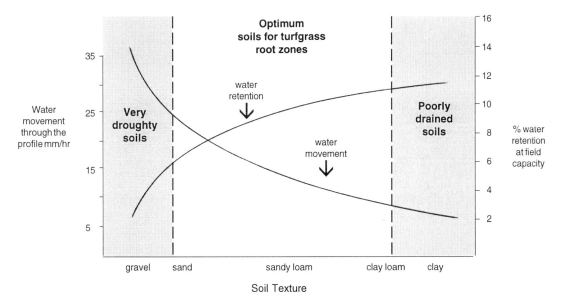

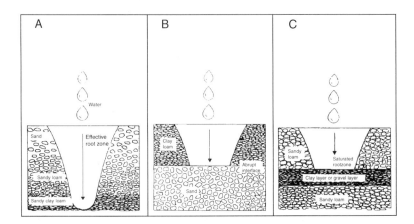

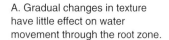

A. Gradual changes in texture have little effect on water movement through the root zone.

B. Abrupt changes in texture interfere with water movements.

C. Layers interfere with water movement.

formity of the topsoil, as well as the drainage characteristics of the subsoil, are more important to the management of turfgrasses.

Chemical properties of root zones also impact turf management practices and the quality of turf produced. Fine-textured soils and soils high in organic matter have much higher nutrient-holding capacities than coarse-textured soils. The nutrient-holding capacity of a soil varies inversely with the size of its particles. The nutrient (cation) exchange capacity (CEC) of soils ranges from 2 to 4 milliequivalents per 100 grams of soil (meg/100 gms) for sands to 40 to 60 meg/100 gms for clay soils. Soils high in organic matter may have CECs over 100 meg/100 gms.

As a result, nutrients may readily leach through a coarse-textured root zone, such as sand or sandy loam, while nutrients are held in reserve in finer-textured soils. The nutrient retention capacity of a root zone is one measure of its fertility. Sandy-textured soils low in organic matter are usually light-colored and considered infertile; while loam and clay loam soils high in organic matter are dark-colored and considered fertile.

The relative amount of each cation held by the clay particles is closely associated with specific properties of the root zone. Highly acid soils (pH below 6.0) have a high percentage of hydrogen ions (H^+) adsorbed on the soil particles and in the soil solution. Alkaline soils (pH 7.5 to 8.5) have a high percentage of calcium ions (Ca^{++}) adsorbed on their soil particles. And highly dispersed soils with low infiltration rates have a high percentage of sodium ions (Na^+) associated with their soil particles (table 5-3).

Thus, the CEC of a root zone and the relative abundance of the various plant nutrients determine the fertility of the soil. Those with high CECs, a high percentage of calcium associated with the soil particles, and an abundance of plant nutrients are considered fertile root zones. Such root zones are typically well aggregated, well drained, and resistant to rapid leaching or loss of plant nutrients.

Table 5-3. pH, Hydrogen Ion (H+) Concentration; Soil Reaction and Grass Adaptation

pH	(H+) Concentration (moles/liter)	Soil Reaction	Grass Adaptation
3	1×10^{-3}	Strongly acid	None
4	1×10^{-4}	Strongly acid	Centipedegrass
5	1×10^{-5}	Acid	Bentgrass, Carpetgrass, Bahiagrass
6	1×10^{-6}	Slightly acid	Bermudagrass, Tall fescue
7	1×10^{-7}	Neutral	Saint Augustine, Zoysia, Kentucky Bluegrass
8	1×10^{-8}	Alkaline	Buffalograss
9	1×10^{-9}	Strongly alkaline	Alkaligrass

Soil reaction, or pH, is a measure of the degree of acidity or alkalinity of a soil, or root zone. The relative amount of hydrogen ions (H+) and hydroxyl ions (OH-) in the soil solution determines the degree of acidity or alkalinity. A predominance of hydrogen ions makes a soil acid; a predominance of hydroxyl ions makes a soil alkaline.

A system of expressing soil reaction in terms of pH was developed by a Danish biochemist. To avoid more complicated terms he defined pH as the hydrogen ion concentration. For example, a soil with a concentration of 1×10^{-7} hydrogen moles per liter has a pH of 7. At a pH of 7 the concentrations of hydrogen and hydroxyl ions in the soil solution are equal and the soil is considered neutral. As the hydrogen ion concentration increases from 1×10^{-7} to 1×10^{-6}, the pH is lowered from 7 to 6 and the soil becomes acid. Since the scale is logarithmic a change of one pH unit represents a tenfold increase or decrease in hydrogen ion concentration. Likewise, a change of two pH units represents a hundredfold increase or decrease.

In soils, hydrogen ions are found in solution and adsorbed on soil particles. As they are removed from the soil solution by plants or microorganisms they are replaced by those on the soil particles. Thus, the soil is resistant to a change in acidity or alkalinity. Only by adding massive amounts of calcium ions to replace hydrogen, or vice versa, can we change soil reaction.

For example, the addition of several tons of limestone per acre may raise the pH of an acid soil by the following reaction:

$$(H^+) \quad + \quad CaCO_3 \quad \rightarrow \quad H_2O \quad + \quad CO_2 \quad + \quad Ca^{++}$$
(acid soil) + (limestone)

In other words, the limestone reacts with the acid soil and the hydrogen ion is replaced by the calcium ion.

Likewise, the addition of elemental sulfur to an alkaline soil reduces the pH by the following reaction:

$$\text{elemental S} + 4H_2O \rightarrow H_2SO_4 + 6H^+$$
$$\phantom{\text{elemental S} + \ \ }\text{(water)} \text{(acid)}$$

In this case, the hydrogen ions (H^+) replace calcium and other cations in the soil solution to reduce soil pH.

In alkali soils (pH above 8.5), the soil particles are saturated with sodium ions (Na^+) which disperse soil particles (destroys soil aggregates) and seal the soil surface. Alkali conditions can be treated with large applications of gypsum ($CaSO_4$). Gypsum reacts with the alkali soil by the following mechanism:

$$CaSO_4 + Na^+ - \text{clay} \rightarrow NaSO_4 + Ca^{++} - \text{clay}$$
$$\text{(gypsum)}$$

If the site has adequate drainage, the soluble $NaSO_4$ is carried away with the drainage water. Sometimes tile drains must be installed for the procedure to be effective. Without adequate drainage the problem is only aggravated by the addition of gypsum. In calcareous soils, elemental sulfur can be added instead of gypsum. Sulfur reacts with calcareous soils to produce gypsum as follows:

$$S + 4H_2O \rightarrow H_2SO_4 + 6H^+$$
$$H_2SO_4 + CaCO_3 \rightarrow CaSO_4 + CO_2$$
$$ \text{(gypsum)}$$

An extremely low or high soil pH is toxic to grass roots and leads to the loss of turfgrasses. Centipedegrass tolerates soil pH to about 4, while alkaligrass tolerates pH above 9. However, nutrient availability is affected by only moderate deviations from a neutral soil pH. At pH levels below 6, nitrogen and phosphorus availability is reduced. And at pH levels above 7.5 the availability of most minor nutrients, iron in particular, is reduced. The chlorotic condition of grasses in alkaline soils is frequently due to an iron deficiency. Soil organisms are also sensitive to only moderate changes in pH. Thus, it is important for the turf manager to monitor soil pH and to add the amendments (limestone, gypsum, or elemental S) needed to neutralize soil acidity or alkalinity.

Organic matter is another component of the turfgrass root zone. The organic fraction of the root zone consists of plant residues in various stages of decay, grass roots, microorganisms, and their amendments (such as peat, rice hulls, etc.) that may have been added to the root zone during preparation. On a weight basis the organic fraction of a turfgrass root zone may range from 1 percent, or less, to 8 to 10 percent. In some areas of the United States, turfgrass is produced on muck soils that contain 30 to 40 percent organic matter on a weight basis.

On a volume basis the organic fraction constitutes a much higher percentage. For example, a one-to-one mixture of peat and soil on a volume basis may be only 5 percent organic matter on a weight basis. Thus, organic matter adds bulk to the soil and reduces the density of mineral soils. A mineral soil may have a bulk density of 1.6 gms/cc; but a muck soil may have a bulk density of only 1.2 gms/cc.

Organic matter contributes significantly to the physical and chemical properties of a turfgrass root zone. Organic matter reduces bulk density, increases porosity, increases nutrient and water holding capacity, increases soil aggregation, increases aeration and water movement, and provides a source of plant nutrients.

Turfgrass root zones that are low in organic matter (less than 1 percent by weight) are typically hard, droughty, compacted, and deficient in plant nutrients. At the other extreme, turfgrass root zones high in organic matter are typically soft (spongy) and waterlogged after rain or irrigation. A heavily thatched turf would be an example of a root zone with excessive organic matter.

Perhaps 2 to 5 percent (by weight) organic matter would be ideal for a turfgrass root zone. That amount of organic matter would add resilience to the turf, increase soil aggregation, provide adequate water and nutrient-holding capacities, and contribute to the nutrition of the turf.

Organic amendments commonly added to turfgrass root zones include peat, rice hulls, sawdust, and bark residues. Fresh organic residues such as rice hulls or sawdust must undergo decomposition before they benefit the soil. Fresh organic residues may tie up plant nutrients and heat the soil to the degree they cause problems. Supplemental nitrogen and limestone may be needed to break down fresh organic materials. Also, uniform mixing with the soil is essential to prevent hot spots in the root zone. Heating, which produces the hot spots, is associated with the decomposition of fresh organic materials and can reach temperatures that kill or injure grass roots.

Biological (microbial) activities of turfgrass root zones are affected by soil texture, soil aggregation, and organic matter. Fine-textured soils, well aggregated soils with good drainage, and soils high in organic matter have high biological activities.

Six major microbial groups are associated with biological activity in turfgrass root zones: bacteria, actinomycetes, fungi, algae, protozoa, and viruses. Biological activities associated with these microbes include turfgrass nutrition, thatch accumulation (or decomposition), chemical (pesticide) decomposition, and soil aggregation (associated with humus, which is a product of microbial activity).

Soil microbes have a major impact on plant nutrition. Nearly all of the nitrogen and much of the phosphorus and sulfur, as well as other plant nutrients, are bound in the soil and unavailable for use by turfgrasses. Through the activity of soil microbes, these nutrients are made available for uptake by grasses and other plants. Nitrogen, for example, is converted from an organic form to a nitrate (NO_3^-) form by bacteria. Sulfur and phosphorus are also converted from unavailable forms to sulfate (SO_4^-) and orthophosphate ($H_2PO_4^-$) which can be utilized by turfgrasses. Likewise, other nutrients tied up in organic matter are made available to plants by the action of microbes on the organic material.

The role of fungi in the decomposition of plant residues can be demonstrated by thatch accumulation in turf frequently treated with fungicides. Other biological organisms, such as earthworms, also have a significant role in the decomposition of plant residues (thatch).

Soil microbes demonstrate remarkable capacities to break down chemical pesticides to compounds that are not considered toxic. Without this microbial degradation we could not use many of the pesticides we depend on today to keep turfgrasses healthy and weed free.

Soil aggregation—the binding together of soil particles—is due in part to the physical binding of soil particles by the structures of fungi and actinomycetes. The formation of humus—the final product of microbial degradations—also aids in the aggregation of soil particles.

All of these biological activities, which are dependent on soil microbes, are sensitive to changes in the environment of the turfgrass root zone. Changes in pH, moisture, temperatures, and aeration can significantly alter the relative composition of soil microbes and, consequently, alter biological activity. For example, reducing soil pH through the use of nitrogen fertilizers over a period of years causes a shift in the population of soil microbes responsible for nutrient conversions. As a result, nitrogen, phosphorus, and other nutrients are not as readily available to the turfgrass. Nitrification, the conversion of organic nitrogen to nitrate (NO_3^-), decreases with increasing acidity and is not observed at pH levels below 4.5. Likewise, increasing pH through prolonged use of high sodium water inhibits microbes that degrade certain groups of pesticides.

Aeration has a dramatic effect on the population of soil microbes. In a well-drained soil aerobic microbes are dominant. Aerobic microbes utilize oxygen to break down organic residues with the release of carbon dioxide (CO_2). In poorly drained soils anaerobic microbes are dominant. Anaerobic microbes reduce sulfur to hydrogen sulfide (H_2S), which produces black layers in soils with the putrid odor of rotten eggs. The H_2S is toxic to grass roots and can lead to the loss of grass. These conditions develop in turfgrass root zones that are overwatered or, where impermeable layers develop, that restrict water movement.

ROOT ZONE MANAGEMENT. Turfgrass managers must consider the soil as the growing medium for their crop—lawns, golf courses, sports fields, etc. For any other crop, particularly horticultural crops, growers go to great efforts and expenses to provide an optimum growing medium. Unfortunately, people tend to assume that grass can grow on any site without regard to soil conditions. People plant grass on hard, compacted soils, poorly drained or waterlogged soils, clay pans or layered soil profiles, and other conditions where one would not consider planting a tree, shrub, or other plant.

If we consider the soil as the growing medium for turfgrass, then we are more likely to be concerned with the environment that a particular soil provides. For example, a hard compacted soil on a poorly drained site provides a harsh environment for plant growth. We would not consider planting a tree or shrub on such a site, but we frequently plant grass on such sites. Ideally, those soils would be modified to provide conditions favorable for plant growth. But usually we are left to manage such soils and are expected to produce fine quality lawns, golf courses, sports fields, etc.

WATER MANAGEMENT. The first priority with respect to root zones for growing turfgrasses is water management. The turf manager who can control water in the root zone has a great advantage over those who cannot. The ideal root zone would hold adequate available moisture for turfgrass growth for 5 to 7 days, yet be permeable enough so that water would not stand on the surface for more than a few minutes following heavy rainfall or irrigation. Deep sandy loam soils with organic amendments incorporated in the root zone usually have those characteristics. As the root zone deviates from this ideal, water management becomes more difficult.

Slowly permeable soils need adequate surface drainage to aid water management, since standing water creates a totally unfavorable root zone environment for turfgrasses. Where standing water consistently occurs after rainfall or irrigation, drains must be installed to remove excess water. Narrow trenches, 10 to 14 inches deep, backfilled with sand or gravel or lined with geotextile fabric-covered drains provide excellent pathways to move excess water. Properly installed, these subsurface drainage systems can remove surface water within 30 minutes following a rainstorm.

Core aeration also helps get water into a slowly permeable soil by increasing the surface area of the root zone and by breaking up surface crusts or impermeable layers near the surface. Aeration provides only temporary improvement in water management and must be repeated when surface crusts and layers develop. Topdressing with a permeable medium, such as sand or sand and organic amendments, helps keep the vertical cores open after aeration. Repeating these practices three or four times for several years can significantly improve surface conditions. However, modifying the few surface inches of the root zone does not solve the drainage problems. The combination of providing surface drainage, installing subsurface drains, and modifying the surface of the root zone improves the ability of the turfgrass manager to manage water in the root zone.

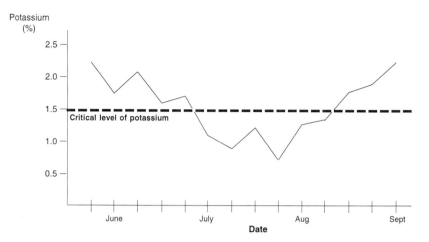

Weekly tissue analyses from bermudagrass golf greens

NUTRIENT MANAGEMENT. The nutrient status of the root zone may be the second priority of the turfgrass manager. Growth rate, density, root development, and color are some of the responses to the turfgrass nutrient status of the root zone. If nutrients are not present in required amounts or are not available to the grass for some reason, then weak turf, poor color, and slow recovery will be apparent.

Growth rate, color, leaf tissue analyses, and soil tests provide the means for the turf manager to determine the nutrient status of the root zone. Each of these indicators provides useful insight into the nutrient status of the root zone, and each should be evaluated on a regular basis. Certainly, growth rate and color should be evaluated weekly, or even daily. Leaf tissue analyses must also be evaluated on a regular basis to develop benchmarks for making comparisons. Monthly tracking of nutrient tissue levels during the growing season may be adequate for all but the most intensively maintained facilities, such as golf greens. Deficiencies of phosphorus, potassium, iron, and other nutrients can be determined from tissue analyses. Soil tests may be conducted annually or semiannually on golf greens to determine the availability of nutrients.

Moisture, pH, texture, and biological activity of the turfgrass root zone all influence the availability of nutrients. Even though nutrients may be present in adequate amounts, they are in soils with very low biological activities. To maintain conditions favorable for nutrient uptake, the turf manager must control soil moisture through irrigation and drainage. Excessive irrigation causes leaching of some nutrients, especially nitrogen and potassium. Also, saturated root zones result in anaerobic conditions where nutrients are not available and gases toxic to grass roots are produced. Denitrification also occurs in saturated soils. Matching irrigation rates to water use rates will reduce problems associated with saturated root zones.

Like soil moisture, soil pH influences the availability of nutrients. At very low and very high pH levels, phosphorus and some minor nutrients are not readily available. The efficiency of nutrient uptake is also reduced at low pH levels. Nitrogen utilization, for example, may be reduced 50 percent at pH 5.5 compared to pH 7.0. At high pH levels, above 8.0, iron availability reaches critical levels. Annual soil tests allow the turf manager to monitor pH levels and identify problem areas. Where pH levels require amendments, more frequent testing should be done.

Soil pH levels can be adjusted with limestone on acid soils and sulfur on alkaline soils. Again, soil test information should be used to determine the amount of limestone or sulfur needed to adjust pH to the desired level. Remember, grasses differ in the pH range to which they are best adapted. Centipedegrass performs best at pH from 5.0 to 5.5; while buffalograss does best at pH levels from 7.5 to 8.0. Perhaps bermudagrass, which does well from pH 5.5 to 8.5, has the widest range of adaptation to soil pH.

Soil texture and structure also influences the nutritional status of a root zone. Coarse-textured soils have very low cation exchange capacities and, consequently, low nutrient retention capacities. Ammonium nitrogen, nitrate nitrogen, potassium, and other nutrients readily leach through a sandy soil. The addition of organic materials greatly improves nutrient retention in coarse-textured soils. In contrast to sandy soils, clay soils and soils high in organic matter have very high cation exchange capacities.

Compacted soils, or soils with poor structural characteristics, do not provide adequate nutrients for good growth of turfgrasses. Aeration and the incorporation of organic matter usually improve the nutritional status of compacted soils.

Soil microbes also play a significant role in the availability of plant nutrients. Nearly all of the nitrogen and most of the phosphorus and sulfur, as well as other nutrients, are bound in soil organic matter. In this form these nutrients are largely, or entirely, unavailable for utilization by grasses. It is only through microbial activity that the vast store of nitrogen and the reserve phosphorus and other nutrients are made available to the grass. Thus, root zone conditions such as compaction, saturation, salinity, acidity, and low organic matter that reduce microbial activity also reduce nutrient availability.

For example, in compacted soils or in poorly drained soils, populations of microbes shift from those that function in aerobic conditions to those that function under anaerobic conditions. As a result, hydrogen sulfide (H_2S) rather than CO_2 becomes the primary product of decomposition, and grass roots deteriorate rapidly.

Also, under compacted soil conditions bacterial reduction of nitrate to nitrogen (denitrification) results in significant losses of nitrogen from the root zone. Denitrification is favored by anaerobic conditions; thus, aeration will reduce those losses from compacted soils.

Grass Selection

Selecting the best adapted turfgrass for a site improves the quality of a lawn, sports field, or golf course and reduces the cost of turf maintenance. Knowledge of the adaptation, use, and maintenance requirements of turfgrasses is essential to selecting the best grass for a site.

Experts have identified certain plant species as being suited for turf, since the needs first arose for close-cropped playing fields. The original turf species were native grasses and legumes that survived close defoliation by grazing animals. Heavy use, frequent defoliation, and the use of commercial fertilizers eliminated all but a few of the grasses for permanent turfs. And increasingly frequent and close defoliation of turf areas narrowed the selection to about 25 species of grasses for turf use. Of those 25 species, only about 10 are used for turfgrasses in the southern states.

Most turf species have been hybridized to produce varieties with specific turf characteristics. Fine texture, high density, and dark green color were the first characteristics selected in turfgrasses. Later, insect and disease resistance, cold tolerance, wear tolerance, salt tolerance, and other special traits were developed. Today, homeowners, golf course superintendents, grounds supervisors, and park managers have numerous turfgrass varieties from which to select a grass for a specific site. In some situations, a mixture of grass varieties may best meet the requirements for a particular use or site.

To select a grass or grass mixture, the homeowner or professional turf manager must have knowledge of environmental conditions, management, and use relative to the site. Some grasses are suited to shade, others are not. Some grasses require supplemental watering to survive, others may not. And some grasses tolerate traffic much better than others.

SELECTION CRITERIA. A wide range of environmental conditions occurs in the southern states, from semiarid western regions to high rainfall regions of the southeast, and from transition climates in the central states to tropical regions in south Texas and south Florida. Most turfgrasses can survive in arid areas with supplemental watering. But temperature limits the adaptation of several species. In the temperate climates of the northern states, cool-season grasses, such as bluegrass, bentgrass, ryegrass, and fescue are grown. In the subtropical areas of the South, the warm-season grasses, such as bermudagrass, centipede, and Saint Augustine grass, are best adapted. In the Transition Zone between the temperate and subtropical climates, both cool- and warm-season grasses can be grown in some situations with good management.

Shade, or light intensity, is a major factor in the adaptation of a turfgrass. Saint Augustine grass or tall fescue, for example, would perform well in an area receiving 50 percent of full sunlight. Bermudagrass would not be satisfactory under the same conditions. However, even the shade-tolerant

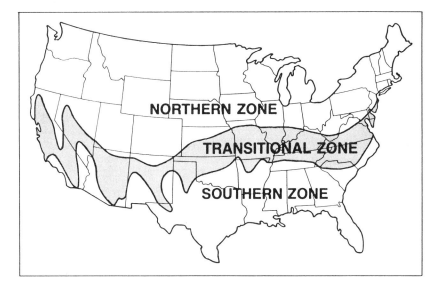

Map showing climate zones

grasses require 30 to 40 percent sunlight to maintain a satisfactory turf.

Interactions between environmental conditions, such as temperature and shade, can also be important. Tall fescue, for example, may not perform well in the northeast in 50 percent shade, but in the Transition Zone it might do well in partial shade. Likewise, temperature and moisture interact to influence the adaptability of a turfgrass. Bentgrass performs poorly on golf greens in the southeast because of the combination of high temperatures and high humidity. But in the arid west where temperatures may be higher, bentgrass performs very well.

Soils also influence the adaptability of turfgrasses to a particular site. The sandy, acid soils of the southeast are well suited to carpetgrass, bahiagrass, and centipedegrass. The heavy (clay or clay loam), alkaline soils of the west are best suited to bermudagrass and buffalograss. Some grasses such as ryegrass, bermudagrass, and zoysia can be successfully grown on most soils.

Management practices often have an overriding influence on turfgrass selection. If a site cannot be watered, a drought-tolerance grass, such as bermudagrass or buffalograss, is required. If a turf is not mowed more than twice a month, only the low maintenance grasses are suitable. In tables 5-4 and 5-5, three levels of maintenance are described. A high level of maintenance implies frequent mowing, regular watering, several applications of fertilizer each year, and a pest control program. In contrast, a low level of maintenance suggests no supplemental watering, monthly mowing, perhaps annual fertilization, and no chemical pest control.

Turf use also influences the selection of grass varieties for specific sites. Some grasses such as the perennial ryegrasses and bermudagrasses tolerate heavy use. Others such as the bentgrasses and hybrid bermudagrasses toler-

Table 5-4. Selection Criteria for Turfgrasses for Lawns, Parks, and Cemeteries

Environmental Conditions	LEVEL OF MAINTENANCE		
	High	Moderate	Low
Arid climates			
Irrigated	1, 2, 4, 6, 9, 10, 11, 12	1, 2, 4, 9, 12	1, 6, 9
Nonirrigated	none	none	1, 6, 9
Humid climates, low winter temperatures	4, 6, 9, 10, 12	4, 6, 9, 10, 12	6, 9
Humid climates, mild winter temperatures	1, 2, 3, 4, 9	1, 2, 3, 4, 5, 6, 8, 9	1, 3, 4, 6, 7, 8, 9
Moderately shaded sites	3, 4, 8	3, 4, 5, 8	3, 5, 7, 8
Poorly drained sites	3, 9, 10	1, 8, 9	3, 7, 8, 9
Saline conditions	1, 2, 3, 9	1, 3, 9	1, 3

1—Common bermudagrass	5—Centipedegrass	9—Tall fescue
2—Hybrid bermudagrass	6—Buffalograss	10—Perennial ryegrass
3—Saint Augustine grass	7—Carpetgrass	11—Creeping bentgrass
4—Zoysiagrass	8—Bahiagrass	12—Kentucky bluegrass

Table 5-5. Selection Criteria for Turfgrasses for Golf Courses and Sports Fields[1]

Environmental Conditions	LEVEL OF MAINTENANCE		
	High	Moderate	Low
Arid climates			
Irrigated	1, 2, 4, 10, 11	1, 2, 4, 9	1, 4, 6, 9
Nonirrigated	none	none	1, 6
Humid climates, low winter temperatures	4, 10, 11	4, 9, 10	4, 6, 9
Humid climates, mild winter temperatures	1, 2, 4	1, 2, 4	1, 4
Poorly drained sites	1, 2, 10	1, 9	1, 7, 8, 9
Saline conditions	1, 2, 11	1, 2, 9	1, 9
Heavy traffic	1, 2, 10, 11	1, 2, 9	1, 9
Closely mowed (½ inch or less)	2, 11	1, 2	1, 6

[1]Refer to code at bottom of Table 5-4 for grass identification.

Table 5-6. Selection Criteria for Turfgrasses for Roadsides, Airports, Golf Course Roughs, and Other Minimum Use Areas[1]

	LEVEL OF MAINTENANCE	
Environmental Conditions	Fertilized	Nonfertilized
Arid climates		
Irrigated	1, 4, 6, 9	6, 9
Nonirrigated	6	6
Humid climates, low winter temperatures	4, 9	4, 9
Humid Climates, mild winter temperatures	1, 3, 4, 5, 7, 8, 9	5, 7, 8, 9
Poorly drained sites	3, 7, 8, 9	7, 8, 9
Shaded sites	3, 4, 5, 7, 8, 9	5, 7, 8, 9
Saline conditions	1, 3, 9	9

[1]Refer to code at bottom of Table 5-4 for grass identification.

ate very close mowing for golf greens and bowling greens. And other grasses are best suited for roadsides, parks, and school grounds because of rapid establishment and low maintenance requirements.

Selecting the best turfgrass for a site does not guarantee success. But planting a grass not adapted to a site ensures failure. An adapted turfgrass properly maintained will provide a beautiful and useful turf. Also turf maintenance costs are less when adapted turfgrasses are used.

To select a turfgrass, use tables 5-4 through 5-6 to identify grasses that meet all environmental conditions for a specific site. Then review the descriptions for each grass that meets those requirements. Finally, select the variety that is best adapted in terms of environment and management to that site. For a thorough discussion of each grass—origin, description, adaptation, and use—refer to chapter 4.

PLANTING

Grasses are established from seed or vegetative material (sprigs or sod), depending on the grass variety selected and the time available to develop a cover. The type of planting material to be used, the method of planting, the quantity of planting material needed, and the best time of year to plant each of the grass species used in the South are shown in table 5-7.

SEEDING. Southern turfgrasses that can be established from seed include common bermudagrass, centipedegrass, carpetgrass, bahiagrass, buffalograss, and all of the cool-season grasses. Saint Augustine grass, zoysia, and the hybrid bermudagrasses are established from vegetative planting rock. When

Table 5-7. Types of Planting Material and Methods, Rates, and Times of Planting

Grass Species	Planting Material	Method of Planting	Quantity per 1,000 sq. ft.	Best Planting Season
Bermudagrass	Seed	Broadcast	½ to 1 lb.	
	Sprigs	Sprig 6 in. apart in 12-in. rows or broadcast	5 to 10 ft. of nursery sod	Spring and early summer
Saint Augustine grass	Sod	Solid-lay as bricks	Same as area to be sodded	Spring and summer
	2-in. sod blocks or runners	2-in. blocks on 12-in. centers, runners planted on 12-in. centers	Sodblocks: 30 sq. ft. nursery sod Runners: 3 to 6 sq. ft. of nursery sod	Spring and early summer
Buffalograss	Treated seed	Broadcast	1 to 2 lbs.	Spring
	Untreated seed	Broadcast	2 to 4 lbs.	Fall
Centipedegrass	Seed	Broadcast	⅓ to ½ lb.	Spring
	Shredded sod (sprigs) or 2-in. sod blocks	Sprig 6 in. apart in 12-in. rows	5 to 10 sq. ft. of nursery sod	Spring and early fall
Zoysiagrass	Sprigs or 2-in. sod blocks	Sprig 2 in. apart in 6-in. rows in a clean seedbed	40 to 45 sq. ft. of nursery sod	Spring and early summer
Ryegrass	Seed	Broadcast	6 to 8 lbs.	Sept. to Nov.
Tall fescue	Seed	Broadcast	6 to 8 lbs.	Sept. to Nov.
Kentucky bluegrass	Seed	Broadcast	2 to 3 lbs.	Sept. to Nov.
Carpetgrass	Seed	Broadcast	1 to 2 lbs.	Spring
Bahiagrass	Seed	Broadcast	6 to 8 lbs.	Spring and fall
Bentgrass	Seed	Broadcast	½ to 1 lb.	Fall

establishing grass from seed, seed quality, seeding rate, seeding date, and seeding method must be considered.

All packages or bags of seed are labeled with information on the variety, purity, and germination percentage of the seed. This information is vital when determining the cost and seeding rate for a particular grass. Both cost and seeding rate need to be determined on some standard basis, and for grass seed the basis for comparison is percent pure live seed, or percent PLS. Percent PLS is calculated by multiplying the percent purity by the percent germination. For example, a 50-pound bag of common bermudagrass seed with a percent purity of 97 and a percent germination of 90 contains 43.65 pounds of pure live seed (0.97 x 0.90 x 50). When comparing seed cost, make the comparison on the basis of PLS. The cheapest bag of seed may be the most expensive on the basis of PLS. Seeding recommendations are also made on a PLS basis.

Another reason to review the label is to determine the weed seed, or crop seed, that may be present. In cool-season grasses, weed seed can present serious problems for turf managers. For example, annual bluegrass seed in bentgrass creates weed problems from the start for the golf course superintendent. Likewise, crabgrass seed in bermudagrass would be undesirable. The cost of seed increases as more of the weed and other crop seeds are removed from a lot of grass seed. Since it would be too expensive to remove all weed or other crop seed from a lot of grass seed, the buyer should purchase the cleanest seed that can be found for critical sites. For low maintenance sites, the less expensive seed may be planted.

Additional information found on the label includes the date of the germination test. If the germination test is more than one year old, the information may not be valid. Generally, germination percentage decreases with time.

Seeding rates depend on grass species, the purpose for the turfgrass, and the time available to develop a cover. Grasses with a creeping-type growth habit are generally seeded at lower rates than bunch-type grasses. Although seeding rates are expressed in terms of pounds per unit area, the number of seed per unit area is more important. Table 5-8 provides information on seed counts and seed densities at recommended seeding rates. In the case of centipedegrass and buffalograss, seed densities as low as 1 seed per square inch are recommended. For all other grasses at least 7 to 10 seeds per square inch are recommended. This discrepancy is the result of the cost of buffalograss and centipedegrass seed compared to the other grasses. Even at such low seeding densities, buffalograss and centipedegrass seed cost more per unit area than all of the other grasses. In the case of buffalograss and centipedegrass, seeding rates are based on cost rather than on desired seed densities.

Seedling vigor, dormancy, and seeding survival also need to be considered when deciding on seeding rates. Bermudagrass, buffalograss, ryegrass, and tall fescue seed all possess good seedling vigor. Thus, seedlings of these grasses could be expected to establish very fast. Bahiagrass, centipedegrass, and bentgrass have low seedling vigor and require much longer to establish a complete cover. However, in the case of centipedegrass, seed cost prevents increasing the seeding rate to compensate for low seedling vigor.

Table 5-8. Seeding Rates for Southern Turfgrasses

Grass Species	No. of Seed (per lb.)	Recommended Seeding Rate (lbs. per 1,000 sq. ft.)	Seed Density (no. per sq. in.)
Bahiagrass	160,000	6–8	7–9
Bermudagrass	2,000,000	½–1	7–14
Buffalograss (burs)	50,000	1–2	0.3–0.6
Carpetgrass	1,000,000	1–2	7–14
Centipedegrass	400,000	⅓–½	1–1.4
Creeping bentgrass	6,000,000	½–1	21–42
Perennial ryegrass	250,000	6–8	10–14
Tall fescue	250,000	6–8	10–14

Another factor, seed dormancy, also influences the seeding rate of some grasses. Bahiagrass and buffalograss seed have a high percentage of dormant seed, 40 percent or more. In the case of bahiagrass, increasing the seeding rate compensates for the dormant seed. But buffalograss seed is too expensive to increase the rate. Therefore, buffalograss seed are generally treated to break dormancy and increase seed germination to 80 percent or more.

Seedling survival, a function of environmental conditions and management practices during the germination period, also influences seeding rates. Any factor that increases the time required for germination or the time the grass is in the seedling stage, also increases seedling losses. Extremely high or low soil temperatures, droughty or excessively wet soils, low soil fertility, seed improperly planted (covered too deep, left uncovered on the surface, or nonuniform distribution), excessive seedling densities, and the presence of some preemergence herbicides all increase seedling losses. Thorough seedbed preparation, proper planting techniques, correct planting date, and proper postplanting care all reduce seedling losses.

Date of planting is critical when establishing grass from seed. Soil temperature and the expected duration of favorable soil temperatures are the primary considerations for selecting the planting date. Cool-season grasses should be planted in the fall when soil temperatures are 70° to 75° F and several months of favorable growing conditions remain. Seed germinates rapidly and seedlings can grow vigorously for the first several months in the fall. If cool-season grasses are planted too early, high soil temperatures create stressful conditions during the seedling stage and result in high seedling losses. Weeds also compete with grass seedlings for a long period if seed are planted too early.

Planting cool-season grasses too late results in immature plants going into the winter months and high seedling losses can occur. Even though soil temperatures may be favorable at the time of planting, the duration of favorable temperatures may not be adequate to develop mature plants and a hard freeze can result in high seedling losses.

In the South, the fall planting dates are best for cool-season grasses. But successful plantings can be made in the spring where cool temperatures are likely through May. In most areas of the South, high springtime temperatures result in high seedling losses. Weed populations are also greater in the spring, and many weeds compete with the turfgrass all summer.

Late spring and early summer are ideal seedling dates for warm-season grasses. Soil temperatures are favorable by late spring and a long growing season is ahead for the warm-season grasses. Late summer is another favorable date for seeding warm grasses, since soil temperatures are favorable and extreme air temperatures are abating.

Early spring seeding dates should be avoided for warm-season grasses, since soil temperatures are low and seedlings are very slow to develop. Weeds often grow faster in the early spring than the grasses. Thus, seedling losses can be high due to competition with weeds.

Late fall plantings of warm-season grasses should generally be avoided because seedlings do not have time to mature prior to winter. However, grasses such as bahiagrass and buffalograss that have a high percentage of dormant seed can be seeded in late fall with the expectation of significant germination in the spring.

Seeding methods have a tremendous influence on the successful establishment of grasses. Ideally, grass seed should be uniformly distributed at recommended seeding rates, covered with ¼-inch of topsoil and rolled to firm the seedbed. Grass drills, or planters, are made to perform all of these tasks in a single pass over the site. The Brillion grass seeder is an example of such a planter that works well for small seeded grasses such as bermudagrass.

Other options include broadcasting the seed uniformly over the surface and covering seed with straw or mulch. The hydroseeder works well for this type of seeding operation. Grass seed, fertilizer, and mulch can be broadcast over the site through a high-pressure nozzle with water. Hydroseeding was developed for planting sites that were difficult to reach with conventional equipment. Steep slopes, rocky slopes, reclamation sites, and other inaccessible areas were well suited to hydroseeding. Since its development the hydroseeder has found much broader use in grass establishment and is used today for seeding lawns, golf courses, sports fields, and other sites.

On small sites seed can be broadcast with a hand seeder or fertilizer distributor over the surface of a lightly raked seedbed. After seeding firm the soil with a roller and lightly water the site. If watering is limited to light, frequent applications, this method works well. But excessive watering will wash the seed and result in a nonuniform stand of grass seedlings.

SPRIGGING. All of the bermudagrasses, the zoysiagrasses, and seashore paspalum are readily established by sprigging. Saint Augustine grass and centipedegrass can also be established from sprigs, but the risks are greater. For large plantings, such as golf courses and sports fields, sprigging provides the most practical method of establishment.

A grass sprig consists of a stem or rhizome segment with at least one node or crown (multiple nodes) and any leaves and roots that might be attached to the node. Usually, three or more nodes are found on a single sprig.

Sprigs are harvested by shredding sod, by rototilling sod and raking, by vericutting, or by using a sprig harvester. Sprigs consisting of rhizomes, crowns, and only a few green leaves are most desirable. Such sprigs will transport and store much better than green, leafy sprigs. They are also more drought tolerant and will survive several days without water; whereas, a green leafy sprig without a crown or rhizome segment may die within hours if not kept moist after planting.

Bermudagrass, zoysia, and seashore paspalum are the only vegetative propagated warm-season grasses with rhizomes. Thus, those grasses are best suited to sprigging. Saint Augustine, centipedegrass, and buffalograss sprigs that consist only of stolons are much more susceptible to drought stress after planting. Such sprigs are also more likely to overheat and deteriorate during shipment. Sprigs that appear moldy when they arrive at the planting site should not be planted. Such sprigs desiccate rapidly after planting, and re-planting is often required.

The quality of sprigs, like that of seeds, is critical to successful establishment. Just as weed seeds are undesirable in a lot of grass seed, off-type grasses are undesirable in a bushel of sprigs. Common bermudagrass sprigs can cause serious problems in a bushel of hybrid bermudagrass sprigs. Likewise, bermudagrass sprigs in zoysia or other turfgrasses lead to serious weed problems for the turf manager.

In addition to purity, sprig vigor is another aspect of sprig quality. Sprigs harvested by digging are usually the most vigorous, since they include rhizomes, crowns, and the large stolons found near the soil surface. Such sprigs are more vigorous than the leafy sprigs harvested above the soil level. The more vigorous sprigs tolerate stress and develop a root system more rapidly than the less vigorous sprigs. Consequently, sprig survival is much greater for the more vigorous sprigs.

Sprigging rates depend on grass varieties, planting method, sprig quality, and the time available for a complete cover. Bermudagrass sprigs spread faster than all other grasses and can be planted at lower rates. Large sites, such as golf course fairways and sports fields, can be sprigged at 250 to 300 bushels per acre with an expected cover in 10 to 12 weeks. Where a faster cover is needed, such as on lawns and golf greens, sprigs can be planted at 10 to 25 bushels per 1,000 square feet. Golf greens sprigged at 25 bushels per 1,000 square feet can be in play in 4 to 6 weeks.

Planting method also influences sprigging rates. Most sprigs are broadcast over the site with a distributor or hydroseeder at rather high rates of sprigs. However, row planters are available for sprigging that use much less planting material. If the row planter functions properly, it places the sprig in a narrow furrow, covering 50 to 80 percent of the sprig with soil. If water is applied immediately (within 30 minutes), a very high percentage of sprigs survive. In contrast, broadcasting sprigs over the surface and, depending on an irrigation system to keep them moist, results in high sprig losses. Covering broadcast sprigs with a mulch helps to reduce their losses.

Sprigging rates can also be reduced by planting high quality sprigs. Sprigs harvested by digging are more vigorous and have a higher survival rate; thus, lower rates of planting can be used. When only the tops of bermudagrass are planted, twice the quantity of planting stock may be needed as when dug sprigs are used.

Finally, the time available to develop a complete cover will significantly influence planting rates. The higher the rate of sprigging, the faster a cover will develop. However, the cost of sprigging also increases with each increase in planting material. By sprigging 3 to 5 bushels of bermudagrass sprigs per 1,000 square feet, a satisfactory cover can be developed in 3 to 4 months. At 10 bushels, a complete cover can develop in 2 months; and at 25 bushels in 1 month. The cost of planting material for those rates may range from $10 to $50 per 1,000 square feet or from $300 per acre to $2,000 per acre. Sometimes, however, the need to use a facility by a certain date precludes the use of the lower planting rates. On small areas, such as golf greens and lawns, the higher planting rates should be used.

PLUGGING. Plugging refers to the setting out of small sod blocks or plugs (2 to 4 inches in diameter), on 6-, 12-, or 18-inch centers to establish a turfgrass. The plugs need to be planted so that the soil on the sod block, or plug, is level with the soil surface. Rooted plugs are available which have been grown in about 2 inches of soil or organic matter. When rooted plugs are planted, a hole about 2-inches deep should be dug. The plugs should not simply be placed on the soil surface.

Saint Augustine, zoysia, and centipedegrasses are frequently established from plugs. Saint Augustine grass plugs spaced on 18-inch centers will cover the site in about 2 months. Centipede and zoysia grasses need to be plugged on 6- to 12- inch centers to cover in one growing season.

Although plugging requires less planting material than sodding, the labor requirement for plugging is greater than for sodding. Rooted plugs, however, require less attention after planting than sod, since their root system was developed prior to planting.

SODDING. Sodding is the laying of blocks or rolls of sod directly over a prepared seedbed to provide an instant lawn. Solid sodding obviously requires more planting materials than other methods, but it eliminates many of the problems associated with seeding, sprigging, or plugging.

When sodding a site, lay sod blocks like bricks on a smooth surface that has been firmed by rolling or settled by rainfall or irrigation. The seedbed needs to be moist, but not wet, at the time sod is laid. After the sod is laid, roll it lightly to eliminate air pockets and to establish firm contact with the soil.

In addition to avoiding many problems with other methods of establishment, sodding can be done any time of the year provided irrigation is available at the site.

A frequent mistake on commercial sites is poor seedbed preparation prior to sodding. Although sod will cover up a lot of problems, the turf manager is left to deal with them. All of the steps of good seedbed preparation should be followed prior to sodding a site.

CARE AFTER ESTABLISHMENT

Water newly planted turf areas regularly. Water lightly and frequently to prevent the surface from drying. As the young seedlings develop or as the sprigs or sod begin to take root and spread, reduce the frequency of watering and increase the amount of water applied per watering. This permits the development of a deep root system and ultimately reduces the amount of water needed.

The time to mow will depend on the species planted. Mow newly planted areas as soon as the grass is 1½ to 2 inches high. Mow frequently enough to prevent removing more than half of the growth at any one mowing.

Fertilize newly planted turfgrasses once a month with a complete fertilizer, at a rate equivalent to 1 pound of nitrogen per 1,000 square feet. Follow soil test recommendations, but in the absence of this information a complete fertilizer should be used. On sandy textured soils, supplement the complete fertilizer with an additional pound of nitrogen between applications. Water after each application of fertilizer.

Cultural Practices 6

Mowing is the primary cultural practice in turf management. Without regular mowing even a fine turf quickly becomes just another weed patch. Good mowing practices enhance a turf more than any other cultural practice. Density, texture, color, root development, wear tolerance, and other aspects of turf quality are all enhanced by proper mowing.

Mowing Practices

Mowing practices have changed considerably since the nineteenth century. In 1859, in a supplemental note to Andrew Jackson Dowing's *A Treatise on the Theory and Practice of Landscape Gardening,* Henry Winthrop Sargent described improved procedures for mowing lawns:

> A very great improvement and economy in the keeping of lawns now-a-days is in the employment of the Lawn-cutter, by which one man, with a horse-machine, will accomplish, in two or three hours, more than a dozen men can in a whole day. The best English lawn-cutters will cut, roll, and gather the grass from one acre, in one hour, where it is good, close turf, and there are no trees to interfere with the action of the machine.
>
> When a lawn is in perfect condition, smooth, free from stones and inequalities, and is cut, as it ought to be, once a week, it is quite surprising how much gratification we derive from what used to be performed with great labor, and often with a very unsatisfactory result. . . . any improvement, which will allow us to cut our lawns throughout the heat of the day, is very desirable. This the mowing machine does. . . . All that remains subsequently to do, is to clip with scythe or sickle around the

edges and verges. . . . We have found more satisfaction in the use of this machine, than in any other thing we have done . . . and have now got our lawn in such a responsive and genial condition, that . . . we have removed our box for catching the grass as it falls from the rollers, and permit it to fly in a little shower all over the lawn, as the cutting progresses.

Luckily for professional turf managers and homeowners alike, mowing practices have improved considerably.

Mowing is primarily a function of the growth rate of grasses. Since grasses continually interact with their environment, the growth rate changes in response to environmental changes. Thus, the turf manager must recognize the need to change mowing practices accordingly. For example, during prolonged periods of drought stress, it might be advantageous to raise the mowing height and reduce the frequency of mowing. Similarly, following the application of fertilizer, it may be necessary to increase the frequency of mowing to avoid excess accumulation of leaf clippings. The skill of the turf manager at making these adjustments determines the quality of turf maintained under the manager's supervision.

Although growth rate largely determines the mowing schedule for a particular site, other factors need to be considered when planning mowing practices. The type and size of mower, frequency of mowing, mowing height, mowing patterns, the management of grass clippings, and the maintenance of mowing equipment all need to be considered when planning mowing practices.

MOWING EQUIPMENT

The type and size of a mower is important to the quality of cut produced and the frequency of cut likely to be achieved. A common reason for shortened life span and high maintenance costs of mowing equipment is the use of a mower in an area and in a situation for which it was not designed. The problem is compounded when a poorly trained or incompetent operator is assigned to run a unit unsuitable for the job. When choosing equipment consider the following:

1. Consider the terrain to be cut. Is it developed or undeveloped? Is it wooded, rough graded, stony, swampy, hilly, or a formal area? If rough or otherwise, decide if a reel- or rotary-type mower is to be purchased.

2. Consider the size of the area or areas and buy the largest mower that is practical. The job gets done faster with less hours when larger capacity equipment is employed. If the mower is to be used for trimming purposes and demands on the mower are not too heavy, a small, low horsepower, light-duty unit may be used, but higher maintenance costs on this type of equipment are inevitable.

3. Look for simplicity of design. A complicated mower may be difficult

to adjust and a trained expert may have to be used for repair. Yet overall maintenance may be lower than for an inappropriate one.

4.   Check for construction, durability, and maneuverability. The mower should be substantially built, well-braced, and have good bearings. The side frames, handles, or drawbars, should be heavy enough to do the job. The bed bars, reels, and blades, should be rigidly constructed. The mower should be highly maneuverable and easy to steer.

Variations in terrain on which the mower is used, the type of lubrication it receives, the correctness of repair, the treatment by the operator, storage, and accuracy of records, all have an influence on cost per mower per year and useful life span of the mower. However, to get the lowest possible operating costs under your conditions, buy quality equipment, buy the right mower for the right job, operate and maintain it properly, and keep adequate records.

Other points to consider when selecting and operating equipment efficiently and at lower total costs include:

1.   Labor. Over the past several years, the greatest increase in cost for turfgrass maintenance has come from labor. In fact, labor comprises the largest part of the total budget, and the costs of labor are growing as fast or faster than those for equipment. Because of this, turf managers must continue to look more closely at total costs and allocate more of their funds for the purchase of higher capacity, labor-saving equipment.

2.   Reel mowers. Generally, reel mowers are more efficient than rotary or flail mowers. The scissors action of the reel mower not only cuts better but requires less power, consequently consuming less fuel. At the same mowing speed, reel mowers will use up to 50 percent less fuel per acre of cut grass than rotary mowers. The number of blades per reel also affects the quality of cut, and impacts fuel consumption. For example, a 5-bladed reel will use 8 to 12 percent less power and fuel than a 6-bladed reel. However, determining the quality of cut for a given area, which in this case is primarily a function of the height of cut, is the responsibility of the turfgrass manager. It is up to the manager to decide whether the economy achieved by raising the height of cut and using fewer blades will produce the quality of turf required.

3.   Diesel engines. Use diesel engines rather than gasoline. It may no longer cost less, but the diesel engine has proved itself to be from 20 to 25 percent more efficient than the gasoline engine. This means fewer gallons and less dollars to perform a given task. The increase in efficiency with resultant lower total cost may be sufficient reason to consider diesel power when selecting and purchasing new equipment.

4.   Equipment maintenance. Clean and properly adjusted equipment is more economical to operate because less power is required to operate it. Proper adjustment of belts, bearings, chains, and shafts can reduce the friction within the mower, allowing for more power for work output. Frequent lubrication of vital parts also reduces friction.

5. Storage. Proper storage of equipment plays an important role in saving money and reducing total costs. When a job is finished and the unit is properly cleaned, the operator should then store it in a clean and dry area. Without adequate storage facilities, total costs for equipment are likely to be excessive.

The two basic types of mowers are the reel and the rotary mower. The reel mower consists of a shaft equipped with blades rotating between two wheels with a stationary bedknife. The grass blades are cut, or sheared, as they are caught between the reel blade and the bedknife. A properly adjusted reel mower cuts the grass just as cleanly as a sharp pair of scissors.

A rotary mower consists of a horizontally rotating steel blade which cuts the grass by impact at a high rate of speed. The rotary mower cuts the grass much like a sickle. As long as the blade is sharp, the quality of cut can be quite good. But a dull blade shreds the leaf blade and leaves the leaf tip frayed. Although rotary mowers are relatively inexpensive and more versatile than the reel mowers, they do not cut as cleanly or as closely as the reel mower. However, because of their lower cost and lower maintenance requirements, the rotary mower is more popular with the homeowner.

On closely mowed turf, such as that on golf greens, fairways, sports fields, and some lawns, the reel mower provides the best cut. However, the quality of cut is influenced by the mowing height, the number of blades on the reel, the rotational speed of the reel, and the forward speed of the mower. The typical reel mower has 5 to 7 blades and is suitable for mowing at heights of ½ to 1½ inches. At lower mowing heights, the turf would develop a wavy or rippled appearance, unless the reel was powered to revolve at a high rate of speed. At mowing heights below ½ inch, 9 or more blades per reel or a hydraulically powered reel are required to produce a smooth cut. The typical golf green mower has 11 to 13 blades on a relatively small diameter reel.

The clip of a reel mower is most readily defined as the distance the mower moves forward between the time that each reel blade engages the bedknife. Most conventional homeowner-type reel mowers have a clip of about one inch. For optimum smoothness of cut with respect to ripple or corrugations, a reel-type mower should have a clip approximately equal to the height of cut. Ground-driven reel mowers have a constant clip and can only provide a smooth cut above a specific height and will show obvious ripples below that height. Power- or hydraulic-driven reels provide a variable clip and extend the application of a given reel mower.

Vertical differences between the peaks and valleys of a reel cut are always present because the valley is the height of the bedknife cutting edge, and the peak is the height to which the grass springs back after being cut. The horizontal distance between peaks, or between valleys, is the clip. When the vertical distance between the peak and valley is minimal, the resulting cut will appear to be smooth. Again, this condition exists when the clip is no greater than the height of cut.

The specific clip of a reel mower is dependent upon the number of blades and the rotational speed of the reel and is independent of reel diameter. The tip speed, however, does increase in direct proportion to an increase in the reel diameter when rotation speed is constant.

If we consider a reel with a certain number of blades, the clip can only vary with the rotational speed of the reel in relation to ground speed. With the same number of blades, the faster reel will produce the shorter clip length.

The relationship of clip to height of cut affects not only the finished appearance of the turf, but the ability of the mower to cut at heights of two or three times the clip distance. A mower with a 1-inch clip will not cut as well at a 2-inch height as a mower with a 2-inch clip.

There are three basic requirements for acceptable reel mower performance: (1) the bedknife must be exactly parallel with the reel; (2) the reel must make only light contact with the bedknife; and (3) the cutting edges of the reel and bedknife must be sharp and straight. A sharp, properly adjusted mower will cleanly cut a piece of paper. Backlapping is the standard procedure used to restore sharp edges on the reel and bedknife.

From time to time, either in the field or after reel service, it may become necessary to reconfirm the reel-to-bedknife contact. Newspaper can be used to help measure the degree of contact along the length of the bedknife. By placing the paper tangent to the reel cylinder between the blade and bedknife, the paper can be used as a shim to bring each of the reel blades in equal contact with the bedknife. The paper should be pinched but not cut. Next, place

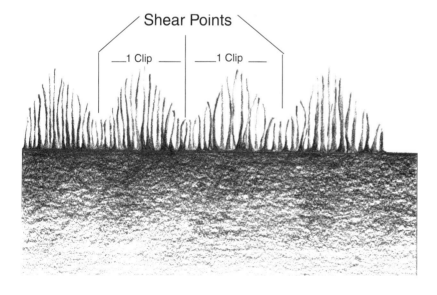

Rippled or wavy appearance caused by mowing too low with five-blade reel

the paper perpendicular to the reel cylinder and refine the adjustment to just cut the paper. Check at least three points along the length for each blade.

At taller mowing heights, 1 ½ inches and more, the rotary mower is generally used. At these taller heights, the quality of cut may not be as important and the rotary mower cuts tall grass, weeds, and seed stalks more effectively than the reel mower.

The rotary mower cuts grass by impact of the blade against the grass at a very high velocity. The first one-half inch of the blade's leading edge cuts the grass. The additional cutting edge length enhances the mowing performance and quality of cut.

Theoretically, the concept of clip also applies to rotary mowers. Rotary mowers are generally designed so that the blade tip cuts the grass at least once every two inches.

In addition to the cutting performance of the rotary blade, good dispersion of grass clippings is also important. Good dispersion is determined by the blade speed, blade design, housing depth, baffling, and other factors that affect airflow and velocity.

The three irregularities which can decrease the blade's quality of cuts are warping, twisting, or dullness. A warped blade is bent in such a way that the blade tips are worn on one or both sides. The situation must be corrected. The twisted blade leaves the cutting edge above the flat surface it is being checked on. With the body of the blade parallel to the flat surface, the blade edges should lay flat on the surface. A twisted blade consumes additional horsepower and causes shredding of the grass blade tips.

To properly sharpen a rotary blade, material should be removed from the top surface of the blade only, trying to maintain the original bevel. If the lower edge of the blade is ground or filed, the cutting edge will be above the heel of the blade, resulting in beating, shredding, and browning of the grass.

The gull wing blade design creates air lift to suspend grass clippings while they are further minced up. The front and rear baffling increase air suction to raise grass into cutting position.

In addition to blade irregularities, damaged housing or improperly mounted engines or decks, bent crankshafts or spindles will result in uneven heights of cut.

Another impact-type cutting unit is the flail mower. The cutting unit on a flail mower consists of a number of small blades attached to a horizontal shaft. As the shaft rotates, the blades are extended by centrifugal force. Each blade becomes an independent, freely revolving, cutting unit. Thus, if the blade strikes a hard object, such as a rock or piece of metal, the blade recoils without damaging the mower or creating a dangerous projectile. The quality of cut still depends on the sharpness of the blade.

FREQUENCY OF MOWING

The single most important aspect of turf management is the frequency of mowing a turf. If there is a secret to turf management, it is frequent mowing—the more often, the better. However, mowing is time-consuming and expensive. Therefore, we often compromise between what is best and what is practical.

Golf greens exemplify fine turf and are usually mowed daily. But those that are mowed twice daily are even finer. However, golf greens make up only a small percentage of the total acreage of a golf course, and efficient mowing equipment makes frequent mowing practical. Fairways, however, constitute a large percentage of a golf course, and more expensive equipment and greater time is required to mow fairways. Thus, fairways are not mowed as often as greens, although fairway turf would be better with daily mowing.

Likewise, the sports field manager who mows three or more times per week will have a finer turf than one who mows less often. The same can be said for the homeowner. The homeowner who mows every 5 days will have a finer lawn than the one who mows at 7- to 10-day intervals.

Several factors influence the recommended mowing frequency. Of course, growth rate (and factors that affect growth rate) and mowing height have the greatest influence on mowing frequency. As a rule of thumb, mow often enough so that no more than 30 percent of the leaf is removed at any one mowing. By following that rule, photosynthesis is only marginally affected by mowing. However, if 50 percent or more of the leaf is removed by mowing, several days are required to restore photosynthesis to its previous level. In contrast, if only 10 percent of the leaf is removed by mowing, the effect on photosynthesis is insignificant. Therefore, to maintain optimum growth, frequent mowing is required.

In addition to minimizing the effect of mowing on photosynthesis, frequent mowing also helps to maintain a high percentage of the leaf surface—a requirement for healthy root development. Following severe defoliation (as a result of infrequent mowing) energy reserves (food) stored in the grass plant are needed to restore leaf surface (Youngner, Nudge, and Ackerson 1976; Hyder 1972). Consequently, root growth may cease for several days since leaves always take priority over roots for energy reserves following defoliation or dormancy. Thus, mowing frequency, which determines the extent of defoliation, has a significant impact on residual leaf surface and root growth.

Growth rate and mowing height must both be considered when deciding on a mowing interval. If we follow the rule of thumb and remove only 30 percent of the leaf surface, the lower the mowing height, the shorter the interval between mowing. For example, consider a growth rate of 0.1 inches per day and a mowing height of 1 inch. In 10 days the grass will be 2 inches tall. Then, the mower would remove 50 percent of the leaf when cut back to

1 inch. The turf would need mowing at 5-day intervals to stay within the 30-percent rule of thumb. The same grass mowed at ½ inch would need mowing at 2 or 3 day intervals to stay within 30 percent. Without exception, the shorter a grass is mowed, the more frequently it must be mowed.

Besides mowing frequency, the turf manager's use of fertilizer has more effect on growth rate than any other cultural practice. High rates of nitrogen fertilizer promote vegetative growth beyond that needed for maintenance. Thus, mowing frequency must be increased as the application of nitrogen increases. During summer months, nitrogen fertilization should be kept at a maintenance level.

Environmental factors also influence mowing frequency through their effect on growth rate. Temperature is the environmental factor that has the greatest impact on growth rate. When temperatures favor growth, mowing frequency needs to be increased. Conversely, when temperature retards growth, mowing frequency can be reduced.

In warm-season grasses, growth (leaf extension) begins at about 65° F. As temperatures increase above 65° F, the rate of leaf extension increases, assuming other requirements (light, moisture, nitrogen, etc.) are met. Consequently, mowing frequency needs to increase as the season progresses from early spring to midsummer. To compensate for the increased growth rate and maintain the same mowing frequency, mowing heights are raised as the season progresses.

The photoperiod (day length) also influences mowing frequencies. During summer months (long days) leaf growth is upright, but during spring and fall (short days) leaf growth is more decumbent (Evans 1940). Consequently, mowing frequencies can be reduced during spring and fall months.

MOWING HEIGHT

Grass variety and turf use have the greatest influence on mowing height. Other factors such as mowing frequency, shade, mowing equipment, and the season of the year need to be considered, but grass variety and turf use are the limiting factors. Tall fescue, for example, performs best at mowing heights between 2 and 3 inches. Tifdwarf bermudagrass and creeping bentgrass perform best at mowing heights below ½ inch. In general, bermudagrasses perform best at mowing heights of 1 inch or less, while other warm-season turfgrasses perform best at mowing heights of 1 to 2 inches. Likewise for the cool-season grasses, bentgrass performs best at mowing heights of ½ inch or less, while bluegrass performs best at a 2-inch or greater mowing height.

The parameters that determine mowing heights for grasses are often fixed by the use of the turf. Golf greens, for example, must be mowed below ¼ inch to provide the smooth, consistent, and fast surfaces that golfers expect. Sports turf for baseball, football, and soccer needs to be mowed near the

1-inch height to reduce interference with the ball and provide fast playing surfaces. Grass bowling greens and tennis courts must also be mowed very short. In contrast, roughs on golf courses are typically mowed at a 2-inch height to penalize the golfer for hitting into the rough.

Grass areas that are mowed infrequently, but where appearance is important, must be mowed between 3 and 4 inches in height to prevent scalping. Roadsides, lawns around commercial and industrial sites, and some park areas often meet these requirements.

On home lawns, grass species, frequency of mowing, shade, and the type of mower determine the optimum height. The turf manager must realize that the shorter a turf is mowed, the more often it must be mowed to prevent scalping. As a result, the homeowner may compromise between the height best suited for the grass and the height best suited for frequency of mowing. For example, bermudagrass provides the finest turf at mowing heights below 1 inch, which requires mowing at 5-day intervals or less. If the homeowner can only mow on a 7-day schedule, the mowing height must be raised to 1½ inches to prevent scalping.

On shaded sites, mowing heights need to be raised 30 to 50 percent to compensate for the more upright growth of leaves under reduced light. Grasses growing in shade typically have long, thin, spindly leaves, and higher mowing heights help maintain leaf surface to carry on photosynthesis (Wilkinson and Beard 1974; Winstead and Ward 1974). If shaded lawns are continuously mowed short, the grass gradually thins out and weeds invade the turf.

The type of mower the homeowner uses may also influence mowing height. Rotary mowers do not usually cut below a 1-inch height and perform best at heights between 1½ and 3 inches. On the other hand, the reel-type mowers cuts best at 1½ inches or less.

The season of the year may also influence recommended mowing heights. In early spring, close mowing is recommended to control thatch and to increase turf density. Also, the more prostrate (decumbent) growth habit of grasses in the early spring allows for close mowing. Mowing heights may be raised slightly during summer months to reduce the frequency of mowing and to reduce watering. Higher mowing heights in the summer also help compensate for the more upright growth of leaves during long days. Mowing heights may be raised again in the fall on warm-season grasses to reduce the risk of winterkill from low temperatures. Then, in the spring as the grass breaks dormancy, the lower mowing heights may be used again to remove excess residues and promote early green up.

Using Saint Augustine grass as an example, the homeowner may mow the lawn at 1½ inches in early spring to remove excess residues and promote early recovery of the lawn. By midsummer the mowing height might be raised to 2 to 2½ inches to reduce mowing frequency. Finally, in areas of the South where winterkill occurs, the mowing height might be raised to 3 inches in the fall to provide more cover and insulation for the stolons and crowns of Saint Augustine grass during winter months.

Mowing patterns are often neglected, but they too can have a significant influence on turf quality. Lawns that are mowed in the same pattern each time because of convenience develop problems during stress periods. If grass clippings are not collected from such lawns, clippings tend to accumulate in rows along the path of the mower. During severe drought or cold stress the thatchy rows are the first to show injury. By changing the mowing pattern each time the lawn is mowed, the grass clippings are uniformly distributed and the problem does not develop.

On golf courses and sports turf, mowing along the same path and direction each mowing produces grainy turf and nonuniform playing conditions. Even on golf course fairways where it is most convenient and much faster to mow the length of the fairway, it is advantageous to occasionally mow across the width of the fairway.

Mowing the same direction between alternate yardage stripes on a football field may be done for the visual effect, but the direction should be reversed occasionally. Likewise, mowing a baseball field or golf green in a checkerboard pattern is fine for the effect it produces, but the direction of mowing should occasionally be reversed.

GRASS CLIPPINGS

Management of grass clippings is critical to the quality of turf produced. On very dense, closely mowed turf areas such as golf greens, grass clippings are routinely removed for aesthetic purposes and to prevent interference with the ball. On turf areas mowed at ½ inch or higher, clippings do not need to be removed if they do not interfere with the use of the turf. If the turf is mowed at appropriate intervals and clippings are uniformly dispersed, the clippings do not present a problem. In fact, by leaving the clippings in place, the nutrients they contain are recycled through the turf and the need for fertilization is significantly reduced. By catching and discarding grass clippings each time a turf is mowed, about 100 to 150 pounds of nitrogen per acre are removed each year.

On large turf areas where it is not practical to remove clippings it may be necessary on occasion to mow several times in one day or several days in a row to uniformly disperse the clippings. This is often necessary following several days of rain or following an application of fertilizer. Grass clippings should not be left in such volume that they appear unsightly or smother the grass.

If a homeowner does not want grass clippings left on the lawn, they can be used for compost in a garden or as a mulch around plants. But other than for aesthetic purposes, there is no need to routinely remove grass clippings from lawns.

Water Management on Turfgrasses

Given the severe water shortages in many sections of the country during the past decade, the value and need for conservation of water can be appreciated. And since scientists forecast more extensive droughts throughout the next decade, the public must become more conscious of water use. Only through careful management of our water resources now can adequate water supplies for turf irrigation be expected through the twenty-first century. In some sections of the country, water use for turf irrigation may seem insignificant, but in other areas it accounts for 50 percent or more of the consumption of city water supplies during the summer months (Gibeault 1985).

If water conservation does not get attention, perhaps improved turf quality should. Both of these effects are products of a properly designed and managed irrigation system. Simply installing an irrigation system to provide coverage to a lawn, golf course, or athletic field does not constitute design. Climatic conditions, root zone properties, grass species, turf use, and water source must all be considered. In addition, pipe size, nozzle diameter, operating pressure, and spacings, which together determine the rate and uniformity of application of water, must also be considered. Efficient use of water will, in time, become the most important design consideration for an irrigation system.

CLIMATIC CONSIDERATIONS

EVAPORATION LOSSES. Direct evaporation from sprinklers can account for a 50 percent or greater loss of water in a desert climate, or for only a negligible loss of water in humid climates (Seginer 1967). Evaporation losses from irrigation increase with solar radiation, temperature, wind movement, and operating pressures, and decrease with relative humidity and nozzle diameter (Frost and Schwalen 1955). Losses due to evaporation are higher for single row irrigation systems with little overlap than for multirow systems with considerable overlap. Low trajectory nozzles also help reduce evaporation losses.

Where climatic conditions favor high losses due to evaporation during summer months, the irrigation system should be designed to operate at a minimum pressure, to have maximum overlap, to use as large a nozzle as practical, to use low trajectory nozzles, and to operate during night and early morning hours. Under conditions that favor evaporation, daytime sprinkler irrigation can require 30 percent more water than night irrigation.

TRANSPIRATION. Transpiration may be defined as the movement of water vapor through the plant to the atmosphere. Most of the water transpired through the plant moves through openings in the leaves called stomates. In actively growing turfgrasses, water continuity exists from the soil (roots), through the plant, to the leaves where evaporation occurs through the stomates.

The primary benefit of transpiration is the cooling effect resulting from the evaporation process. In the absence of transpirational cooling, leaf temperatures can approach 130° F (Beard and Green 1994). In some locations with grasses such as bentgrass, transpirational cooling must be supplemented with syringing in midday to increase evaporative cooling on very hot, summer days.

The amount of water lost through transpiration is a function of the rate of plant growth (transpiration is very low during the dormant season) and several environmental factors—soil moisture, solar radiation, temperature, humidity, and wind. Transpiration rates are highest during summer months when soil moisture, solar radiation, temperature, and wind speeds are high. Transpiration rates are also higher in arid climates than in humid climates because of the greater water vapor deficit between the leaf and the atmosphere in dry air. Thus, transpiration losses may be as high as 0.35 inches of water per day in desert climates during summer months; whereas, under similar temperature conditions in humid climates the daily losses may be only 0.20 inches of water.

In addition to transpirational water losses from turf, evaporative losses from the soil also occur. With the exception of plant growth rate, evaporation losses are dependent on the same environmental variables as transpiration—soil moisture, temperature, solar radiation, humidity, and wind.

The loss of water from the soil by evaporation and through the plant growing on the soil by transpiration is called evapotranspiration (ET). During the growing season, transpiration accounts for most of the ET losses from established turfgrass sites.

Because of the difficulty of measuring ET rates in the field, great efforts have been made to relate ET to readily available climatic data. Thornthwaite, Penman, and Blaney-Criddle all developed rather complex equations to relate ET to climatic data (Sellers 1965). In an effort to simplify these relationships, researchers found that reasonable estimates of ET can be made from pan evaporation data collected by most weather stations (Shih and Snyder 1985). For warm-season grasses ET can be estimated by the following relationship:

ET (warm-season grasses) = (0.75 x pan evaporation rate)

For cool-season grasses the rate is increased to 0.85 times the pan evaporation rate. These estimates are most accurate during the growing season for the respective grasses. Estimated monthly ET rates for selected Texas cities are shown in table 6-1.

In the absence of official pan evaporation data you can collect your own data using a 4-foot diameter, 10-inch deep pan with vertical sides. The pan

Table 6-1. Evapotranspiration Rates (ET) in Inches

City	Jan.	Feb.	Mar.	Apr.	May	June	July	Aug.	Sep.	Oct.	Nov.	Dec.	Total
Abilene	3.06	3.80	6.60	8.40	9.63	11.33	11.90	10.32	7.31	5.79	3.72	3.14	85.01
Amarillo	2.57	3.27	5.79	8.06	9.46	10.72	11.08	9.49	6.87	5.43	3.13	2.52	78.39
Austin	2.97	3.61	5.70	6.62	7.79	9.34	10.48	9.53	6.96	5.39	3.55	2.97	74.91
Brownsville	3.20	3.92	5.86	7.27	9.31	9.64	10.59	9.42	7.17	5.76	3.99	3.23	79.36
Corpus Christi	2.98	3.75	5.81	6.92	8.08	9.43	10.84	9.55	7.18	5.73	3.86	3.13	77.23
Dallas/Ft. Worth	2.60	3.17	5.44	7.04	8.33	9.94	11.55	10.09	7.26	5.17	3.46	2.71	76.76
Del Rio	3.31	4.09	6.58	7.33	7.66	9.11	10.24	9.13	6.81	5.47	3.92	3.21	76.86
El Paso	3.07	4.18	7.25	9.44	11.49	11.77	10.73	9.48	7.28	5.59	3.53	2.83	86.64
Galveston	1.98	3.07	4.06	5.71	8.10	9.71	9.45	8.39	6.34	4.83	2.64	1.89	66.17
Houston	2.52	3.18	4.75	5.95	7.53	8.37	8.76	7.63	5.98	4.61	3.03	2.62	64.93
Lubbock	2.64	3.41	6.20	8.12	9.84	11.04	10.83	9.27	6.65	5.05	3.22	2.61	78.88
Midland	3.45	3.84	6.84	8.50	10.69	11.46	11.88	9.35	6.59	4.84	3.43	3.00	83.57
Port Arthur	2.42	3.19	5.56	5.95	7.79	8.48	8.27	7.45	6.15	4.92	3.20	2.42	65.80
San Angelo	3.00	3.64	6.13	7.46	8.34	9.58	10.06	9.03	6.45	5.39	3.41	2.92	75.41
San Antonio	2.22	3.03	5.07	6.41	7.82	9.59	10.37	9.12	6.35	4.47	2.74	2.08	69.27
Victoria	2.76	3.37	4.98	5.70	7.49	7.50	7.91	7.24	5.84	4.99	3.53	2.77	64.08
Waco	2.55	3.09	5.20	6.15	7.33	9.04	10.28	9.25	6.53	5.11	3.30	2.46	70.29
Wichita Falls	2.46	3.08	5.30	6.79	8.05	9.58	10.70	9.53	6.71	5.08	3.09	2.44	72.81

should be placed on blocks so that it is about 6 inches above soil level. You can measure the loss of water, in inches, by measuring the depth of water in the pan each morning at the same time. If you are just interested in average ET rates, measure the depth of water at 3-day intervals and divide the loss by 3. Also, for warm-season grasses multiply the pan evaporation loss by 0.75 to estimate ET rates.

ROOT ZONE PROPERTIES

POROSITY. Soils consist of solid particles and pore spaces which are filled with either air or water. Pore space may account for 40 to 50 percent of the soil, depending on texture, structure, degree of compaction, and other variables. Individual pore spaces are classified as small pores (capillary pores) or large pores (noncapillary pores). Small pores are generally filled with water, and large pores are filled by air. Total pore space and pore size distribution determine most of the physical properties of soils that are important to irrigation practices.

Water moves downward in a soil through the large pore spaces until the flow is interrupted by a significant change in pore size. A barrier such as a compacted soil, gravel layer, or clay pan will impede the downward movement of water. Where these barriers are near the surface of the soil, irrigation rates and schedules must be adjusted to prevent excessive surface runoff or leaching, depending on the nature of the barrier.

INFILTRATION AND PERCOLATION. The rate of movement of water

Soil profile graphs A–E

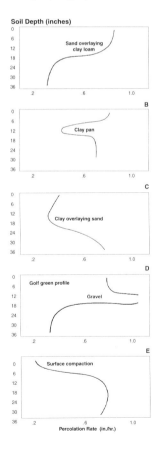

into a soil is called the infiltration rate. A dry soil may have a very high initial infiltration rate, but as the soil pores become filled with water (saturated), the infiltration rate decreases sharply. In a saturated soil the infiltration rate is equal to the rate at which water moves through the soil profile—the percolation rate. The infiltration rate and percolation rate are critical physical properties of the soil that must be considered when designing and operating an irrigation system. Both of these properties determine the rate at which water can be effectively applied to a soil.

WATER RETENTION. The soil serves as a reservoir for water storage. A clay soil may store 2 to 2½ inches of available water per foot, whereas a sandy loam soil may hold only 1 to 1½ inches per foot. For an irrigation system to be efficient, the water in the root zone of the soil should be completely recharged by irrigation when 50 to 60 percent of the available water has been depleted. For some turfs this practice may require as little as ½ inch of water or as much as 1½ inches per application. Few sprinkler irrigation systems are designed to apply more than 1 inch of water per application. Obviously, the more available water the root zone will hold, the longer the irrigation interval (days between irrigations) can be.

SURFACE CONDITIONS

Turf development and soil surface conditions can restrict water infiltration rates in the same way that soil profile characteristics restrict percolation rates. A dense thatch layer, surface crusts, or a nonwettable sand can severely reduce water infiltration rates. Unlike soil profile characteristics, these surface conditions can be readily corrected through cultivation, soil amendments, or wetting agents. Cultivation (aeration, vertical mowing, and topdressing) provides an effective means of removing and controlling thatch accumulation in turf.

Where thatch accumulation is excessive, significant amounts of irrigation water may be required just to wet the thatch layer. Evaporation losses are considerably higher from thatch than from soil. A heavily thatched turf is usually shallow-rooted, which also prevents effective utilization of irrigation water. Where the root system is restricted to the thatch layer, light and frequent applications of water are more efficient than more thorough irrigations.

Soil amendments such as organic matter, calcined clay aggregates (Greens Choice, and Turface), gypsum, or lime may be used to alleviate surface compaction and increase infiltration rates. When sodium salts from saline irrigation water disperse the soil particles and seal the soil surface, gypsum may be used to improve surface conditions.

Under some conditions sandy soils may develop nonwettable properties. This characteristic has been attributed to an organic substance produced by soil microorganisms that coats the sand particles and binds them together. Some wetting agents in combination with aeration have been effective in alleviating this condition.

Several types of soil profiles are illustrated in graphs A through E. Graph A represents the ideal situation where soil can be effectively wetted to a depth of 18 to 24 inches. In graph B the clay pan limits the time that the irrigation system can be operated at one setting, because only the upper 6 inches of soil can be effectively wetted. If water continues to be applied after the top 6 inches are wet, the soil will become saturated and runoff will occur.

In graph C the rate of application of water is limited by the percolation rate of the upper 6 inches of soil. Graph D represents a typical USGA golf green profile. In this case, irrigation should be stopped after the top 8 to 10 inches of soil are wet. Continued irrigation after that point would result in excess water losses due to leaching. Graph E illustrates a situation where surface compaction restricts the movement of water into the soil profile.

RUNOFF. Runoff occurs when root zones are saturated or when precipitation rate exceeds the infiltration rate of the root zone. Runoff is highest in humid climates and is greater during the cool season than during summer if rainfall is evenly distributed. For a given annual precipitation, total runoff varies greatly across the United States. For example, a mean annual precipitation of 30 inches is accompanied by runoff in the range of 3 inches in Nebraska, 6 inches in Tennessee, 12 inches in New York, and 22 inches in the Rockies. These differences are largely due to seasonal distribution of rainfall. Areas where runoff is greatest receive most of the rainfall in the winter when only limited radiant energy is available for evaporation.

For the range of precipitation normally found in the U.S., a simple equation can be used to estimate runoff:

Runoff [as a % of precipitation (P)] = $a\, P^2$

where a is a variable based on precipitation distribution and radiant energy (Sellers 1965).

For much of Texas a is 0.005 and runoff ranges from 15 to 25 percent. For estimating runoff on an annual basis, I suggest using 15 percent on level areas, 20 percent on areas with about 1-percent slope, and 30 percent on a 2-percent slope. A football field, for example, with an 18-inch crown down the center line of the field would have about a 2 percent slope. Most golf course fairways and lawns have a 1 to 2 percent slope so that 25 percent might be a good estimate for runoff on those sites.

Such information is useful when estimating water needs for irrigation. For example, a golf course superintendent in Dallas, Texas, could estimate annual water needs by the following equation:

Water Needs (in./yr.)	=	ET (annual) – [Rainfall – Runoff]
	=	60 – [36 – (.25) (36)]
	=	60 – [36 – 9]
	=	60 – 27
	=	33 inches per year

Thus, an average of 33 inches of water would be needed to maintain growth at a maximum level. On a bermudagrass golf course, good playing conditions could be maintained with 60 to 70 percent of the 33 inches or 20 to 23 inches of effective irrigation.

SPECIES AND USE

Grasses differ in their water requirements, as some can survive much greater moisture stress than others (Biran et al. 1981). The cool-season grasses are generally more susceptible to moisture stress than warm-season grasses. Buffalograss, for example, can survive long periods of severe moisture stress, whereas bluegrass would be killed by the same conditions. Buffalograss may not look any better than the other grasses during this period, but it would recover when moisture was restored. However, where turf is maintained for its aesthetics or for recreation, mere survival is not satisfactory. All turfgrasses require supplemental irrigation during stress periods to maintain color and growth. During peak water use periods cool-season grasses use about 0.3 inch per day; whereas warm-season grasses use about 0.25 inch per day.

Depth of rooting is the most important factor in the drought resistance of a turf. A shallow-rooted turf is much more susceptible to drought injury than a deep-rooted turf. Management practices, root zone properties, and turf use have a greater effect on the depth of rooting than grass species. However, grass species and varieties differ significantly in depth of rooting. Close mowing, overwatering, excessive fertilization, soil compaction, and thatch accumulation all lead to shallow-rooted turf. Golf course putting greens are excellent examples of turf that are managed to favor shallow rooting. The roots of most bentgrass putting greens occupy the surface 2 to 4 inches. Consequently, irrigation schedules must be adjusted to a light and frequent schedule.

Management practices that promote deep rooting include aeration, thatch control, proper mowing, proper fertilization, and infrequent irrigation. A deep-rooted turf uses water more efficiently than a shallow-rooted turf because it can go longer between irrigations.

IRRIGATION PRACTICES

To maximize efficiency of water use by turfgrasses, irrigation programs should be based on cumulative evapotranspiration losses, soil moisture retention, effective depth of rooting, infiltration rate, and type of turf being irrigated. An irrigation program set up on a calendar basis is much less efficient than one based on the above criteria. Water use on a daily basis can be estimated from pan evaporation measurements, which are available from weather stations throughout the United States.

Today, computerized irrigation controllers are available that provide irrigation programs based on evaporation data entered several times an hour and accumulated on a daily basis. Also, automatic adjustments in the program are made daily based on rainfall, temperature and other environmental parameters. These controllers take the art out of water management and replace it with science.

Irrigation systems should be designed to meet the water requirements of turf during the months of maximum use. For example, locations that have a net evaporation loss of 15 cm (6 inches) during the month of July should have the capability of applying about 4 cm (1½ inches) of water per week. Whether the 1½ inches of water is applied in two or more applications will depend on turf use, soil moisture retention, infiltration rate, and depth of rooting. If the turf is deep-rooted and in a soil capable of holding 1 ½ inches of water in the effective root zone, the entire amount could be applied in a single irrigation. Or, where the infiltration rate restricts the rate of water movement into the rootzone, the water could be applied in a series of intermittent irrigations. If the turf is shallow-rooted or if the soil will hold only 1 inch of water in the root zone, the water should be applied in 2 or more irrigations.

On an annual basis, warm-season grasses will use 40 to 60 inches of water per year, depending on the availability of water. A well watered bermudagrass fairway will use about 60 inches of water per year, or 1.6 million gallons per acre. The same fairway could be maintained in equally good condition with about 40 inches of water, a 33 percent savings in water alone. In addition, energy needed to pump the water, wear on the equipment, and fertilizer losses are also significantly reduced.

Under intensive maintenance such as lawns, sports fields, and golf course fairways, rainfall meets about half of the water needs in southern states; irrigation must provide the remainder. Thus, irrigation must provide 20 to 30 inches of water per year in the South and 40 to 50 inches in the West, for warm-season turfgrasses. These numbers equal 0.5 to 1.5 million gallons of water per acre, or 12 to 36 thousand gallons per 1,000 square feet of turf. Obviously, these quantities of water represent significant dollars.

By promoting deep rooting through thatch control, aeration, moderate fertilization, and infrequent irrigation, significant quantities of water can be saved. Further savings can be achieved by planting drought-resistant grass varieties.

TENSIOMETERS

Moisture-indicating instruments called tensiometers may be used to measure the moisture status of the soil and indicate when irrigation is required. They consist of a porous cup, a vacuum gauge, and a water-filled connecting tube between the cup and the gauge. When the cup is placed in the root zone of the soil, water is free to move through the porous wall and come to equilibrium with the soil water. As the soil dries, water moves from the cup and causes a vacuum to be indicated on the gauge; thus, the drier the soil, the higher the gauge reading. When irrigation water is applied or rainfall occurs, water returns through the porous cup and releases the vacuum, which lowers the gauge reading.

By placing the tensiometers at several depths and observing them daily or weekly, it is possible to estimate how often irrigation is needed and the depth to which water should penetrate to recharge the rootzone.

Moisture readings with these instruments represent only a small area of soil that surrounds the cup; therefore, sufficient locations over the area should be established so that a representative measurement of soil moisture can be obtained.

Irrigation schedules based on tensiometer readings that indicate moisture stress are much more efficient in terms of water use than schedules established on a calendar basis.

PRACTICAL WATER MANAGEMENT

The objective of a turfgrass manager is to provide as fine a lawn or playing surface as desired with a minimum use of labor and resources such as water. Although much of the previous discussion concerned the maximum, or potential, use of water by turfgrass; in practice, grasses can only use the water that is available to them. Thus, where precipitation is below the potential water use rate, the actual water use equals the effective precipitation (rainfall + irrigation − runoff). In situations where the rootzone is very shallow, leaching losses must also be considered. Otherwise, for simplicity, we can disregard leaching.

For example, in a nonirrigated site in central Texas where rainfall for 1992 was 30 inches, the water use rate can be calculated as follows:

$$\text{Water Use Rate (in./yr.)} = \text{Rainfall} - \text{Runoff}$$
$$= 30 - [.005\,(30)^2]$$
$$= 30 - 4.5$$
$$= 25.5$$

Thus, even though the potential water use rate for central Texas is about 60 inches, the actual water use rate for 1992 was only about 25 inches. The turf manager must decide if the quality of turf is adequate for that site. If it is not adequate, then how much additional water is necessary?

Observations in Texas indicate that bermudagrass will survive with about 20 inches of water per year. Research indicates that bermudagrass can be kept green during the growing season with only about 50 percent of the potential water use rate, or about 30 inches per year, if the applications of water are timely. For a lawn 30 inches of water may be all that is needed. But for a sports field or golf course where growth is needed for recovery, more than 30 inches might be needed.

Therefore, if your objective is water conservation, 20 inches is needed for survival, 30 inches for acceptable color, and about 40 inches for adequate color and growth. Those values are for common bermudagrass. Hybrid bermudagrass such as Tifway and Tifgreen require slightly more water for the same level of maintenance.

Buffalograss is similar to common bermudagrass, but buffalograss will survive with only about 15 inches of effective rainfall. However, water requirements for maintenance of color and growth are about the same as for common bermudagrass.

For Saint Augustine grass those same parameters might be 30 inches for survival, 40 inches for color, and 45 inches for color and growth. Zoysiagrasses are similar to Saint Augustine grass.

Tall fescue and bluegrass have the highest water requirements for Texas lawns. Although these grasses can survive with only 30 to 35 inches of water, they require in excess of 50 inches to maintain acceptable color and growth.

To maintain turfgrasses with the amount of water previously indicated, turf managers must apply water effectively. One method of effective water management is to recharge the root zone at intervals that allow the grass to show slight moisture stress—wilting and discoloration. For example, bermudagrass growing in deep sand might be irrigated at 5- to 7-day intervals with 1 inch of water. The same grass in the Texas Hill Country, where root zones are typically shallow, may require 0.5 inch of water at 2- to 3-day intervals. Extending the interval between irrigations to the point of showing moisture stress promotes deep rooting of turfgrasses. However, the entire root zone must be recharged when water is applied.

Sloping sites and sites with very low infiltration rates must be irrigated intermittently to reduce runoff. For example, the site may require 0.75 inches of water to recharge the root zone, but the infiltration rate may be only 0.25 inches of water per hour. Putting out all the water needed in one irrigation cycle would result in significant runoff. However, by applying 0.25 inches of water per cycle and repeating the cycle at 1- to 2-hour intervals, runoff can be significantly reduced.

Through conscientious water management homeowners and professional turfgrass managers can conserve water resources and still provide attractive lawns and sports fields.

Potential water deficits for turfgrasses in Texas (inches per year)

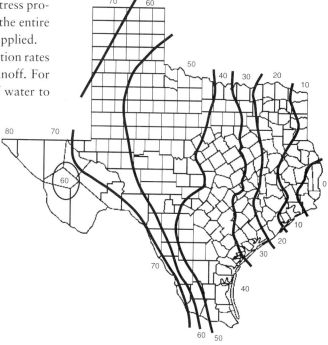

Water Budget

Water Deficit

	J	F	M	A	M	J	J	A	S	O	N	D
Evapotranspiration (inches)												
Rainfall (inches)												
Runoff (inches)												
Water Deficit												

Water Requirement

Water Requirements = ET + Irrigation Losses + Runoff − Rainfall

    1. Total ins. x no. of 1,000 sq. ft. x 620 = gals. of water
    2. Total ins. x acres irrigated x 27,152 = gals. of water

Example: A 10,000 sq. ft. lawn requiring 30 inches of water per year.
    30 (ins./yr.) x 10 (10,000 sq. ft. lawn) x 620 = 186,000 gals.

WATER COST

    Acre feet   _____
    Acre inches   _____
    1,000 gallons   _____

    3. No. of 1,000 gals. x cost per 1,000 gals. = cost

Example: Residential water costs $2.25 per 1,000 gals. at College Station
    186 (from above example) x $2.25 = $418.50/yr.

    Total   _____

LABOR COST

	J	F	M	A	M	J	J	A	S	O	N	D
Labor (hours)												

    Total hours   _____
    Cost per hour   _____
    Total   _____

EQUIPMENT COSTS PER YEAR

Controller/20 years _____

Sprinkler System/20 years _____

Pumps/10 years _____

Hoses/5 years _____

Sprinklers/5 years _____

Total _____

OPERATING COSTS

Electricity _____

Repairs _____

Total _____

Total Irrigation Costs (see previous totals)

Water _____

Labor _____

Equipment _____

Operating _____

Grand Total _____

Water Budgeting Example

Total Costs for Irrigation

Example:

Total Irrigation Costs = Water + Labor + Equipment + Operating

For a 10,000 square foot residential lawn requiring 30 inches of water per year, the total irrigation costs might include:

Water Costs

$418.50 (see above calculation)

Labor Costs

50 hours (to monitor, operate, and repair the sytem) at $8.50 per hour equals $425.00

Equipment Costs

$2,500 for system installation depreciated over 20 years or $125.00

Operating Costs

$35.00 for repairs plus $75.00 sewage charge for residential water use

Total Irrigation Costs

$418.50 + $425.00 + $125.00 + $35.00 + $75.00 = $1,078.50

If the homeowner provided the labor, the $425.00 labor costs can be deducted. Nevertheless, the example shows that water costs are only a portion of the total irrigation costs to a homeowner or client.

Table 6-2. Root Zone Deficits for College Station, Texas (30-year average)

	J	F	M	A	M	J	J	A	S	O	N	D	Total
Rainfall	3.0	3.2	2.7	4.0	4.2	3.3	2.7	2.5	3.0	2.7	3.3	3.5	38.1
ET	2.5	2.5	4.2	5.1	6.5	6.3	6.5	6.5	6.0	4.8	4.2	2.5	57.6
Runoff	0.75	0.8	0.67	1.0	1.0	0.82	0.67	0.62	0.75	0.67	0.82	0.87	9.5
Root zone deficit	0.25	0.10	2.17	2.1	3.30	3.82	4.47	4.62	3.75	2.77	1.72	–0.13	29.0

$$
\begin{aligned}
\text{Root Zone Deficit} &= \text{ET} - (\text{Rainfall} - \text{Runoff}) \\
&= 57.6 - (38.1 - 9.5) \\
&= 57.6 - 28.6 \\
&= 29
\end{aligned}
$$

Table 6-3. Turfgrass Adaptation Based on Potential Water Deficits and Other Environmental Factors

Turfgrass Species	Potential Water Deficit	Other Environmental Factors
Centipedegrass	0–30	Alkaline soil in western section limits this species.
Saint Augustine	0–40	Low winter temperatures limit this species to coastal regions of the South.
Zoysiagrass	0–40	
Bermudagrass	0–50	
Buffalograss	20–60	Sandy soil limits this species in some sections.
Blue Grama, Western wheatgrass, curly mesquite	30–70	

Turfgrass Fertilization

Plants are unique in that they derive their energy for growth from the basic elements of soil minerals, light, water, and air. They do not require any organic constituents for growth. Since the early work of German chemist Justus von Liebig in the mid-1800s that established the role of minerals in plant growth, there has been a tendency to emphasize fertilization as the solution to plant nutrition problems. Yet the fertilizer nutrients (NO_3^-, NH_4^+, K^+, $H_2PO_4^-$) do not provide the energy plants need for growth. These nutrients are only the raw materials which together with sunlight, water, and carbon dioxide enable the plant to produce the organic compounds necessary for growth—sugars, starch, amino acids, etc. Consequently, when we evaluate the nutrient needs of a turf we must consider factors such as nutrient levels, nutrient availability, and interactions among nutrients; and we must also consider environmental conditions that determine the availability of the nutrients to the grass.

NUTRIENT AVAILABILITY. Grass obtains the nutrients it needs from soil minerals, organic matter, fertilizer, and, to a lesser extent, from the atmosphere. Deficiencies of one or more nutrients may occur because of several reasons: (1) the nutrient may be lacking in the soil or in the environment, (2) the nutrient may be too slowly available, or (3) there may be an imbalance between nutrients.

For nutrients to be taken up by the grass, they must be present in a form that the plant can use. Nitrogen, for example, is not taken up as elemental nitrogen (N_2) from the air, but as nitrate (NO_3^-) or ammonium (NH_4^+) from the soil. Likewise, phosphorus and potassium may be present in the mineral form in large concentrations, but they must be in available forms ($H_2PO_4^-$, and K^+) to be taken up by the grass. Nutrients in the available form are readily soluble in water and are taken up with water by grass roots. However, depending on management and environmental conditions, these nutrients may be lost by leaching or volatilization, or they may be utilized by soil microorganisms before being taken up by the grass. A brief discussion of nutrient availability in relation to each fertilizer nutrient may help explain some of the responses obtained from fertilizer applications.

NITROGEN. Grasses may obtain nitrogen from organic matter, but fertilizers provide the major source of nitrogen to turfgrasses. Organic matter, organic fertilizers, and some slow-release fertilizers must be broken down by soil microorganisms before the nitrogen can be used by the grass. This transformation is called mineralization and may be described as follows:

$$R\text{—}NH_2 \quad + \quad H_2O \quad \rightarrow \quad NH_4^+$$
$$\text{(organic N)} \quad \text{(water)} \quad \text{(ammonium)}$$

The ammonium (NH_4^+) form of nitrogen may be taken up by the grass or may be transformed to nitrate (NO_3^-). The latter transformation is called nitrification and may be described as follows:

$$NH_4^+ \quad + \quad 2\,O_2 \quad + \quad \text{microbes} \quad \rightarrow \quad NO_3^- \quad + \quad H_2O \quad + \quad 2H^+$$
$$\text{(ammonium N)} \quad\quad\quad\quad\quad \text{(nitrate N)}$$

Note the acidifying effect of nitrification (2 hydrogen ions). These transformations are dependent upon soil microbes and are sensitive to a number of environmental conditions. They do not occur below freezing temperatures and are slow to take place in poorly aerated soils, very dry soils, or very wet soils, and in highly acid soils. Thus, the application of an organic source of nitrogen or urea-formaldehyde does not necessarily provide the grass with its nitrogen requirement. Environmental conditions (temperature, moisture, compaction, pH, etc.) may prevent or restrict the transformations necessary for conversion to available forms of nitrogen. Since aeration is not adequate

Leaching

NO_3^- NO_3^- NO_3^-
↓   ↓   ↓

Dentrification
Urea
Ammonium sulfate

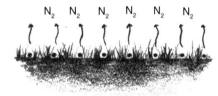

N_2 N_2 N_2 N_2 N_2 N_2

Wet soils
High temperature

Volatilization
Urea
Ammonium sulfate

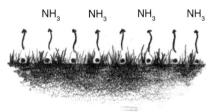

NH_3 NH_3 NH_3 NH_3

Alkaline soil
High temperature

due to compaction or overwatering in many soils on which turfgrasses are maintained, nitrification is often inhibited and ammonium (NH_4^+) tends to accumulate. Where NH_4^+ accumulates, nitrogen losses due to volatilization (loss of nitrogen as ammonia [NH_3] gas) may be excessive.

On the other hand, nitrification may be very rapid in soils moistened by rain or irrigation after being dry for a prolonged period. In this case, the grass may be overstimulated or nitrogen losses due to leaching may be excessive.

Since the nitrate (NO_3^-) form of nitrogen is highly soluble in water, it is readily moved below the root zone of grasses following heavy rainfall or irrigation. This leaching is most likely to occur during dormant periods or when the grass is not growing vigorously. Thus, leaching may account for a significant loss of nitrogen during the winter.

Nitrification does not occur below freezing and is insignificant above 105° F. It is slow in acid soils, very slow in compacted or poorly aerated soils, and is limited in dry or wet soils.

Mineralization and nitrification serve to convert nitrogen from an organic source to a form that is available to the grass. However, environmental conditions may favor plant uptake or nitrogen loss through leaching or volatilization.

Denitrification is the conversion of nitrate nitrogen to gaseous elemental nitrogen which is lost to the atmosphere. This process is favored by low oxygen levels in the soil, high soil moisture, alkaline soils, and high temperatures. Denitrification can account for 10 to 30 percent losses of applied nitrogen under compacted soil conditions or waterlogged soils, particularly where soils are alkaline (pH 7.5-8.5).

$$NO_3^- \rightarrow NO_2 \rightarrow N_2O \rightarrow N_2 \uparrow$$
(nitrate N)   (elemental nitrogen)

Other soil conditions may favor the loss of nitrogen through volatilization. Volatilization involves the conversion of ammonium nitrogen to ammonia gas, which is lost to the atmosphere. This process is favored by alkaline soils, warm temperatures, dry soils, and soils with a low exchange capacity. Where conditions favor volatilization, 30 percent or more of the applied nitrogen may be lost to the atmosphere. The classic example of this method of losing nitrogen is the application of ammonium fertilizer to alkaline soils:

$$2NH_4^+ + CaCO_3 \rightarrow 2NH_3 \uparrow + H_2CO_3 + Ca^{++}$$
(lime)   (ammonia)

Nitrate (NO_3^-) is lost from soil by leaching and soil microorganisms. It is taken up by grass, denitrified, and volatilized.

Nitrogen fixation is the conversion of elemental nitrogen (N_2) from the air to a form that can be used by plants. Nitrogen is fixed by nodules formed on the roots of grasses and legumes by bacteria that grow in close association with the roots. The nitrogen fixed by the nodules is recycled through the turf following the decay of plant parts. Thus, the need for nitrogen fertilizer may be reduced. Grasses and legumes can be inoculated with the bacteria to promote the biological fixation of nitrogen. Inoculated legume plants grown on U.S. cropland are estimated to fix 12 million tons of atmospheric nitrogen per year.

To date, there are no known bacteria and host grasses that produce sufficient nitrogen for turf maintenance. Although some grasses may be able to survive on the nitrogen levels produced, they would not be suitable for turf.

NITROGEN SOURCES FOR TURFGRASS

Turf can be grown without N fertilizers, but not to today's standards. Mineralization of organic matter, nitrogen-fixing microorganisms, and nitrogen oxidized by lightning and dispersed by rainfall all contribute to the natural supply of nitrogen. Where demands on grass are low, these natural sources may be adequate. But hybrid turfgrasses, the promotion of dark green color as being standard, the development of automatic lawn sprinklers, and the advent of commercial lawn care have all prompted greater use of nitrogen fertilizers.

When evaluating a nitrogen source for turfgrass use, availability from suppliers, nitrogen release rate, mechanism of nitrogen release, cost, burning potential, nitrogen residual, salinity hazard, and turf response must be considered. Perhaps the most important, yet most difficult to measure, characteristic of nitrogen sources is turf response. Traditionally, turf response has been evaluated by color and growth rate (yield). These responses are relatively easy to measure, but they are not the most important criteria for determining turf quality. Root growth, carbohydrate reserves, shoot density, and stress tolerance are the most important turf responses to nitrogen; however, they are more difficult to measure than color and growth rate. Thus, we frequently rely on color and growth rate to evaluate the response of turfgrasses to nitrogen sources.

When using growth rate to evaluate the response of nitrogen sources, we must consider the seasonal growth patterns of turfgrasses. Even with no supplemental nitrogen, grasses have periods of high and very low growth rates. Warm-season turfgrasses should not be fertilized with high rates (above 1 pound/1,000 square feet) of nitrogen sources immediately prior to or during periods of rapid growth (late spring and summer). Likewise, cool-season turfgrasses should not receive high rates of nitrogen in the early spring or summer. By carefully timing nitrogen applications, the growth periods can be extended and the peaks and valleys moderated to some extent. Also, using slow-release and organic nitrogen sources along with soluble sources to build up levels of residual nitrogen can help to maintain uniform growth rates.

SOLUBLE NITROGEN SOURCES. Urea, ammonium sulfate, potassium nitrate, and ammonium nitrate are commonly used soluble nitrogen sources. A soluble nitrogen source provides a readily available supply of nitrogen to the turf. Following the application of a soluble nitrogen source to turf, the growth rate increases sharply about 2 days after application, reaches a peak growth rate in 7 to 10 days after application, and tapers off to the original growth rate in 4 to 6 weeks, depending on the rate of application. If this response were carried to the extreme and very small amounts of soluble nitrogen were applied on a daily schedule, a uniform growth rate could be produced. The only practical method of applying nitrogen on a daily schedule would require applying nitrogen through the irrigation system—fertigation.

The peaks and valleys in growth rate observed between applications of soluble nitrogen fertilizers may not be obvious on frequently mowed turf areas, but they can have a detrimental effect on the grass. Short bursts of growth after fertilizer application followed by a period of slow growth can deplete carbohydrate reserves in the grass, reduce root development, and eventually thin a turf. These effects are not readily apparent by observing growth rate and color responses to fertilization. Long-term observations and responses to stress would more accurately establish the effect of soluble nitrogen sources on turf.

At rates of application above 1.0 pound of N per 1,000 square feet, soluble sources may desiccate or burn the foliage if not watered into the turf shortly after application. A commercial lawn service organization cannot depend on the homeowner to water the lawn as needed. Also, at rates above 1.0 pound of N per 1,000 square feet, soluble N fertilizers produce a burst of growth for a short period after application. This is not desirable from the standpoint of mowing, watering, and other maintenance requirements. Also, excessive leaf growth depletes the grass of energy reserves, retards root growth, and increases the susceptibility of the grass to insects and diseases. Finally, soluble N sources have only a 4- to 6-week residual after which N supply is exhausted.

In their favor, soluble N sources are the lowest cost per pound of N, produce a rapid greening response, are effective at all temperature extremes, and are suited to either liquid or dry programs. Where N can be applied at rates between ½ and 1 pound per 1,000 square feet at monthly intervals, the soluble products are the choice of most applicators. However, the need for frequent applications limits their use in most lawn service operations.

A relatively new product, Formolene (methylol urea), overcomes several of the shortcomings of the soluble N sources but does not have a long residual. The methylol urea has a greatly reduced burn potential and 1 to 1½ pounds of N per 1,000 square feet can be applied in a single application without burning the foliage. Also, the product does not produce the rapid burst of growth produced by other soluble N fertilizers. However, the residual is only slightly greater than soluble N fertilizers. A further disadvantage is that the product is tightly bound to the foliage, and clipping removal after application can remove significant amounts of nitrogen. Formolene is a liquid concentration with 25 to 30 percent nitrogen. It mixes readily with other fertilizer nutrients and pesticides and is well suited to liquid applications. The user should be advised not to remove the grass clippings for at least 2 mowings after application.

SLOW RELEASE NITROGEN SOURCES. A low, uniform supply of available nitrogen during the growing season is the objective of most turfgrass fertilizer programs. Such a program is difficult to accomplish without the use of slow-release sources of nitrogen. Residual soil nitrogen, that which becomes available to the grass over a relatively long period of time, cannot be built up with soluble materials. Slow-release nitrogen sources build up residual soil nitrogen that is made available to the grass at varying rates. The rate at which residual nitrogen is made available (released) may vary with nitrogen source, temperature, moisture, pH, particle size, and time of application. Knowledge of a particular nitrogen source and of conditions favorable for nitrogen release is necessary for a turf manager to determine the timing and rates of application of slow-release fertilizers (Waddington et al. 1976; Wilkinson 1977).

UREA-FORMALDEHYDE. Urea-formaldehydes (UF) are products of reacting urea with formaldehyde under carefully controlled temperatures, pH, and reaction times. The nitrogen-release characteristics of the UF produced are determined by the ratio of urea to formaldehyde in the product (Kaempffe and Lung 1967). Methylene urea has a 1.9-to-1 ratio and is ⅔ water soluble and ⅓ water insoluble. Other UF products such as Nitroform and Fluf have a ⅓-to-1 ratio of urea to formaldehyde and are ⅓ water soluble and ⅔ water insoluble. The rate of nitrogen release of these products is closely related to the solubility of the UF. Methylene urea has a faster nitrogen release and greening response than Nitroform, but the residual nitrogen is much greater for Nitroform.

All of the nitrogen in UF is dependent on soil microorganisms to break down the methylene urea chains to urea before nitrogen can be released. But the short chain (water soluble) methylene urea polymers are broken down much faster than the long chain (water insoluble) polymers. The water insoluble fraction of UF may not be completely broken down in the first year. And with relatively short growing seasons, significant carryover (residual) can be expected into the second and third seasons. Where normal rates of UF are applied, 2 or 3 years may be required to build up residual nitrogen to a level that annual applications of UF release an adequate amount of nitrogen. To overcome this lag in nitrogen availability, higher initial rates of UF can be applied or supplemental soluble nitrogen can be used.

Since microorganisms are required to break down UF, environmental conditions (high temperatures, neutral soils, and an adequate supply of moisture and oxygen) that favor microbial activity also promote nitrogen release from UF. Conversely, low temperatures, nutrient deficiencies, and acid soils inhibit the release of nitrogen from UF.

Losses of nitrogen due to leaching and volatilization are less from UF than from soluble nitrogen sources. Thus, if we evaluate the efficiency over a period of several years, UF sources are at least equal to soluble sources in terms of nitrogen use efficiency. And under conditions that favor leaching and volatilization UF sources are more efficient. Nitrogen losses due to removal of fertilizer granules with grass clippings can be significant on closely mowed turf. Losses may be as high as 20 percent on golf greens. For the first several days after application, the grass should be allowed to dry before mowing.

Urea-formaldehyde has little effect on soil pH or salinity. Thus, even at high rates of application, UF does not burn the grass.

ISOBUTYLIDENE DIUREA (IBDU). IBDU, a condensation product of urea and isobutyraldehyde with slow-release characteristics, is a nitrogen fertilizer (Waddington, Duich, and Turner 1977; Wilkinson 1977). Contrary to UF, IBDU does not depend on soil microorganisms for release of nitrogen. In the presence of water, IBDU is hydrolyzed to urea. The rate of hydrolysis varies with soil pH, temperature, particle size, and moisture. IBDU is effective as a controlled release nitrogen source for turfgrasses between pH 5 and 8. Below pH 5, the rate of hydrolysis is very rapid and above pH 8 the rate of hydrolysis is quite slow.

Temperature does not influence the release of nitrogen from IBDU to the degree that it does for UF and organic nitrogen sources. But high temperatures favor the hydrolysis of IBDU and significantly increase nitrogen release. The rate of nitrogen release from IBDU is 2 to 3 times as fast at 75° F than at 50° F; whereas, for UF and organic sources the same temperature difference may result in a tenfold increase in nitrogen release rates.

Particle size of IBDU granules has a significant influence on hydrolysis rates and nitrogen release. The finer the particle, the greater the surface area and the faster is the rate of hydrolysis. Thus, by varying the size of the IBDU granules, nitrogen release can be distributed over a longer period of time. A material with a range of particle sizes between 8 and 24 mesh is recommended for turfgrasses. Particle size does not influence the rate of nitrogen release from UF.

Since water hydrolysis is the rate-controlling process, soil moisture levels also influence the release of nitrogen from IBDU. Wet soil conditions favor the release of nitrogen from IBDU. Soil moisture levels of 40 to 70 percent of field capacity are favorable for a controlled release rate of nitrogen from IBDU. Above these levels nitrogen release is very rapid, and below these levels nitrogen release is very slow. IBDU would not provide a uniform level of available nitrogen where turf is exposed to prolonged wet and dry cycles.

Nitrogen losses due to leaching and volatilization are quite low from IBDU. And efficiency, in terms of nitrogen recovery, is similar to other slow-release nitrogen sources. Nitrogen losses due to mower pickup of the IBDU granules are similar to those that occur with UF sources,

Unlike UF sources, IBDU does not require a buildup of residual nitrogen to provide adequate levels of available nitrogen. Unless particle sizes of IBDU granules are quite large, greater than 2 mm in diameter, most of the nitrogen is hydrolyzed within 60 days after application. However, where particles are much over 2 mm in diameter, mowers will pick up significant quantities of IBDU granules on closely mowed turf.

IBDU has little effect on soil pH, although a temporary increase in pH may occur following a high rate of application. Also, IBDU does not affect turfgrasses at normal rates of application. However, temporary chlorosis has developed 3 to 4 weeks after the application of very high rates of IBDU (above 6 lbs. N/1,000 sq. ft.). This chlorosis has been attributed to excessive absorption of ammonia by the grass.

SULFUR-COATED UREA (SCU). Sulfur-coated urea is produced by spraying preheated urea with molten sulfur in a rotating drum. A wax coating may be applied on top of the sulfur coating to seal the pinholes and cracks in the sulfur coating. Finally, the product is cooled and a clay conditioner applied to reduce cracking. The product is screened to remove any oversize granules.

Sulfur-coated urea granules have been shown to provide a slow-release nitrogen source (Wilkinson 1977). The rate of release of nitrogen from SCU depends on the time required for microorganisms to break down the sulfur coating. Thus, the nitrogen release rate can be decreased by heavier sulfur coating and by inclusion of a microbial inhibitor in the coating. However, a problem occurs with heavy sulfur coatings for turfgrass fertilizers because the mower crushes or picks up the larger fertilizer granules.

Factors that influence the release of nitrogen from UF (temperature, pH, and moisture) also affect nitrogen release from SCU. High temperatures, neutral pH, and moist soils favor the release of nitrogen from SCU.

Sulfur-coated urea is the least uniform of the slow-release nitrogen sources discussed. Imperfections exist in the coatings of SCU because of irregularities on the surface of urea. Also, the sulfur coating may not be uniformly applied to the urea granule. These defects together with incompletely covered granules and cracks in the coatings provide the sites for urea to be released when SCU is exposed to water. Thus, each SCU granule will have a slightly different rate of nitrogen release depending on the extent of the imperfections. Whereas, UF and IBDU granules are homogenous and are not affected by imperfections in the coating. Sulfur-coated urea granules are also subject to being crushed by the fertilizer distributor during application or by the mower reel, roller, or wheel during mowing.

Dissolution (solubility) rates for SCU are expressed as the percent urea released when the product is placed in water at 100° F for seven days. Commercial products usually have a dissolution rate between 20 and 30 percent. Below 20 percent the product is considered too slowly available, but much above 30 percent the product would not be considered a slow-release nitrogen source.

Nitrogen losses from SCU due to leaching and volatilization are intermediate between urea and UF or IBDU. Perhaps the greatest losses of nitrogen from SCU occur when the sulfur coating is broken and urea is readily released, or when the SCU granules are picked up with the grass clippings by the mower. SCU has little effect on salinity but may reduce soil pH. The sulfur released by SCU after the coating is broken down tends to reduce soil pH. When sulfur is deficient in soils, SCU provides an additional benefit with the release of sulfur that eventually becomes available to the grass.

Nitrogen recovery for SCU is greater than for urea and other soluble nitrogen sources. However, recovery would need to be measured over a longer period of time for SCU than for soluble sources.

POLYMER-COATED NITROGEN SOURCES. Polymer-coated nitrogen sources such as Grace Sierra's Once and Pursell Industries' Polygon provide controlled release of nitrogen by diffusion through a polymer membrane (coating). Release rates are dependent on moisture and temperature and by the composition and thickness of the coating. Such products are very uniform and provide predictable release rates of nitrogen.

ORGANIC NITROGEN SOURCES. The oldest sources of nitrogen used for turfgrass fertilization have been natural organic materials—manure, composted crop residues, sludges, and humus. These materials are quite low in nitrogen content, difficult to store and apply, expensive, and, in some cases, contain undesirable substances such as salts, heavy metals, and weed seeds.

Nevertheless, organic nitrogen sources can be effectively used in most turf maintenance programs. Nitrogen release from organic sources is dependent on microorganisms; thus, factors that favor microbial activity increase the rate of nitrogen release from these materials. Organic materials are not considered good nitrogen sources for winter months because of the low activity of microbes. During other seasons organic sources are very effective.

Organic sources should not be considered slow-release sources. When conditions favor nitrogen release from organic sources, the nitrogen usually becomes available to the grass within four to six weeks. A significant amount of the nitrogen from organic sources may remain tied up in the organic form for years.

Organic sources have the advantage that they will not burn the grass, have little effect on pH, contain nutrients other than nitrogen, and may raise soil temperatures during cool periods. Also, some of these materials such as manures, sludges, and composts may improve the physical condition of soils.

MILORGANITE. The most widely used organic nitrogen source on fine turf is Milorganite, a product of the Milwaukee Sewage Commission. Milorganite is an activated sewage sludge that contains 6 percent nitrogen. The product is granulated, screened, and packaged for application to fine turf. It is, perhaps, the most widely recognized nitrogen source for golf green turf.

Advantages of Milorganite for putting green turf include a uniform nitrogen release rate over a period of three to four weeks, a very low burning potential, the addition of phosphorus and iron, soil warming during cool periods, and a minimum effect on soil pH and salinity. Leaching and volatilization losses of nitrogen from Milorganite are also very small.

Disadvantages of Milorganite include a low nitrogen content, a short nitrogen residual, a relatively high cost per pound of nitrogen, and a poor winter response. The limited availability of the product might also be considered a disadvantage.

Turf response to Milorganite in terms of growth rate and color are excellent during the spring, summer, and fall. Additionally, turf researchers have reported lower disease and insect activity and less thatch accumulation where Milorganite was used in place of soluble nitrogen sources.

COMBINATIONS OF NITROGEN SOURCES FOR TURFGRASS. In low-maintenance areas a single source of nitrogen may meet the needs of the turf. But where demands are greater as for lawns, golf courses and athletic fields, combinations of nitrogen sources provide the most uniform level of nitrogen to the turf.

The objectives of the fertilization program have a significant influence on the source of nitrogen needed. The objective of fertilization is to simply maintain a grass cover, a single application of a slow-release fertilizer, or perhaps, two applications of a soluble fertilizer which will meet the requirement of the grass. But, when a continuous supply of nitrogen is needed to maintain growth, to recover from wear, or to maintain good color, a combination of nitrogen sources will best meet the needs.

For lawns, fairways, athletic fields, and other intensively maintained turf areas mowed at a ½-inch height or greater, SCU, UF, or IBDU can provide the residual nitrogen, while soluble sources can be used to produce rapid green-up. For closely mowed turf areas such as golf greens, tennis courts, and bowling greens, UF and IBDU should be used for residual nitrogen, and Milorganite or similar organic sources should be used for rapid green-up. In cold temperatures IBDU or soluble sources must be used to produce a fast greening response.

Other factors that must be considered include the acidifying potential of SCU or ammonium sulfate, the salinity hazard of ammonium nitrate and ammonium sulfate, and the cost of the slow-release and organic nitrogen sources.

On a cost-per-pound-of-nitrogen basis relative to urea, SCU is about 2 times greater, UF and IBDU are 3 to 4 times greater, and organic sources are

5 to 6 times greater than urea. Thus, for larger turf areas where soluble sources can be safely used, they may be the logical choice for nitrogen fertilization. The most important factors when using soluble sources include the rate and timing of applications. Single applications should not exceed 1 pound of nitrogen per 1,000 square feet and should not be made prior to or during a period of rapid growth.

RESPONSE OF TURF TO NITROGEN

Turfgrass response to nitrogen fertilizers is generally measured in terms of yield (dry matter production), color, or turf density. These are the responses that are most readily measured or observed. Other more difficult to measure responses to nitrogen such as water use, disease resistance, thatch accumulation, root growth, and cold tolerance may be more important to the turf manager. The rate and timing of nitrogen applications, nitrogen source, environmental conditions, and turf management practices determine the response of these grasses to nitrogen.

GROWTH RATE, COLOR AND DENSITY. Bermudagrass readily responds to nitrogen in terms of growth, color, and density. Yellow leaves, thin turf, and little growth characterizes nitrogen deficient bermudagrass. When temperature and moisture are not limiting and grass clippings are removed, bermudagrass produces a yield response to nitrogen at rates as high as 20 pounds per 1,000 square feet and a color and density response up to 12 pounds per 1,000 square feet.

In contrast, a Saint Augustine grass lawn where clippings are not removed is much less responsive to nitrogen. Saint Augustine shows a yield response up to about 8 pounds of nitrogen per 1,000 square feet and a color and density response up to only 4 pounds of nitrogen.

How does that kind of information help? To begin with, it provides a range of nitrogen rates to consider. For example, if you are maintaining a Saint Augustine grass turf, you can expect a response to between 4 and 8 pounds of nitrogen per year; you would not expect significant improvement in color or density in Saint Augustine grass to rates above 4 pounds of nitrogen if clippings are not removed. The only apparent response to higher rates of nitrogen would be increased growth (dry matter production). There are other undesirable responses to excessive rates of nitrogen, such as greater water use, increased disease susceptibility, and thatch accumulation. Excessive rates of nitrogen (rates above those that produce a color response) significantly increase water use by turfgrass. A Saint Augustine grass turf fertilized with 8 pounds of nitrogen per 1,000 square feet per year would require about 30 percent more water than one fertilized with only 4 pounds of nitrogen. Also, heavily fertilized turfgrasses are always the first to wilt during periods of drought stress.

Leaf spot, brownpatch, dollar spot, and other warm-season diseases of turfgrasses are also increased by improper nitrogen fertilization. Gray leaf spot and brownpatch on Saint Augustine grass, for example, can be a serious problem following excessive applications of nitrogen fertilizers. In contrast, *Helminthosporium* leaf spot and dollar spot can be severe on warm-season turfgrasses maintained at very low nitrogen levels. In some cases, the application of soluble nitrogen fertilizer will correct the problem. In general, turfgrasses fertilized with adequate, but not excessive, rates of nitrogen are more resistant to diseases.

Bermudagrass and Saint Augustine grass continue to produce a growth response to nitrogen at rates above those that produce maximum color response. Tifgreen bermudagrass, for example, produces a growth response up to about 3 pounds of nitrogen per month. Of course, thatch accumulation is a concern where growth rate becomes excessive. To demonstrate this concern, we measured thatch accumulation in a Tifgreen bermudagrass putting green six months after beginning monthly applications of soluble nitrogen at 1 and 3 pounds per 1,000 square feet (table 6-4).

As expected, the color of the grass was significantly darker at the higher rate of nitrogen. Thatch accumulation, as measured by depth, was also 30 percent greater at the higher rate of nitrogen. The greater level of thatch was evidenced by the degree of scalping on the higher nitrogen plots. Certainly, 3 pounds nitrogen per 1,000 square feet per month is excessive on a bermudagrass green, and 1 pound is probably minimal. Thus, ½ pound of nitrogen at 7- to 10-day intervals should produce satisfactory color and growth without contributing to thatch accumulation.

Table 6-4. Color Response of Saint Augustine and Bermudagrass to Nitrogen

Nitrogen (lbs. per 1,000 sq. ft. per month)	COLOR RATINGS*													
	June			July				August				September		
	14	21	28	9	16	23	30	6	13	20	27	10	24	Avg.
Saint Augustine grass														
0	3.3	5.2	5.3	6.0	5.0	5.0	6.0	5.3	6.0	6.0	6.0	6.1	6.3	5.5
1	6.0	5.8	6.5	6.3	6.5	6.3	7.0	6.3	6.0	6.5	6.5	6.8	7.3	6.5
2	7.0	5.5	6.5	5.8	6.0	6.0	5.8	6.3	6.5	7.0	7.0	7.8	6.8	6.5
Tifgreen burmudagrass														
0	5.0	4.8	5.3	5.3	5.3	6.0	6.3	5.5	5.3	5.3	4.8	5.0	3.3	5.5
1	6.5	7.5	6.5	6.5	5.8	7.0	7.0	6.3	6.0	7.5	7.3	7.0	7.0	6.5
2	7.8	8.0	8.8	7.0	7.0	8.3	8.3	8.3	8.0	8.5	8.3	7.5	8.0	8.0

*Ratings made on a scale of 1 to 9, with 1 being extremely chlorotic and 9 being dark green.

In addition to annual rates of application of nitrogen, the rate per application and the source of nitrogen influence the response produced. As a general rule, do not apply more than 1 pound of soluble nitrogen per application. Again, the only apparent response for higher rates would be more growth. Since Saint Augustine grass requires ½ pound of nitrogen per month during the growing season to maintain optimum color and density, 1 pound of nitrogen should last for 2 months. Therefore, at least 50 percent of the nitrogen should be from a slow release source, or only ½ pound of soluble nitrogen should be applied every month on Saint Augustine grass lawns.

Bermudagrass, particularly hybrid bermudagrass such as Tifgreen, requires about 1 pound of nitrogen every 2 weeks to maintain optimum color and density. Again, no more than 1 pound of soluble nitrogen should be applied per application.

To support these recommendations, I applied soluble nitrogen at 1 and 2 pounds per month to a Saint Augustine lawn and a Tifgreen bermudagrass putting green from May through September. Color ratings made in June, July, August, and September show that Saint Augustine grass does not respond to more than 1 pound of soluble nitrogen per month. In contrast, Tifgreen bermudagrass continued to show a color response up to 2 pounds of soluble nitrogen per month. Thus, ½ pound of soluble nitrogen every week should produce maximum color and density on Tifgreen bermudagrass. Certainly, only the most intensive culture of bermudagrass, such as that used on golf greens, would require that level of nitrogen.

NITROGEN SUPPRESSES ROOTS. Deterioration of roots is another undesirable response to excessive rates of nitrogen (Oswalt, Bertrand, and Teel 1959). At high rates of nitrogen, root diameter generally increases, but root number and root elongation decrease. The net result is a decrease in root weight. Thus, the shoot-(leaves and stems)-to-root ratio increases significantly with nitrogen fertilization. Tifgreen bermudagrass demonstrates this response quite well. In greenhouse investigations significant reductions in roots were observed in Tifgreen bermudagrass grown in sand and in hydroponic culture at high rates of nitrogen. Tifgreen bermudagrass growing in a low-nitrogen medium produced twice as much root growth as that growing in a high-nitrogen medium. Similar responses to nitrogen by other grasses are reported in the literature.

Considering the increased leaf production and shoot growth at high rates of nitrogen, the shoot-to-root ratio gets way out of balance at high rates of nitrogen. Ideally, we would like to see a shoot-to-root ratio of about 1.5 to 2 on regularly mowed turf. At high rates of nitrogen the ratio would likely be above 3, but at very low levels of nitrogen the ratio would be about 1.

Turf responses to high rates of nitrogen such as rapid wilting under drought stress and increased winterkill support the evidence that high nitrogen suppresses root growth. In cool-season grasses, the deleterious effects of high nitrogen rates on root systems are much better documented.

COLD TOLERANCE. Lush, rapid growth that generally follows the application of soluble nitrogen fertilizers usually causes a decrease in cold tolerance in grasses. Again, much of the work on cold tolerance has been conducted on cool-season grasses. Kentucky bluegrass and bentgrass withstand cold temperatures better at low levels of nitrogen fertilizers.

Work conducted at North Carolina showed that Tifgreen and Tifdwarf bermudagrasses fertilized in the fall with nitrogen only were less resistant to low temperatures than those fertilized with a complete fertilizer (Gilbert and Davis 1971). In their study the fertilizer that produced the greatest cold tolerance was a 4-1-6 ratio fertilizer. Researchers in Texas have demonstrated similar responses to nitrogen (Reeves, McBee, and Bloodworth 1970). Tifgreen bermudagrass receiving high nitrogen and potassium demonstrated the greatest resistance to cold temperatures. In their study high nitrogen levels in the grass did not show much effect on cold tolerance, but high nitrogen levels were associated with high potassium levels which did increase cold tolerance. It was apparent from their work that nitrogen was required to increase potassium uptake by the grass.

In the Texas study high levels of phosphorus in the plant had a detrimental effect on cold tolerance. However, when potassium was applied, it appeared to counteract the detrimental effect of phosphorus.

Saint Augustine grass does not show the same cold-tolerance response to nitrogen fertilization as bermudagrass. Work in Texas has shown no significant difference in cold tolerance between fertilizer treatments (Reeves and McBee 1972). Saint Augustine grass is much less cold tolerant than bermudagrass, and it seems to suffer significant winterkill when temperatures drop below 10° F regardless of nitrogen fertilization. The only apparent nitrogen response with respect to cold tolerance was that Saint Augustine which was fertilized with nitrogen recovered faster in the spring from winter injury.

GRASS ESTABLISHMENT. During establishment from seed, sprigs, or plugs, both bermudagrass and Saint Augustine show a tremendous response to nitrogen fertilization. On a sandy soil the rate of cover of bermudagrass is greatest with weekly applications of soluble nitrogen at ½ pound per 1,000 square feet. On clay or clay loam soils, applications of soluble nitrogen at 1 pound per 1,000 square feet every 2 weeks will produce the fastest rate of cover. Unfertilized bermudagrass seed or sprigs are very slow to spread on most soils.

Saint Augustine grass plugs planted on 2-foot spacings will cover in about 10 weeks if fertilized monthly with 1 pound of soluble nitrogen per 1,000 square feet. Higher rates of nitrogen do not produce significantly faster cover with Saint Augustine. Unfertilized Saint Augustine planted the same way would only produce 30 to 40 percent coverage after 10 weeks.

In addition to nitrogen, phosphorus is also important in promoting grass establishment. In the Texas study Saint Augustine grass plugs fertilized monthly with a 2-to-1 phosphorus-to-nitrogen ratio fertilizer at 1 pound nitrogen per 1,000 square feet produced the fastest rate of cover of all fertilizer treatments; but a one-to-one ratio of phosphorus-to-nitrogen fertilizer produced about the same response as a straight nitrogen fertilizer.

PHOSPHORUS

Grasses take up phosphorus primarily in the orthophosphate ($H_2PO_4^-$) form. Although soils may contain relatively large amounts of phosphorus, much of it is in forms not available to grasses. Some phosphorus is provided by soil minerals and soil organic matter, but it is very slowly available from these sources:

$$Ca_3(PO_4)_2 \quad + \quad 4H^+ \quad \rightarrow \quad Ca(H_2PO_4)_2 \quad + \quad 2Ca^{++}$$
(rock phosphate) + (acid) (superphosphate)

Other phosphorus sources include superphosphate and polyphosphate fertilizers:

$$Ca(H_2PO_4)_2 \quad + water \quad \rightarrow \quad 2(H_2PO_4^-) \quad + CA^{++}$$
(superphosphate) (orthophosphate)

$$(H_2PO_4^-)n \quad + \quad water \quad \rightarrow \quad H_2PO_4^-$$
(polyphosphate) (orthophosphate)

Fertilizer applications provide the major source of phosphorus for turfgrasses. Since phosphorus moves very little through the soil, it usually accumulates in the surface layer of soil. Thus, cultivation with a coring type aerator prior to applications of phosphorus helps to move the phosphorus into the root zone.

Phosphorus is provided by soil minerals, organic matter, fertilizers, and exists in only small amounts present in the soil. Phosphorus is readily fixed by Ca, Fe, Al, and microorganisms and is very slowly available.

Phosphorus availability is also influenced by soil pH. At a pH below 5.5 iron and aluminum become soluble and form a complex with phosphorus that is not available to the grass. At a pH above 7.5 calcium complexes with phosphorus so that it is not available. Phosphorus is most available between pH 6.0 and 7.0.

$$Ca(H_2PO_4)_2 \quad + \quad free\ CaCO_3 \quad \rightarrow \quad CaHPO_4\ or\ Ca_3(PO_4)_2$$
(superphosate) (alkaline soil) (insoluble)

Maintaining a sufficient supply of phosphorus in the soil requires more than the application of fertilizer. Adequate cultivation and the addition of lime or sulfur to adjust pH may be just as important.

Phosphorus availability is influenced by pH; soluble Fe, Al (low soil pH), soluble Ca (high soil pH); the amount of organic matter; and the activity of microorganisms.

POTASSIUM

Potassium is often present in large quantities in soils, but very small amounts may be in the available form (K^+). Potassium is a constituent of many soil minerals and is held very strongly by clay particles. For potassium to be taken up by the grass, it must be in the solution in the potassium ion (K^+) form. An equilibrium exists between the K^+ in solution and that held by clay particles (see illustration). As the grass root takes up the K^+ from the soil solution, additional K^+ is released from the soil solution to the clay particles. Clay particles, thus, serve as a reservoir for K^+ and help to reduce the amount of K^+ lost by leaching.

Soil microorganisms also require considerable amounts of potassium, and they compete with grass for the available potassium. Removal of grass clippings also severely depletes the soil of potassium since the grass contains higher amounts of potassium than any other fertilizer nutrient except nitrogen. Where high levels of potassium are available the grass will absorb much more than it requires for growth. High potassium levels in plant tissue are associated with improved cold tolerance, drought tolerance, wear tolerance, and disease resistance.

Potassium is often present in large amounts in soil minerals and organic matter. Potassium loss from soils occurs by its removal by plants, its tendency to be readily leached from sandy soils, and microorganisms utilizing K^+.

To maintain adequate levels of K^+ in the soil, apply light, frequent applications of potassium fertilizer, return grass clippings when possible, and avoid overwatering to reduce leaching losses.

NUTRIENT INTERACTIONS

Nutrient uptake is a function of nutrient levels and interactions between nutrients. The level of one nutrient can affect the uptake of another nutrient. For example, a high concentration of NH^+ can reduce the uptake of K^+ by the grass. Also where NO_3^- levels are deficient, K^+ uptake will be restricted even though high levels of K^+ may be present. These interactions between nitrogen and potassium can have a significant influence on the growth of turfgrasses.

In turfgrasses interactions between phosphorus and iron are quite common. Where phosphorus levels are excessive, iron which would be available to the grass becomes insoluble and unavailable. This problem can be prevented by monitoring soil levels of available phosphorus and avoiding excessive phosphorus fertilization.

Traces of nutrients or micronutrients, including iron (Fe), manganese (Mn), zinc (Zn), copper (Cu), boron (Bo), molybdenum (Mo), chlorine (Cl), and sodium (Na) are present in soils minerals, organic matter, and fertilizers.

Iron deficiency may also occur because of excessive levels of zinc,

Nutrient Uptake

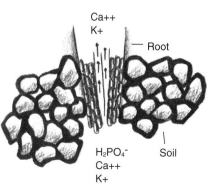

manganese, or copper. In sandy soils these interactions among nutrients can present a problem. In highly buffered clay soils these interactions are less likely to present a problem.

Conditions that are conducive to micronutrient deficiencies are sandy soils, high soil pH, and clipping removal.

ENVIRONMENTAL CONDITIONS. Environmental conditions, including aeration, temperature, light, moisture, and soil pH, have a significant effect on turf response to fertilization. When soils are poorly aerated due to compaction or overwatering, biological activity required to convert nitrogen to an available form is inhibited. Thus, nitrogen efficiency is greatly reduced and the expected response may not occur. When soils are compacted or waterlogged, aeration should be a routine cultural practice in conjunction with fertilization. Soil amendments such as organic matter, calcined clay aggregates, sand, and gypsum should be considered for topdressing mixtures.

Temperature and light also influence fertilizer response, but there is little that turf managers can do to alter these factors. Fertilizer applications should be timed to coincide with favorable temperatures for growth of turfgrasses. Also, nitrogen sources should be selected based on their availability to grasses under expected temperature conditions. Organic nitrogen sources and urea-formaldehyde do not release nitrogen at sufficient rates for turf growth when soil temperatures are below 50° F. Conversely, at high soil temperatures, these sources release nitrogen very rapidly.

Soil moisture is required for the grass to use fertilizer nutrients effectively. All biological activity requires adequate soil moisture for the conversion of nutrients to an available form. Also, the utilization of fertilizer nutrients requires adequate soil moisture for root growth and nutrient uptake. Where grass is grown under dry conditions, fertilizer application rates should be much less than where water is not limiting.

Some nitrogen fertilizers such as IBDU require moisture for the release of nitrogen. Since most turfgrasses are irrigated, this characteristic of IBDU could be considered ideal. However, soil pH also affects the release of nitrogen from IBDU. At a pH of 7.5 or greater the effectiveness of IBDU is significantly reduced. Soil pH also influences the availability of phosphorus, iron, and most other micronutrients.

Soil pH can be increased by liming acid soils, or decreased by adding elemental sulfur to alkaline soils:

$$CaCO_3 \;+\; H^+ \;\rightarrow\; H_2O \;+\; CO_2 \;+\; Ca^{++}$$
(lime) (acid soils)   (neutralizing)

$$Elemental\ S \;+\; H_2O \;+\; alkaline\ soil \;\rightarrow\; SO_4^- + 2H^+$$
                                        (acidifying)

Adjusting soil pH to near neutral conditions (pH 6.5–7.2) increases the availability of phosphorus, iron, and other nutrients. In some soils such an adjustment is practical, but in many calcareous soils there is too much lime-stone present to significantly lower soil pH.

All of these factors (aeration, temperature, moisture, pH, etc.) must be considered when planning a turf fertilization program. Applying a fertilizer without consideration of its effect on the level of nutrients present, the availability of nutrients, or the interactions with environmental factors can only increase turf nutrition problems. To meet the nutritional requirements of a turf, factors other than fertilization must be considered.

Factors that affect nutrient availability include (1) oxidation, the reduction state of the nutrient; (2) concentration of the nutrient; (3) water content of soil; (4) oxygen; (5) temperature; and (6) pH. Refer to tables 6-5 through 6-12, the fertilizer requirements example, and list of nutrient sources.

Table 6-5. Fertilization Requirements and Soil Test Levels

	PPM				
	Very High	*High*	*Medium*	*Low*	*Very Low*
Nitrogen (NO$_3$)		**> 10**	5–10	< 5	
Phosphorus (P)	> 40	**21–40**	11–20	5–10	< 5
Potassium (K)	> 300	173–300	**121–175**	70–120	< 70
Calcium (Ca)	> 3560	751–3560	**461–750**	180–460	< 180
Magnesium (Mg)		> 100	**50–100**	< 50	
Sulfur (S)		> 25	**8–25**	< 8	
Zinc (Zn)		> 0.8	**0.3–0.8**	< 0.3	
Iron (Fe)		> 4.2	**3.2–4.2**	< 3.2	
Manganese (Mn)		> 1.5	**1–1.5**	< 1.0	

Boldface indicates levels needed for most turfgrasses.

Table 6-6. Soil Test Levels

	LBS./1,000 SQ. FT.				
	Very High	*High*	*Medium*	*Low*	*Very Low*
Nitrogen (NO$_3$)		**> .5**	.25–.5	< .25	
Phosphorus (P)	> 2.2	**1.0–2.2**	.5–1.0	.25–.5	< .25
Potassium (K)	> 14	8–14	**5.5–8.0**	3.2–5.5	< 3.2
Calcium (Ca)	> 164	34–164	21–34	8.3–2.1	< 8.3
Magnesium (Mg)		> 4.6	**2.3–4.6**	< 2.3	
Sulfur (S)		> 1.1	**0.4–1.1**	< 0.4	
Zinc (Zn)		> 0.02	**0.007–.02**	< 0.007	
Iron (Fe)		> 0.1	**.07–0.1**	< 0.07	
Manganese (Mn)		> 0.35	**0.02–0.035**	< 0.02	

Boldface indicates levels needed for most turfgrasses.

Table 6-7. Conversion Table for Soil Nutrients

ppm nutrients in the top 6 inches of soil x 2 = lbs. nutrient per acre ÷ 43.5 = lbs. per 1,000 sq. ft.

ppm (top 6 ins. of soil)	Lbs. per Acre	Lbs. per 1,000 sq. ft.
5	10	.25
10	20	.5
30	60	1.4
50	100	2.3
100	200	4.6
200	400	9.2
300	600	13.8
400	800	18.4
500	1000	23.0

Table 6-8. Nutrients Removed by Clippings per Month (lbs./1,000 sq. ft.) in Bermudagrass—Lawns, Golf Courses, Sports Fields

	J	F	M	A	M	J	J	A	S	O	N	D	Total
Nitrogen (N)			.25	1.0	1.5	2.0	2.0	2.0	1.5	1.0	.25		12.0
Phosphorus (P)			.05	.2	.3	.4	.4	.4	.3	.2	.05		2.3
Potassium (K)			.2	.8	1.0	1.5	1.5	1.5	1.0	.8	.2		8.5
Calcium (Ca)			.1	.4	.6	.8	.8	.8	.6	.4	.1		4.6
Magnesium (Mg)			.05	.2	.3	.4	.4	.4	.3	.2	.05		2.3
Sulfur (S)			.03	.1	.2	.25	.25	.25	.2	.1	.03		1.4
Zinc (Zn)		x 10⁻³	.25	1.0	1.5	2.0	2.0	2.0	1.5	1.0	.25		.012
Iron (Fe)		x 10⁻³	1.0	4.0	6.0	8.0	8.0	8.0	6.0	4.0	1.0		.046
Manganese (Mn)		x 10⁻³	.25	1.0	1.5	2.0	2.0	2.0	1.5	1.0	.25		.012

Table 6-9. Nutrients Removed by Clippings per Month (lbs./1,000 sq. ft.) in Saint Augustine Grass, Zoysia—Lawns, Golf Courses, Sports Fields

	J	F	M	A	M	J	J	A	S	O	N	D	Total
Nitrogen (N)			.25	.75	1.0	1.0	1.0	1.0	1.0	.75	.25		7.0
Phosphorus (P)			.05	.15	.2	.2	.25	.25	.2	.15	.05		1.5
Potassium (K)			.15	.5	.7	.8	.8	.7	.7	.5	.15		5.0
Calcium (Ca)			.2	.3	.4	.5	.5	.5	.4	.3	.2		3.3
Magnesium (Mg)			.05	.15	.2	.25	.25	.25	.2	.15	.05		1.5
Sulfur (S)			.05	.1	.15	.15	.15	.15	.1	.1	.05		1.0
Zinc (Zn)		x 10⁻³	.25	.75	1.0	1.0	1.0	1.0	1.0	.75	.25		.007
Iron (Fe)		x 10⁻³	1.0	2.0	3.0	4.0	4.0	3.0	3.0	2.0	1.0		.023
Manganese (Mn)		x 10⁻³	.25	.75	1.0	1.0	1.0	1.0	1.0	.75	.25		.007

Table 6-10. Nutrients Removed by Clippings per Month (lbs./1,000 sq. ft.) in Centipedegrass, Buffalograss, Bahiagrass—Lawns, Golf Courses, Sports Fields

	J	F	M	A	M	J	J	A	S	O	N	D	Total
Nitrogen (N)			.2	.4	.6	.8	.8	.8	.4	.4	.22		4.6
Phosphorus (P)			.05	.1	.15	.2	.2	.15	.15	.1	.05		1.1
Potassium (K)			.1	.25	.4	.5	.5	.4	.4	.25	.1		2.9
Calcium (Ca)			.1	.2	.3	.4	.4	.3	.3	.2	.1		2.5
Magnesium (Mg)			.05	.1	.15	.2	.2	.15	.15	.1	.05		1.1
Sulfur (S)			.03	.05	.4	.1	.1	.05	.05	.05	.03		.6
Zinc (Zn)		x 10^{-3}	.25	.5	.75	1.0	1.0	.75	.75	.5	.25		.006
Iron (Fe)		x 10^{-3}	1.0	2.0	3.0	4.0	4.0	3.0	3.0	2.0	1.0		.013
Manganese (Mn)		x 10^{-3}	.25	.5	.75	1.0	1.0	.75	.75	.5	.25		.006

Table 6-11. Nutrients Removed by Clippings per Month (lbs./1,000 sq. ft.) in Tall Fescue, Bluegrass—Lawns, Golf Courses, Sports Fields

	J	F	M	A	M	J	J	A	S	O	N	D	Total
Nitrogen (N)	.2	.3	.9	1.2	.9	.6	.2	.2	.3	.6	.9	.4	6.7
Phosphorus (P)	.05	.07	.2	.3	.2	.15	.05	.05	.07	.15	.2	.1	1.6
Potassium (K)	.1	.2	.6	1.0	.6	.5	.2	.2	.2	.5	.6	.3	5.0
Calcium (Ca)	.06	.1	.3	.4	.3	.2	.06	.06	.1	.2	.3	.14	2.2
Magnesium (Mg)	.03	.05	.15	.2	.15	.1	.03	.03	.05	.1	.15	.07	1.1
Sulfur (S)	.02	.03	.09	.12	.09	.06	.02	.02	.03	.06	.09	.04	.07
Zinc (Zn)	.15	.25	.75	1.0	.75	.5	.15	.15	.25	.5	.75	.35	.006
Iron (Fe)	2.4	4.0	12.	16.	12.	8.	2.4	2.4	4.0	8.0	12.	5.6	.09
Manganese (Mn)	.15	.25	.75	1.0	.75	.5	.15	.15	.25	.5	.75	.35	.006

Table 6-12. Fertilizer Calculations

Nutrient	Pounds Nutrient Needed per 1,000 sq. ft. A	Percent Nutrient in Fertilizer B	Pounds Fertilizer Needed per 1,000 sq. ft. C (C = A/B x 100)	Pounds Fertilizer Needed for the Property D (D = C x No. of 1,000 sq. ft.)
Nitrogen (N)				
Phosphorus (P)				
Potassium (K)				
Sulfur (S)				
Magnesium (Mg)				

Fertilizer Requirements Example

Bermudagrass Sports Field

Fertilizer Recommendation:
   6.0 lbs. N per 1,000 sq. ft per year
   1.5 lbs. P per 1,000 sq. ft per year
   4.0 lbs. K per 1,000 sq. ft per year

Fertilizer Sources:
   Sulfur coated urea (32-0-0)
   Ammonium sulfate (21-0-0)
   Complete fertilizer (15-5-10)

Amounts needed:
Since the 15-5-10 fertilizer is the only source of P and K on hand, the 1.5 pounds of P and 4.0 pounds of K recommended must be provided by that source. Since P and K are in a 1-to-2 ratio in the 15-5-10 fertilizer, 2 pounds of P must be applied to provide 4 pounds of K.

$$\frac{\text{lbs. K needed}}{\text{\% K in fertilizer}} \times 100 = \text{lbs. fertilizer needed}$$

The 15-5-10 fertilizer contains the following nutrients: 15% N, 5% P, 10% K.

Thus, to get 4 lbs. of K we need

$$\frac{4}{10 \ (\text{\% K in fertilizer})} \times 100 = 40 \text{ lbs. of 15-5-10 fertilizer}$$

In addition to 4 pounds K and 2 pounds P, 40 pounds of 15-5-10 fertilizer also provides 6 pounds of N (40 x 15/100). Therefore, additional nitrogen is not needed to meet the fertilizer recommendation. Applications of 10 pounds 15-5-10 fertilizer per 1,000 square feet in March, June, August, and October would provide 1.5, .5, and 1.0 pounds of N, P, and K per 1,000 square feet per application. Although that schedule would not exactly meet the recommendations made for a bermudagrass sports field, it would be satisfactory if at least 50 percent of the nitrogen in the 15-5-10 fertilizer was slow release.

Assume the same set of conditions where the following sources were available:

Sulfur-coated urea	(32-0-0)
Ammonium phosphate	(18-46-0)
Muriate of potash	(0-0-60)

Since the 18-46-0 is the only source of P, determine how much is needed to provide 1.5 pounds of P by the following equation:

$$\frac{\text{lbs. P needed}}{\text{\% P in fertilizer}} \times 100 = \text{lbs. fertilizer}$$

$$\frac{1.5 \text{ (lbs. P needed)}}{46 \text{ (\% P in 18-46-0)}} \times 100 = 3.3 \text{ lbs. of 18-46-0}$$

Remember, the 18-46-0 fertilizer provides 18 percent nitrogen in addition to 46 percent P. Thus, 3.3 pounds of 18-46-0 fertilizer provides 0.6 pounds (3.3 x 18/100) of nitrogen. The remaining N (6-0.6), or 5.4 pounds, must be provided by S-coated urea.

$$\frac{5.4 \text{ (lbs. N needed)}}{32 \text{ (\% N in SCU)}} \times 100 = 16.9 \text{ lbs. of SCU}$$

Muriate of potash (0-0-60) is the only source of K; therefore,

$$\frac{4 \text{ (lbs. K needed)}}{60 \text{ (\% K in potash)}} \times 100 = 6.7 \text{ lbs. potash needed}$$

These amounts (3.3 lbs. of 18-46-0, 16.9 lbs. SCU and 6.7 lbs. of potash) are needed per 1,000 square feet per year. To determine the total amount needed for the athletic fields, multiply these numbers by the number of 1,000 square feet in the football field (the typical area of a football field is about 60,000 square feet).

60 x 3.3 = 198 lbs. of 18-46-0
60 x 16.9 = 1,014 lbs. of SCU
60 x 6.7 = 402 lbs. of muriate of potash

Therefore, for a typical football field, you would purchase 200 pounds of 18-46-0, 1,000 pounds of sulfur-coated urea and 400 pounds of muriate of potash to meet the 6-1.5-4 fertilizer recommendation per 1,000 square feet.

Nutrient Sources

Nitrogen Sources

Urea	(45-0-0)
Sulfur-coated urea	(32-0-0)
IBDU	(31-0-0)
Ureaform	(38-0-0)
Ammonium sulfate	(21-0-0) plus 24% S
Ammonium nitrate	(33-0-0)
Potassium nitrate	(13-0-45)
Milorganite	(6-4-0)

Phosphorus Sources

Triple superphosphate	(0-46-0) plus 12% Ca
Diammonium phosphate	(18-46-0)
Milorganite	(6-4-0)

Potassium Sources

Muriate of potash	(0-0-60)
Potassium nitrate	(13-0-45)
Potassium sulfate	(0-0-50) plus 18% S
K-Mag	(0-0-22) plus 22% S, 11 Mg

Sulfur Sources

Gypsum	16–18% S
Ferrous sulfate	12% S (20% Fe)
Elemental sulfur	99% S
Ammonium thiosulfate	26% S (12% N)
K-Mag	22% S (22% K, 11% Mg)

Micronutrient Sources

Copper sulfate	25% Cu
Ferrous sulfate	20% Fe
Manganese sulfate	25% Mn
Zinc sulfate	35% Zn

SOIL ACIDITY

Soil acidity is determined by a pH meter that measures the hydrogen ion concentration in the soil solution. The hydrogen ion concentration is expressed in pH units with 5 being strongly acid, 6.6 being neutral, and 8.2 being strongly alkaline. Each pH unit decrease below 7 represents a tenfold increase in hydrogen concentration, or acidity (table 6-13).

Strongly acid soils reduce the effectiveness of some fertilizer nutrients, inhibit microbial activity, inhibit the decomposition of thatch, and reduce the effectiveness of some herbicides. Table 6-14 shows the reduction in nutrient recovery by turfgrasses as soil acidity increases (or soil pH decreases).

LIMING SOILS TO SORRECT SOIL ACIDITY. The amount of limestone ($CaCO_3$) needed to neutralize soil acidity is based on soil pH and soil texture. In general, the amount of limestone needed increases as soil pH decreases and as soil texture changes from sands to loams to clays. Table 6-15 can be used as a guideline to estimate the pounds of limestone needed per 1,000 square feet of turf.

Table 6-13. pH Range

5.0 or less is strongly acid.
5.0 to 5.5 is moderately acid.
5.6 to 6.5 is slightly acid.
6.6 to 7.2 is neutral.
7.2 to 8.2 is slightly alkaline.
8.2 and above is moderately to strongly alkaline.

Table 6-14. Percent Nutrient Recovery

Soil pH	Nitrogen	Phosphorus	Potassium
7.0	70	30	60
6.0	63	15	60
5.5	52	15	45
5.0	38	10	30
4.5	21	8	21

Table 6-15. Limestone Needed per 1,000 sq. ft.

Soil pH	Sands, Loamy Sands	Sandy Loam	Clay Loam, Clay
> 6.0	0	0	0
5.1–6.0	50	75	100
< 5.0	100	125	175

The benefits of liming acid soils are that it increases soil pH, fertilizer use efficiency, microbial activity, and thatch decomposition, and enhances the effectiveness of some herbicides, especially triazines such as atrazine and metribuzin.

SOIL SALINITY

Soils which have high enough levels of soluble salts to affect plant growth are classified as saline soils. Saline soils may be recognized by white crusts on high spots, stunted plants, or spotty stands of grass, but these symptoms are not always obvious. In South Texas and throughout the southwestern U.S. saline soils are a significant problem on irrigated sites. In most cases, these problems are increased by poor quality irrigation water. Generally, warm-season turfgrasses are quite tolerant to soluble salts. Bermudagrass, for example, tolerates 4,500 ppm, or more soluble salts in the soil, without apparent injury, whereas cool-season grasses such as tall fescue may be severely injured by only 2,500 ppm soluble salts (Maas 1986). Even within turfgrass species, significant differences are found in tolerance to salts (Dudeck and Peacock 1985). For example, Santa Ana bermudagrass tolerates much higher salt levels than common bermudagrass. However, plant response to soluble salts is greatly influenced by environmental conditions and management practices.

Salts affect plants both directly and indirectly. Direct effects include the accumulation of specific salts (sodium, chlorine, boron, etc.) within the plant to toxic levels and the burning of foliage by salt residues from sprinkler irrigation. These effects are most common on woody and herbaceous plants.

Indirect effects of salts on plants include desiccation, deterioration of soil physical conditions, and an imbalance of plant nutrients. Grasses are generally injured by one or more of these indirect effects (table 6-16).

The first visible symptom of salt injury is stunted appearing plants—reduced growth rate, short leaf blades, and short internodes. In grasses leaf growth decreases linearly with increasing salt levels after reaching a threshold level, but root growth usually increases at moderate salt levels, then decreases sharply as salinity increases.

HOW SALT PROBLEMS DEVELOP. Salt problems usually develop because of poor drainage, high groundwater tables, and poor quality (salty) irrigation water. Where soils are poorly drained because of an impermeable layer or impermeable topsoil, salts accumulate in the surface soil. Where high groundwater tables are present, salts move upward with the water through the finer capillary pores and accumulate as water evaporates. In clay soils salts have been known to accumulate 20 to 30 feet above a water table over a long period of time.

Most salt problems develop, however, directly from salts added by the irrigation water. This problem usually develops over a long period of time because large amounts of salt must accumulate before salts affect the growth of grasses. The amounts of salt added to a soil by irrigation waters over a period of years when 36 inches of water are applied per acre per year are shown in table 6-17 (Longenecker and Lyerly 1974).

Water containing 735 ppm soluble salts is considered good quality irrigation water, yet in several years enough salt would be added to affect most

Table 6-16. Soil Salinity

SCALE OF CONDUCTIVITY*		
mmhos/cm	*ppm Soluble Salts*	*Grass Response*
0	0	Salinity negligible
2	1,300	Sensitive plants may be affected.
4	2,600	Sensitive grasses affected (cool-season grasses)
8	5,200	Only salt-tolerant grasses thrive (bermudagass, meyer zoysia)
16	10,400	Only very salt tolerant grasses thrive (seashore paspalum, alkali saccaton)

*Electrical conductivity of saturated soil paste

Table 6-17. Amount of Salt Added to Soil by Irrigation Water

ppm Salt in Irrigation Water	TONS OF SALT ADDED PER ACRE* (BY YEARS)					
	1	2	3	4	5	6
368	1.5	3	4.5	6	7.5	9
735	3	6	9	12	15	18
1470	6	12	18	24	30	36
2940	12	24	36	48	60	72
4410	18	36	54	72	90	108

*Assumes that 36 in. of water applied per year

plants. Thus, salts must be removed by leaching before they accumulate and become a problem.

MANAGEMENT OF SALINE SOILS. Proper irrigation management (occasional leaching) and adequate drainage are essential to prevent salinity problems. The only way to remove salts from the soil is by leaching them below the root zone.

In areas with adequate rainfall, leaching may not be required. But in arid climates periodic leaching by applying excessive irrigation water is necessary to prevent salinity problems. Where restrictive soil layers prevent the downward movement of water, lateral tile drains installed directly above this layer are needed.

To leach salts below the root zone, extra water is needed beyond that required to wet the root zone. The amount of the extra water needed to leach salts increases with turfgrass sensitivity and with the salt content of the water. The percentage extra water can be approximated from table 6-18.

To effectively use the approximation of extra water needed for leaching salts, the turf manager must know the salt content of the water and the amount of water needed to wet the root zone. The latter value can be estimated from table 6-19.

For example, a tall fescue lawn growing on a sandy loam soil irrigated with water containing 2,000 ppm soluble salts would need the following amount of water to leach salts below a 6-inch deep root zone.

From table 6-19, 12 inches of a sandy loam soil would hold approximately 1.5 inches of available water following irrigation. During the summer this amount of water would be gone in 5 to 6 days. To effectively leach salts below the 12-inch root zone, 1.5 inch of water plus 23 percent of 1.5 inches, or 1.85 inches, should be applied during the next irrigation. If the lawn is irrigated every other day, 0.62 inches of water are needed (.5 inches replacement water plus 0.12 inches [23 percent] of extra water).

Such a watering practice would be wasteful of water, but there are no other means of removing salts from the root zone during periods of limited rainfall.

Where restrictive layers develop in the root zone, cultivation or aeration

Table 6-18. Percent Extra Water Necessary for Leaching

Salt Content of Irrigation Water (ppm soluble salts)	PERCENT EXTRA WATER NECESSARY FOR LEACHING	
	Ryegrass, Bluegrass, Tall Fescue, Centipede, Buffalograss, Bahia	*Bermudagrass, Saint Augustine, Zoysia*
735	10%	5%
2200	25%	10%
3675	35%	20%

Table 6-19. Salt Content and Amount of Water Needed to Wet Root Zone

Soil Texture	Available Water Per Foot of Soil (in inches)
Sands	0.8–1.1
Sandy Loam	1.2–1.7
Silt Loam and Loam	1.7–1.9
Clay Loam	1.9–2.3
Clay	2.1–2.7

may be required before attempting to leach salts through the soil. Deep-tine aeration is an effective way to improve water movement through a layer in the top 10 to 12 inches of the root zone. Such a procedure may need to be repeated several times each year to prevent salt problems.

When sodium constitutes a significant amount of the salts found in soil or in the irrigation water, additions of gypsum or sulfur may be necessary. The calcium in gypsum, or in the gypsum produced by the addition of sulfur, replaces the sodium on the soil particles and allows water to move the sodium below the root zone. Soil tests will indicate the need for amendments such as gypsum and sulfur.

Fall Fertilization

After being concerned with grass clippings all summer, many turfgrass managers are simply too busy to think about fertilizing turf in the fall, and most are probably ready for the grass to go dormant. Traditionally, fall application of nitrogen was avoided to induce hardening of the grass and, thereby, increase its cold hardiness. Hardening of the grass was reported to be favored by reduced growth which, in turn, was favored by low nitrogen. But turf research has given us a reason to consider late fall fertilization of lawns, golf courses, and athletic fields.

COLD HARDINESS

Contrary to earlier beliefs high nitrogen and potassium content in the foliage may actually increase the cold hardiness of turfgrasses (Gilbert and Davis 1971; Reeves, McBee, and Bloodworth 1970). Apparently, it is not the nutrient content that affects cold hardiness. Rather, it is the succulent shoot growth produced by early fall fertilization and the ratio among nitrogen, phosphorus, and potassium that affects cold hardiness. When the ratio of potassium to phosphorus is high, low temperature kill is reduced regardless of the nitrogen content of the tissue (Reeves, McBee, and Bloodworth 1970).

Nitrogen levels in grass tissue show little effect on winterkill but have a great influence on the uptake of potassium. Thus, a fertilizer high in nitrogen and potassium and low in phosphorus should be used for late fall fertilization of turfgrass. If soil tests indicate high levels of phosphorus, only nitrogen and potassium need to be applied.

ENHANCED COLOR AND GREATER TURF DENSITY
Late fall applications of nitrogen prolong color retention and extend the usefulness of the turf (Wilkinson and Duff 1972). Throughout the South where golf courses and athletic fields are used year-round, a green foliage presents a more attractive and resilient surface than a semidormant turf. Although turfgrasses (warm-season or cool-season grasses) may not produce abundant growth during the late fall or early winter, turf density and recuperative capacity are greater where the grass has been fertilized in the late fall. Thus, late fall fertilization enhances wear tolerance. Also, turfgrasses are more competitive with weeds when fertilized in the fall. Even cool-season turfgrasses retain color and density throughout the winter in southern latitudes as a result of late fall fertilization.

ROOT GROWTH AND CARBOHYDRATE STORAGE
Environmental conditions in late fall (cool temperatures, short days, and high light intensity) favor root growth and carbohydrate accumulation. Fall nitrogen fertilization was not recommended because it was thought to increase growth and deplete the plants' carbohydrate (energy) reserves, thus, increasing the danger of winterkill. Research has shown, however, that due to favorable environmental conditions in the late fall, fertilization actually increases root growth and carbohydrate accumulation (Powell et al. 1967b). However, excessive nitrogen rates may have the opposite effect.

The importance of iron in late fall should not be overlooked. Foliar applications of iron enhance turf color and increase both root growth and carbohydrate reserves. Where iron deficiencies commonly exist, foliar applications of iron are essential.

SPRING RECOVERY
Late fall applications of nitrogen increase spring clipping yields and improve turf quality. Grass fertilized in the late fall also resumes growth earlier in the

spring than grass not receiving a late application of fertilizer. In addition, the timing of spring fertilization is not as critical when a late fall application of fertilizer was made.

OTHER CONSIDERATIONS

Nitrogen must be available to the grass in late fall in order to obtain the benefits of iron and potassium. Nitrogen sources that are dependent on microbial activity for nitrogen release are not as effective for fall fertilization as the more soluble sources. Thus, soluble sources such as ammonium sulfate and slow-release sources that are not dependent on temperature should be used for late fall fertilization. Rates of fertilization should not exceed 1 pound of nitrogen per 1,000 square feet per application for soluble sources and 1 ½ pounds for slow-release sources. When the color and density of permanent grasses are maintained throughout the winter, applications of soluble nitrogen at a rate of ½ pound per 1,000 square feet should be repeated at monthly intervals.

Grasses are not the only plants that benefit from late fall fertilization. Although trees and shrubs appear dormant, plant roots absorb nutrients very readily in the fall and winter. Also, tree leaves retain their color and remain on the plant longer when late fall applications of fertilizer are made. Spring growth of trees that receive late fall applications of fertilizer is superior to that of plants not fertilized in late fall. Tree height and trunk diameter also respond to fall applications of fertilizer.

Despite appearance to the contrary, there may be some negative effects of late fall fertilization. Some turfgrass diseases are favored by late fall fertilization. *Typhula* snow mold, *Fusarium*, and *Rhizoctonia* brownpatch activities may be increased by early fall applications of nitrogen. However, knowing this, managers can apply fungicides to prevent injury of turf. Also, potassium levels may be increased in the plant tissue to help reduce the incidence of diseases.

Excessive rates of nitrogen applied in early or late fall may produce succulent shoot growth and reduce cold hardiness in turfgrasses. Also, high levels of nitrogen and phosphorus may reduce cold hardiness. But these problems can be avoided by applying low rates of a fertilizer high in nitrogen, iron, and potassium in the late fall.

Iron Chlorosis in Turfgrass

Iron chlorosis presents a significant problem to crop production in the southwestern United States. It is most prevalent in high pH, calcareous soils. In such soils the growth and appearance of many plants, including turfgrasses, are impaired by iron deficiencies.

Iron chlorosis results when green chlorophyll in leaf tissue fails to develop. Although iron is not part of the chlorophyll molecule, it is one of the nutrients essential for chlorophyll synthesis. Iron chlorosis first develops in new growth and appears as yellowish-green leaves, usually as an interveinal yellowing, giving the leaf a striped appearance. As the condition worsens leaves appear yellow to almost white. In severe cases of iron chlorosis, loss of turfgrass and other plants occur in irregular patterns.

Iron chlorosis is attributed to reduced availability of iron in calcareous soils and may also be associated with high levels of bicarbonate and phosphate in plant tissue.

Management practices can also contribute to iron deficiencies. Well aerated soil is needed for plants to take up iron. Excessive irrigation and soil compaction result in poorly aerated soils and reduced iron uptake. High phosphorus levels resulting from excessive fertilization and high levels of bicarbonate in irrigation water also interfere with iron uptake by plants.

Environmental factors such as temperature, rainfall, and light intensity also impact iron uptake and assimilation by plants. Low soil temperatures reduce soil microbial activity which, in turn, reduces iron uptake. Wet soils, or excessively dry soils, and low light intensities also reduce iron uptake. For example, iron chlorosis is common in Saint Augustine grass under shaded conditions.

Plant genetics is a dominant factor influencing the plant's ability to take up iron. Grasses of the same species may differ considerably in their ability to take up iron. Floratam Saint Augustine grass, for example, is much less likely to show iron chlorosis than other varieties of Saint Augustine grass. Bermudagrass varieties also differ in their ability to take up iron.

CORRECTING IRON CHLOROSIS

One approach to correcting iron chlorosis has been to reduce soil alkalinity with acidifying materials such as elemental sulfur and sulfuric acid. In soils elemental sulfur is oxidized by microorganisms to form sulfuric acid. Under acid conditions iron is more soluble and, consequently, may be more available to the plant.

In turfgrasses 5 to 20 pounds of elemental sulfur per 1,000 square feet are applied to reduce soil pH and iron chlorosis. Also, sulfuric acid may be added through the irrigation system in dilute concentrations to lower soil pH. Both methods of acidification have been shown to reduce iron chlorosis in some soils. However, both methods have as an additional effect increased soluble salts. On poorly drained sites, where salts would accumulate, these methods should not be used without first correcting the drainage problem. Also, care must be taken not to over acidify the soil.

The application of products containing iron to the soil or directly to the plant is the most widely used method to correct iron chlorosis. The problem with this method is the short longevity of the effect. Typically, iron applications improve the color of turfgrasses for only 3 to 4 weeks. In soils iron is rapidly oxidized to form insoluble iron oxides. In grasses iron is immobile and is removed with the clippings. Thus, the response is of short duration.

Iron-Sul, a product of Duval Sales Corporation, has demonstrated promise as an effective means of correcting iron chlorosis. A single application of Iron-Sul at 10 pounds per 1,000 square feet to bluegrass turf significantly improved the color of the turf for 16 weeks. Similar responses have been reported on Saint Augustine and bermudagrass turf. Other products, including Ruffin and Milorganite, have been shown to temporarily correct iron chlorosis in turfgrasses.

Phosphorus fertilization can also interact with soil-applied iron to cancel the greening effect of iron. Even at relatively high rates of Iron-Sul (400 pounds per acre), no greening effect was observed where phosphorus was applied at rates greater than 1 pound per 1,000 square feet. Similar interactions between phosphorus and iron have been demonstrated on centipedegrass and other plants.

Foliar applications of iron sulfate and iron chelates provide a temporary solution to iron chlorosis. Again, the effect of a foliar application to turf usually disappears after 2 or 3 mowings since iron is not mobile in the plant. Ferrous sulfate produces a dramatic greening response on warm-season grasses at 4 to 6 ounces per 1,000 square feet and on cool-season grasses at much lower rates. Iron chelates produce similar responses when applied to the foliage at recommended rates. The addition of nitrogen (5 pounds of urea per 100 gallons) to the spray solution of iron greatly increases the level of response.

Finally, high levels of organic matter in the soil favor iron uptake, and management practices to maintain high levels of organic matter promote good iron nutrition. Likewise, maintaining good soil aeration and adjusting soil pH help promote good iron nutrition.

Leaf Analysis

Turfgrass nutrition involves more than the simple application of fertilizers. Salinity, pH, nutrient levels, temperature, grasses, and soil interact to influence nutrient uptake and fertilizer response. Turfgrass appearance and soil analysis have been widely used as a basis for the development of fertilizer recommendations. Leaf analysis has been generally overlooked as an aid to making turf fertilizer recommendations or to diagnosing turf problems. Yet, leaf analysis provides a check on the effectiveness of our fertilization program and an indication of nutrient deficiencies before visual symptoms appear. For example, high soil pH values may limit the availability of phosphorus, iron, and other nutrients, and leaf analysis would indicate low levels of these nutrients, although the grass may not show deficiency symptoms. In saline soils, calcium, magnesium, or sodium may compete with potassium and other nutrients for uptake by the grass. Thus, potassium may be present in the soil at adequate levels but may be deficient in the leaf tissue. Another reason for leaf analysis is that an imbalance of plant nutrients in the soil may interfere with nutrient uptake and create a deficiency in the plant. For example, high levels of phosphorus in the soil can create deficiencies of iron, zinc, and other nutrients in the leaf tissue of grasses. Leaf tissue analysis would bring these problems to the attention of the turf manager.

Leaf analysis is not recommended for the homeowner or the manager of a small turfgrass facility. These people do not usually have the expertise to interpret leaf analyses or to use the information to their advantage. Leaf analysis is recommended for the professional turfgrass manager, the golf course superintendent, the grounds maintenance, and athletic field manager of the professional lawn service operator. The professional turfgrass managers can use leaf analysis as a means of monitoring the effectiveness of fertilization programs and as a means of diagnosing turfgrass problems. Certainly the demand for high quality turf on these facilities together with the increasing cost of fertilizer materials and the need to conserve fertilizer resources would justify leaf analysis as a backup to soil testing.

LEAF SAMPLING AND PREPARATION
Just as with a soil test, a leaf analysis is not any better than the sample sent to the laboratory. The leaf sample must be representative of the turf whether it be from a lawn, golf green, or a football field. Hand-collected samples should not be contaminated with soil from roots or with weedy species, nor should they be collected from a single location. Samples should consist of young tissue or new growth such as would be collected from the basket of a mower. If samples are collected by hand, stainless steel clippers should be used. Only one or two days regrowth should be allowed before collecting samples for leaf analysis, as some nutrients accumulate in older leaves. For example, iron may be present in adequate levels in older (lower) leaves but deficient in new leaves. Samples should not be collected within five days of the application of fertilizers or pesticides. Likewise, several weeks may be required before sampling a turf that has been topdressed with soil or other amendments.

As soon as samples are collected they should be dried in a warm, clean location. The grass clippings should be spread on a clean piece of paper and allowed to dry for two to three days before mailing or delivering to a laboratory. If a microwave oven is available, samples can be oven-dried and mailed to the laboratory immediately.

To dry leaf clippings effectively in a microwave, operate the unit for 3 or 4 cycles at 2-minute periods. Place a cup half filled with water in the microwave to prevent combustion of the clippings, and place clippings on a plate (do not use a brown paper bag).

Each sample collected for analysis should consist of about 1 pound of fresh clippings so that about 1 ounce of dry grass clippings can be sent to the laboratory.

NITROGEN (N)

Soil analysis for nitrogen has little value for turf because grasses take up soluble N in the soil as rapidly as it becomes available. Thus, nitrogen always appears deficient from soil analyses under turf conditions. Nitrogen levels in the plant also change faster than for any other nutrient. Although leaf tissue level of nitrogen may have been adequate the day the sample was collected, it could become deficient in leaves in several days. Nitrogen levels below 2.5 percent are considered deficient in leaf clipping from turfgrasses, while N levels above 4.0 percent might be considered excessive and could lead to an imbalance of other nutrients (Menn and McBee 1970; Thomas 1994). Light green color, slow growth rate, and excessive seedhead production may all be associated with nitrogen deficiencies and are all readily visible symptoms. However, these symptoms could develop because of other problems. Pale green color and stunted growth are visual symptoms of deficiencies of iron, magnesium, and sulfur, as well of N. Thus, the application of N to a sulfur-deficient turf would not correct the observed symptoms. Leaf analysis made before the N application could have indicated a sulfur, iron, or magnesium deficiency and might have prevented an unnecessary application of N fertilizer.

Because the N level in the grass varies with fertilization, leaf age, season, drought stress, etc., a single analysis would have little value as a basis for a fertilizer recommendation. A trend established by sampling over a period of several days would have a greater value for determining N fertilizer needs.

PHOSPHORUS (P)

Symptoms of P deficiency are difficult to identify by visual inspection of the turf. Soil analysis is an excellent indication of the level of available P in the soil, but it tells us little about the rate at which P becomes available. Although the amount of available P in the soil may be low at any one time, the rate at which it becomes available may be adequate to meet plant needs. Thus, leaf analysis together with soil analysis would provide the essential information on the P status of the turf to develop a fertilization program.

Phosphorus is considered to be adequate in the plant at levels above 0.3 percent, but a response in terms of growth can be obtained at levels to 0.6 percent or higher (Thomas 1994). This response helps explain the recommendation for higher P fertilization during the establishment period. However, excessive P levels in the leaf have been shown to cause deficiencies of other nutrients, particularly iron. Apparently, excess P prevents the movements of iron from the root to the leaves. Thus, foliar applications of iron are required to overcome the effect of high P levels in the plant tissue. High P levels in the leaf tissue also change the levels of other nutrients in the leaf.

A relationship between P and K levels in the leaf tissue has also been shown to influence cold hardiness in warm-season grasses. High P to K ratios in the leaf tissue have been associated with increased winterkill in bermudagrass and Saint Augustine grass.

POTASSIUM (K)

Turfgrass requirements for K increase with increasing rates of N fertilization, heavy irrigation, and clipping removal. Deficiency symptoms for K include spindly growth (narrow leaves, thin turf), leaf tip burn, reduced wear, cold and disease tolerance, and reduced growth rate. These symptoms may develop when leaf levels of K drop below 1.5 percent. Optimum levels of K in leaf tissue of turfgrasses range from 2.0 to 2.5 percent, although little response to K fertilization in terms of color and growth rate may be observed when tissue levels are above 2.0 percent. Benefits may be realized in terms of greater wear, drought and cold tolerance and greater resistance to turfgrass diseases.

Soil test information usually provides an accurate estimate of the K status of the grass. However, environmental factors may complicate the relationship between K levels in the soil and in the grass. For example, high levels of sodium in the soil or in irrigation water may significantly reduce the uptake of K by the grass, even though K levels in the soil are high. In this case, the recommendation might be to apply gypsum to leach the excess sodium through the profile (a golf green with tile drain) and apply a foliar application of K (as technical grade potassium sulfate). Without reducing the sodium levels in the soil, additional applications of K to the soil would only increase the salt problem. In this example, the problem may not be properly diagnosed without the aid of the leaf analysis.

Low K levels may also be associated with low N fertilization. Where K levels in the soil are adequate, N fertilization increases the uptake of K by the grass.

CALCIUM (Ca)

Turfgrasses utilize Ca as a structural nutrient to cement adjacent cells and give rigidity to cell walls. The Ca level in leaf tissue varies greatly with the age of the leaf. Older leaves (lower leaves) may contain over 1.0 percent Ca, but younger leaves may obtain only 0.1 percent Ca. Calcium is an immobile nutrient (it does not move from older leaves to new leaves) and consequently, must be supplied continuously. Grasses are able to take up Ca under a wide range of soil conditions, and it is rarely deficient in grasses. Grass clippings would not be considered deficient in Ca above 0.2 percent (Thomas 1994). Under highly acid soil condition or where soils are saturated with sodium, Ca may approach this deficiency level. Ca may be supplied to the grass by granular application, so add limestone to acid soils and gypsum to alkaline soils.

MAGNESIUM (Mg)

Magnesium deficiencies in grass are found on sandy soils such as on golf greens, where high rates of N and K are applied and clippings are continuously removed. Highly acid soils may also produce turf deficient in Mg. Symptoms of Mg deficiency are similar to those of iron deficiency—pale green appearance, stunted growth. For these symptoms to become apparent the Mg content of the leaf tissue would need to be below 0.1 percent. Magnesium levels between 0.2 and 0.5 percent would be considered normal in leaf tissue (Thomas 1994).

Soil tests for Mg usually provide a good estimate of the Mg status of the grass. However, as with K, Mg levels in the grass cannot always be predicted from soil test information. Granular sources of Mg include dolomite (acid soils), Sul-Po-Mag and K-Mag.

SULFUR (S)

Sulfur is a component of plant protein and in grasses is found at levels between 0.25 percent and 0.4 percent. The ratio of N to S in the grasses is perhaps more important than the S content and should be about 14 to 1. Deficiency symptoms of S are very similar to those of N and can occur when the N to S ratio is greater than 20 to 1, or when S levels are below 0.15 percent in leaf tissue. Leaf clippings with a high N to S ratio are also slow to decompose and can increase the rate of thatch accumulation since microorganisms require S to decompose plant residues.

Sulfur is a component of most low analysis fertilizer and is an atmospheric pollutant where high S fuels are burned. However, the trend toward high analysis fertilizer and Environmental Protection Agency (EPA) restrictions on high S fuels has reduced these sources of S to levels where S deficiencies are found in plants. Roy L. Goss (1969) at Washington State University has reported a good response on bentgrass to S-containing materials. Similar responses to S have been reported for bermudagrasses in sandy soils in Texas and Florida. Sulfur can be added as a foliar spray or as a soil application with gypsum ($CaSO_4$), elemental sulfur, or sulfur fertilizers.

MICRONUTRIENTS

Soil analyses for the essential micronutrients (Fe, Mn, Zn, Cu, Mo, B, Cl) for turfgrasses do not adequately predict their concentrations in leaf tissue. For example, the Mn content may range from 1 to 4 ppm in the soil but the grass growing on those soils may range from less than 20 ppm to over 400 ppm Mn in leaf tissue. Thus, it is difficult to predict a Mn deficiency in grass from soil test information. Even more critical, Fe levels in the soil may appear adequate, yet Fe may be deficient in the grass. Iron is tied up by excess P in the roots of the grass plant. Leaf analysis for these micronutrients can provide information not readily obtained from soil tests.

IRON (Fe)

Iron deficiencies are common in turfgrasses where soils have a high pH (above pH 7.0), during periods of cool temperatures or where grasses are overwatered. Iron deficiency symptoms usually show when the leaf tissue is below 50 ppm Fe and are characterized by yellow leaves with green veins, which gives the leaf a striped appearance. The upper or newer leaves are the first to show Fe deficiency symptoms. Turfgrasses might be considered low in Fe when leaf levels are below 50 ppm and adequate at levels between 200 and 1,000 ppm (Thomas 1994). At excessively high levels in the leaf, Fe can induce a manganese deficiency. Soil application of Fe materials may not readily correct Fe deficiencies. Foliar application of iron sulfate or iron chelates to Fe-deficient turf at recommended rates produces an immediate response. However, repeat applications may be required indefinitely to prevent reoccurrence of the deficiency symptoms.

ZINC (Zn)

Zinc deficiencies, like Fe deficiencies, are difficult to identify through soil test results. Deficiency symptoms include a mottled, chlorotic leaf, rolled and thin leaf blades, and stunted growth. These conditions occur most frequently under alkaline soil conditions, in soils high in P or under compacted, waterlogged soil conditions. Zinc deficiencies may occur when leaf tissue levels are below 10 ppm Zn (Thomas 1994). Satisfactory levels of Zn would normally range from 20 to 50 ppm in the leaf. As with Fe deficiencies, Zn deficiencies may be readily corrected with foliar applications of zinc sulfate or zinc chelate.

MANGANESE (Mn)

Manganese may come deficient in grasses at levels below 20 ppm in leaf tissue (Thomas 1994). Deficiency symptoms include a chlorotic appearance and stunted growth. Leaf tissue between the veins turns yellow while veins remain green. Deficiencies may occur where soil pH is above 6.0 and where organic matter in soil is low. Mn deficiencies can be corrected with foliar applications of manganese sulfate or manganese chelate.

Manganese toxicity can occur in turfgrasses when soil pH is below 5.5 or when soils are consistently overwatered. Crews and Gilbert (1974) at North Carolina State University have reported Mn toxicity in bentgrass on acid soils that were also overwatered. They reported toxicity symptoms developing when leaf clippings contained over 1,300 ppm Mn. Toxicity symptoms for Mn included stunted growth, thinning of leaves, and the development of brown spots on leaf blades. Mn toxicity can be readily corrected through liming and proper irrigation practices, or by improving drainage on waterlogged soils.

MOLYBDENUM, BORON, COPPER, AND CHLORINE

Deficiencies of these nutrients have not been observed on turfgrasses in the United States, although toxicities have occurred. Toxicities from one or more of these nutrients are usually associated with high concentrations of the nutrient in irrigation water. The use of sewage effluent for turf irrigation purposes requires close monitoring of the water and the grass for possible toxicities from one or more of these nutrients.

Tissue analysis is not proposed as a substitute for soil testing or as a solution to nutrition problems. But it is recommended to professional turfgrass managers as another management aid and as a backup to soil testing. Not all soil testing laboratories conduct tissue analysis, but there are laboratories throughout the U.S. that will conduct these analyses. Consult your state soil testing laboratories for additional information on leaf analysis. Soil testing laboratories at Texas A&M University, Mississippi State University, University of Georgia, Auburn University, and University of Florida presently conduct leaf tissue analyses.

Special Cultural Practices

7

Lawns, golf courses, sports fields, and other turf areas often deteriorate because of compacted soil, excessive thatch buildup, and excessive use. When this happens, physical disturbance (cultivation) of the sod is often required to restore its vitality.

Turfgrass Cultivation

Unlike conventional crops which can be plowed, turfgrass areas must be cultivated so that the surface is opened up without destroying the aesthetic value of its appearance and its function. Cultivation of turfgrasses can be accomplished by vertical mowing, core aeration, spiking, and topdressing.

Vertical mowing, coring, and spiking are methods of cultivating intact turfgrass sod to improve the growing environment within the thatch layer or in the soil immediately below the surface. Each practice requires specialized equipment.

VERTICAL MOWING

The vertical mower cuts by impact of whirling knives, which turn in a vertical plane on a high-speed horizontal shaft. These blades are usually fixed, but may be free-swinging. They vary in thickness from $1/32$ to $1/4$ inch. The thinner blades are used on golf greens, where the surface must not be drastically disturbed. The interval of space between blades on the shaft can be varied. The spacing interval is determined by the desired effect and the horsepower of the engine on the unit. Power requirements for vertical mowing are two to three times that required for reel mowing.

Originally, the vertical mower was a hand-operated unit with a cutting head 18 to 22 inches in width. It was used at monthly or seasonal intervals to cut vertically into the sod and lift out a large portion of the thatch layer. This practice was very time-consuming and was usually limited to golf greens. Vertical mowing with these units marred the appearance of the turf and required several weeks to restore color and density to the turf. A once-over with the vertical mower and the site looked as though a football scrimmage had been held on it. The practice was ultimately good for the grass, because it (1) partially eliminated the excess thatch layer, (2) cut and often reduced graininess, and (3) promoted growth of many new shoots.

In heavily thatched turf it may be necessary to set the vertical mower to cut deeply into the turf. This will groove the surface, thereby necessitating topdressing with a soil mix to smooth the surface and cover exposed stolons.

With the advent of the riding triplex greens mower came multiple-head vertical mowing units, which are interchangeable with the cutting reels. This equipment enables the turf manager to vertical mow fine turf very rapidly and to simultaneously collect the clippings. The latter equipment necessitated that a vacuum or sweeper be passed over the turf following vertical mowing.

With the triplex vertical mowing units, it is practical to vertical mow at weekly intervals when the turf is actively growing. The cutting blades should be set to only nick the grass surface so that the turf is not impaired. Frequent vertical mowing, together with aerification, eliminates the need to renovate turf by severe vertical mowing.

A more recent improvement in vertical mowing units is the grooming mower. The grooming mower has a vertical mowing attachment just in front of the reel cutting unit of a triplex greens mower. With the grooming mower, turf is lightly vertically mowed (or groomed) each time the turf is mowed. Thus, light and frequent vertical mowing is very practical.

In summary, routine vertical mowing of fine turf will improve the playing surface by (1) truing the surface by removing grain, (2) stimulating new shoot development, and (3) removing some thatch.

Core aerating golf greens

In addition, the vertical mower is useful at the time of overseeding bermudagrass turf with winter grasses. Turf to be overseeded may be vertical mowed several days prior to seeding. This vertical mowing may be more severe than routinely used during the warm months. It will (1) retard the growth of bermudagrass, thus reducing competition for the seedlings; (2) open the turf somewhat for better penetration of the overseeded grasses; and (3) reduce thatch accumulation.

Vertical mowing is not totally beneficial to turf. It may encourage more weeds, and if the height of cut is too low, it will weaken the turf and lower the quality. On bentgrass putting greens, vertical mowing should be avoided during stress periods when growth of the grass is slow.

Vertical mowing of larger turf areas is accomplished with tractor-drawn vertical mowing units which operate off the power take-off (PTO). Such units usually have large blades which are set to groove the turf to the soil surface or deeper. The main purpose of this type of vertical mowing is to remove thatch and to prepare a site for overseeding. Using such a mower once or twice a year to dethatch bermudagrass lawns, fairways, or sports fields is a common practice. Where bermudagrass lawns, fairways, or sports fields are overseeded each fall, the ideal time to vertical mow is several weeks prior to overseeding.

AERIFICATION

Aerification may be defined as the removal of small soil cores or plugs from turf areas, leaving a hole or cavity in the sod. Such holes aid in the movement of air, water, nutrients, nematicides, and other compounds into and through the upper portion of the soil. Machines for coring turf may have hollow tines or open spoons about 4 inches in length, which are ¼- to ¾-inch in diameter. The depth of penetration of the tines or spoons depends on the degree of soil compaction, soil moisture, and the capacity of the aerifier. Increasing soil moisture usually facilitates deeper penetration. Soil cores brought to the surface may be removed or pulverized and worked back into the thatch layer. When worked into the sod, the soil intermingles with the thatch layer and aids in its biological decomposition. This is one of the most effective ways to control thatch buildup.

Aerification is most beneficial on soils with an impermeable layer near the surface and on highly compacted soils. The frequency of aerification needed depends on the degree of soil compaction. Golf greens, tees, and sports fields need more frequent aerification than lower traffic areas. In general, turf responds to aerification best in spring and late summer. Generally, three to four aerifications annually are adequate for intensively used turf areas.

Deep tine core aerifiers are available that extract a ¾- to 1-inch diameter core 8 to 10 inches deep. The deep tine aerifier is beneficial on golf greens with layered profiles, impermeable layers, sand layers, or other boundaries that interfere with water movement, aeration, or root development. The deep aerifier is more of a renovation tool than a regularly scheduled maintenance practice.

Equipment is also available for slicing thin holes in the soil without removal of soil cores. Slicing is less effective than coring, but it can be done much faster and is often more practical for large turf areas. Most slicing machines have blades shaped like those on a sickle mower. These blades are bolted at intervals to the perimeter of metal wheels spaced 6 to 12 inches apart on a long axle. As the wheels turn, the blade slices into the turf, cutting a narrow slit 3 to 5 inches deep and about ¼ inch wide. Such openings do not interfere with the use of the turf.

It is often best to irrigate the turf immediately after slicing or coring to prevent excessive drying of turf at the edge of the openings made by the blades or tines.

If the soil on which the turf is growing were ideal in physical makeup, it is doubtful if aerification would even be needed. However, such an ideal soil mixture is rarely attained; hence, aerification should be a standard practice on most turf areas receiving regular traffic, whether foot or vehicular.

SPIKING

Spiking is a variation of slicing. Spiking is accomplished by forcing the small solid teeth of metal discs into the soil surface to a depth of ½ to 2 inches. A typical spiking machine has about 20 disc-shaped blades which have teeth-like rowels on a spur. Wider units or tandem groups of smaller spikers are available for use on large turf areas. The spiker does not remove a soil core.

The spiker is most useful in breaking up surface crusting of soil or algae. Since a single pass of a spiker creates about 10 to 20 thousand holes per 1,000 square feet, it is effective in helping to dry out poorly drained turf areas. It also improves water penetration. When such conditions exist on golf courses or sports fields, spiking is a beneficial practice.

Since spiking causes only minor disruptions of surface conditions, it can be practiced more than core aerification.

TOPDRESSING

Any discussion of cultivation would be incomplete without giving consideration to topdressing—the spreading of a thin layer of soil or soil mix over a turf. Improperly done, topdressing can add to existing problems. Apply too much and the grass becomes smothered. Apply the wrong material or change materials frequently and topdressing contributes to layering. If topdressing components are not sterilized, weeds are introduced. There are other advantages, not the least of which is the inconvenience to golfers or others using the facility and the cost in terms of time, equipment, and materials. But the benefits of topdressing are too great to overlook.

Topdressing is the turf industry's castor oil. It is a bitter medicine to take, but it certainly accomplishes a lot of good. On established turf, topdressing aids in thatch decomposition, smoothing the playing surface, promoting recovery from injury or disease, reducing graininess on golf greens, and producing a denser and finer textured turf. In addition, topdressing can be used to modify existing soils and to aid in overseeding.

Selecting a soil or soil mixture for use in topdressing is critical to the success of the practice. If the existing soil or soil mixture is satisfactory, it is desirable to topdress with similar material. If the existing soil is compacted and impermeable it may be beneficial to modify the surface conditions by topdressing with a more permeable soil mixture. For golf putting greens, specifications for topdressing mixtures should approach those for soil mixtures used for greens construction (Hummel 1993).

A problem often associated with topdressing is layering—a nonuniform soil profile with boundaries that restrict water and air movement and root growth. For example, the application of a loam or clay loam soil to what may be called a sand creates a boundary that disrupts the profile.

Where a layer of sand exists in a profile, a condition that develops when a sand topdressing is followed by a soil or soil mixture topdressing, the soil above the sand is often wet, and root growth is restricted. Even relatively small differences in topdressing materials can have an adverse effect on the turfgrass root zone. By following a regular schedule of core aerification together with topdressing, the development of layers should be reduced.

When it is possible to topdress with an existing soil or soil mixture, the problem of layering should not develop. Light applications of topdressing, 1 to 2 cubic yards per 5,000 square feet, followed by aerification to partially incorporate the topdressing, would not lead to layering. However, heavier topdressing which might bury the thatch could lead to layering. Likewise, changing topdressing materials can lead to layering problems.

The frequency of topdressing depends on the objectives of the practice. If smoothing large irregularities on a playing surface is the objective, frequent and heavy topdressing may be required. If maintaining good putting conditions is the goal, light and frequent topdressing is needed. The frequency of topdressing for thatch control depends on the intensity of maintenance of the turf. Golf greens may require eight to ten applications of topdressing, but lawns or sports fields may need only one. When turf vigor is low, topdressing is not required for thatch control.

If materials are to be mixed to formulate a topdressing, take care to mix materials in the recommended ratio and to blend the materials uniformly. With some materials screening is required to remove large particles and aggregates. Sterilization by composting or with methyl bromide is also recommended when soil is a component of the topdressing. Washed sand and organic mixes may not require sterilization.

Proper handling of topdressing materials includes storage in a place that will keep them uncontaminated and dry. Polyethylene covers may be used in the absence of better storage facilities.

Getting the prepared topdressing from the storage area to the site efficiently and economically requires only three steps: (1) loading into a truck or other carrier, (2) transporting to the site, and (3) loading into a topdressing machine from the truck.

Topdressing for improved surface

In many efficient operations, topdressing is never touched by human hands. It is loaded into the truck with a bucket loader and transported and unloaded directly into the topdressing machine.

Topdressing machines usually apply the material quite uniformly, but smoothing and working the material into the turf may require dragging. Smoothing is best accomplished with a power drag mat going over the site several times. The object is to remove soil from high spots and deposit it in the depressions to obtain a smooth and true surface. Following the drag mat operation, the new soil should be further settled into place by light watering.

The advantages of a good topdressing are many and where the finest quality putting greens are desired, this practice is a must.

Thatch Control in Turf

How often have you heard a homeowner say that walking on a neighbor's lawn is like walking on a carpet? How often do you hear golfers talk about how well the greens cushion shoots? To some people such a lawn or golf green is considered ideal, a luxury. However, the characteristic that contributes most to this luxury is thatch—an accumulation of living and dead plant tissues between the soil and the green vegetative cover.

THE PROBLEM

A limited amount of thatch, perhaps ¼ inch on a golf green or ½ inch on a lawn, is desirable because it contributes resilience to the turf, increases its wear tolerance, and conserves soil moisture. However, when thatch increases beyond those depths, the negative aspects of thatched turf often results in an unsightly scalped appearance, and watering results in excess runoff which carries nutrients with it. Thus, not only is water wasted, but nutrients are also lost. While thatch reduces the effectiveness of pesticides, it provides a favorable habitat for insects and disease organisms. Thus, insect and disease control become more troublesome.

Excess thatch also leads to shallow root systems which complicate all aspects of turf management. Shallow-rooted turf is highly susceptible to low temperature kill, drought, heat stress, herbicide injury, and other adverse conditions.

THE CAUSES

Thatch originates from undecomposed organic residues that accumulate under intensified turf management (Meinhold et al. 1973; Kleinig 1965; Ledeboer and Skogley 1967). Thatch consists of a layer of stems and roots entwined in partially decayed leaf, stem, and root tissue between the soil and the green leaves. This layer is characterized as being fibrous in nature and highly resistant to microbial breakdown. Grass clippings, on the other hand, consist of leaf blades which are high in cellulose and are rapidly decomposed by soil microbes. As a result, grass clippings do not greatly contribute to thatch accumulation. This is contrary to the often repeated recommendation to remove grass clippings to prevent thatch accumulation. Vigorous grass varieties, excess fertilization, watering, mowing practices, and extensive use of pesticides all contribute to thatch accumulation.

Grasses differ in growth rate and in chemical composition, which leads to different rates of production and decomposition of plant tissues. Pee Dee bermudagrass, which has a faster growth than other turf-type bermudagrasses, develops thatch very rapidly. Zoysiagrasses have a high silica content and the fine fescues a high lignin content, which both slow decomposition and increase thatch accumulation. Evansville bentgrass is unusual in that it has extensive surface root development which contributes to thatch accumulation.

Fertilization practices contribute to most thatch problems. Excessive application of nitrogen fertilizers, particularly soluble nitrogen, stimulates leaf and stem production and leads to thatch accumulation. Organic and slow-release nitrogen fertilizers do not increase thatch as much as the soluble nitrogen fertilizers. This difference can be attributed to the uniform growth response from organic and slow-release fertilizers. Although nitrogen sources influence thatch accumulation, the amount of nitrogen applied to the turf has an even greater effect. The critical nitrogen fertilization rate might be defined as the rate above which thatch accumulates rapidly and below which thatch accumulates very slowly. The critical nitrogen fertilization rate differs among grass varieties and among management programs for the same grass variety. For example, this rate may be 4 pounds of nitrogen per 1,000 square feet for bentgrass putting greens, but only 2 pounds for bentgrass fairways. Or, if we compare grasses under lawn conditions, it may be 2 pounds for tall fescue and Saint Augustine grass and 4 pounds for bluegrass and

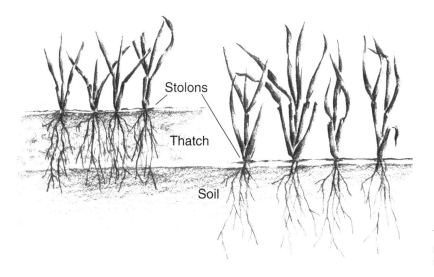

Thatched turf *(left)* and new planting *(right)*. Note root system in thatch.

bermudagrasses. Certainly, we cannot exceed the critical nitrogen fertilization rate without using cultural practices to control thatch—remove grass clippings, topdress, vertical mow, aerify, etc. Since these cultural practices are routine on golf greens, the critical nitrogen fertilization rate for golf greens is much higher than for fairways, even though the same grass may be used.

Watering practices may also promote thatch accumulation in turf. Since microbial decomposition of thatch requires the presence of free oxygen, saturated soil conditions created by frequent watering retard thatch decomposition. Also, intermittent wetting and drying of the thatch layer increased the physical breakdown of plant tissues which increases the rate of microbial decomposition. Thus, the practice of keeping golf greens moist to hold golf shots favors thatch accumulation.

Mowing heights that promote tillering and rhizome development also favor thatch accumulation. Bluegrass mowed at a height of 1½ inches will develop a greater thatch layer than that mowed at a height of ½ to ¾ inch. In contrast, bermudagrass mowed at a height of less than 1 inch develops thatch more rapidly than when mowed at greater heights. In these cases, turf density would have to be sacrificed to reduce thatch. Mowing frequency can also affect thatch accumulation in turfgrasses. Mowing frequencies should be such that only 30 to 40 percent of the leaf growth is removed. Long, stemmy grass clippings do not work into the turf as readily as short clippings. Also, the mature grass clippings are much higher in lignin and more slowly decomposed than the more succulent leaf blades. The relationship between mowing height and mowing frequency should not be overlooked—the shorter the grass is mowed, the more often it will need to be mowed. Grass clippings that consist largely of leaf blades and are short enough to work into the turf disappear very rapidly. Thus, grass clippings from turf mowed at the proper height and frequency will not contribute to thatch, but their removal increases the fertilizer requirements of the turf. Grass clippings are relatively high in nitrogen, potassium, soluble sugars, and cellulose, all of which are utilized by soil microbes to break down more complex compounds. Thus, the grass clippings may serve as an energy source and as an inoculant for microbes that break down thatch.

Pesticides applied routinely for the control of weeds, insects, and diseases may also contribute to the accumulation of thatch. For many years lead and calcium arsenates used for weed control and chlordane, a residual insecticide, were associated with increased thatch. Both the arsenates and chlordane reduced the earthworm populations to the level that thatch accumulated. Earthworms are instrumental in the soil incorporation of organic matter which promotes its decomposition. Reducing earthworm populations leads to surface accumulation of organic matter (thatch).

Broad-spectrum fungicides used on a preventative schedule may also promote thatch accumulation. These fungicides reduce the populations of saprophytic fungi as well as the population of the parasitic fungi. Since the saprophytic fungi help break down organic residues, they are essential to prevent thatch accumulation. The specific fungicides which kill only selective fungi do not increase thatch accumulation. In turf maintenance programs where both earthworm and fungi populations have been greatly reduced, thatch becomes a serious problem.

THE SOLUTION

Maintaining a heavily thatched turf is not an impossible task, but the problems encountered in mowing, watering, and pest control often lead to turf renovation. Short of complete turf renovation, cultivation practices can be used to control thatch. Vertical mowing, aeration, and topdressing, when performed on a timely basis, will control thatch. In addition, other maintenance practices such as fertilization, mowing, watering, and pest management must be adjusted to reduce thatch accumulation.

Vertical mowing of a thatched turf slices through the thatch layer and pulls some of the organic residues to the surface where they can be removed. Vertical mowing also cuts shoots and stolons which can be removed with close mowing. When performed on a timely basis, vertical mowing can thin a turf and reduce or prevent thatch. Intensively maintained bermudagrass turf responds very well to light vertical mowing on a weekly schedule throughout the summer. Bentgrass requires vertical mowing during spring and fall, and bluegrass responds very well to early fall vertical mowing. If a heavy thatch is present, vertical mowing alone will not solve the problem.

Aeration with hollow tines or spoons increases air and water penetration of the thatch layer and improves conditions for thatch decomposition. The soil cores brought to the surface by aeration also serve as topdressing, which further aids thatch decomposition. The combination of vertical mowing and aeration serves as a method of cultivating a turf, much like the cultivation of crop residues with a disc or tiller. Certainly, the soil incorporation of crop residues aids their decomposition. Since a turf cannot be disced on an annual basis, vertical mowing and aeration offer the most practical alternative.

Topdressing a turf with a soil or soil mixture is another cultivation practice that aids thatch decomposition by increasing the contact between soil particles and thatch and by re-

Plug from bermudagrass turf showing thatch layer

Dethatching a bermudagrass turf

Sweeping the residue after dethatching

Thatch removed from one baseball field

taining enough moisture to sustain microbial activity for longer periods. In some European countries topdressing is the only cultivation practice used to prevent thatch. John Madison, turf scientist at the University of California at Davis, has developed a turf management program that uses topdressing as the only means of thatch control (Madison, Paul, and Davis 1974).

Soil activators and inoculants are promoted as cure-alls for thatch. Some of these products contain small amounts of plant nutrients and microorganisms which are reported to stimulate microbial decomposition of thatch. Other products are promoted on the basis of their humus content and the so-called miraculous results associated with adding humus to the soil. The promotion of such products is almost entirely based on testimonials with little factual information to support their claims. Research conducted on these products has generally not supported manufacturers' claims that they eliminate or reduce thatch. In research conducted in eight southern states in cooperation with the USDA, applications of two of these products at manufacturers recommended rates did not increase decomposition of plant residues, nor did they increase the number or the activity of soil microorganisms (Weaver, Dunigan, and Parr 1974). Research has suggested that topdressing with a soil or soil mixture controls thatch more effectively than the so-called soil activators or biological dethatchers.

In summary, thatch represents an accumulation of organic debris between the soil surface and the green grass cover. It contributes resiliency to the turf, increases wear tolerance, and helps conserve soil moisture. However, excess thatch interferes with mowing and watering practices, reduces the effectiveness of fertilizers and pesticides, and increases winterkill and desiccation. Thus, excess thatch is undesirable but can be controlled with a good maintenance program. Fertilization rates should be kept as low as possible without sacrificing turf quality. Watering practices should be adjusted to provide intermittent wetting and drying of the thatch, and mowing frequency should be such that only 30 to 40 percent of the leaf growth is removed at one time. Pesticides that reduce populations of earthworms and microorganisms should be used only as needed. Also, where microbial activity has been reduced by acid soil conditions, the addition of limestone will aid thatch decomposition. Cultivation practices on a timely basis will also help control thatch. Vertical mowing, aeration, and topdressing provide the most effective means of reducing thatch.

Growing Turfgrasses in Shade

A significant portion of the total acreage of turf grown in the United States is produced under some degree of shade. Estimates as high as 20 to 25 percent are widely used in the turfgrass industry (Winstead and Ward 1974). Turfgrass managers frequently report shade as their number one problem in growing grass. Yet, no one recommends the simple solution to the problem—remove the trees. In most adequate landscape situations, trees and shrubs are more important and more valuable than grass. Imagine a home landscape, a park, or golf course without trees. It would not be very attractive and certainly would not be used as often as a similar area with trees. Given a choice between trees or grass, most people prefer trees.

In landscape plans, trees and grasses can be selected that grow very well together. Often, however, we are left with the plan that nature or someone else provided. In association with oak, crape myrtle, sycamore, golden raintree, and others, shade-tolerant grasses will do very well. But when grown under shallow-rooted trees that also have dense canopies such as sweet gum, ash, magnolia, and elm, grasses do very poorly.

THE SHADE ENVIRONMENT

Trees significantly alter the environment in the shaded area. They drastically decrease the amount of light available to the grass in the shaded area. Some trees also filter out part of the photosynthetically active light spectrum and, thus, affect the quality of light reaching the grass. Tree shade affects the duration of light and the time of day that light is available to the grass. All of these effects of shade interfere with growth and development of the grass.

Some grasses are adapted to low light intensity. For example, creeping red fescue and Saint Augustine maintain a horizontal leaf arrangement (prostrate growth habit) at low light intensities. Thus, red fescue and Saint Augustine grass intercept more of the light reaching the turf than bluegrass or bermudagrass.

Plants grown in 60 percent shade are weak and spindly.

In addition to the intensity, which is the quality and duration of light under a canopy of trees, trees also modify temperature, humidity, moisture, and wind movement in the shaded area. All of these factors affect the growth of turfgrasses. The moderation of temperature extremes has a positive effect on grasses. However, the moderation of temperature extremes has the same effect on disease pathogens, which often become the factor limiting growth of turfgrasses in shade. Also, higher relative humidities and decreased wind movement favor the development of diseases. Disease resistance or tolerance is often a characteristic of a shade-tolerant grass.

Soil moisture relationships are altered around trees because the tree canopy intercepts and collects a significant portion of rainfall, and tree roots compete with grass for uptake of soil moisture. During extended droughts trees have the advantage over grass for extracting soil moisture, and the grass is always the first to show moisture stress. Some grasses such as the fescues and Saint Augustine grass, maintain a satisfactory root system in spite of tree competition. But, in other grasses, such as bermudagrass, rooting is severely restricted by tree root competition. Root inhibition of some grasses under trees may be due to something other than competition for light, moisture, and nutrients; chemical inhibitors may be implicated.

The type (evergreen or deciduous) and age of trees involved in the shade also has a significant effect on the compatibility of trees and grasses. Deciduous trees that lose their foliage in late fall are more compatible with grass than evergreen trees such as cedar, pine, or holly. The canopy of deciduous trees thins in the fall and does not become dense until late spring. Thus, the underlying grasses have late fall and early spring to recover and accumulate carbohydrates to survive summer stress. Furthermore, with cool-season grasses in the South, the tree canopy protects the grass from temperature extremes in midsummer.

Dense canopies created when young trees and shrubs underlie taller trees also create environmental conditions unsuitable for the growth of grasses. Such situations are very common in home landscapes where tree and shrub planting continues for a number of years.

GRASS RESPONSE TO SHADE

As previously discussed, some grasses are better adapted to shade than others. The mechanism of adaptation may be leaf orientation, root development, photosynthetic efficiency, recuperative potential, disease resistance, or a combination of these factors (Beard 1965). It is also widely believed that a light-sensitive system, phytochrome, which controls the growth habit of grasses is primarily responsible for shade tolerance in turfgrasses. Control of this system would likely be through enzymes and plant growth substances that are inherent in some grasses.

Fine-leaved fescues, *Poa trivialis,* creeping bentgrass, and tall fescue are cool-season turfgrasses considered to have good shade tolerance. Colonial bentgrass, perennial ryegrass, and meadow fescue have fair shade tolerance. But Kentucky bluegrass with the exception of a few cultivars has poor shade tolerance. A-34 and Nugget Kentucky bluegrass have fair shade tolerance due to their resistance to powdery mildew and leaf spot. Within these groups there needs to be further delineations in shade tolerance because the fine-leaved fescues require dry shade. *P. trivialis* prefers moist shade, ryegrass and tall fescue must be in the warmer portions of the cool humid climate where winterkill is not serious, and bentgrasses require preventative disease-control programs to persist in shade.

Among warm-season turfgrasses Saint Augustine and zoysia have good shade tolerance, bahia and centipede fair shade tolerance, and bermudagrass and buffalograss poor shade tolerance (Barrios et al. 1986; McBee and Holt

1966). As with bluegrasses, some varieties of bermudagrass, such as Tifway, have more shade tolerance than others. Unfortunately, the only grasses suitable for playgrounds or sports fields in the South are the bermudagrasses which have poor shade tolerance.

All grasses require some degree of direct sunlight for normal growth and development. Grasses growing under low light intensity with tree root competition develop long, narrow leaves, long internodes, weak root systems, reduced shoot density, reduced tillering, upright growth habit, and increased chlorophyll content (Whitcomb 1972). Grasses grown under reduced light may also develop a thinner cutin layer, thinner cell walls, and increased succulence. As a result of these structural changes, grasses growing in shade are more susceptible to environmental stresses such as drought, temperature extremes, and disease development.

Other responses to shade include reduced photosynthesis, reduced carbohydrate reserves, lower respiration rates, and lower transpiration rates. The net result of these responses to shade is weak, spindly turf with greater susceptibility to environmental stress and disease. The importance of disease in determining shade adaptability should not be disregarded. Some evidence suggests that disease susceptibility is the limiting factor in shade adaptation of turfgrasses (Beard 1965). Powdery mildew, for example, eliminates many Kentucky bluegrass cultivars in shade. *Helminthosporium* leaf spot and fading-out eliminate some of the fescues from shade. And in warm-season grasses, gray leaf spot and *Helminthosporium* present serious problems to grasses in shaded environments.

MANAGEMENT AFFECTS
PERSISTENCE OF TURFGRASS IN SHADE

Persistence of grasses in shaded environments depends largely on management and use of the turf (Kurtz 1975). Either Kentucky bluegrass or bermudagrass can survive in moderately shaded areas. However, if these areas serve as recreational or playground areas, the grass would soon disappear. Fescue may appear weak in midsummer under shaded conditions, but if properly managed, it can recover enough during the fall to survive. Likewise, bermudagrass tolerates 30 to 40 percent shade but would tolerate very little use under these conditions.

Mowing practices have an important effect on persistence of grasses in shade. Even shade-tolerant species perform best when mowed higher in shade than in full sun. Mowing heights of 2 to 3 inches are recommended for lawns, parks, and golf course roughs in shade. Mowing frequency should be adequate to avoid severe defoliation of shaded turfgrasses. Severe defoliation shocks the grass which is already weakened by shade. In lawn management insufficient mowing frequencies account for many failures. Mowing height and frequency must be such that leaf area is maintained as high as possible.

CULTURAL PRACTICES

Irrigation practices are also critical for grasses growing in shade since their root systems are severely weakened. Under light, frequent irrigation practices, tree roots have the competitive advantage for surface moisture. But with thorough irrigation practices tree roots utilize the deeper moisture while grasses use the surface moisture. Also, water should be applied to shaded turfgrasses in the early morning hours to remove dew from the grass and to allow for rapid drying. Late evening watering keeps the foliage moist and promotes disease activity on shaded turfs.

Fertilization schedules must be adjusted under shaded conditions to avoid stimulation of grasses during stress periods and to promote recovery when conditions are favorable. Grasses growing in shade require less fertilizer than those growing in full sun. However, trees also utilize surface-applied fertilizer. Thus, the total amount of fertilizer applied to shaded areas may be only slightly less than that applied to grass growing in full sun. Timing of fertilizer applications is critical. Nitrogen fertilizer applied in late spring or early summer increases the succulence of grasses, which in shade increases their susceptibility to disease. Fall fertilization promotes the recovery of grass and reduces losses due to winterkill. And spring applications before tree foliage is fully developed helps to increase turf density and vigor. If only a single fertilizer application is made, the fall application is more important. If three or more fertilizer applications are made to shaded turfs, summer application of soluble nitrogen should not exceed ½ pound per 1,000 square feet per month on warm-season grasses and should be avoided on cool-season grasses.

DISEASE CONTROL

Perhaps disease control is the most important management practice for the maintenance of turf in shade. Powdery mildew, *Helminthosporium* leaf spot, and gray leaf spot are serious problems to the management of Kentucky bluegrass, fescue, and Saint Augustine grass, respectively, in shaded environments. Where these diseases are controlled, turf quality is usually satisfactory. Disease control requires good management as well as the use of preventative fungicides. In cool, humid climates the use of grass mixtures or blends can help reduce losses to disease problems, but fungicides are frequently needed to prevent serious losses of turf.

Pruning tree branches and removing fallen tree leaves from the turf can also help turfgrasses persist under tree shade. Both of these practices increase the amount of light available to the grass and modify the microclimate that favors disease development. Lower tree branches should be removed 6 to 8 feet up the trunk. Selective thinning of branches in the crown of the tree also helps the grass. Vigorous pruning increases light exposure and wind movement in the shaded area.

When all of these practices still fail to produce acceptable turf, annual grasses, ground covers of nonliving surfaces, should be used.

Overseeding Bermudagrass Turf

To some, overseeding is a simple operation—just scatter some seed and wait until they germinate. But to the professional turfgrass manager or golf course superintendent, whose success depends on the quality of the product, overseeding is a complex operation that requires preparation, timing, and luck. Unfortunately, knowledge and experience do not always suffice. Just plain bad luck, usually unfavorable weather conditions, can sometimes ruin sound procedures.

The objective of a skilled turfgrass manager is to minimize the chance for failure by proper seedbed preparation, planting adapted grass varieties at the proper time, and careful management during the seedling stage.

PREPLANT PRACTICES

Seedbed preparation is just as important for establishment of a new turf. Perhaps one of the greatest causes of a poor stand of winter grasses is poor seedbed preparation. Thatch, compacted soils, and weeds in the seedbed can result in seedling diseases and thin stands of grass during the early stages of overseeding.

Seedbed preparation does not begin two weeks before the date of seeding. It begins several months prior to seeding. Light vertical mowing during late summer and fall helps to reduce thatch in bermudagrass turf. Aeration and topdressing also help control thatch, provide a smooth surface, and create favorable conditions for germination of winter grasses. Timing of each of these practices is crucial to their success.

Light vertical mowing should begin in midsummer and continue through fall when bermudagrass growth slows. Frequent vertical mowing so that the effects are not noticeable after several days is the most successful program to follow. Vertical mow golf greens weekly and lawns monthly during this period. The use of grooming mowers several times each week may substitute for vertical mowing on golf greens. Infrequent and severe vertical mowing results in unsightly turf and poor putting surfaces during late summer.

Aeration is also important to seedbed preparation. Early spring, late spring, and late summer are ideal times to aerify to alleviate compaction, reduce thatch, and help develop a seedbed. Overseeded sites should not be aerated after September 1 because it promotes germination of annual bluegrass. Core aeration within a month of the date of planting also results in the seed emerging in clumps rather than in a uniform stand over the site. Sloping sites can be aerated as needed during the spring and summer to reduce runoff and increase water retention in soils.

Light and frequent topdressing also helps prepare a bermudagrass golf green for overseeding. Topdressing materials may vary among golf courses, but most topdressings consist of a high percentage of medium-textured sand. Topdressings should be free of sand particles larger than 1.0 mm in diameter and should contain less than 10 percent of particles (sand, silt, and clay) below 0.1 mm in diameter. Organic amendments may be added to the sand to soften the mix and increase its moisture and nutrient retention. Where organic amendments are high in fine sand, silt, and clay, the final mix should not contain more that 10 percent (by weight) of particles below 0.1 mm in diameter.

Topdress lawns with soil similar to that which exists at the site. Generally, sandy loam soils are ideal for topdressing lawns. More important than helping to prepare a seedbed, all of these practices (vertical mowing, aeration, and topdressing) help maintain an attractive, smooth, resilient surface up to the time of overseeding. Of course, routine mowing is the unwritten requirement that must go along with the other practices to maintain fine bermudagrass lawns and putting surfaces.

Where these cultural practices are followed, there is little else that needs to be done at the time of overseeding. Disease control prior to the date of planting is the only other requirement of seedbed preparation. A broad-spectrum fungicide should be applied one to two weeks prior to planting. The fungicide application will reduce populations of soilborne disease organisms that attack seedling grasses. Fungicide treated seed can also be planted to reduce seedling disease such as Pythium.

ANNUAL BLUEGRASS CONTROL

Annual bluegrass (*Poa annua*) can be controlled but not eliminated through cultural practices. If greens are prepared as previously described, perennial ryegrasses are the dominant overseeded grasses, planting date is properly timed, and seedling diseases are controlled, annual bluegrass should not be a serious problem on overseeded sites. On the other hand, where bermudagrass is severely thinned by vertical mowing immediately prior to planting, the site is aerated in September or October when annual bluegrass is germinating, and a dense stand of overseeded grasses does not develop rapidly, annual bluegrass readily invades the winter grasses.

Where turf managers find it necessary to use preemerge herbicides or Rubigan for annual bluegrass control, they should be applied 60 days prior to the expected planting date. Preemerge herbicides should not be used on poorly drained sites or on sites that are moderately shaded. And, when used, herbicides must be applied uniformly at recommended rates. Rubigan can be used on sites not suitable for other preemerge products. Ideally 2 applications of Rubigan 60 days and 30 days before seeding should be made. Finally, perennial ryegrasses should be the dominant overseeded grasses planted where preemerge herbicides are applied prior to seeding. *P. trivialis*, fescues, and bentgrasses are more sensitive to preemerge herbicides than the perennial ryegrasses.

The use of preemerge herbicides, proper seedbed preparation, and perennial ryegrasses can effectively eliminate annual bluegrass as a problem on overseeded sites.

GRASS VARIETIES

The choice of grass varieties for overseeding influences cost, texture, color, time required for a complete cover, cold tolerance, wear tolerance, and, to some degree, spring transition. But as for the success of the overseeding program, the choice of grass varieties is secondary to seedbed preparation.

The most expensive grasses in terms of seed cost per 1,000 square feet are the perennial ryegrasses. Mixing fescues, bentgrasses, and/or *Poa trivialis* with the ryegrasses reduces seed costs per 1,000 square feet and may improve the characteristics of the mix in terms of cold tolerance, texture, and spring transition. Perhaps the least expensive overseeding grass that produces attractive lawns and good playing surfaces is *P. trivialis*. The only weakness of pure stands of *P. trivialis* are wear tolerance and annual bluegrass invasion.

Even with higher seed costs, golf course superintendents prefer the perennial ryegrasses or mixtures with a high percentage of perennial ryegrass. Their fast establishment, wear tolerance, and competitiveness with annual bluegrass give the superintendent greater opportunity for success. And in overseeding operations, reducing opportunities for failure is important to the superintendent and the golf club.

Varieties of perennial ryegrass that consistently perform well include Birdie, Caravelle, Citation, Delray, Derby, Fiesta, Gator, Goalie, Loretta, Manhattan, Omega, Palmer, Pennant, Pennfine, Prelude, Regal, and Yorktown. Grass mixtures or blends containing perennial ryegrasses have also performed well.

P. trivialis in combination with the perennial ryegrass improves the density, texture, and cold tolerance of overseeded sites compared to ryegrass alone. Usually, 15 to 20 percent *P. trivialis* is required to make a noticeable difference. The addition of as much as 20 percent *P. trivialis* also reduces the cost of seeding. Varieties of *P. trivialis* that have been consistently outstanding include Sabre, Laser, and Cypress.

Fine fescue, bentgrass, and bluegrass can also be added to mixtures with perennial ryegrasses to improve the color, texture, and cold tolerance of the overseeded greens. Fine fescues are desired because of their very fine, stiff texture and good wear tolerance. However, the fescues do poorly under wet conditions and do not persist in hot weather. Improved varieties of fine fescues that have performed well include Atlanta, Banner, Dawson, Highlight, Jamestown, Marker, Scarlet, Southport, Vista, and Warick.

Creeping bentgrasses are often used in overseeding mixtures because of their fine texture and persistence into early summer. Cobra, Seaside, Pennfine, Pennlinks, Putter, SR1020, Penneagle, and Emerald creeping bentgrasses are most often used in overseeding mixtures. A relatively slow rate of establishment is the major drawback to creeping bentgrass for overseeding purposes.

Kentucky bluegrasses are used in overseeding mixtures to provide a dark green color. They also have excellent cold tolerance and retain their green color under freezing temperatures. However, Kentucky bluegrasses are very slow to establish a cover and contribute very little to an overseeding mixture for the first several months. Varieties of Kentucky bluegrass that have performed well in overseeding trials include Able-1, Arista, Baron, Mystic, Nugget, Pennstar, RAM, Touchdown, Vantage, and Victa.

SEED QUALITY

Seed quality is an important consideration when purchasing seed. In addition to certification of grass variety, seed labels contain information on purity, germination, and weed seed content. Since seeding rates are based on a pure live seed basis, information on purity and percent germination is required to calculate the amount of seed to plant. A typical seed label may appear as follows:

VARIETY:	GULF ANNUAL RYEGRASS
Purity:	98%
Inert:	1.5%
Crop:	0.4%
Weeds:	0.1%
Germination:	90%

Perennial ryegrass seed are large and vigorous relative to other grasses.

To calculate the pure live seed in this seed lot multiply the percent purity by the percent germination. In the above example, the seed lot contains 88.2 percent pure live seed (98% x 90%). If seeding specifications require 20 pounds of Gulf ryegrass per 1,000 square feet, then 22.7 pounds of the above seed lot must be planted (20 ÷ 88.2%). A weak stand of winter grasses may result if planting rates are not determined on a pure live seed basis.

Another important aspect of the seed label is the weed seed content. In the above example 0.1 percent weed seed may seem insignificant, but it may represent several hundred *Poa annua,* chickweed, or other weed seed in every pound of seed. When seed is used for temporary winter cover, percent crop seed is usually of little concern. In the lot of Gulf ryegrasses, crop seed may include Kentucky bluegrass or fescue. These other grasses (or crops) would not cause as serious a problem in a temporary winter turf as would *P. annua,* chickweed, or other broadleaved weeds.

PLANTING PROCEDURES

Most golf courses and sports fields are played straight through the overseeding operation. Thus, it is important to maintain good playing conditions throughout the period of overseeding. Playing condition is only one reason to begin preparing for overseeding several months in advance of planting time. Other reasons include maintaining an attractive appearance and giving the over-seeding operation every opportunity to succeed.

If the site has been prepared as described above (aerated, dethatched, and topdressed during late summer), only regular mowing is necessary immediately prior to seeding.

Distribute seed in several directions to obtain uniform distribution. Water lightly for several days to work the seed into the turf. Then topdress with sand or a topdressing mixture and smooth with a brush or carpet drag.

Watering is critical during the establishment period, but avoid over-watering. Wet, water-soaked sites are not playable and are prone to disease problems during seedling establishment. On the other hand, the surface must be lightly watered at frequent intervals to obtain rapid germination. Uniform application of water is essential to uniform emergence of seedlings. Light watering 2 to 3 times a day for 7 to 10 days is ideal. After seedlings emerge, water frequency can be gradually reduced to your regular schedule. Do not continue the light, frequent irrigation schedule past the germination period. Thorough irrigation at less frequent intervals is important to leach salts below the root zone and to promote root development.

Planting date plays an important role in the success of an overseeding program. Planting too early increases problems with seedling diseases and with bermudagrass competition. These two factors can seriously weaken and thin overseeded turfgrasses. On the other hand, planting too late can prolong the time required to obtain a complete cover because of low temperatures. Generally, the ideal time to plant is after bermudagrass has nearly ceased growing but before freezing temperatures are expected. A more specific date would be when soil temperature at the 4-inch depth reaches 72° F or two to three weeks before the average first frost date. In the northern half of the bermudagrass belt (North Texas, Oklahoma, Arkansas, Tennessee, North Carolina, and the northern regions of Mississippi, Alabama, and Georgia) this date would be October 1-15. In the southern half of the zone the optimum date would be October 15-November 1, and in southern extremes of Texas and Florida, November 1-November 15 (table 7-1).

Seeding rate is also important to establishing a fast, dense cover of overseeded grasses and to competing with annual bluegrass. Low seeding rates result in thinning stands of winter grasses and high populations of annual bluegrass. On golf greens, perennial ryegrasses should be planted at 35 pounds of pure live seed per 1,000 square feet, *Poa trivialis* at 10 pounds; fine fescues at 25 pounds, and bentgrass at 3 pounds. Mixtures of these grasses should be planted at rates according to the percentage of each grass in the mixture. For example, an 80-20 mix of perennial ryegrass and *P. trivialis* should be planted at 30 pounds per 1,000 square feet (80% of 35 pounds + 20% of 10 pounds, or 28 pounds of ryegrass and 2 pounds of *Poa*) (table 7-2).

Lawns, golf course fairways, and sports fields are planted at about 25

Table 7-1. Planting Dates for Overseeding Bermudagrass Turf

Location	PLANTING DATE		
	Earliest	Optimum	Latest
Extreme South[1]	Oct. 15	Nov. 1–15	Dec. 1
Central region[2]	Oct. 1	Oct. 15–Nov. 1	Nov. 15
Northern region[3]	Sept. 15	Oct. 1–15	Nov. 1

[1]South Texas and the southern half of Florida
[2]Central regions of the coastal states
[3]Northern sections of the bermudagrass belt

Table 7-2. Seeding Rates of Turfgrass Species for Winter Putting Greens

Grass Species	Lbs. per 1,000 sq. ft.
Annual ryegrass	45
Perennial ryegrass	35
Poa trivialis	10
Creeping bentgrass	3
Fine fescues	25
Mixtures	
Perennial ryegrass, fescue	25, 15
Perennial ryegrass, *Poa trivialis*, bent	20, 6, 1
Perennial ryegrass, fescue, bent	20, 10, 1
Poa trivialis, fescue, bent	6, 10, 1
Poa trivialis, fescue, bluegrass	6, 10, 4
Poa trivialis, bluegrass, bent	6, 4, 1
Poa trivialis, fescue, bluegrass, bent	6, 10, 4, 1

percent of the seeding rate of golf greens. Fairways, football fields, and lawns require 6 to 8 pounds of perennial ryegrass per 1,000 square feet or 2 to 3 pounds of *P. trivialis*. Only the infield of a baseball field needs a higher seeding rate. The infield needs about 75 percent of the seeding rate of golf greens.

MAINTENANCE PRACTICES

Mowing, watering, fertilization, and pest management are all critical to the successful establishment of newly overseeded winter grasses. Mistakes or poor judgement with any of these practices can lead to poor stands of winter grasses and heavy infestations of annual bluegrass.

Since play is continuous on newly overseeded golf greens, superintendents must mow greens daily. Raising the mowing height to ¼ inch and removing grass catchers for about two weeks after planting will help develop a fast cover. It is absolutely necessary to keep the mower razor sharp during this period to prevent pulling up the young seedlings. Daily mowing at ¼ inch during this time will produce slow but playable greens. After two weeks the mowing height can be reduced at $\frac{1}{32}$-inch increments to about $\frac{3}{16}$ inch, 4 to 6 weeks after planting. Daily mowing with sharp mowers is essential throughout this period. Greens should be mowed when the grass is dry to prevent tracking seed onto the collars. It may be helpful to lightly water the greens at daylight to wash dew off the foliage. Not only will that speed drying, but it may help reduce disease development and leaf tip burning attributed to leaf exudates.

Newly overseeded sites should not be kept wet and should not be allowed to become excessively dry. Close attention to watering is important for the first several weeks after planting to establish the grass and provide playable conditions. Avoid late evening watering that keeps grass moist all night. Diseases can develop and spread rapidly when grass remains moist overnight.

Fertilize overseeded sites with a complete fertilizer such as 12-4-8 at about 1 pound of nitrogen per 1,000 square feet. Apply fertilizer immediately after seeding so as not to burn the young seedlings. After seedlings emerge, light applications of nitrogen will help produce a dense, healthy stand of grass. Soluble nitrogen sources, such as urea or ammonia sulfate, can be applied most effectively as a foliar spray at rates not exceeding $\frac{1}{2}$ pound of nitrogen per 1,000 square feet per week. Nitrogen sources with a low burn potential, such as Nutralene, IBDU, or Milorganite, can be applied in dry applications at rates between $\frac{1}{2}$ and 1 pound of nitrogen per 1,000 square feet. Very low rates of soluble nitrogen, such as 2 to 4 ounces per 1,000 square feet, can be applied as a foliar spray along with fungicides.

Seedling diseases such as *Pythium* and brownpatch must be controlled to maintain a thick, healthy stand of winter grasses. Application of a preplant fungicide and the use of treated seed will go a long way toward producing a disease-free turf. Diseases are much more effectively controlled on a preventative rather than a curative basis. Once a disease becomes a problem it can set overseeded grasses back several weeks. Strict attention must be given to spray schedules for disease prevention for the first several weeks after planting.

Broadleaved weeds such as lawn burweed, chickweed, and clover can be controlled after winter grasses are established. Products such as Trimec, Weedone DPC, Turflon II Amine, and Confront can be used if label directions are followed.

SET UP A SCHEDULE

It is important to develop an overseeding schedule well in advance of planting time. A suggested program might include the following:

1. Select the grass seed.
   —Measure overseeded sites to determine the quantity of seed needed.
   —Decide on a variety or mixture and order seed in mid summer.

—Select several new grasses or mixtures to observe on a practice putting green or test location.

2. Prepare the seedbed.
   —Set up a vertical mowing schedule during midsummer.
   —Aerate in late summer.
   —Topdress (prepare topdressing material ahead of time).
   —Use preemerge herbicide or Rubigan (optional).
   —Preplant fungicide.
3. Seed the site.
   —Determine seeding rate (calibrate sprayers).
   —Determine seeding date.
4. Set up a watering schedule during and after seedling emergence.
5. Set up a spray schedule.
   —Use fungicides (*Pythium* and brownpatch).
   —Use herbicides (broadleaved weeds).
6. Fertilize before and after seeding.
7. Mow the site.
   —Determine appropriate height.
   —Determine appropriate frequency.

The most common causes of failure include (1) poor seedbed preparation, (2) planting too early or too late, (3) seedling diseases, (4) herbicide injury (pre- and postemerge), (5) overwatering and excessive rain, (6) fertilizer burn, and (7) mowing with dull mowers.

Weed Control in Turf 8

Weeds are the number one pest problem in lawns, golf courses, and sports fields. Aggressive competitors for sunlight, moisture, and nutrients and prolific multipliers even under adverse conditions, weeds present a challenge for even the most experienced turfgrass managers.

The color, texture, and growth rate of weeds often contrast markedly with that of the turfgrasses they may be associated with in a lawn or sports field. Consequently, weeds detract from the uniformity of a turf and add to its maintenance requirements.

The origin of weeds is as varied as that of turfgrasses. Most are introduced species that were inadvertently brought to this country from Asia and Europe. Many were unintentional stowaways in animal fodder or ship ballasts or, simply, contaminants in seed of food supplies brought to this country.

In lawns and sports fields, weeds are often the result of poor quality turf rather than the cause of poor quality turf. The aggressive nature of weeds and their prolific reproductive capacity enable them to invade thin, weak turf areas. Cultural practices should always be viewed as the first step to effective weed control. By determining why weeds established a foothold, one can correct those deficiencies. If the basic problem is not corrected, weeds will continue to occur.

An effective weed control program also requires identifying the undesirable species' classification as a grassy weed, a broadleaved weed, an annual, or a perennial. Most turf weeds belong to two principal categories—grasses and broadleaved plants. Chemical controls for these two categories of plants frequently differ.

Grassy weeds have jointed, hollow stems; leaf blades have veins parallel to leaf margins and several times longer than they are wide. Roots are fibrous and multibranching and flowers are usually inconspicuous. In contrast, broadleaved plants often have showy flowers; leaves have a network of veins at diverse angles to one another; stems are often pithy and a taproot is usually present.

Another group of turf weeds, sedges, have grass-like characteristics but require a different group of chemicals for control. Sedges are characterized by three-sided stems (triangular cross section) which bear leaves in three directions (in contrast to the two-ranked arrangement of grass leaves).

Weeds can be further grouped according to their life span—annual or perennial. From the standpoint of chemical control, the grouping is most important because preemerge herbicides are only effective for control of annual weeds (table 8-1).

Annual weeds germinate from seed each year; mature in one growing season and die in less than 12 months. Crabgrass and henbit are examples of annual weeds—crabgrass being a summer annual and henbit being a winter annual. Preemerge herbicides must be applied according to the expected date of emergence for each targeted species.

Perennial weeds live more than one year and recover or regrow from dormant stolons, rhizomes, or tubers as well as from seed. Control of perennial weeds requires a postemerge herbicide during its season of active growth.

Broadleaf weeds
Annuals:
  burweed
  henbit
  spurge
Perennials:
  buttonweed
  dandelion

Grassy weeds
Annuals:
  annual bluegrass
  grassburs
  crabgrass
  goosegrass
Perennials:
  dallisgrass

Sedges:
yellow nutsedge
purple nutsedge

Effective chemical weed control requires identifying the weed's classification (grass, broadleaf, sedge, etc.), life span (annual or perennial), and season of active growth (cool season or warm season). Effective chemical control also requires accurate timing of applications, proper rate of application, and uniformity of application. Always follow label directions for a product and observe all warnings and precautions relative to safety of the application.

Broadleaved Weed Control

DANDELION

The dandelion (*Taraxacum officinale*) is a troublesome weed in bluegrass lawns throughout the Transition Zone. Although it is found in every southern state, it is most troublesome in the cooler regions where it persists year-round. The bright yellow flower of the dandelion appears from early spring through summer in the Transition Zone, where it contrasts sharply with the color and texture of turfgrasses. In the Gulf States the flowering period ends in late spring.

DESCRIPTION. The dandelion is a perennial plant with a deep, thick taproot. A rosette of basal leaves emerges from the crown of the plant. The leaves are long, narrow, deeply notched, with backward pointed lobes. The leaves and flower stalk contain a milk-like juice. Flower stalks are long and slender and terminate in a single flower. The flower is 1 to 1½ inches across and consists of bright yellow to orange-yellow petals. The flower head is surrounded by narrow pointed bracts with the outer ones curved backwards. The seeds are brown, ¼-inch long, narrow, with a parachute-like pappus attached to a long beak at the upper end. The dandelion flowers from April through June, and seed mature and disperse quickly after the bloom appears.

CONTROL. Dandelions are readily controlled by 2,4-D, or products containing 2,4-D, if applications are made in fall or early spring before the plants begin to flower. After flowering begins, 2,4-D will twist and curl the leaves and flower stalks, but the plants often survive the treatment.

HENBIT

Henbit (*Lamium amplexicaule*) is a cool-season, annual broadleaved weed. Seedlings begin to emerge in early fall and grow throughout the fall, winter, and spring. Henbit can dominate turfgrass in the spring throughout the southern region.

DESCRIPTION. Henbit, a member of the mint family, has characteristic square stems. Stems are slender, ascending or prostrate,

Dandelion

Henbit

Table 8-1. Weed Classification

Broadleaved Weeds	Grassy Weeds	Sedges
Annuals:	Annuals:	yellow nutsedge
burweed	annual bluegrass	purple nutsedge
henbit	grassburs	
spurge	crabgrass	
	goosegrass	
Perennials:		
buttonweed	Perennials:	
dandelion	dallisgrass	

and freely branched at the base. Stems may root at the lower nodes. Leaves are opposite, nearly circular, deeply veined, hairy, and petioled. Upper leaves clasp the stem, and the lower leaves are distinctly petioled. Roots are shallow and fibrous.

Flowers, conspicuous in early spring, are tubular, pink to purple, and borne in the leaf axile. Seeds are borne in a pod.

CONTROL. Henbit is most effectively controlled with herbicides in the fall, while plants are small and immature. Products containing dicamba, MCPP, and 2,4-D have demonstrated effective control in the fall and early spring. In dormant bermudagrass, glyphosate, diquat, or metribuzin will control henbit. In the spring close mowing will control henbit.

If applied prior to germination, products such as surflan, bensulide, prodiamine, pendimethalin, and simazine also provide good control of henbit. Follow label directions on all products recommended for henbit to obtain the best control.

COMMON CHICKWEED

Common chickweed (*Stellaria media*) is a matted, herbaceous, winter annual broadleaved plant. Chickweed is a prolific spring weed, as it thrives under cool, wet conditions. It rarely tolerates hot, dry conditions that occur in late spring or early summer. Other common names for chickweed include starweed, winterweed, satin flower, and tongue grass.

DESCRIPTION. Common chickweed develops prostrate, tender, freely branching stems that root at nodes; opposite, smooth, oval, or elliptic leaves, lower leaves with long petioles, upper leaves sessile; shallow, fibrous, and very frail roots. Flowers are solitary or in small clusters at ends of stems, flower stalks fragile, petals white, and seeds are produced in oval, five-segmented capsule. Seeds are circular, flattened, and reddish-brown in color. Plants form a thick mat of succulent or tender vegetation in the early spring that is not eradicated by close mowing.

CONTROL. Common chickweed is effectively controlled by timely applications of preemerge herbicides, such as simazine, dithiopyr, dacthal, oryzalin, prodiamine, pendimethalin, and isoxaben. Preemerge applications should be made in early fall prior to the emergence of chickweed.

Postemerge control of chickweed during winter and early spring can be achieved with products containing dicamba, dichlorprop, and triclopyr. The latter product is only labelled for use on cool-season turfgrasses such as tall fescue, bluegrass, and perennial ryegrass.

CLOVERS (WHITE CLOVER, BURCLOVER)

Several species of clover are troublesome in turfgrass, since they develop dense patches of lush vegetation that compete with grasses in the early spring. White clover is a desirable species in pastures and rangelands, as it provides nutritious forage and adds nitrogen to the soil. White clover is a perennial plant in areas where summer rainfall is adequate. In other areas it reestablishes each fall from seed. Burclover is an annual plant with little forage value.

DESCRIPTION. White clover (*Trifolium repens*), also called Dutch clover, is a perennial, mat-forming herbaceous plant with a creeping stem that roots at the nodes. Leaves are trifoliate with long, erect petioles; leaflets are widely elliptic with toothed margins and usually with a white splotch near the base of the upper surface. Blooms are a spherical cluster of white or pinkish flowers that develop on long stalks. Flower clusters are about one inch wide and appear slightly above the leaves. Plants bloom from March to October. Seeds are kidney-shaped or circular in outline and reddish brown in color with a smooth surface.

Burclover (*Medicago* spp.) is an annual species whose vegetative characteristics are similar to white clover. In place of the whitish splotches on the upper leaf surfaces characteristic of white clover, burclover has purplish markings (spotted burclover) or no distinct markings. Flowers develop in small clusters, and the yellow petals fall soon after blooming. Seed develops in pods, usually in clusters, with a double row of soft spines forming the bur. Burclover blooms from March through May.

CONTROL. Burclover can be controlled preemerge in warm-season turfgrasses with simazine (Princep) or isoxaben (Gallery). Postemerge, both white clover and burclover, can be controlled with hormone products such as MCPP (Chipco Turf Herbicide MCPP), dicamba (Banvel), 2,4-D, MCPP and dicamba (Trimec), 2,4-D and dichlorprop (Weedone DPC) and 2,4-D and triclopyr (Turflon II Amine).

PROSTRATE OR SPOTTED SPURGE

Prostrate spurge (*Euphorbia supina*) and spotted spurge (*E. maculata*) are warm-season annual weeds found throughout the southeastern states. Both species have a rather deep taproot, are freely branching, and form a circular mat or clump several inches to several feet in diameter. Both species produce abundant seed that germinate throughout the summer and readily invade turf.

Prostrate spurge

DESCRIPTION. Leaves are opposite, ovate to oblong, slightly serrated, sparsely pubescent with a tinge of red or purple in the center. A milky latex drips from cut leaves, stems, or roots of both plants. In an unmowed location, spotted spurge develops a more erect plant than prostrate spurge. Also, seedlings of the spotted spurge have a pink or green stem.

Like most broadleaved weeds, spurge is most susceptible to postemerge herbicides when plants are in the seedling or immature stage. Mature plants are quite tolerant to most herbicides.

Spurge begins to germinate in late spring and continues to emerge throughout the summer. Controls are most effective when applied in early summer. A second application may be required 4 to 6 weeks after the initial application to control new seedlings.

CONTROL. Products such as dicamba and Trimec provide good control of immature spurge plants, but only fair control of mature plants. These products can be used on most turfgrasses. In bermudagrass turf, MSMA and Trimec can be used for postemerge control of spurge.

Dacthal, pendimethalin, prodiamine, and oryzalin have provided good preemerge control of spurge in warm-season turfgrasses. To be effective, they must be applied in early spring prior to germination of weeds at recommended rates of application. A second application may be required sixty days after the initial application to provide season-long control of spurge.

YELLOW WOODSORREL

Yellow woodsorrel (*Oxalis stricta*), also commonly called oxalis or sheep sorrel, is a spring or summer annual weed throughout the South, Midwest,

Buffalograss, a warm-season
perennial grass, is the only
native species widely used
for turf.

Bermudagrass lawns need full sunlight.

Spring dead spot is a troublesome disease in bermudagrass turf.

Winterkill is a serious problem on overseeded bermudagrass golf greens.

Brownpatch is a serious disease on Saint Augustine grass lawns.

Saint Augustine grass leaf blades showing healthy *(left)*, SAD-infected *(center)*, and iron chlorosis *(right)* symptoms.

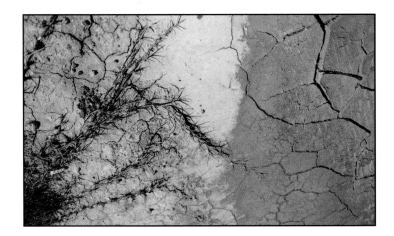

Adalayd growing on a salt-encrusted site

Adalayd growing at the edge of a brackish pond

Carpetgrass produces a low-maintenance lawn.

Tall fescue lawns contrast with
dormant bermudagrass lawns.

Saint Augustine grass has good shade tolerance, but poor drought tolerance and coarse texture.

Centipede has good shade tolerance, good drought tolerance, and medium texture.

Emerald zoysia has good shade tolerance, good drought tolerance, and fine texture.

Hybrid bermudagrasses have multiple uses in the South.

Nutrient deficiency
symptoms

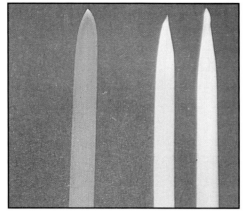

Nitrogen

Potassium

Calcium

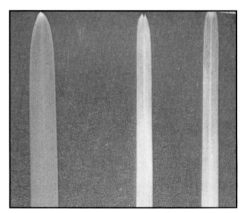

Magnesium

Sulfur

Centipedegrass in early
spring

Stems of henbit are slender,
ascending, and freely
branched.

Spurge competes strongly
with turfgrasses.

Annual broadleaf weeds:

Mouseear chickweed

Common chickweed

Mustard

Purslane

Sow thistle

Carolina geranium

Dichondra

White clover

Burclover

Dollarweed

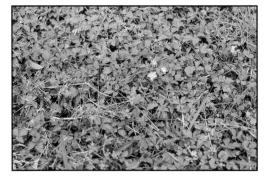

Wild strawberry

Dandelion

Interveinal chlorosis is a
symptom of triazine herbicides
on elm and pear leaves.

Leaf margin necrosis is a
symptom of severe injury
from triazine herbicides on
live oak and Shumard oak.

Lesions on stolons distinguish Nigrospora stolon rot.

Overall symptoms of stolon rot resemble chinch bug injury or drought.

Bermudagrass decline

Bermuda decline with brown roots and few rhizomes

Helminthosporium leaf spot on bermudagrass

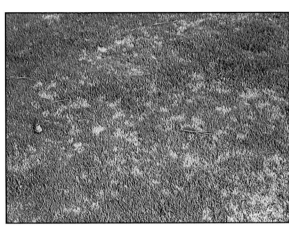

Dollar spot

Saint Augustine decline symptoms

Gray leaf spot

Cinch bug injury in St. Augustine grass resembles drought stress.

Immature stages *(left)* to adult chinch bug *(right)*

White grub feed on the roots of turfgrasses.

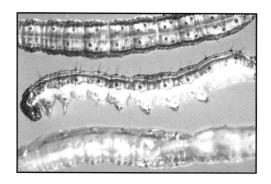

Armyworms

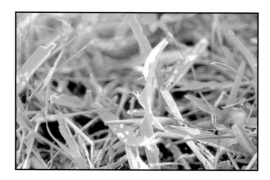

Skeletonized leaf blades
produced by armyworms

and eastern states. Yellow woodsorrel is a problem weed found in lawns as well as in ornamental plantings. In lawns the weed develops a creeping growth habit, often rooting at the nodes of low-growing stems. In ornamental beds or gardens the plant develops an upright or bushy growth habit.

DESCRIPTION. Yellow woodsorrel leaves are divided into 3 heart-shaped leaflets, green to purplish in color, with long petioles attached to a weak, branching stem. Stems may be prostrate or erect up to 50 cm tall. Plants have a taproot, but some species spread by weak rhizomes.

Flowers of yellow woodsorrel have 5 bright yellow petals and are about 2 cm wide. Flowers develop in clusters in an unequally branched umbel. Seed develops in a slender capsule 5 to 15 mm long with five ridges and a pointed tip. Mature seed scatter several feet when the capsule bursts.

CONTROL. Yellow woodsorrel is most effectively controlled by preemerge herbicides, such as dacthal, oryzalin (Surflan), pendimethalin (Pre-M), prodiamine (Barricade), isoxaben (Gallery), dithiopyr (Dimension), and oxadiazon (Ronstar). Preemerge products must be applied in early spring for effective control of early emerging weeds. Repeat applications may be needed with some products to obtain season-long control.

Yellow woodsorrel is resistant to postemergent products such as 2,4-D and MCPP. Postemerge products containing dichlorprop (Weedone DPC) and triclopyr (Turflon D) are effective on yellow woodsorrel if applied early postemerge. Repeat applications may be required to control more mature plants.

BURWEED

Carpet burweed, or lawn burweed (*Soliva* spp.), a cool-season annual introduced from South America, has become a nuisance on golf courses, sports fields, parks, and lawns throughout much of Texas and the Southwest. The weed becomes a real nuisance when the seed matures in the spring because the sharply pointed spines on the seed can easily pierce the skin. Burweed becomes a deterrent to the use of sports fields, parks, and playgrounds in the spring when the seed mature. On golf courses burweed invades even the most closely mowed putting greens as well as fairways, tees, and roughs.

DESCRIPTION. Burweed is a small, low-growing annual plant. In an unmowed site it only reaches 2 inches in height and the individual plants may spread out to about 6 inches in diameter. Leaves are pinnately divided, giving the plant a feathery appearance. The seed enclosures are flattened, callous structures terminating in teeth on spines.

Burweed emerges in early fall and matures in the spring. The vegetative part of the plant dries up in May, and the seeds remain to germinate the next fall. Populations of the weed may become so high that

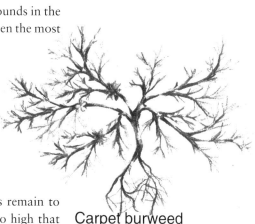

Carpet burweed

plants cover the ground like a carpet—thus, the name carpet burweed. Where grassy weeds such as annual bluegrass are eliminated by the use of preemerge herbicides, populations of burweed increase dramatically in following years.

CONTROL. Like most broadleaved weeds, burweed is easily controlled in the seedling stage with hormone-type herbicides. Products containing 2,4-D, MCPP, and dicamba will control burweed in the seedling stage.

Preemerge herbicides are generally not effective for burweed control. In fact, burweed populations increase where preemerge herbicides reduce the competition. Simazine and atrazine are exceptions in that they effectively control burweed.

BUTTONWEED

Buttonweed (*Diodia virginiana*) is becoming an increasingly troublesome weed in lawns, golf courses, and other turfgrass areas. Buttonweed is found through the southeastern states and is particularly well adapted to low, wet areas. In Texas it is a serious lawn problem in the eastern half of the state.

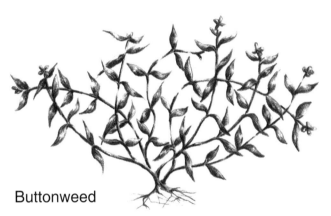

Buttonweed

DESCRIPTION. Buttonweed is a warm-season perennial with a sprawling, widely branched growth habit. Leaves are opposite, margins slightly serrated, oblong, or nearly linear, generally 2 to 3 inches long and leathery in texture. Leaves often develop a purplish color. The plant has an extensive root system and develops underground rhizomes.

The plant produces small, white flowers during the summer and fall. Fruit develop along the stolons, or stems, in summer and fall. Fruit are oval-shaped with vertical ridges and usually 6 to 10 mm long. The fruit develops into leathery pods in rows along the stolons and gives the plant its name, buttonweed.

Plants develop in early spring from dormant rhizomes and seed. Emergence occurs about the time Saint Augustine grass begins growth and continues throughout the spring. The aboveground part of the plant is killed in the fall by the first frost.

CONTROL. Preemerge herbicides are not effective, since buttonweed emerges from dormant rhizomes as well as seed. Postemerge control requires repeated treatments in the spring and summer. In bermudagrass turf MSMA will provide temporary control. Combinations of MSMA with Trimec (or similar products) have provided good control with only two applications (spring and summer).

In Saint Augustine grass lawns, dicamba (Banvel) or products containing dicamba (Trimec) provide some control with two or more applications in spring and summer. Products with only 2,4-D have not demonstrated control of buttonweed.

Winter Broadleaved Weeds

Winter broadleaved weeds are a major problem throughout the South where mild temperatures occur. These weeds, including clover, chickweed, henbit, dandelion, and burweed, are particularly troublesome in early spring when warm-season turfgrasses are dormant. Not only are these weeds unsightly, but they increase mowing requirements and compete with desirable grasses for sunlight, water, and nutrients.

Controlling broadleaved weeds with chemicals in the winter and early spring helps grasses develop a dense, uniform turf that resists invasion by summer weeds. Weed control also helps to reduce mowing in the early spring and to improve the appearance of lawns, golf courses, and other turfgrass areas.

Regular mowing in the late winter and early spring reduces the competition from broadleaved weeds but does not eliminate them from the turf. Chemical control with nonselective herbicides on dormant bermudagrass or with selective herbicides will remove the weeds from the turf.

On dormant bermudagrass turf in January and early February, nonselective herbicides such as Roundup or Diquat can be used to control broadleaved and grassy weeds. In some cases repeat applications, two to four weeks after the initial application, are required for complete control. Sencor can also be used on dormant bermudagrass fairways for control of certain broadleaved weeds.

Applications of selective herbicides, such as those containing 2,4-D, MCPP, and/or dicamba, can be used during winter and early spring for control of many broadleaved weeds. Identification of weeds is important with these materials, since some species require combinations of the materials for effective control. Generally, repeat applications of these materials are required for complete control.

For all of the products the rate of application is critical to their safe and effective use (table 8-2). Label directions should be observed for all products used.

Grassy Weeds

CRABGRASS

Crabgrass has plagued turf managers for fifty years and still tops the list of most troublesome weeds. Since lead arsenate first showed promise for crabgrass control, turf managers have sought better chemical controls. Several products have come and gone, and new products appear frequently, but crabgrass remains.

DESCRIPTION. Two species of crabgrass are found throughout the semitropical and temperate zones of the United States—smooth crabgrass (*Digitaria ischamum*) and hairy crabgrass (*D. sanguinalis*). Both are an-

Table 8-2. Chemical Control of Broadleaved Weeds in Turf

Product	Rate and Volume	Remarks
Dormant bermudagrass		
Glyphosate (Roundup)	1 pt./acre in 25–40 gals. water	Apply when temperature is above 50°F. Bermudagrass must be dormant at the time of application.
Diquat	1 pt./acre in 50 gals. water	Repeat if necessary. Add surfactant.
Sencor 75	0.5 lb. active/acre in 40 gals. water	Only one application per year to dormant turf. Use on common bermudagrass only.
Dormant and actively growing turf		
2,4-D amine	1 lb. active/acre in 25–40 gals. water	Apply when between 60–80° F. Repeat if necessary.
2,4-D + dicamba	1 lb. active/acre in 25–40 gals. water	Same as above.
2,4-D + MCPP + dicamba	1 lb. active/acre in 25–40 gals. water	Same as above.
Triclopyr	1 lb. active/acre in 25–40 gals. water	Same as above.
Preemerge (apply before annual weeds emerge)		
Simazine	1–2 lbs. active/acre	Make initial application after Sept. 1. Second application must be made before June 1.
Atrazine	1–2 lbs. active/acre in 50 gals. water	For use on Saint Augustine, centipede and dormant bermudagrass. Has some postemerge activity. Apply between Oct. 1 and April 15.
DCPA	10.5 lbs. active/acre in 50 gals. water	Repeat application at same rate 6 to 8 weeks later.
Oryzalin	1.5 lbs. active/acre in 50 gals. water	Repeat application at same rate 8 to 10 weeks later.
Pendimethalin	1.5–2 lbs. active/acre in 50 gals. water	Apply before weeds emerge.
Prodiamine	0.5–1 lb. active/acre in 50 gals. water	Apply before weeds emerge.

nual grasses that emerge in early to midspring and are killed by the first frost in fall. Crabgrass flowers throughout the summer and is a prolific seed producer.

Crabgrass has one significant weakness in that the seed requires light to germinate. Consequently, a dense turf cover effectively resists invasion by crabgrass. But conditions that weaken the turf during the spring and summer, such as disease, insect damage, traffic, or winterkill, increases the likelihood of a crabgrass invasion. Often, cultural practices such as aeration and dethatching increase the crabgrass problem by exposing the seed to favorable conditions—sunlight, moisture, and high temperatures.

Once crabgrass germinates it rapidly dominates a turf. Crabgrass is a vigorous plant that grows faster than the most desirable turfgrasses. It grows under stress conditions such as drought, heat, and low fertility that make

Crabgrass

turfgrasses suffer. Crabgrass thrives under low mowing heights because of its prostrate growth habit.

CONTROL. Crabgrass control requires a sound turf maintenance program together with a planned herbicide program. A dense turf is the best protection against invasion by crabgrass. Cultural practices that promote a dense, healthy turf include regular mowing and watering together with timely fertilization, aeration, and dethatching. Pest management including insect and disease control is also essential to preventing crabgrass invasions.

For the past twenty-five years, preemergence control of crabgrass has been the target of considerable research. A number of very good herbicides have been developed for turf as a result of that research. DCPA (Dacthal), simazine (Princep), besulide (Betasan, Presan), benefin (Balan), dithiopyr (Dimension), oxadiazon (Ronstar), oryzalin (Surflan), pendimethalin (Pre-M), napropamide (Devrinol), prodiamine (Barricade), and fenoxaprop (Acclaim) are some of the materials available for preemergence crabgrass control.

Since crabgrass germinates from April through September in most areas of the country (slightly shorter periods in other areas), few of these herbicides provide season-long control. All of these products should be applied about two weeks prior to the expected date of emergence of crabgrass. Since this date varies from North to South and from year to year, a specific date must be developed by turf managers from past experiences, climatic conditions, and, perhaps, biological indicators.

The presence of thatch is another factor that influences the effectiveness of preemergence herbicides. Some products such as benefin and oxadiazon are more injurious to turf where a thatch layer is present. Other products, including DCPA and benefin, break down more rapidly in thatch than in soil. Thus lighter and more frequent applications of preemergence herbicides may be required for effective season-long control of crabgrass in thatchy turf.

Occasionally, turfgrass injury may appear during stress periods after the application of preemergence materials. Injury usually resembles drought stress and may be attributed to root injury by the herbicide. The symptoms should be treated as drought stress by increasing the frequency of irrigation and applying fungicides to reduce disease occurrence on the weakened grass.

Selective postemergence control of crabgrass with chemicals is effective in many situations. The organic arsenicals, including MSMA, DSMA, AMA, and CAMA, effectively control crabgrass with little injury to bermudagrass or zoysia when used properly. These materials should not be applied to fescue, Saint Augustine, centipede, or bahia turf. A single application of one of these materials at 2 pounds active per acre in 80 to 100 gallons of water per acre will control seedling crabgrass. Repeat applications at 14-day intervals may be required to control more mature crabgrass plants. For best crabgrass control, turf should not be mowed for 2 to 3 days prior to application or 2 to 3 days after application and temperatures should be 80° to 90° F at the time of application.

In some states Asulox is labeled for postemergence control in Saint Augustine grass turf. A single application at 5 pints per acre is recommended for crabgrass control in Saint Augustine grass.

Dimension Turf Herbicide (dithiopyr) is a preemerge product that provides effective postemerge control of crabgrass when plants are in the 3- to 4-leaf stage. Dimension will control more mature crabgrass plants but may require 4 to 6 weeks to kill the plants.

When crabgrass and other weeds are dominant and renovation is required, nonselective herbicides such as glyphosate (Roundup) can be used. These products will kill existing weeds and grasses prior to planting. Again, label recommendations with respect to turf renovation should be followed. Keep in mind that crabgrass and other weeds will germinate from seed after treatment with these products. Thus, selective postemergence materials may be required after planting.

GOOSEGRASS

Goosegrass (*Eleusine indica*) is a troublesome weed in turfgrasses throughout the South. It is most frequently found in high traffic areas where the turfgrass cover is thin. Sports fields and golf courses are prime sites for an infestation of goosegrass. The name goosegrass is commonly used for this species, but it is also called silver crabgrass, crowfoot, or wiregrass.

DESCRIPTION. Goosegrass, a warm-season annual grass, develops in leafy, commonly reclining, tufts. Goosegrass is a prolific seeder and, in most cases,

Goosegrass is a prolific seeding annual weed.

has 3 to 7 fingerlike racemes on a single stem. Often, 15 to 20 stems are produced by a mature plant and as many as 50,000 seed can be produced by a single plant. Once goosegrass becomes established, annual reinfestations are likely to occur.

Goosegrass has a strong, extensive root system and readily invades hard, compacted soils found in high traffic areas. It adapts well to close, frequent mowing and even produces seed when mowed at putting green heights.

Mature leaf blades of goosegrass are extremely difficult to cut with a mower. Often the leaf blades are frayed by the mower and the tips develop a whitish cast. Mower blades must be kept sharp to maintain a satisfactory cut on goosegrass-infested turf.

Goosegrass emergence from seed begins as early as March in Florida and South Texas and as late as June in the northern portions of the South. Emergence continues throughout the summer months. Plants are usually killed by the first frost in the fall.

CONTROL. Cultural practices that promote vigorous turf and maintain a complete grass cover will keep goosegrass populations to a minimum. But where the grass cover is weakened by traffic or by competition with overseeded grasses, goosegrass emerges in the spring and summer.

Preemerge herbicides such as Ronstar, Surflan, Pre-M, Devrinol, and Barricade will control goosegrass in warm-season grasses. The rate and timing of application is critical to effective goosegrass control. A single application of Ronstar at 3 pounds active per acre several weeks prior to the expected emergence date will provide season-long control of goosegrass. Other products may require split applications for season-long control.

In bermudagrass turf, goosegrass can be controlled postemerge with repeated applications of MSMA at 2 to 3 pounds active per acre at 10- to 14-day intervals. Sencor is also labeled for goosegrass control in common bermudagrass fairways and commercial sod farms. Illoxan is a restricted use product for postemergence goosegrass control in bermudagrass presently approved in Florida, Alabama, North Carolina, South Carolina, Mississippi, Georgia, and Texas (table 8-3).

ANNUAL BLUEGRASS (*POA ANNUA*)

Annual bluegrass invades desirable turfgrasses each fall in the southern states. Annual bluegrass is a particularly serious weed problem in closely mowed areas such as golf greens and fairways.

DESCRIPTION. Two types of *Poa annua* are found in the southern states— an upright growing plant with a bunch-type growth pattern and a decumbent type with creeping stolons. The upright type is a prolific seed producer and is an annual. The decumbent type produces very little seed and is perennial in nature, although it dies during the summer in the deep South.

Annual bluegrass begins to emerge in late summer and early fall when

Table 8-3. Chemical Control of Goosegrass in Established Bermudagrass Turf

Product	Rate of Application (pounds product/acre)	Remarks
Preemergence Control		
Ronstar 2G	150	Two weeks prior to expected date of emergence. Do not use on putting greens or tees.
Devrinol 5G	40	Use two applications at 40 lbs. each, 8–10 weeks apart.
Barricade 65 WG	2.3	Use two applications, the first at 1.15 lbs. and the second at 1.15 lbs., 60 days apart. Do not use on putting greens.
Surflan AS	2 qts.	For split applications use two applications at 2 qts. per acre, 8–10 weeks apart. Do not use on putting greens.
PreM 60 DG	5	Do not use on putting greens.
Postemergence Control (bermudagrass only)		
Sencor	$\frac{1}{3}$–$\frac{2}{3}$	Use *only* on common bermudagrass fairways and sod farms. Repeat application if necessary. Do not make more than two applications per year.
MSMA	2 qts.	Do not mow or water-treat area for 48 hours after application. Repeat treatment in 10–14 days.
Illoxan	1–2 qts.	Young actively growing plants are more easily controlled than mature plants. The lower rate may be used on plants in the 1- to 3-leaf stage. Do not apply more than 2 qts. per acre per year. Do not overseed treated area for at least 3 months after application.

night temperatures are in the sixties and moisture is abundant. Annual bluegrass seeds continue to germinate through the fall, winter, and spring—a characteristic that makes chemical control more difficult.

Germination and growth of annual bluegrass are favored by moist soil conditions and cool temperatures. Thus, it has a strong competitive advantage over warm-season grasses from fall through spring. On closely mowed and irrigated turf, annual bluegrass will dominate a stand of bermudagrass by late spring if herbicides are not used. Populations of annual bluegrass are greatly reduced by taller mowing heights and limited use of water. Thus, little annual bluegrass is found in golf course roughs, lawns, parks, and

Annual bluegrass

other areas maintained at taller mowing heights and with less irrigation.

Annual bluegrass initiates seedheads in late fall and winter, but seedhead development is greatest in the spring and early summer. Until those seedheads appear, annual bluegrass is not too objectionable. After seedhead appearance, the turf develops a yellowish-white color and an uneven appearance.

CONTROL. Annual bluegrass can be effectively controlled with pre- and postemergence herbicides in warm-season turfgrasses. Preemerge products must be applied prior to the emergence of annual bluegrass in the fall. The date of emergence varies between locations and years but generally begins when night temperatures are in the sixties and daytime temperatures are below 85° F. Where winter grasses are to be overseeded on bermudagrass turf, applications of preemergence products must be made 60 to 90 days before seeding (table 8-4). Follow label directions for all products.

GRASSBURS (SANDBURS)

In recent years drought has aggravated the grassbur problem in lawns, golf courses, and playgrounds throughout the South. Where drought-weakened turf gets some spring and summer rainfall, grassburs are a problem. Grassburs (*Cenchrus* spp.) include annual and perennial species. Plants are bunch-type with low branching stems terminating in a raceme of burs. The burs readily fall off the stem when mature. Grassburs are commonly found in open fields and meadows where competition from other plants is not great; they are seldom found in dense, vigorous turf.

DESCRIPTION. Lawns damaged or weakened by insects, drought, or wear are susceptible to invasion by grassburs. The seed (burs) for this weed may lie dormant in the soil for several years until environmental conditions favor germination, or the seed may be carried in by birds, small animals, or people.

Once grassburs get started, where there were only a few plants one year, there may be hundreds of plants the following year. All the grassbur needs to become a problem is a weak turf and favorable moisture conditions during the late spring and early summer. The plants may go unnoticed most of the summer, but once burs develop, they are unavoidable. Close mowing and catching the clippings will improve the appearance of the turf and reduce seed for next year, but enough burs will remain to reinfest the area for several years.

CONTROL. It takes a good turf management program to eliminate grassburs. Preemergence herbicides applied in the spring for crabgrass control before emergence of the grassburs have been shown to reduce grassbur populations.

Herbicides or fertilizer-herbicide (weed and feed) combinations containing benefin (Balan), DCPA (Dacthal), oryzalin (Surflan), oxadiazon (Ronstar) or simazine are effective against the grassbur if the timing and rate of application are correct. As for all pesticides, follow label instructions closely and carefully.

Grassbur

Table 8.4. Chemical Control of Annual Bluegrass in Warm-Season Grass Lawns and Fairways

Product (formulation)	Chemical Name	Rate of Application (product/acre)	Time of Application
Postemergence Control (bermudagrass only)			
Kerb 50 WP	pronamide	2–3 lbs.	Use lighter rate during fall and higher rate in spring. Use on bermudagrass only.
Roundup (liquid, 4 lbs./gal.)	glyphosate	¾ pint or 12 fl. oz.	Apply only to dormant bermudagrass turf.
For overseeded bermudagrass turf:			
Prograss (liquid, 4 lbs./gal.)	ethofumesate	Initial Application: 2–4 pints Supplemental Application: at 30- to 60-day intervals, 2 pints	Apply only to dormant bermudagrass 15 to 30 days after overseeding with perennial ryegrass. Do not apply after February 1.
Preemergence control			
Balan 2.5G	benefin	120 lbs.	Apply two weeks prior to germination.
Dacthal 75 WP	DCPA	20 lbs.	Apply two weeks prior to germination.
Pre-M 60 DG	pendimethalin	3 lbs.	Apply two weeks prior to germination.
Princep 4G	simazine	25 lbs.	Apply after October 1.
Ronstar 2G	oxadiazon	200 lbs.	Apply two weeks prior to germination.
Barricade 65 WG	prodiamine	1 lb.	Apply two weeks prior to germination.
May be used on golf greens:			
Pre-San 12.5 G	bensulide	100 lbs.	Apply at least two weeks prior to germination.
For bermudagrass turf only:			
Kerb 50 WP	pronamide	1–2 lbs.	Has both pre- and postemerge activity.

In bermudagrass lawns postemergence herbicides can be used for grassbur control. Products containing one of the organic arsenical herbicides, such as DSMA or MSMA, can be used for postemergence grassbur control in bermudagrass lawns, but label instructions must be followed for effective control.

In warm-season grasses, Image (imazaquin) is labeled for postemerge control of grassburs. In Saint Augustine grass Asulox (asulam) is also labeled for grassbur control.

Always keep in mind that herbicides only provide a temporary solution to the grassbur problem. A healthy, vigorous turf is the ultimate solution. Regular mowing, proper fertilization and watering, and pest control are all required for satisfactory control of grassburs.

Fertilize lawns in the spring and summer to promote desirable grasses. If the grassburs are already established in the lawn, fertilization will stimulate them as well as the desirable grasses. But a more vigorous turf will reduce the grassbur population the following year. Late fall fertilization, after grassburs have matured, is worthwhile.

Water lawns as needed to maintain a complete turf cover, since thin turf is more susceptible to invasion by grassburs. Avoid light, frequent watering which keeps the soil surface moist and is ideal for weed seed germination. Instead, water lawn thoroughly and infrequently to promote deep-rooted grasses.

DALLISGRASS

Dallisgrass (*Paspalum dilatatum*) is a perennial, warm-season grass that readily invades turfgrass areas throughout Texas and the southeastern states. Dallisgrass is native to South America and was introduced into the United States for its value as a forage plant. Records indicate that it was first introduced into the U.S. in the vicinity of New Orleans, Louisiana. It was found in Texas as early as 1875. The grass was named for A. T. Dallis of La Grange, Georgia, who was an enthusiastic proponent of the plant around 1900.

DESCRIPTION. Dallisgrass grows in clumps, or bunches. Leaves are produced near the base of the plant on shoots that arise from a knotty base of very short rhizomes. Relative to turfgrasses, especially bermudagrass, the leaves of dallisgrass are much coarser textured. Dallisgrass also produces unsightly seed stalks several feet above the turf. After mowing, dallisgrass leaves elongate much faster than bermudagrass turf and significantly increase the mowing needs for bermudagrass turf areas.

The color, texture, and growth rate of dallisgrass contrast sharply with bermudagrass.

CONTROL. In bermudagrass, dallisgrass is effectively controlled by 2 applications of MSMA or similar materials at 3 pounds per acre. Applications in early spring are most effective and should be repeated at 2-week intervals. MSMA should be applied with a boom or broadcast sprayer in 100 gallons or less of water per acre.

Make applications of MSMA 3 to 4 days after mowing to provide more leaf surface to absorb the herbicide. Do not water for at least 24 hours after treatment and delay mowing for several more days. Dallisgrass leaves will begin to show discoloration 3 to 5 days after treatment, and significant leaf burning should be apparent after 7 to 10 days. Within 2 weeks some regrowth may occur, and a second application of MSMA is necessary.

In Saint Augustine and centipedegrass lawns, spot treatment of dallisgrass with glyphosate (Roundup) is most effective. Treated areas need to be plugged or sodded with Saint Augustine or centipedegrass after dallisgrass dies to prevent other weeds from becoming established in the dead areas. Preemerge herbicides may also be helpful in Saint Augustine or centipede turf to prevent the spread of dallisgrass from seed.

Nutsedge (Nutgrass)

Nutsedge, commonly called nutgrass, is one of the world's most annoying weeds. In fine turfgrass areas nutgrass is particularly unsightly because of its coarse texture and rapid shoot growth.

In addition to being unsightly in turf, nutsedge is very difficult to control because of its prolific seed production and its underground network of rhizomes and tubers. It is virtually impossible to eradicate, but by using good cultural practices and herbicides, nutsedge can be controlled.

DESCRIPTION. Nutsedge is a perennial plant that reproduces by seed, rhizomes, and tubers. Two prevalent species of nutsedge in the southeastern U.S. are purple nutsedge (*Cyperus rotundus*) and yellow nutsedge (*C. esculentus*). Yellow nutsedge is the most widespread species in the U.S.; purple nutsedge, the more persistent species, is primarily found in Texas and along the Gulf Coast states.

Yellow nutsedge plants are yellowish-green in color with straw-colored flowers (seedheads). Plants grow to 30 inches in height with new shoots emerging from apical buds borne on the end of short rhizomes.

Purple nutsedge is similar to yellow except that plants are dark green in color, produce reddish-purple seedheads, and grow to only about 12 inches in height. Unlike yellow nutsedge, purple nutsedge produces a chain of underground tubers. Each tuber has the potential to produce new plants and a whole new series of tubers.

CONTROL. Soil sterilization with products such as methyl bromide or Vapam prior to planting is the only method of eradicating nutsedge from lawns and gardens. Postemergence herbicides provide some degree of con-

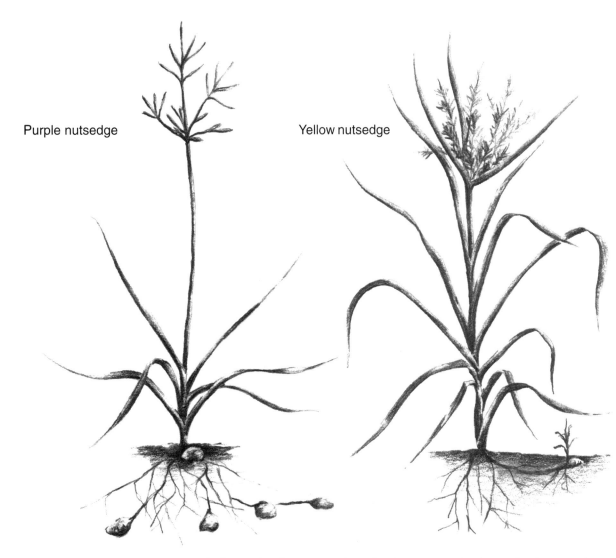

Purple nutsedge   Yellow nutsedge

trol of nutsedge, but repeated applications are required to maintain control.

In bermudagrass turf, the methyl arsonates (MSMA, DSMA, CMA, etc.) provide selective control of both yellow and purple nutsedge. Applications must be repeated after regrowth to maintain control of nutsedge.

In bermudagrass, zoysia, centipede, and Saint Augustine lawns, Basagran is effective against yellow nutsedge, and Image can be used for both yellow and purple nutsedge (tables 8-5 through 8-7).

Herbicide Injury Symptoms on Selected Trees and Shrubs

Injury to trees and shrubs in the landscape is a concern of every professional turf manager and homeowner when using herbicides for weed control in turfgrass. Today, a number of herbicides are available that effectively control grassy type weeds in and around shrub beds. Many of these materials have

Table 8-5. Turf Weed Control

TURF, HOME LAWNS

POSTEMERGENCE CONTROL

Weeds Controlled	Product and Product Rate per 1,000 sq. ft.	Herbicide Common Name (active ingredient)	Spray Volume per 1,000 sq. ft.	Time to Apply	Remarks
Broadleaved weeds including clover, chickweed, dandelion, dichondra, dock, henbit, oxalis, plantain, wild carrot, wild onion & wild garlic, spotted spurge & shepherdpurse	Dacamine 4D ¾ oz. of 3.6 lbs./gal. product	2,4-D amine	2 gals.	Spring, early summer, and fall	May cause discoloration on Tifdwarf and Tifgreen bermudagrass, Saint Augustine grass, and centipedegrass lawns. Late summer or early fall applications of the hormonal-type herbicides appear to predispose Saint Augustine grass to greater damage from brownpatch.
	Weedar 64 ¾ oz. of 3.8 lbs./gal. of product	2,4-D amine	2 gals.	Same as above	Same as above
	Chipco Turf Kleen 4 ozs. of 1 lb./gal. of product	2,4-D amine & MCPP	2 gals.	Same as above	Same as above
	Ortho Chickweed and Clover Killer 3.3 ozs. of 1.3 lbs./gal. product	MCPP	5 gals.	Same as above	Same as above
	Ortho Weed-B-Gon Lawn Weed Killer 3.3 ozs. of product	2,4-D and MCPP	5 gals.	Same as above	Same as above
	Ortho Weed-B-Gon for Southern Lawns 5 ozs. of product	MCPP and Chlorflurenol	5 gals.	Same as above	For use on Saint Augustine, bermuda, zoysia, centipede, and bahia lawns.
	2 Plus 2 (MCPP + 2,4-D amine) 2 ozs. of 3.7 lbs./gal. product	2,4-D and MCPP	2 gals.	Same as above	May injure bentgrass, Saint Augustine, and buffalograss.
	Banvel 1/10 to 1/5 oz. of 4 lbs./gal. product	Dicambra	2 gals.	Same as above	Same as above
	Turflon II Amine 1.2 to 1½ ozs. of 3 lbs./gal. product	Triclopyr	2 gals.	Same as above	For use on bluegrass, tall fescue, and ryegrass turf. Do not use on other grasses unless injury can be tolerated.
	Turflon D 1 to 1½ ozs. of 3 lbs./gal. product	2,4-D and Triclopyr	2 gals.	Same as above	Same as above
	Lesco's Weedone DPC Herbicide 1.1 to 1.5 ozs. of 3.7 lbs./gal. product	2,4-DP and 2,4-D	2 gals.	Same as above	Use half rate on Saint Augustine and centipede lawns.

Weeds Controlled	Product and Product Rate per 1,000 sq. ft.	Herbicide Common Name (active ingredient)	Spray Volume per 1,000 sq. ft.	Time to Apply	Remarks
	Greenlight's Wipeout Broadleaf Weed Killer 4 ozs. of product	2,4-D, MCPP plus dicamba	2 gals.	Spring, early summer, and fall	
	Ortho Chickweed, Spurge and Oxalis Killer D 4 ozs. of product	2,4-D, MCPP, and dicamba	2 gals.	Same as above	
	Gordon's Trimec or Lesco's Three-Way 1.2 to 1.5 ozs. of 4 lbs./gal. product	2,4-D, MCPP, and dicamba	2 gals.	Same as above	Do not use on Saint Augustine, centipede, or bentgrass.
Warm-season grassy weeds, including crabgrass, goosegrass, barnyardgrass, dallisgrass, nut grass, and sandbur	Daconate 6, Bueno 6 1 oz. of 6 lbs./gal. product	MSMA	2.5 gals.	Spring and early summer	Do not use on carpet, Saint Augustine, or centipede grasses. Repeat application in 7–10 days.
	Ortho Crabgrass Killer 8 ozs. of product	CMA	2.5 gals.	Same as above	Same as above
	Chipco DSMA Liquid 3 ozs. of 3.6 lbs./gal. Hexahydrate product	DSMA	2.5 gals.	Same as above	Same as above
	Greenlight's MSMA Crabgrass Killer 1.6 ozs. of product	MSMA	2.5 gals.	Same as above	Same as above
Nutgrass (yellow nutsedge and purple nutsedge)	Image 1/2 to 1 oz. of 1.5 lbs./gal. product	Imazaquin	2 gals.	Spring and early summer	For use on bermudagrass, centipede, Saint Augustine, and Zoysia.
	Basagran 3/4 to 1 1/2 ozs. of 4 lbs./gal. product	Bentazon	2 gals.	Same as above	For control of yellow nutsedge only

PREEMERGENCE WEED CONTROL

Weeds Controlled	Product and Product Rate per 1,000 sq. ft.	Herbicide Common Name (active ingredient)	Spray Volume per 1,000 sq. ft.	Time to Apply	Remarks
Control of Poa annua, crabgrass, goosegrass, rescuegrass, little barley, ryegrass, and certain broad-leaved weeds*	Balan 2.5G 3 lbs. of 2.5% granular product	Benefin	Dry	Prior to weed emergence Feb. 15–Mar. 15 for warm-season weeds, Aug 15–Sept. 15 for cool-season weeds	May be used on established warm-season turf grasses.

Weeds Controlled	Product and Product Rate per 1,000 sq. ft.	Herbicide Common Name (active ingredient)	Spray Volume per 1,000 sq. ft.	Time to Apply	Remarks
	Ronstar 2G 2.5 lbs. of 2% granular product	Oxadiazon	Dry	Same as above	Same as above
	Dacthal W-75 Turf 5.3 ozs. of 75% product	DCPA	2–3 gals.	Same as above	Same as above
	Dacthal 2.5G 10 lbs. of 2.5% granular product	DCPA	Dry	Same as above	Same as above
	Betasan 3.6G 5–6 lbs. of 3.6% granular product	Bensulide	Dry	Same as above	Same as above
	Lesocan 7G 2.5–3 lbs. of 7% granular product	Bensulide	Dry	Same as above	Same as above
	Surflan AS 1.5 ozs. of 3.6 lbs./gal. product	Oryzalin	2–3 gals.	Same as above	Same as above
	Devrinol 2G 3 lbs. of 2% granular product	Napropamide	Dry	Same as above	Same as above
	Princep 4G 0.5 to 1.0 lb. of 4% granular product	Simazine	Dry	Fall and late winter	Apply after Sept. 1 for winter annuals. For summer annuals apply in early spring (before June 1). Do not exceed two applications per year. Do not use on muck or alkaline soils.
	Aatrex 4L 1.5 ozs. of 4 lbs./gal. of product	Atrazine	1 gal.	Fall and late winter	Apply after Oct. 1 for winter annuals and before April 15. Do not exceed two applications per year. Do not use on muck or alkaline soils.
	Pennant 5G 0.9 to 1.4 lbs. of 5% granular product	Metolachlor	Dry	Spring and early fall	Treated area must be dry before people enter the site.
	Scott's Halts Crabgrass Preventer 2 lbs. of 1.7% granular product	Pendimethalin	Dry	Spring	

Weeds Controlled	Product and Product Rate per 1,000 sq. ft.	Herbicide Common Name (active ingredient)	Spray Volume per 1,000 sq. ft.	Time to Apply	Remarks
Preemerge control of broadleaf weeds in turfgrasses such as chickweed, henbit, clover, knotweed, oxalis, spurge, purslane, and some annual grasses*	Gallery ½ oz. of 75% dry flowable product	Isoxaben	2 gals.	Spring and fall prior to weed germination	Gallery must be activated with rainfall or irrigation within 21 days of application.
	Dimension 2 to 3 ozs. of 1 lb./gal. of product	Dithiopyr	2 gals.	Spring and early fall	For pre- and early post-emergence control of annual broadleaved weeds and grasses.
PREPLANT WEED CONTROL					
Control of all grassy and broadleaved plants, including bermudagrass	Dowfume MC-2 1–2 lbs. product per 100 sq. ft.	Methyl bromide	Gas	When grass and weeds are actively growing and soil is moist	Must be applied under polyethylene cover. Leave cover in place 48 hours. Do not apply over the root zone of desirable trees and shrubs. Poisonous gas. Follow manufacturer's directions.
	Vapam 1 qt. of 4 lbs./gal. product per 100 sq. ft.	SMDC	1 gal. per 100 sq. ft.	Same as above	Area to be treated should be irrigated prior to treatment. Water thoroughly after treatment. Do not apply within 3 ft. of drip line of desirable trees and shrubs. Follow label directions.
	Roundup 3 ozs. of 4 lbs./gal. product	Glyphosate	2 gals.	Same as above	Do not mow area to be treated for 2 weeks before or 10 days after treatment.
	Ortho Kleen Up Systemic Weed and Grass Killer 1 qt. of 5% glyphosate	Glyphosate	2 gals.	Same as above	Same as above

*See label instructions

Table 8-6. Partial List of Turf Weeds and Suggested Chemical Controls

Common Name	Scientific Name	Chemical Control*
Annual bluegrass	*Poa annua*	8, 9, 10, 11, 12, 13, 14, 15, 16, 17, 18, 19
Aster	*Aster exilis*	3, 4, 6, 8
Bermudagrass	*Cynodon dactylon*	20
Betony	*Stachys sieboldii*	3, 4, 6, 8
Bindweed	*Convolvulus arvensis*	1, 2, 3, 4, 5, 6
Black medic	*Medicago lupulina*	2, 3, 4, 5, 6, 8
Burclover	*Medicago hispida*	1, 2, 3, 4, 6, 8
Carolina geranium	*Geranium carolinianum*	3, 4, 5, 6, 18, 19
Carpet burweed	*Soliva nasturtiifolia*	1, 2, 4, 5, 6, 8
Chickweed	*Stella media*	2, 3, 4, 5, 6, 7, 8, 10, 11, 18, 19
Crabgrass	*Digitaria* spp.	7, 8, 9, 10, 11, 12, 13, 14, 15, 16, 17, 18, 19
Cudweed	*Gnaphalium*	1, 3, 4, 5, 6, 8
Dallisgrass	*Paspalum dilatatum*	7
Dandelion	*Taraxacum*	1, 2, 3, 4, 5, 6, 8
Dichondra (ponyfoot)	*Dichondra* spp.	1, 2, 3, 4, 6, 8
Dock	*Rumex crispus*	1, 2, 3, 4, 5, 6
Evening primrose	*Oenothera* spp.	1, 3, 4, 6
Goathead (Puncturevine)	*Tribulus terrestris*	1, 3, 4, 6
Goosegrass	*Eleusine indica*	7, 8, 9, 10, 11, 12, 13, 14, 15, 16, 17, 18, 19
Henbit	*Lamium amplexicaule*	3, 4, 5, 6, 12, 14, 15, 18, 19
Little barley	*Hordeum pusillum*	8, 9
Mallow	*Malva neglecta*	2, 3, 4, 5, 6, 18
Mat chafflower	*Alternanthera peploides*	3, 4, 6
Matchweed	*Lippia nodiflora*	3, 4, 5, 6, 8
Nightshade	*Solanum* spp.	3, 4, 5, 6
Oxalis (yellow woodsorrel)	*Oxalis stricta*	2, 3, 4, 5, 6, 7, 8, 14, 15, 18, 19
Pennywort	*Hydrocotyle* spp.	1, 3
Pepperweed	*Lepidium* spp.	1, 2, 3, 4, 5, 6
Plantain	*Plantago* spp.	1, 2, 3, 5
Prostrate knotweed	*Polygonum aviculare*	2, 3, 4, 6, 11, 18
Prostrate pigweed	*Amaranthus* spp.	1, 4, 5, 6, 8, 9, 18
Purple nutsedge (nutgrass)	*Cyperus rotundus*	7, 20, 21
Purslane	*Portulaca oleracea*	3, 4, 6, 8, 9, 10, 11, 18
Rescuegrass	*Bromus catharticus*	8, 9, 10, 11, 12, 13, 14, 15, 16, 17
Ryegrass	*Lolium multiflorum*	8, 9, 10, 11, 12, 13, 14, 15, 16, 17, 18
Sandbur	*Cenchrus* spp.	7, 9, 14, 21
Shepherd's purse	*Capsella bursa-pastoris*	1, 2, 3, 4, 5, 6, 18, 19
Smutgrass	*Sporobolus poiretti*	20
Sow thistle	*Sonchus oleraceus*	1, 2, 3, 4, 5, 6, 18
Spurge, spotted	*Euphorbia supina*	2, 3, 4, 5, 6, 8, 18, 19
Whiteclover	*Trifolium repens*	2, 3, 4, 6, 18
Wild carrot	*Daucus carota*	1, 2, 3, 4, 5, 6
Wild onion & garlic	*Allium* spp.	1, 4, 6, 21
Yellow nutsedge	*Cyperus esculentus*	7, 17, 20, 21, 22

*Numbers refer to herbicides listed on table 8-7.

Table 8-7. Partial List of Turf Weed Control Herbicides

Common Name	Trade Names (partial list)
1. 2,4-D Amine*	Decamine 4 D; Weedar 64; Hi-Yield 2,4-D Amine; numerous mixtures with MCPP, and/or dicamba
2. Mecoprop (MCPP)*	Ortho Weed-B-Gon Lawn Weed Killer; 2 Plus 2; Chipco Turf Kleen; numerous mixtures with 2,4-D, and/or dicamba
3. Trimec*	Greenlight's Wipeout; Ortho Chickweed, Spurge and Oxalis; Gordon's Trimec; Lesco's Three-Way
4. Dicamba*	Banvel; numerous mixtures with 2,4-D, and/or MCPP
5. Triclopyr*	Turflon II Amine, Turflon D
6. Dicloroprop*	Weedone DPC Herbicide
7. Organic arsenicals (MSMA, DSMA, CMA, AMA)	Daconate 6, Bueno 6, Ortho Crabgrass Killer, Chipco DSMA Liquid
8. Atrazine*	Atarex 4L, Purge
9. Simazine	Princep 4G
10. DCPA	Dacthal W-75 Turf
11. Benefin	Balan 2.5G
12. Bensulide	Batason 3.6G; Lescosan 7G
13. Oxadiazon	Chipco Ronstar 2G
14. Oryzalin	Surflan AS
15. Pendimethalin	Lesco Pre-M 60 DG; Scott's Halt Crabgrass Preventer
16. Napropamide	Devrinol 2G
17. Metolachlor	Pennant 5G
18. Isoxaben	Gallery 75 Dry Flowable
19. Dithiopyr	Dimension Turf Herbicide
20. Glyphosate	Roundup, Ortho Kleenup Systemic Weed & Grass Killer
21. Imazaquin	Image
22. Bentazon	Basagran

*State limited or restricted use products (must have a State Department of Agriculture private applicator or commercial applicator's license to purchase).

demonstrated wide safety margins to trees and shrubs. These products include both pre- and postemerge herbicides for grassy weed control.

Most of the herbicides that are suspect in regard to injury to trees and shrubs are those used for broadleaved weed control—the hormone-type and the triazine-type herbicides. These herbicides include products that contain 2,4-D, dicamba, and atrazine. To evaluate the safety of these herbicides in the landscape and to demonstrate injury symptoms produced by them, an experimental nursery was established with 6 species of trees and shrubs—Shumard red oak, dwarf yaupon holly, dwarf Chinese holly, juniper procumbens, dwarf crape myrtle, and a hybrid tea rose (Duble 1987). Experimental units consisted of the 6 species of plants in rows 6 feet apart. The

Table 8-8. Herbicide Treatment Applied to Turf around Trees and Shrubs

Treatment No.	Herbicide	Formulation	Rate of Application (lbs. active/acre)
1	dicamba (Banvel)	4 lbs./gal. E. C.	0.125
2	dicamba (Banvel)	4 lbs./gal. E. C.	0.25
3	dicamba (Banvel)	4 lbs./gal. E. C.	0.50
4	dicamba plus 2,4-D amine	4 lbs./gal. E. C.	0.25 + 0.50
5	atrazine (Aatrex)	4 lbs./gal. flow-able	1.5
6	untreated	—	—

experimental unit included 4 plants of each species spaced 3 feet apart in the row. Species were randomized within each experimental unit and 3 replications were established. Centipedegrass was sodded between rows with 18 inches of bare soil on each side of the plants.

Herbicide treatments included dicamba (0.125, 0.25, and 0.50 pounds per acre), a mixture of dicamba plus 2,4-D amine (0.25 + 0.50 pounds per acre), atrazine (1.5 pounds per acre), and an untreated control (table 8-8). Treatments were applied in 3-foot strips between rows with a Weed-Miser applicator in a volume of water equivalent to 2 gallons per 1,000 square feet. Treatments were applied 4 times per year at approximately 6-weed intervals beginning in late May.

With the exception of the Shumard red oak trees and the roses, plants were established from 1-gallon container-grown plants. The roses and oaks were established from 2- and 5-gallon container plants, respectively. The plants were irrigated with a drip system and fertilized each spring and fall. At the time of planting, the oak trees averaged 0.75 inches in diameter and 5 feet in height. The yaupon holly and Chinese holly plants were 8 inches in height and 10 inches in diameter. After 2 years, the oaks averaged 2 inches in diameter and 10 feet in height. The yaupon and Chinese holly plants averaged 15 inches in height and 25 inches in diameter. All of the plants made significant growth during the experimental period suggesting that water and nutrient uptake was optimum. Roots also demonstrated good growth. In 2 years tree roots enlarged from the original 5-gallon container to a spread of 10 feet in diameter. The roots of shrubs expanded from the 1- and 2-gallon containers to a diameter of 6 feet. Again, the growth of the plants suggests that water and nutrient uptake was optimum. Thus, conditions should have been favorable for plants to take up the herbicides through their root system.

In fact, plants did take up herbicides, and injury symptoms were expressed as abnormalities in leaf shape, texture, color, and growth. However, not a single plant out of the 432 in the study was killed, defoliated, or permanently damaged. As expected, the treatment that demonstrated the greatest effect on the plants was the 0.5 pound per acre rate of dicamba. But even after 4 applications at 6-week intervals for 2 years, only foliage abnormali-

Table 8-9. Growth Measurement on Trees and Shrubs Exposed to Herbicides

Treatment No.	DWARF YAUPON HOLLY		DWARF CHINESE HOLLY		SHUMARD RED OAK	
	Ht[1]	Dia[1]	Ht[1]	Dia[1]	Ht[2]	Dia[2]
1	13.3	23.5	12.8	23.6	8.3	1.9
2	13.1	20.7	12.9	21.5	8.8	2.0
3	13.2	21.5	12.1	21.1	8.0	2.1
4	12.8	19.9	13.0	21.9	8.0	1.9
5	13.9	21.5	13.1	20.7	8.5	2.1
6	13.3	22.8	12.4	21.4	9.1	2.1

[1]Measurements of plant height (in inches) and canopy diameter (in inches).
[2]Measurements of plant height (in feet) and trunk diameter (in inches).

ties were apparent. The growth of the oak trees in terms of height, trunk diameter, and canopy diameter was not affected by any of the herbicide treatments (table 8-9).

EFFECTS OF HORMONE-TYPE HERBICIDES ON TREES AND SHRUBS

Expected symptoms on ornamental plants from hormone-type herbicides, such as 2,4-D and dicamba, include leaf cupping, leaf petiole curling, parallel venation, changes in leaf texture, stem twisting, and abnormal leaf size and shape. All of these symptoms occurred on one or more of the species included in this investigation.

The hybrid tea roses were most noticeably affected by the hormone-type herbicides. Symptoms became apparent on roses after the second applica-

Hormone herbicide injury symptoms on Shumard oak trees.

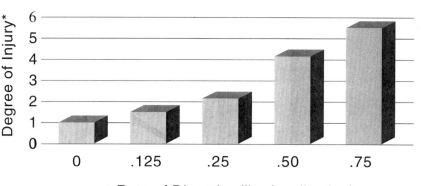

Rate of Dicamba (lbs./application)

*1 equals no injury, 9 equals severe injury.

tion of the 0.25 pound per acre rate. Symptoms were expressed as abnormally shaped leaves near the terminal bud. Leaf size was greatly reduced and leaf shape was abnormal. Leaf petioles on the bud stem appeared normal, but the leaflets remained minute.

Terminal bud stems were also twisted and distorted, and the flower bud was easily separated or broken from the stem. Finally, flower color was faded and variegated.

Two months after the last application of the hormone-type herbicides, the roses had outgrown those symptoms, and fall flowers appeared normal. The following spring, prior to beginning herbicide treatments, treated roses could not be distinguished from untreated roses.

The Shumard red oak trees were the only other plants to show injury symptoms from the hormone-type herbicides. Again, as with the roses, symptoms only became apparent after the second application of dicamba at or above the 0.25 pound per acre rate.

Symptoms included leaf cupping, parallel venation, changes in leaf texture (treated plants exhibited leathery-textured leaves), exaggerated leaf margins, and twisted petioles.

Upon casual observation, treated trees could not be distinguished from untreated trees. Close observation of the foliage was required to notice herbicide injury symptoms. As previously mentioned, the growth of trees in terms of trunk diameter (measured 6 inches above the soil) and tree height was not affected by herbicide treatments. Some of the foliage symptoms described could be found in spring growth before the third year of treatments was begun, but the appearance and growth of the trees were not impaired.

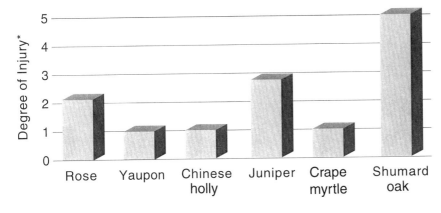

Atrazine injury symptoms on trees and shrubs

(at 4.5 lbs. per acre per year)

*1 equals no injury, 9 equals severe injury.

EFFECTS OF ATRAZINE ON TREES AND SHRUBS

The classical symptoms of triazine herbicide injury to ornamental plants include interveinal chlorosis on new growth followed by the development of necrotic tissue on leaf margins and between leaf veins. These symptoms could lead to complete defoliation of plants.

After a total of seven applications of atrazine at 1.5 lbs. per acre, over a 2-year period, only chlorosis in some plants was apparent. The juniper plants were the first to show injury to atrazine. The chlorosis persisted throughout the season, but new growth the following season appeared normal. None of the juniper plants was permanently injured by atrazine.

The Shumard red oak trees showed injury symptoms from atrazine on new growth in the spring after two years of treatments. Terminal leaves on new branches produced in the spring developed interveinal chlorosis and marginal necrosis. Without additional applications of atrazine during the third year, it appeared that the trees would outgrow these symptoms. The growth of trees in terms of trunk diameter and height was not affected by atrazine.

None of the other plants included in the study showed symptoms of injury from atrazine (fig. 10).

Turfgrass Diseases 9

Identifying turf problems requires expertise, experience, and, sometimes, good detective work. An experienced turf manager might correctly identify a turf problem 60 percent of the time. The expert might correctly identify a problem 70 or 80 percent of the time, but neither will be correct 100 percent of the time. The problems and their interactions are often too numerous and complex to identify correctly.

Identification of Turfgrass Diseases

Recognizing that a turf problem exists does not require a great deal of skill, but identifying the problem correctly does. Often a turf manager inherits problems. At least, that is the rationale that is often used. Other problems result from environmental stress, such as shade, drought, or extreme temperatures. Some problems are the result of turf pests. However, the most common problems, those we are least likely to identify, are the ones we create through our own management.

Early recognition and identification of a problem is essential to the maintenance of fine turfs. Early symptoms of a turf problem rarely attract the attention of a nonprofessional. A subtle change in color or growth rate, wilting or footprinting earlier in the day than normal, cottony growth on the grass in the early morning, birds or other animals actively feeding in the turf, or a combination of these symptoms may be the tip-off to a serious turf problem. After the turf thins out or brown patches appear in the turf, the opportunities for effective control are greatly reduced.

The turf manager must make regular inspections of the turf to establish a reference by which abnormalities can be readily recognized. For example, differences in soil conditions may cause the grass in one area to wilt sooner than in another area. Also, changes in the color or growth rate of a turf may indicate a nutrient deficiency and require frequent observation to detect. The height of the grass before mowing, the number of baskets of clippings removed from a golf green, or the frequency of mowing required all provide a reference to detect changes in growth rate. Color changes require even closer observations, but they can be an early warning to a serious turf problem. A subtle change in color may signal a nutrient deficiency, a disease occurrence, or an insect infestation. A turf manager that is familiar with the normal color and growth rate of a particular turf is most likely to recognize these early symptoms of a problem.

Keep a daily log in enough detail to show what, when, why, and how management practices are performed. Fertilization records can help explain changes in turf color or growth rate. Cultural practices, such as mowing, watering, aeration, vertical mowing, and topdressing, should also be included in the daily records. Insect, disease, and weed control treatments must be recorded along with the response obtained. The turf manager trying to identify a problem without these records is at a serious disadvantage. Often, by reviewing well-kept records, some potential causes of the problem can be eliminated. For example, a recent application of nitrogen to a turf that appears chlorotic and stunted along with a soil test report that shows adequate levels of other nutrients suggests that nutrition is not the problem.

In addition to the records of daily operations, keep soil tests, water, and plant analyses for several years for reference purposes. In critical situations these analyses could provide helpful information.

Extension publications, conference proceedings, trade journal articles, and turfgrass newsletters can provide valuable reference information. This printed information can be added to this logbook for reference purposes.

CLASSIFYING PROBLEMS AS TO ORIGIN

Turf problems should first be identified by their nature—cultural, environmental, or pest. Often two or more of these factors contribute to the problem. For example, a grass that has limited shade tolerance (environmental) should not be mowed too close (cultural). Likewise, a nitrogen deficiency (cultural) can be a contributing factor to an outbreak of dollar spot (pest), or shade (environmental) and overfertilization (cultural) can contribute to an occurrence of leaf spot (pest). When two or more factors contribute to the problem, all factors must be identified before the problem can be effectively corrected.

Too often only one factor contributing to a turfgrass problem is identified, when, in fact, several factors contribute to the problem. For example, many pest problems are a result of environmental conditions and cultural practices. In fact, pest-related problems, such as dollar spot, may be controlled most effectively by changing the cultural practices that contributed to the problem.

Pest management programs must consist of more than the shot-in-the-dark application of pesticides to turf. Accurate identification of factors contributing to the problem and timely application of pesticides is a better alternative.

Disease problems require accurate identification to obtain effective and safe control. In addition to the symptoms shown by the grass, environmental conditions, grass species, and previous cultural practices should be considered when identifying pest-related problems. Turfgrass diseases are particularly difficult to identify. Often environmental conditions modify the disease. Also, after the grass has been killed, it becomes increasingly difficult to identify the cause. In many cases, microscopic examination by experts is required to accurately diagnose a turfgrass disease problem.

A KEY TO THE IDENTIFICATION OF COMMON TURFGRASS DISEASES
DIRECTIONS: This key is arranged so that you may identify the turfgrass disease by a process of elimination. First, read the characteristics for Group I. If they do not apply, continue to Group II. If characteristics for Group I do apply, continue to A. If characteristics for A apply, go to B; if not, go to AA, and so on.

GROUP I. Grass affected in distinct patches.
  A. Individual patches 2 to 3 inches in diameter, leaf lesions present.
    1. Dollar Spot. Diseased spots are light tan or straw-colored; light tan lesions may be found near the top of the grass blade; fine, cobwebby, mycelial growth can be seen covering the spots in the early morning when dew is present.
AA. Individual patches usually larger than 2 to 3 inches in diameter; leaf lesions not present.
  B. Dark green halo or half-moon shaped rings; mushrooms present in circular pattern outside of dark green ring.
    1. Fairy Ring.
 BB. Dark green halo or mushrooms not present in circular pattern.
    1. Pythium Blight. Grass blades matted together in affected area; greasy, water-soaked appearance, fading to a light tan as grass blades dry and shrivel; cottony appearance in early morning hours; blighted areas may merge to form large irregular areas or long streaks.
    2. Brownpatch. Outer edge of circular patch is yellowish brown in color giving it a smoke ring appearance, grass blades in this smoke-ring can be easily pulled from the stem or crown.
    3. Take-all Patch. Outer edge of circular patch is straw-colored, grass within the border is straw-colored and crisp; leaves not easily pulled from the stolon.
    4. Fusarium Blight. Circular, doughnut-shaped patches of chlorotic, tan or straw-colored grass; patches no more than 3 feet in diameter with green grass in the center producing a frog-eye pattern, chiefly on cool-season grasses.

5. Spring Dead Spot. Circular patches of grass appear brown in early spring; grass does not recover from winter dormancy (bermudagrass only).

GROUP II. Grass not affected in distinct patches.

A. Spots distinct on leaf blades.

1. Rust. Orange or red bumps on leaf surface, rust-colored spores readily rub off the leaf surface.

2. Saint Augustine Decline. Leaf blades show chlorotic mottling (Saint Augustine grass only).

3. Gray Leaf Spot. Oval-shaped spots with tan or gray-colored center and brown margin surrounded by chlorotic tissue; spots apparent on leaves and stems.

4. *Bipolaris* and *Exserohilum* (*Helminthosporium*) Leaf Spot. Small, elongated spots with dark brown or purple margins; spots increase in size and the centers fade to a brown or straw color; where leaf spots are numerous, leaves may be completely killed; spots apparent on leaves and stems.

5. Powdery Mildew. Small superficial patches of white to light gray dusty fungus growth on leaves; lower leaves often completely covered; leaf tissue under the mildew becomes yellow and fades to brown; heavily infected leaves gradually dry up and die.

AA. Spots not distinct on leaf blades.

B. Grass appears chlorotic

1. Fading-out, summer brownpatch, or *Nigrospora* stolon rot (on centipedegrass, centipede decline). Affected areas appear yellow, thin, and generally unhealthy; grass roots appear normal.

2. Nematodes. Affected areas appear yellow, thin, not responsive to treatment; grass roots stunted, swollen, or blackened.

3. Nitrogen or iron deficiency. (Check soil analysis for other possible nutrient deficiencies.) Grass appears chlorotic, seed stalks abundant, growth rate noticeably slower than normal, no distinct boundaries or patterns to the affected area (except possible fertilizer distribution pattern), root system appears normal.

BB. Grass not generally chlorotic.

C. Leaf tips frayed, grass not wilted; turf has a brown appearance several days after mowing; mowing patterns noticeable.

1. Mower blade dull or not properly adjusted.

CC. Leaf tips not frayed.

D. Grass wilted in localized spots; turf has a gray cast in wilted areas and turns brown where condition persists; leaves rolled.

1. Localized dry spot. Drought stress, soil compaction, or hydrophobic soil (common on sandy soils).

2. Wet wilt, poor drainage. Water stands in places after rainfall or irrigation; weak root system.

3. Fertilizer burn or improper application of chemicals. Grass appears burned in spots or streaks; leaf tips are first to turn brown; occurs shortly after application of soluble fertilizer or other chemicals.

4. Gas, oil, hydraulic fluid, or fertilizer spill. Grass leaves rolled; bleached or brown grass in spots or streaks.

D. Grass not wilted.

1. Grass scalped; excessive thatch accumulation. Turf has a brown appearance shortly after mowing; grass stems or crowns exposed.

2. Too much nitrogen. Turf has healthy color but appears to be thinning out; grass grows rapidly after mowing; grass is shallow-rooted.

Characteristics of Turfgrass Diseases

BROWNPATCH

Brownpatch, a fungus disease caused by *Rhizoctonia solani*, presents a serious threat to most turfgrasses each fall. With the onset of slightly cooler temperatures and wet conditions, turf managers throughout the South will be plagued by brownpatch.

Conditions most favorable for brownpatch development include (1) the presence of active fungi, (2) vigorous growth of a susceptible grass, (3) daytime temperature ranges between 75° and 85° F, and (4) the presence of free moisture on the foliage. When night temperatures drop below 68° F in late summer or early fall, expect to find brownpatch on turfgrasses.

SYMPTOMS. On warm-season turfgrasses, the disease is characterized by at least two different types of symptoms. The most common symptom is a circular pattern of yellow grass with a grayish colored ring (smoke ring) of wilted grass at the perimeter of the diseased area. The leaves can be easily pulled from the stolons within the smoke ring because the fungus destroys the tissue at the base of the leaf sheath. Symptoms first appear as small circular patches of water-soaked, dark grass that soon wilt and turn light brown. Stolons often remain green. As the disease develops, the circular patches enlarge, smoke rings become more apparent, and new green leaves may emerge in the center of the circular areas.

Disease development occurs most rapidly when air temperatures are between 75° and 85° F and free moisture is present. Those conditions occur most often and for longer duration in the fall. High levels of nitrogen may also increase the severity of the disease. Fungal activity generally stops when air temperatures reach 90° F.

On cool-season grasses the disease first appears as dark green, water-soaked circular patches that range from a few inches to several feet in diameter. The affected leaves wilt and turn light brown but remain upright. A dark, grayish black ring (smoke ring) of wilted grass often is present around the perimeter of the diseased areas in the early morning.

CONTROL. When environmental conditions are favorable, brownpatch is likely to develop on susceptible turfgrasses. The severity of the disease can be somewhat controlled by avoiding heavy applications of nitrogen during spring and fall, by watering early in the morning to remove dew and allow the grass to dry quickly, and, where possible, by removing grass clippings during periods of disease activity (table 9-1).

HELMINTHOSPORIUM DISEASES

Warm-season turfgrasses are susceptible to various diseases caused by *Helminthosporium* spp. Leaf spot, root rot, and other diseases are incited by *Helminthosporium* fungi.

SYMPTOMS. On bermudagrass small purplish spots may appear on the leaves, stems, or crowns of the plant. On leaves these spots increase in size, the centers turn brown and fade to a light tan with purplish borders. During warm (60°–85° F), moist conditions leaf blighting may occur as a rapid collapse and drying of the leaves. Under favorable conditions, the disease may complete this whole cycle in a period of several days. The overall pattern appears as brownish fading-out of turfgrass areas of various sizes.

On bermudagrass stems symptoms begin as small purple spots on stems and crown. Leaves close to the stem lesions become chlorotic but may not show any spots or lesions. Diseased areas become stunted and spindly.

On bentgrass the disease first appears as irregularly shaped, smoky blue areas varying from 1 to 4 feet in diameter. Soon after these areas appear, yellowing and complete killing of the grass occurs. Finally, these areas appear water-soaked and matted down. On leaves the first symptoms are small yellow flecks that progress to irregularly shaped water-soaked blotches.

DISEASE CYCLE. The disease-causing fungus survives the winter as mycelium in the tissue of infected plants and as spores in the thatch layer of the turfgrass. As the temperatures warm in the spring, the disease first appears as small spots on the leaves or stems. The severity of the disease increases with temperature and humidity. At 78° F, a period of 8 to 10 hours with 100 percent relative humidity is all that is required for a high level of infection to develop.

The severity of these diseases seems to be greater when grass is maintained at low levels of nitrogen and potassium. Also, any stress situation, such as drought, herbicide injury, or heavy traffic seems to increase the severity of the disease.

CONTROL. Healthy turfgrass is the best protection against turf diseases. Managers should maintain vigorous turf through proper fertilization and give special attention to maintaining adequate levels of nitrogen and potassium. Excessive applications of nitrogen should be avoided.

Efforts should be made to reduce stress during periods favorable for disease development. The turf should not be allowed to become extremely dry during warm weather. At the same time, good surface and internal drainage

Table 9-1. Fungicides for Control of Brownpatch *(Rhizoctonia solani)*

Product Name	Chemical Name	Rate of Application (oz. product/1,000 sq. ft.)	Interval of Application (days)
Acti-dione RZ	Cycloheximide-PCNB	6.0–8.0	7–14
Bayleton	Triadimeton	1.0–2.0	30
Chipco 26019	Iprodione	2.0	14–21
Daconil 2787	Chlorothalonil	4.0–8.0	7–10
Dyrene	Anilazine	4.0–6.0	7–10
Eagle WSP	Myclobutanil	0.6	14
Fore	Mancozeb	4.0	7
Rubigan	Fenarimol	0.4–0.8	7–14
Tersan LSR	Maneb	4.0–6.0	7–10
Tersan 1991	Benomyl	2.0	10–14
Terraclor 75 WP	PCNB	16.0 (1 lb.)	21–28
Turfcide 10G	PCNB	120.0 (7.5 lbs.)	21–28

Table 9-2. Fungicides for Control of *Helminthosporium*

Product Name	Chemical Name	RATE OF APPLICATION (OZ. PRODUCT/1,000 SQ. FT.)		Interval of Application (days)
		Preventative	Curative	
Dyrene	Anilazine	2–4	4–6	7–10
Daconil 2787	Chlorothalonil	3–6	6–11	7–10
Cyclohexamide/Thiram	Acti-dione/Thiram	2	4	7–10
Chipco 26019	Iprodione	2	2	14–21
Fore, Tersan LSR	Maneb	4	4	7–14
Terraclor 75 WP	PCNB	7	10	21–28
Turfcide 10G	PCNB	80 (5 lbs.)	120 (7.5 lbs.)	21–28

is important during wet conditions. Herbicide applications during critical periods of disease activity should be avoided. Traffic in high traffic areas such as golf greens should be dispersed by moving the cup frequently.

During periods of high disease activity, fungicides can protect the turf from severe injury by *Helminthosporium* diseases. Preventative applications of fungicides on a regular schedule is much more effective than treating a severe outbreak of any *Helminthosporium* disease. During periods of high disease activity, applications of fungicides at 7 to 14 day intervals may be required (table 9-2).

DOLLAR SPOT

Dollar spot, a disease of turfgrasses caused by the fungus *Sclerotinia homeocarpa* attacks most turfgrasses grown in the South. Bentgrass, hybrid bermudagrasses, and zoysia are most susceptible to dollar spot. The disease occurs from spring through fall and is most active during moist periods of warm days (70°–85° F) and cool nights (60° F) in the spring, early summer, and fall. The disease is spread from one area to another by water, mowers, equipment, or shoes.

SYMPTOMS. On fine-textured and close-cut turf, the disease appears as round, brown to straw-colored, and somewhat sunken spots approximately the size of a silver dollar; thus, the name dollar spot. In coarse-textured grasses maintained at taller cutting heights, the dead spots are larger and more diffuse. Under these conditions dollar spot can be confused with brownpatch, *R. solani*. Dollar spot is readily distinguished, however, by characteristic lesions on the leaf blades of live plants near the border of the affected area. Lesions are light tan with a reddish brown border and usually radiate from the margins of the leaf blade. On fine-bladed grasses, such as bentgrass, the lesions usually girdle the leaf blade.

If the turf is examined when the disease is active early in the day before the dew dries, cobweb-like mycelium of the fungus can be seen growing on affected areas. During early stages of the disease, affected plants may appear water-soaked and wilted, but spots quickly fade to a characteristic straw color.

DISEASE DEVELOPMENT. Several factors influence the occurrence and severity of dollar spot. Bentgrass, hybrid bermudagrass, and zoysia are most susceptible; while Saint Augustine and centipede are less frequently attacked by dollar spot.

Low soil moisture has been reported to enhance dollar spot activity, but moisture from dew, light rain, or irrigation must be present on the foliage for the disease to develop.

The dollar spot fungus is capable of growth over a wide range of temperatures (50°–90° F), but disease development is greatest at temperatures between 70° and 80° F. The dollar spot fungus survives unfavorable temperature and moisture conditions in plant tissue, and thatch as dormant masses of mycelium, called sclerotia.

Low nitrogen and potassium levels in the soil have been reported to increase the severity of dollar spot. Some rather severe outbreaks of dollar spot have been brought under control by the application of soluble nitrogen fertilizer. However, the beneficial effect of nitrogen is thought to be due to rapid recovery of the grass during periods of reduced disease activity. Research has shown that nitrogen increases the susceptibility of grass to dollar spot.

CONTROL. Cultural practices that promote healthy turf help to reduce the occurrence and severity of dollar spot. Control measures include (1) removing excess thatch; (2) keeping fertility levels adequate; (3) avoiding light, frequent watering; (4) mowing frequently at recommended heights; and (5) aerating compacted soils.

To prevent dollar spot apply a fungicide labeled for the disease at recommended rates and intervals. Applications are most critical during moist weather in the spring, early summer, and fall when temperatures are between

70° and 80° F. Fungicides recommended for dollar spot include, but are not limited to, those shown in table 9-3.

SAINT AUGUSTINE DECLINE

Saint Augustine Decline (SAD) is a virus causing a chlorotic mottling or stippling of Saint Augustine grass leaves. Saint Augustine grass and centipedegrass are the only turfgrasses that the virus is known to affect. The virus is widespread in Texas and has been reported in Louisiana and Arkansas.

DESCRIPTION. After the chlorotic mottling or stippling, present in the early stages of SAD, diminishes, the mottling progresses, with leaves developing a chlorotic appearance. Usually three or more years after the early symptoms are observed, Saint Augustine grass becomes weakened to the extent that bermudagrass invades the lawn. Also, grass infected with SAD and growing under shade or other stress conditions will begin to thin out and be replaced by weeds.

Saint Augustine grass infected with SAD is also slower than healthy grass to recover. In the spring following an unusually cold winter, much of the diseased Saint Augustine does not recover.

Lawns infected with SAD will respond to fertilization, but the symptoms remain. Early fall and late spring applications of complete fertilizer and summer applications of iron will help maintain good color of SAD-infected lawns.

Early stages of SAD are often confused with iron chlorosis, but the two can be readily distinguished. Leaves showing chlorosis caused by iron deficiency are either uniformly yellow or show characteristic yellow stripes parallel to the midvein of the leaf. Iron chlorosis also appears first in the new, or young leaves; whereas, SAD produces the mottling in young and older leaves. Iron chlorosis is readily corrected by a foliar application of iron sulfate or iron chelate.

The SAD virus, like all viruses, is a microscopic particle found inside the cells of Saint Augustine grass. Inside the plant cell, the virus reproduces and

Table 9-3. Fungicides for Control of Dollar Spot *(Sclerotinia homeocarpa)*

Product Name	Chemical Name	Rate of Application (oz. product/1,000 sq. ft.)	Interval of Application (days)
Acti-dione/Thiram	Cycloheximide/Thiram	2.0–4.0	7–10
Bayleton	Triadimeton	1.0–2.0	30
Chipco 26019	Iprodione	1.0–2.0	14–21
Daconil 2787	Chlorothalonil	3.6–6.0	7–14
Dyrene	Anilazine	4.0–8.0	7–14
Eagle WSP	Myclobutanil	0.6	14
Fore	Maneb	6.0–8.0	7–14
Rubigan	Fenarimol	.2–.4	14–21
Tersan 1991	Benomyl	1.0	10–14
Terraclor 75WP	PCNB	7.0–10.0	21–28

spreads to other cells throughout the plant. As more and more cells become infected with the virus, the vigor of the plant is reduced, rendering it more vulnerable to other diseases and environmental stresses.

CONTROL. The SAD virus is mechanically transmitted by mowing equipment, edgers, and other tools. Mowing companies that mow several lawns with the same equipment can transmit the virus from an infected lawn to a healthy lawn. Cleaning the mowing equipment with steam or a 10 percent chlorine bleach solution will help prevent the spread of the virus.

However, the best control for the virus is to introduce resistant varieties of Saint Augustine into the lawn. Presently, Floratam, Floralawn, Raleigh, and Seville are SAD-resistant varieties of Saint Augustine grass.

PYTHIUM BLIGHT

Pythium blight, also called cottony blight or grease spot, is a fungal disease of turfgrasses. All turfgrasses, warm and cool season, are susceptible to attack. The disease is most severe during hot, humid conditions and where there is little air movement. Poorly drained soils also favor the occurrence of the disease.

SYMPTOMS. Pythium blight is most readily recognized as small spots or patches of blighted grass that suddenly appear during warm, wet periods. In the early stages the grass leaves appear water-soaked, slimy (greasy), and dark. As the disease progresses, the leaves shrivel and the patches fade from green to light brown. When observing these patches in the early morning, cottony fungal growth can usually be seen on the foliage.

In many cases these patches develop into diffused streaks that follow water drainage patterns or mowing patterns. These streaks are caused by the water or equipment picking up the causal fungus and spreading it along its path. Under favorable conditions for disease development, these streaks may coalesce to form large areas of dead grass. If a sudden drop in temperature or humidity or the application of a fungicide checks the development of Pythium blight, distinct straw-colored spots, resembling dollar spot, develop.

In the South, Pythium blight was not identified as a problem on turfgrass until 1954. By 1970 twenty species of *Pythium* were identified on turfgrasses from the South. *Pythium aphanidermatum* is the most frequently found causal agent of turf blights.

Pythium spp. also cause more root rot and injury to the crown of grass plants than is generally recognized. Infection results in slower growth, poor color, and a general thinning of turfgrasses. Pythium blight is one of the major causes of a poor transition from overseeded grasses to bermudagrasses in late spring. Damage to the crown and roots of bermudagrass during early spring severely weakens the grass and slows its recovery. Such injury goes unnoticed until it is too late too prevent.

DISEASE DEVELOPMENT. The mycelium or spores of *Pythium* spp. are commonly present in diseased grass tissue, thatch, and in soils. Under favor-

Table 9-4. Fungicides for Control of *Pythium* spp.

Product Name	Chemical Name	Rate of Application (oz. product/1,000 sq. ft.)	Interval of Application (days)
Aliette 80 WP	Fosetyl-Al	4–8	14–21
Banol	Propamocarb	3–4	7–21
Koban 30 WP	Etridiazole	2–4	5–10
Subdue 2E	Metalaxyl	1–2	10–21

able temperature and moisture conditions, the mycelium resumes growth, and the spores germinate (much like the stolons and seeds of the grass plant). The spores can germinate and infect the grass plant within an hour or two.

Disease development occurs rapidly from these centers of origin by a cobweb-like, mycelial growth of the fungus from leaf to leaf. Rapid spread occurs when the mycelial strands or spores are moved by water or equipment across the turf.

Pythium blight develops most rapidly under humid conditions when air temperature is above 80° F. As temperatures approach 90° F, only a few hours are required to destroy a strand of grass.

CONTROL. Cultural practices can go a long way toward preventing Pythium blight. Preventative measures include removing thatch on a regular basis through frequent vertical mowing and topdressing; avoiding lush growth produced by overfertilization and overwatering; improving air circulation by pruning or selectively removing trees bordering the site; and improving drainage through aeration and the use of soil amendments.

During extended periods of warm, humid weather a preventative fungicide program may be needed to check the development of *Pythium*. Applications of fungicides recommended for control of Pythium blight should be made to areas with a history of *Pythium* activity when conditions are favorable for development or when symptoms first appear. Applications should be repeated as necessary.

On overseeded bermudagrass greens, Apron- or Koban-treated seed can be used to prevent Pythium blight during the establishment period. Fungicide applications may be needed 7 to 21 days after planting to protect the young seedlings (table 9-4).

BERMUDAGRASS DECLINE

Most specific disease problems are caused by only one pathogen and are given a disease name such as brownpatch, dollar spot, or anthracnose that reflects that pathogen. Until recently bermudagrass decline was thought to be a complex problem caused by several disease organisms. No one had been able to isolate any pathogen associated with these decline areas. Through the correction of poor management practices, the turf would recover slowly. Pathologists in general considered the problem of declining bermudagrass to be a complex management problem; hence, the name bermudagrass decline.

Researchers working on this problem have isolated the disease organism from declining areas. Results of these isolations show the fungus, *Gaeumannomyces graminis,* to be associated with these declining areas. Another species of *Gaeumannomyces* is the fungus associated with take-all patch, a disease on bentgrass golf greens.

Initial symptoms of bermudagrass decline include chlorotic patches of turf 8 to 24 inches in diameter. The turf thins out and may eventually be completely killed in these patches. Chlorotic leaf blades may develop next to green shoots at the margins of the diseased area. Roots of diseased bermudagrass are brown and without feeder roots and root hairs. Signs of the fungus on the root surface appear as dark brown hypal runners.

Fungicides have been tested for control, but only Rubigan has shown good activity against the *Gaeumannomyces.* The disease occurs on weakened or damaged turf, which indicates that management could be the key to control. If disease occurs, managers should try to identify the predisposing factors and correct them through proper management practices. On golf greens, raising the mowing height is the most effective management practice to correct the problem.

NIGROSPORA STOLON ROT

A relatively new disease, *Nigrospora* stolon rot, of Saint Augustine grass has resulted in serious deterioration of Saint Augustine lawns. The disease appears to girdle the stolon (stem or runner) of Saint Augustine grass and deprive the stolon of water and nutrients. Leaves and stolons appear to be under severe moisture stress and soon become totally desiccated.

The disease has been especially severe during dry spring and early summer months. High temperatures and drought conditions favor development of stolon rot in Saint Augustine grass. Symptoms of the disease include dark brown lesions on stolons. As conditions favor the fungus, the lesions enlarge and eventually completely girdle the stolon. The girdling of the stolons stops the movement of water and nutrients to the leaves. The leaves soon wilt, turn yellow, and die. New growth on the terminal end of diseased stolons is typically thin and yellow, reflecting a limited supply of nutrients to the growing point. Overall symptoms are similar to those caused by chinch bugs on Saint Augustine grass.

Laboratory observations of stolons from diseased areas may show the presence of *Nigrospora* as well as *Curvularia.* Both fungal organisms are weak pathogens and usually only attack plants under stress. Environmental conditions such as unusually low winter temperatures, extreme drought, and extremely high temperatures during spring and summer contribute to the occurrence of stolon rot. Providing adequate moisture, raising the mowing height, and making two applications of Daconil 2787 at 8 ounces per 1,000 square feet at 14- to 21-day intervals has provided good control of the disease.

SEEDLING DISEASE

Seedling diseases create problems for those tying to establish grass from seed in the fall. *Pythium, Rhizoctonia, Helminthosporium, Curcularia,* and *Fusarium* all contribute to a disease complex causing damping-off, fading-out, or seedling blight. The disease attacks seemingly healthy vigorous stands of seedlings and kills the young plants in patches. Seedling diseases are especially damaging during adverse weather conditions—unusually warm periods in the fall; continued wet conditions; or cool, wet periods in early fall. Planting too early (or too late) also increases the incidence of seedling diseases.

The terms "damping-off" or "seedling blight" are used to describe several seedling diseases. The diseases may be incited by fungi or by environmental conditions. Excessive or inadequate soil moisture, cool soil temperatures, saline soils, compacted soils, or other environmental stresses can lead to damping off or seedling blight.

SYMPTOMS. Damping-off and seedling blight can occur before seedling emergence (preemergence) or after seedling emergence (postemergence). *Pythium*-incited damping-off is characterized by a high order of preemergence killing of seedlings. In this case the deterioration process begins soon after the seed coat is broken.

In the case of postemergence damping-off, seedlings emerge above the soil and begin deteriorating at the soil level. As the deterioration progresses upward, the seedlings appear water-soaked. As the tissue collapses, the seedlings shrivel and turn brown. *Pythium, Fusarium, Rhizoctonia, Helminthosporium,* and *Curvularia* may all cause postemergence damping-off.

The effect of these seedling diseases is a significantly reduced stand of grass that usually requires replanting. If the disease outbreak is treated in time, the stand may only be thinned by the attack.

CONTROL. To reduce the incidence of seedling diseases, plant only top quality seed. Seeds that germinate quickly and produce vigorous plants are more likely to survive the seedling stage. Also, seeds should be planted at the proper date. Planting too early greatly increases the risk of seedling diseases. Depending on location, cool-season grasses should be planted from mid-September through November. Ideal temperatures for planting cool-season grasses occur when nighttime temperatures are in the mid-60s and daytime temperatures in the mid-80s. To ensure the availability of nitrogen, an application of a soluble nitrogen fertilizer should be made several days prior to planting. And, most important, the seedbed should not be overwatered.

Preemergence damping-off caused by *Pythium* can be reduced by using seed treated with a fungicide such as Apron or Koban. Also, treating the seedbed with a broad-spectrum fungicide prior to seeding can reduce the incidence of preemergence seedling losses.

After seedling emergence, fungicide applications can effectively control damping-off, fading-out, or seedling blight. Fungicide applications should alternate between a broad-spectrum fungicide and a *Pythium*-specific fungicide at 7- to 10-day intervals during the seedling stage.

During the seedling stage, soil moisture should be maintained sufficiently to avoid drought stress. Heavy applications of soluble nitrogen should be avoided. And mowing with a sharp mower is recommended to avoid pulling up the young seedlings. Early morning syringing to wash dew off foliage will also reduce the incidence of seedling diseases.

FAIRY RING

Fairy rings appear in lawns, golf courses, and other turf areas during spring and summer months. The rings appear as either dark green or brown circular bands, ranging in size from a few inches to 50 feet in diameter. The fairy ring fungus grows outward from a central point at a rate varying from a few inches to as much as two feet a year. Where several distinct rings converge, fungus activity stops at the points of contact. As a result, the circular shape of the original rings is replaced by a scalloped effect.

Mushrooms frequently develop in a circle outside of the dark green or brown ring during spring and fall after a period of heavy rainfall or irrigation. Centuries ago people thought that the mushrooms appeared where fairies had danced the night before.

DISEASE CYCLE. The disease is caused by any one of a number of soil-inhabiting fungi. Development of the fairy rings starts with a germinating spore or a strand of mycelium and grows outward in all directions. The fungus feeds on organic matter in the soil. Fungal strands (mycelium) spread throughout the soil to a depth of 10 to 12 inches. As the fungus grows, the first visible evidence of a new fairy ring is a cluster of mushrooms (the fruiting structure of the fungus) or a tuft of stimulated dark green grass. Later, as the fungi spread outward from the point of origin the ring-like pattern develops.

The initial tuft of dark green grass and the ring of stimulated grass that develops later results from the nitrogen released after the fungus breaks down the organic matter in the soil. The ring of brown or dead grass is caused by the depletion of soil moisture in the area where the fungus is concentrated. If the area of brown or dead grass is dug up, a dense growth of white mycelium will be exposed. Water will not penetrate this zone of dense mycelial growth.

During periods of unfavorable conditions, low temperatures, and drought, mushroom production and fungal activity stops and may not be resumed for months or years.

CONTROL. Fairy rings are very difficult to control with fungicides, since the soil in the infected area is almost impervious to water. Some success has been achieved by aerating the soil and drenching the infected area with fungicide. A new fungicide, Prostar from AgrEvo Chemical Company, has shown good control of fairy ring.

Masking the symptoms of fairy rings is also effective. Aerating and drenching the soil with a wetting agent will help prevent the development of the zone of brown or dead grass in the area of dense mycelial growth. Keeping the fertility level of the turf high will also help to mask the appearance of the ring of stimulated, or dark green, growth. Also, regular mowing removes the mushrooms, the other symptom of the fairy ring disease.

SPRING DEAD SPOT IN BERMUDAGRASS

One of the most noticeable and destructive diseases of bermudagrass is known as Spring Dead Spot (SDS). The disease was first described in a publication in Oklahoma in 1960. It is thought to have been present in Oklahoma since 1936. Since that time, SDS has been observed in most states where bermudagrass is grown. The prevalence and severity of the disease has been increasing for several years, and it may be the most destructive disease of bermudagrass in some states. In Texas SDS has been observed in all areas except extreme South Texas. The disease has been particularly severe in North Texas and the Texas Panhandle.

In North America three fungi have been shown to cause SDS; *Leptosphaeria korrae, Ophiosphaerella herpotricha,* and *Gaeumannomyces graminis* var. *graminis.*

SYMPTOMS. The symptoms of SDS are circular dead areas of bermudagrass 6 inches to several feet in diameter in the spring as bermudagrass resumes growth from winter dormancy. The bermudagrass roots and stolons in affected spots appear dark and rotted. The grass recovers very slowly during the summer months from stolons creeping in from the border of affected areas. Bermudagrass stolons that grow into the affected areas usually produce short, stubby roots. It is usually midsummer before the affected areas are covered by bermudagrass, and the areas are visible throughout the summer because of thin turf and weeds. The disease develops again the following year in the same areas. The spots enlarge each year, and after 2 to 3 years may develop into circular areas where bermudagrass survives in the center. At this stage the symptoms can be confused with those of fairy ring.

All varieties of bermudagrass are susceptible to SDS. Hybrid varieties such as Tifgreen appear to be the most commonly affected. The disease does not usually develop until 3 to 4 years after establishment and may be associated with moderately thatchy turf.

CONTROL. In California and Australia the disease has been controlled by repeated applications of fungicides such as Banner, Tersan 1991, and Rubigan. The applications must begin in late summer when the fungus is thought to be active. Judicious use of nitrogen fertilizer helps to reduce disease severity. Ammonium-based nitrogen fertilizer combined with potassium help reduce SDS over time.

GRAY LEAF SPOT ON SAINT AUGUSTINE GRASS

Gray leaf spot, caused by the fungal organism *Piricularia grisea*, develops rapidly with abundant moisture and warm weather in the spring and early summer on Saint Augustine grass lawns. The disease is especially troublesome in shaded areas.

SYMPTOMS. Gray leaf spot causes oval or circular, tan-colored lesions with brown or purplish borders on the leaf blades of Saint Augustine grass. In severe cases of gray leaf spot, lesions develop on leaf sheaths and stems, and the leaves wither and die. Under these conditions the disease causes serious thinning of Saint Augustine turf. Unless the disease is controlled, a stand of Saint Augustine grass may be lost.

CONTROL. To reduce the severity of gray leaf spot, applications of soluble nitrogen fertilizers should be avoided on moderately shaded lawns during summer months. Herbicide applications which may weaken Saint Augustine grass should also be avoided on shaded lawns. Water should be applied to the lawn in early morning when water is needed. Late afternoon and evening watering should be avoided which keeps the leaf surface moist for long periods. Also, grass clippings should be gathered in lawns where gray leaf spot is a problem.

Preventative fungicides for gray leaf spot include Daconil 2787 at 4 ounces per 1,000 square feet at 7- to 10-day intervals and Acti-dione Thiram at 2 ounces per 1,000 square feet at 7- to 10-day intervals. Curative rates of these fungicides are 6 to 8 ounces of Daconil and 4 ounces of Acti-dione Thiram at 7- to 10-day intervals.

POWDERY MILDEW

Powdery mildew is primarily a problem on Kentucky bluegrass turf growing in partial shade or in areas with poor air circulation. The disease is most often found in the spring and fall when days are cloudy and nights are cool and damp.

SYMPTOMS. The disease appears as a white to light gray powdery growth on the upper surfaces of leaves and leaf sheaths. It spreads rapidly in shaded areas and the powdery growth becomes increasingly dense. The lower leaves of Kentucky bluegrass may be completely covered by the powdery growth. Infected leaves turn yellow, become tan or light brown, and gradually shrivel and die.

Repeated infestations of the disease result in greatly reduced growth and eventual death of plants. Surviving plants often remain in a weakened condition.

CONTROL. Reduced shading and increased air circulation will help control powdery mildew. Where these conditions cannot be changed, fungicides are available for control. Acti-dione RZ, Banner, and Bayleton are fungicides labeled for control of powdery mildew.

RUST

Rust diseases are found throughout the U.S. on most species of grasses. Bluegrass, ryegrass, and zoysiagrass are most commonly affected. Rust diseases are favored by warm and humid conditions and develop most frequently on grasses subject to stress—droughty conditions, low nitrogen fertility, and shade. Low mowing heights, particularly on Kentucky bluegrass, also increase the susceptibility of grasses to rust.

SYMPTOMS. The disease first appears on grass leaves as small orange to reddish brown flecks that enlarge to form raised pustules on leaves and stems. Individual pustules are usually oval or elongated and contain a powdery mass of orange to reddish brown spores. As the pustules mature they turn brown to black. Heavily infested turf becomes thin with an overall yellow-orange to reddish brown color. Infected leaves turn yellow, wither, and die.

In southern states ryegrasses are highly susceptible to rust in the spring, particularly where nitrogen fertility is low. Zoysiagrasses are most often affected by rust in the fall as the growth rate of grass slows and environmental conditions favor disease development.

CONTROL. Cultural practices which improve the vigor of the turf help prevent rust. To reduce the incidence of rust, nitrogen levels should be kept adequate for turf growth, moisture stress or overwatering should be avoided, and mowing heights should be adjusted according to the grass needs. In the case of Kentucky bluegrass and perennial ryegrass, varieties that have good resistance to rust should be used where the disease is a problem.

When these measures fail to provide adequate control of rust diseases, fungicides are available for its control. Banner, Bayleton, Daconil, and Fore are some of the fungicides labeled for the control of rust on turfgrasses.

FUSARIUM BLIGHT

Fusarium blight is caused by the widespread fungi *Fusarium roseum* and *F. tricinctum*. The disease is most troublesome on cool-season grasses such as bentgrass, bluegrass, and tall fescue, but it occasionally attacks the warm-season grasses as well. The disease is most serious during hot, humid conditions when the turfgrasses are under drought stress.

SYMPTOMS. Initially, affected grasses display light green patches 2 to 6 inches in diameter. The shape of the affected areas may appear as circular patches, elongated streaks, or crescents. At high temperatures the patches quickly change from light green to reddish brown, then tan, and finally a straw color. The most characteristic symptom at this stage is a doughnut-shaped area up to 3 feet in diameter with healthy grass in the center, giving a frog-eye pattern to the diseased area. When conditions of high temperature and high humidity persist for an extended time, these diseased areas become numerous and may overlap. As a result, large areas of turf may appear blighted. As the disease progresses, grass dies as the crown and root tissues are destroyed.

On individual leaves, dark green blotches envelope the full width of the leaf blade. As the disease progresses these symptoms extend from the cut leaf tip to the base. The color changes from dark green to reddish brown and finally to a dull tan.

DISEASE CYCLE. The fungi that cause Fusarium blight survive the winter in the thatch layer and on infected grass roots, crowns, and rhizomes. As temperatures increase above 70° F spore production begins. When air temperatures are between 75° and 90° F and humidity is high, spore production becomes profuse, and affected grass may die in 4 to 7 days after the first symptoms appear. The fungi show little activity when air temperatures are below 70° F or when humidity is very low.

High nitrogen levels favor Fusarium blight because of the greater accumulations of thatch. Also, excessive watering creates conditions more favorable for the fungi.

CONTROL. In bluegrass areas Fusarium blight can be prevented by planting mixtures of bluegrass with perennial ryegrass. Otherwise, a fungicide together with a program to control thatch is essential for effective control of Fusarium blight. Bayleton, Chipco 26019, Cleary's 3336, and Rubigan are labelled for control of Fusarium blight.

NEMATODES

Nematodes are microscopic roundworms living in soil and feeding on the roots of grasses and other plants. Most species of nematodes are harmless to grass since they feed upon decaying organic matter and other soil organisms. A few species of nematodes are beneficial to grass since they are parasitic on grass-feeding organisms.

Nematodes that cause problems for grasses do so by penetrating into grass roots or sucking sap from the root surface with a spearlike stylet. In addition to the damage caused by their feeding, the wounds they leave in root tissue provide an entry for parasitic fungi.

Nematodes overwinter in soil debris or within living roots as eggs, cysts, or larvae. When the soil warms in the spring, they become active and begin feeding on plant roots. Most species have a life cycle of 30 to 60 days. Nematodes can move on their own up to 2 to 3 feet a year but are more rapidly spread by the movement of soil.

SYMPTOMS. Nematode-infested turf appears off-color and stunted and generally lacks vigor. Such symptoms occur in spotty, irregular patterns in the turf. During stress periods such as drought, infested areas are the first to show injury through wilting, discoloration, and thinning. The severity of injury varies with the species and population of nematodes.

Such symptoms are frequently mistaken for drought, nutrient deficiency, soil compaction, or pest problems. However, nematode-infested turf does not respond as readily to water and fertilizer as turf stressed by drought.

Also, turf damaged by nematodes usually has short, stubby roots that appear dark brown instead of white.

Positive identification of parasitic nematodes requires microscopic examination by a competent laboratory. Soil samples for nematode analysis should be taken from the top 4 to 6 inches of soil when moisture conditions are good. Dry soils should be irrigated several days prior to sampling.

CONTROL. When plant parasitic nematodes have been identified in populations high enough to cause damage to intensively maintained turf areas, treatment with approved nematicides may be needed.

CENTIPEDE DECLINE

In mature (3 years or older) centipedegrass lawns problem areas appear in the spring and enlarge throughout the summer. These problem areas usually develop in thatchy turf, compacted soils, droughty spots, or areas under some stress. Since a specific disease organism has not been identified as the causal agent, the problem has been broadly named centipede decline.

SYMPTOMS. Centipede decline is descriptive of the problem as the grass gradually deteriorates and is replaced by weeds or other grasses. Frequently, the grass greens up in early spring and gradually turns off color, wilts, and dies. These areas may initially be less than 1 foot in diameter, but by midsummer may have expanded to 3 to 6 feet in diameter. Individual areas may coalesce to produce large irregular-shaped patterns of wilted and discolored turf. Such areas resemble centipedegrass suffering from drought conditions.

Examination of turf in these declining areas reveals very little root development. In fact, many of the stolons, or runners, have no root attachment to the soil. Some small discolored roots may be found in the thatch, or the organic layer. The grass may be dead in the center of the areas with discolored, often dark green, leaves radiating into the healthy grass.

CONTROL. Cultural practices provide the most effective means of preventing centipede decline. Mowing heights above 2 inches tend to promote centipede decline, but mowing heights of 1½ inches or less at weekly intervals lessen the problem. Mowing height does not provide absolute control but reduces the potential for centipede decline.

Application of nitrogen at rates above 2 pounds per year has been shown to increase problems with centipede decline. Ideal fertilization of centipedegrass would be 0.5 pounds N per 1,000 square feet in April, June, August, and October.

TAKE-ALL PATCH

Take-all patch, caused by the fungus *Gaeumannomyces graminis* var. *graminis*, is a serious disease of Saint Augustine grass and can also cause problems in bermudagrass. The causal organism seems to be most active during the fall, winter, and spring, when there is abundant moisture and temperatures are moderate. The disease has the ability to destroy large sections of turfgrass if left untreated.

SYMPTOMS. When the disease is active, the first symptom is often a yellowing of the leaves and a darkening of roots. The area of discolored and dying leaves may be circular to irregular in shape and up to 20 feet in diameter. A thinning of the turfgrass within the affected area occurs as stolons become infected and decline. Unlike brownpatch, the leaves of take-all–infected plants do not easily separate from the plant, and the stolons will often have discolored areas with brown to black roots. The roots are sometimes so rotted that damaged stolons are easily pulled from the ground. Roots and stolons of brownpatch-infected plants usually have a healthy appearance. Regrowth of the grass into the affected area is often slow and unsuccessful as the new growth becomes infected. During the stressful summer months, the weakened, infected turfgrass will continue to decline.

DISEASE CYCLE. The pathogen survives on infested debris and on infected perennial parts of living grass plants. When conditions are favorable (cool, moist weather), the fungus grows on the surface of roots, stolons, rhizomes, crown, and leaf sheaths of the grass and then penetrates and infects the tissues. As the weather becomes warmer and dryer, the infected plants are stressed, and symptoms become more evident. The pathogen can be spread over long distances when infected plants or plant debris are transported mechanically. Infected sod may serve as a source of inoculum even if it shows no immediate symptoms of the disease.

CONTROL. Controlling take-all patch is not easy and much has yet to be learned about this disease. Control efforts should consider both cultural and chemical methods. Good surface and subsurface drainage is important. Excessive watering can also be favorable to development of take-all patch. Irrigating only when required to maintain good plant growth and vigor is suggested, and infrequent but thorough watering is preferred to frequent shallow watering.

Since the pathogen can survive on infested thatch, prevention of thatch buildup is suggested. Efforts to dethatch and to prevent thatch accumulation may prove helpful. If soil compaction exists, aerification will help to alleviate this condition and allow the grass to establish a deeper, more vigorous root system.

The fungicide Rubigan is labelled for the control of take-all patch caused by *Gaeumannomyces graminis*. Since infection is thought to occur primarily in the fall, with disease progression continuing during the fall and winter months under cool, moist conditions, fall applications may be the best time for fungicides to be applied.

Managing Turfgrass Insects 10

For 250 million years insects have flourished on land, and for the last several million years they have successfully competed with humans for food and shelter. Approximately 100 thousand different species of insects are found in the United States, with several million kinds found throughout the world. They outnumber people 500 thousand to 1.

Many insects are beneficial to the turf manager in that they aid in the decomposition of organic matter and improve soil structure and soil aeration; some are predators of harmful organisms. Nonetheless, many insects present problems for the turf manager.

In spite of human efforts to control them, insects have survived and increased in number. In competition with all other forms of life on land, insects stand supreme in numbers of species and individuals. Some of the weapons insects have to counter efforts to control them include: (1) a prolific potential to reproduce (A single chinch bug in spring can multiply to a million by late summer.); (2) a hard, elastic, tough exoskeleton to resist destruction; (3) protective colorations for camouflage; (4) defensive structures such as spines, scales, odors, and hairs to repel predators; (5) unique habitats in soil and plant tissues to escape detection; (6) complicated life cycles; (7) mobility; (8) high adaptability to new environments and hosts; and (9) a high degree of organization in some species.

In turn, humans have a large arsenal of weapons which help keep insects in check. With the development of DDT and its widespread use in the 1940s and 50s, many thought our insect problems had been solved. For example, a single application of DDT at 25 pounds per acre provided complete control of grubs and other soil insects for a number of years. Later, chlordane and other cyclodiene insecticides proved to be even more effective against these turf insects.

However, after a number of years of use of DDT and chlordane, grubs developed resistance to these insecticides to the point that they were no longer effective.

In Florida frequent use of the cyclodiene and organophosphate insecticides for chinch bug control resulted in resistance of the insect to both classes of insecticides. Other examples of insecticide-resistant insect populations have also been reported (Tashiro 1982).

In addition to insecticides, a number of biological controls have been used for insects. Perhaps one of the most successful examples of biological control of a turfgrass insect has been the introduction of a parasite, *Neodusmetia sangwani,* for the control of Rhodesgrass scale (mealybug) in Texas (Dean et al. 1979). The scale attacked most turfgrasses and was a serious problem in South Texas lawns in the 1950s and 60s. Chemical control of the insect was not effective because of its habitat and complex life cycle. The adult scales, which have a waxy coating, are found in the crown of the plant lodged between the leaf sheath and the stem. Only during the crawler stage, the first larval instar of the insect, could the pest be effectively controlled with chemicals. Today, some ten years after widespread introduction of the parasite, Rhodesgrass scale has been effectively controlled.

Other biological insect controls include the milky spore disease for control of Japanese beetle larvae and *Bacillus thuringiensis* for control of other larvae. The milky spore disease has the potential to increase under natural conditions to a high enough population for effective control of the larvae of the Japanese beetle for a number of years (Klein 1982).

Another weapon is the use of turfgrass varieties with resistance to specific insects. Perhaps Floratam Saint Augustine grass represents the best illustration of the effectiveness of insect-resistant varieties (Reinert 1982). The southern lawn chinch bug, *Blissus insularis,* has caused widespread damage to Saint Augustine lawns for twenty-five years. In Texas over 25 million dollars are spent annually for the control of the chinch bug. In 1974 the Florida and Texas Agricultural Experiment Stations released a Saint Augustine grass variety, Floratam, that was resistant to the chinch bug. Instead of the insect killing the grass, chinch bugs restricted to Floratam soon died.

Unfortunately, biological controls are not available for most turf insects. With the removal of the persistent cyclodiene insecticides (DDT, chlordane, etc.) from the manager's arsenal and with insects developing resistance to others, insects are no longer a nuisance but a serious problem to turf managers.

Soil-inhibiting pests such as grubs can be difficult to control with the insecticides labeled for use today. The organophosphate insecticides are effective for grub control, but some are bound very strongly to the thatch layer in turf (Niemczyk and Krueger 1982). Thus, the insecticides do not reach the target—a grub in the soil under the thatch—in concentrations required for control. Also, the residual of organophosphates is so short that timing of the application becomes critical.

Other insects also present serious problems. In some areas of the country, particularly south Florida, chinch bugs have developed resistance to a number of insecticides (Reinert and Niemczyk 1982). Also, the list of replacement materials is short, and few new ones are being researched. Thus, control of chinch bugs is, and probably will continue to be, difficult and expensive to achieve.

Sod webworms and cutworms present another example of the increased difficulty of control. Materials available today require repeated applications for year-round control. Although the organophosphate and carbamate insecticides are effective against the sod webworm, monthly or biweekly applications may be required for control during late spring and summer.

Thus, although it was once only a nuisance to control turf insects, today it requires a serious effort based on knowledge and life histories of the problem pests as well as knowledge of insecticides. A brief discussion of several of the more troublesome insect pests of turfgrass and control measures follows.

WHITE GRUBS

At least four different kinds of grubs attack turfgrasses in the United States. In the Northeast larvae of the European chafer have caused extensive damage in New York for many years. In the Midwest the northern masked chafer and the Japanese beetle are serious problems. And in the South larvae of the southern masked chafer and the June beetle present a serious problem to turf. All of these grubs are soil-inhabiting species that feed on the roots of turfgrasses and other plants.

JAPANESE BEETLE. Adult beetles usually appear on the foliage of trees and shrubs in June and early July. The head, thorax, and abdomen of Japanese beetles are metallic-green while the other wings are coppery-brown. Two tufts of white hair appear on the abdomen just behind the wings with five

Life history of common white grubs.

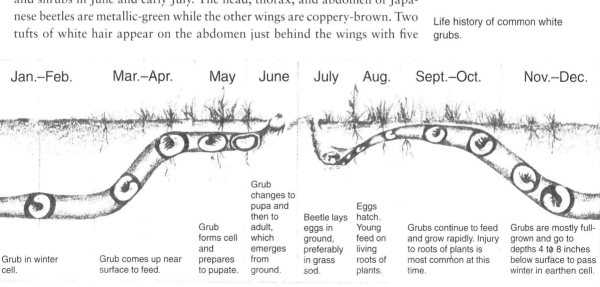

| Jan.–Feb. | Mar.–Apr. | May | June | July | Aug. | Sept.–Oct. | Nov.–Dec. |

Grub in winter cell.

Grub comes up near surface to feed.

Grub forms cell and prepares to pupate.

Grub changes to pupa and then to adult, which emerges from ground.

Beetle lays eggs in ground, preferably in grass sod.

Eggs hatch. Young feed on living roots of plants.

Grubs continue to feed and grow rapidly. Injury to roots of plants is most common at this time.

Grubs are mostly full-grown and go to depths 4 to 8 inches below surface to pass winter in earthen cell.

tufts along each side of the body. The beetles are midday fliers, in contrast to chafers and June beetles which fly at night.

Female Japanese beetles feed on foliage for several days, then dig into the turf to deposit eggs. They emerge again in a few days and, after feeding for several more days, return to the soil to deposit another cluster of eggs. The adult beetle lives for 30 to 45 days during which time she deposits 40 to 60 eggs.

Eggs hatch into tiny grubs in about 10 days and immediately begin to feed on grass roots. The grubs increase in size rapidly and continue feeding through the summer and fall. By the latter part of September the grubs are about 1 inch long and are white to grayish white in color. With the approach of cold weather, they move downward in the soil where they spend the winter.

In late March or April of the following year, the grubs move back toward the surface and continue feeding until the latter part of May, when they change into the pupal stage. During the pupal stage, the insect transforms into the adult beetle that emerges in June or July. The life cycle of this species requires one year.

The critical period during the life cycle of the insect—the period when an insecticide application has the best chance of achieving control—is the early larval stage, usually the month of August. By this time, most of the eggs have hatched, and even the larvae of those that hatched early are small enough to be controlled by insecticides. Insecticide applications prior to that time will not control the eggs. Later-stage larvae occurring in September and October are harder to control. Thus, the most vulnerable period in the life cycle with respect to effective chemical control is the early larval stage.

To be effective the chemical must reach the target—the soil level where grubs feed. Thus, the presence of a thatch layer presents a serious barrier to the movement of insecticides to the target. When materials such as chlordane were used the insecticide eventually reached the soil level, where it remained active for years. But the organophosphate and carbamate insecticides are active for only a few weeks. Therefore, they must reach the pest immediately. Dethatching prior to applications helps, but drenching the insecticide into the turf immediately after application is needed to move the material to the soil level where the target pest is feeding. Thorough watering of the turf 24 to 48 hours prior to application also helps move the grubs closer to the surface.

Liquid formations of these insecticides should not be allowed to dry on the turf before irrigation. In heavily thatched turf applying a wetting agent to the turf before spraying with an insecticide and following with a thorough irrigation will improve the effectiveness of the insecticide. Granular formulations of organophosphate insecticides have proven to be more effective in heavily thatched turf. Granular formulations must be watered in, but the urgency is not as great as for liquid formulations.

Grubs of the Japanese beetle can also be controlled with a dust containing

White grub

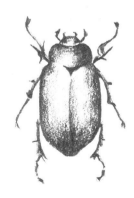

Adult beetle

spores of milky disease, *Bacillus popilliae*. The dust should be applied by treating spots at 5-foot spacings with 1 teaspoon of material. The dust should not be used in combination with insecticides. The disease organism requires several years to infect existing grubs and develop adequate bacteria population for effective control. Thus, milky spore disease does not provide an immediate control method for grub problem.

Another parasite, a nematode, that attacks the larvae of the Japanese beetle has been found in the Northeast. The parasite is being studied as another possible biological control of the Japanese beetle larvae (Klein 1982).

MASKED CHAFERS. The beetles of the masked chafers are about ½ inch long and tan-brown. Adult beetles emerge from the soil in June and July. Unlike the Japanese beetle, masked chafers are night fliers and are strongly attracted to light. The northern masked chafer is found from Connecticut to Alabama and west to California. The southern masked chafer is found throughout the southwest and in Texas, Oklahoma, Iowa, and Illinois.

Adults lay eggs that hatch into tiny grubs in about 3 weeks. The grubs begin to feed on roots of plants and organic debris in the soil almost immediately after hatching. They work their way toward the surface as they continue to feed upon the roots of grasses. At the approach of cold weather, the grubs begin to descend into the soil where they overwinter at a depth of 14 to 16 inches.

The following spring the grubs move upward and by early May they are feeding near the surface. In early June, they move back down to about 6 inches where they transform in the pupal stage. They spend 18 days in this stage before emerging as adult beetles. The life cycle of masked chafers requires 1 year.

Information relative to chemical control on Japanese beetle larvae also applies to control of the masked chafer. Again, the optimal period for control of the grub with short-residual insecticides would be late July and August.

JUNE BEETLES. Numerous species of May or June beetles are found in the South and Midwest. One species, *Phyllophaga crinita*, has caused extensive damage to turfgrasses in Texas and neighboring states. The adults are ½ to ⅝ inch long and light brown with a reddish tinge just behind the head. The adults begin to emerge from the soil in February with peak emergence in May or June, usually after a period of significant rainfall. At least two flights of the June beetle are observed each year. During these flight periods large numbers of adults can be seen flying around street lights at night.

The females lay 30 to 40 eggs at soil depths of 2 to 5 inches. The eggs hatch in about 3 weeks, and the larvae begin feeding on grass roots. The insect passes through 3 larval stages (instars). The third instar is the mature white grub that causes extensive damage, feeding on grass roots in the fall and early spring. The stage of the insect most susceptible to control with insecticides is the early larval stage, which is found during July and August, depending on when the major flight of the beetles occurred. Insecticide treatments for white grub control should be made 4 to 6 weeks after the major flight of the June beetle is observed (table 10-1).

CHINCH BUGS

Chinch bugs are serious pests of cool- and warm-season turfgrasses. In northern states, the hairy chinch bug (*Blissus leucopterus hirtus*) causes extensive damage to bluegrass, fine fescue, and bent lawns in mid- to late summer. In southern states the lawn chinch bug (*Blissus insularis*) is the most destructive pest of Saint Augustine grass lawns, with more than 50 million dollars spent annually for its control. Many homeowners have planted grasses other than Saint Augustine because of the chinch bug problem.

The adult chinch bug is about ⅛ inch long, having black with white patches on its wings that fold over the back. Adults overwinter in thatch and other protected areas. In the spring female chinch bugs begin laying eggs. The eggs are pushed into protected places, often being found between the leaf sheath and the stem. Females lay only a few eggs for several weeks. Eggs hatch in about two weeks.

Newly hatched nymphs are very small, bright red insects with a white band across the back. With each of five molts, the nymphs become darker and more closely resemble the adults. The newly hatched nymphs are vigorous and begin feeding immediately on tender portions of grass stems. The nymphal stages of the insect cause most of the damage by clogging the plant's conductive tissues, thus, preventing water and nutrients from reaching leaves and new shoots. Damage first appears as scattered yellow areas that rapidly enlarge to brown, dead spots.

Within a given lawn or area, chinch bugs occur aggregated in scattered patches rather than uniformly distributed. These aggregations move rather slowly, usually completely killing the grass in infested patches before moving. When chlorotic or wilted patches are noticed, ample time remains to apply controls before large areas are damaged.

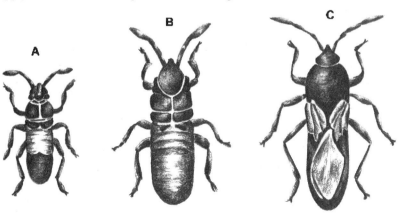

Chinch bug: A, First stage, or red nymph; B, second-stage nymph; C, winged adult

Table 10-1. Chemical Control of White Grubs

Insecticides	Rate of Application per 1,000 sq. ft.	Remarks
Crusade 5G	1.8 lbs.	Apply ¼ to ½ inch of water after application. Do not pre-water.
Diazinon 5G (Not for use on golf courses or sod farms)	2.5 lbs.	Apply 1 inch of water 24 to 48 hours before application and ½ to 1 inch immediately after application.
Dursban Turf Insecticide	1.5–3 fl. ozs.	Same as above
Dylox/Proxol 80SP	3.75 ozs.	Same as above
Oftanol 5G	0.9 lb.	Same as above
Triumph 4E	1.5 fl. ozs.	Do not treat areas that border lakes, streams, or ponds. Do not apply on sand or loamy sands. Maximum of 1 application per year.

In northern states two generations of chinch bugs usually occur each year. The first generation appears in June and the second in August. The greatest injury is caused during July and August when the turf is under moisture stress. In southern states as many as four complete generations may occur, with each generation larger than the preceding generation. Southern Florida has as many as seven generations per year.

Insecticide applications should be made when injury symptoms are first noticed. Organophosphate and carbamate insecticides labeled for use on chinch bugs will control both adults and nymphs. Most materials will control newly hatched nymphs for about a two-week period after application.

Evidence suggests that heavy applications of soluble nitrogen fertilizers increased the occurrence of chinch bug damage. Populations apparently develop more rapidly and cause more injury on heavily fertilized grass.

Moisture also has a significant effect on chinch bug populations. Heavy irrigation or rainfall suppresses chinch bug numbers to the degree that they do not cause serious damage.

Perhaps most promising is the development of resistant grass varieties. Floratam and Floralawn Saint Augustine grass varieties are resistant to the lawn chinch bug and can be sprigged into other Saint Augustine grass lawns (table 10-2).

SOD WEBWORMS, CUTWORMS, AND ARMYWORMS

The larvae of several kinds of moths, such as sod webworms, cutworms, and armyworms, feed on grass leaves and damage turf extensively. The insects can be distinguished by their feeding habits and injury symptoms. Sod web-

Table 10-2. Chemical Control of Southern Lawn Chinch Bugs

Insecticides	Rate of Application per 1,000 sq. ft.	Remarks
Crusade 5G	1.5–1.8 lbs.	Irrigate treated area for 10 to 15 minutes after application.
Diazinon 5G	2.0 lbs.	Not for use on golf courses and sod farms.
Dursban Turf Insecticide	0.75 fl. oz.	Do not allow public use of treated area until spray has dried.
Orthene Turf and Ornamental	1.2–2.4 ozs.	Use minimum of 5 gals. water per 1,000 sq. ft.
Triumph 4E	0.75 fl. oz.	Do not treat areas that border lakes, streams, or ponds. Do not apply on sand or loamy sands. Maximum of 2 applications per year for the 0.75 oz. per 1,000 sq. ft. rate.

worms and cutworms are night-feeding caterpillars. Both insects feed around a small burrow or tunnel in the turf and carry the leaf blades into the tunnel. Silken threads can be seen in the early morning covering the tunnel of the sod webworm. The cutworm is often found on golf greens after greens are aerated. The aeration holes provide an ideal habitat for the cutworm larvae during the day while feeding around the hole at night. Armyworms are appropriately named because they can be seen moving across turf in large numbers. In contrast to sod webworms and cutworms, armyworms feed during the day and night and leave the turf with a white skeletonized appearance.

Sod webworm adults are small, white to gray moths, with a snout-like projection on the front of the head. While resting, the wings of the moth are closely folded about the body.

The moths are frequently seen fluttering over the turf in the early evening. The females scatter their eggs at random as they fly over the turf. Apparently the moths are attracted to dark green, healthy turf. Eggs hatch in 7 to 10 days and larvae begin feeding on grass leaves. As they mature, the larvae build silk-lined tunnels through the thatch layer and into the soil. The slender larvae reach ¾ inch in length and are characterized by a light brown color with several rows of dark spots along the entire length of the body. The first signs of sod webworm damage are areas of unevenly clipped grass and patches of brown or closely clipped grass. The larvae remain active for several weeks, then pupate. Adults appear about 1 week later. A life cycle is completed in 5 to 6 weeks with several generations per year.

Sod webworms are readily controlled by organophosphate (diazinon, trichlorfon, chlorpyrifos) and carbamate (carbaryl) insecticides. However, these are short residual materials and repeat applications are required to control the next generation of larvae.

Cutworm moths exhibit a grayish brown to black color and a wingspread of 1 to 2 inches. The moths are active only at night. Females lay their eggs singly or in groups of 2 to 3 on the leaves and stems of grasses. Eggs hatch in 7 to 10 days, and the larvae begin feeding. Cutworm larvae are grayish-black, smooth worms that curl into a ball, or C-shape, when disturbed. The cutworms grow into a length of 1½ to 2 inches, are usually plump (in contrast to the slender sod webworm), and may be spotted or striped. There are several generations of cutworms produced annually.

Cutworms often appear in the early spring when temperatures are slightly above freezing. Damage appears as closely clipped grass in patterns radiating from their tunnel or hiding place. Cutworms are readily controlled by organophosphate and carbamate insecticides.

The fall armyworm is the most common armyworm found on turf. The adults are grayish-colored moths with gray or white mottled wings that measure about 1½ inches across. The females lay eggs in masses of 100 or more on grass leaves and other foliage. The eggs hatch in 2 to 4 days, and the tiny larvae begin feeding on tender grass blades. Newly hatched larvae are white with black heads. Their bodies darken as they feed until they are full grown. Full-grown fall armyworms are about 1½ inches long and light green to almost black in color with several light stripes along the body.

Fall armyworms feed for 2 to 3 weeks, then burrow into the soil to pupate. In 10 days to 2 weeks, the moths emerge. Several generations may occur annually.

Damage may first appear as whitish patches in the lawn where the grass

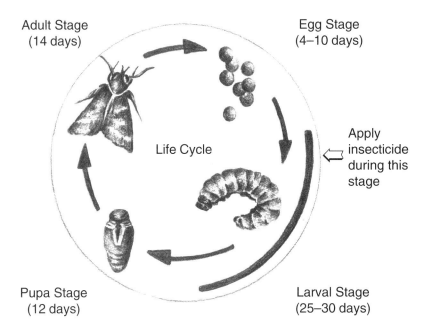

Adult Stage
(14 days)

Egg Stage
(4–10 days)

Life Cycle

Apply
insecticide
during this
stage

Pupa Stage
(12 days)

Larval Stage
(25–30 days)

Moth life cycle

has been skeletonized. Later, as the larvae grow, they devour all foliage except grass stems. Fall armyworms may be seen migrating across the grass in the daytime, but they feed mostly at night.

Fall armyworms can be controlled by the same materials recommended for sod webworms and cutworms.

MOLE CRICKETS

Next to hurricanes, mole crickets may be the scariest critters a golf course superintendent can experience in the sandy Deep South.

The burrowing crickets, with muscular forelegs and shovels for feet, waste little time in killing turf on greens, tees, fairways, and roughs. Cricket-infested ground appears cultivated. Soil is loosened and exposed grass is left to die. The tunneling insects, sometimes covering 10 to 20 feet in a night, can drag uprooted grass into their burrows for nesting material.

Areas in warmer climates, which encourage year-round infestations, have experienced cricket infestations for two decades or more, causing large turf areas to be annihilated within one week. In parts of Georgia mole crickets were controlled with pesticide bait treatments, but they are a continuing threat in the lower third of the state's sandier soils.

Areas of Louisiana and Texas also present favorable habitats, and entomologists in those states say damaging infestations are found.

NO NATURAL PREDATORS. With no known locally occurring natural predators, the mole cricket has existed with impunity since arriving at five Gulf Coast ports less than a century ago. The insects' east-to-west pattern of spread and corresponding infestation levels apparently relate to the length of time they have been on U.S. soil. Natives of either Puerto Rico or Central America (Walker and Nickle 1981), crickets initially settled near Brunswick, Georgia, near the Florida state line, in 1899 and later at Savannah (1904), Charleston (1915), and Galveston (1925).

In Florida researchers hope that a parasitic wasp which they introduced several years ago will prove successful in naturally controlling crickets as it has in its native habitat in Puerto Rico. However, sufficient generations of the predator wasp have not yet been established (Klein 1982).

In the meantime, effective pesticide controls are available. From mid- to late summer is usually the ideal time in most areas to initiate treatments, when adult crickets are feeding near the surface and are most susceptible to the attractant of baits.

During cooler weather the mole crickets tunnel farther into the soil to escape freezing temperatures. The nocturnal insects are most active when nighttime temperatures are above 60° F. It is during these times that tunneling is concentrated in the upper inch or two, giving turf the fearsome cultivated appearance.

SPOT TREATING. Spot treating usually produces desired results within

Mole cricket

Table 10-3. Chemical Control of Mole Crickets

Insecticides	Rate of Application per 1,000 sq. ft.	Remarks
Crusade 5G	1.8 lbs.	Irrigate after treatment with ½ inch of water.
Dursban Turf Insecticide	1.5 fl. ozs.	Apply in 2 gals. of water per 1,000 sq. ft.
Orthene Turf & Ornamental	1–2 ozs.	Apply in 2 gals. of water per 1,000 sq. ft.
Oftanol 5G	0.9 lb.	Irrigate after treatment with ½ to 1 inch of water
Sevimol (Chipco)	5 fl. ozs.	Apply in 2 gals. of water per 1,000 sq. ft.
Triumph 4E	1.5 fl. ozs.	Apply in 2 gals. of water per 1,000 sq. ft. Do not use on golf course fairways.

a reasonable time if infestations are caught early. Suspected turf can be tested by applying a soap flush made of one ounce of liquid detergent to one gallon of water and applied over four square feet of turf. If more than two crickets surface within three minutes, control probably is needed. A more precise method—though one usually impractical on golf courses—involves physically removing a soil plug and ascertaining the number of crickets. One per square foot indicates the need for treatment (table 10-3).

Integrated Pest Management Program

Integrated pest management (IPM) is a familiar term in agriculture, but the concept is not well known in the turfgrass industry. The IPM concept was originally developed as a means of producing high quality crops with a minimum use of pesticides. This program also reduced the producers' dependence on pesticides and protected the environment. Today the public focus on pesticide residues in food crops and in drinking water and the effects of those residues on the environment compels the turfgrass industry to adapt the principles of IPM to the maintenance of lawns, golf courses, athletic fields, sod farms, and other turfgrass areas. With prudent use, these integrated pest management techniques will maintain or even improve the aesthetic value of a property. Using proper management practices for turfgrass care will maintain the turf and benefit the soil, water, and atmosphere around the site. A thick healthy lawn can prevent erosion, moderate summer heat, and filter rainwater from roofs, downspouts, and driveways. Healthy lawns help improve soil structure and increase infiltration by adding organic matter to the soil while helping retain nutrients and other plant protection chemicals useful in deterring pests.

Over 20 million acres of lawns, 2 million acres of golf courses, and millions of acres of playgrounds, athletic fields, cemeteries, etc. in the United States could benefit from integrated pest management. If fertilizers or pesticides are used indiscriminately on lawns, golf courses, athletic fields, or sod farms, pollution can occur. One potential pollution hazard is leaching of fertilizers and crop protection chemicals into groundwater. Overwatering or excessive rainfall can cause fertilizers and pesticides to seep below the root zone of grasses. Once these chemicals enter the soil and leach beyond the plant root zone, they may harmlessly degrade, or they may become potential hazards in deeper soil layers or even in groundwater.

With wise management, however, these potential problems can be avoided. In fact, a healthy, vigorous stand of grass can actually outcompete most weeds and withstand damage from diseases and insects. This natural resistance will lessen the amount of fertilizer or pesticide needed.

IPM does not preclude the use of pesticides but emphasizes instead the importance of planting adapted turfgrasses, following recommended cultural practices, keeping detailed records, monitoring weed and pest populations, targeting pesticide applications, and using biological controls, including resistant grass varieties when available.

ADAPTED TURFGRASS VARIETIES

The use of adapted turfgrass varieties reduces many pest-related problems. For example, growing Kentucky bluegrass in shaded sites frequently leads to problems with powdery mildew. Also, growing susceptible varieties of Saint Augustine grass in full sun leads to problems with chinch bugs. In both of these examples, using a different grass species or planting a resistant variety would avoid the problem. Likewise, where mole crickets are a serious problem, grasses such as bahia which are highly susceptible to the insect should be avoided.

On golf courses in southern states the use of bentgrass on putting greens often increases the need for fungicide applications. In areas where bentgrass is adapted, it should be first choice, but where its adaptation is marginal, Tifdwarf bermudagrass would be a better choice.

CULTURAL PRACTICES

Following recommended turfgrass management practices helps to reduce pest problems in turfgrass areas. Seeding rates, mowing practices, fertilization, watering, and cultivation are all management practices that affect pest activity in lawns, golf courses, athletic fields, and other turf areas.

Seeding at recommended rates reduces the time required to establish a turf and, consequently, reduces weed problems. Overseeding golf greens with perennial ryegrass at 30 to 35 pounds per 1,000 square feet reduces infestations of annual bluegrass compared to lower seeding rates. Conversely, seeding bermudagrass lawns at ½ to 1 pound per 1,000 square feet reduces the incidence of seedling disease compared to much higher seeding rates.

Mowing practices also have a significant effect on weed and pest problems in turfgrasses. For example, mowing Kentucky bluegrass turf below 1 inch increases invasion by annual bluegrass. Likewise, mowing golf greens too short during summer months increases weed invasion and susceptibility to turfgrass diseases.

Mowing turfgrasses at recommended heights and frequencies increases turf density and vigor and reduces weed and pest problems. The turf manager must decide on the best mowing schedule based on grass variety, environmental conditions, and turf use.

Perhaps fertilization practices have a greater impact on pest problems than any other cultural practice. Inadequate fertilization can lead to invasion by weeds and increased disease activity (dollar spot and rust). Excessive fertilization leads to greater insect activity (chinch bugs and sod webworms), increased disease activity (leaf spot, brownpatch, and *Pythium*), and potential environmental problems. Moderate fertilization based on grass species, environmental conditions, turf use, and mowing practices is a critical component of an integrated pest management program. Healthy grass that is neither deficient in nutrients nor succulent from too much nitrogen is most resistant to weed and pest infestations.

Watering practices also have a significant impact on weed populations and pest activity. Overwatered lawns, golf courses, and athletic fields always have higher weed populations than properly watered sites. Keeping the soil surface moist promotes weed seed germination and growth. Excess watering also promotes brownpatch, *Pythium,* and other turfgrass disease problems. Frequently, weed populations and disease activity can be reduced to acceptable levels by adjusting watering schedules. This practice will allow more of the fertilizer and pest control chemicals to remain in the top layer of soil where they can be utilized. Proper watering will also reduce losses of these chemicals through runoff or leaching.

Cultivation practices (vertical mowing, aeration, and topdressing) impact pest problems by their effect on thatch. Both insect and disease activity increase as thatch levels increase in turf. At the same time, the effectiveness of chemical controls decreases as thatch increases. Chinch bugs in Saint Augustine grass are seldom a problem in newly planted lawns but become serious problems in mature, thatchy lawns. White grubs can be readily controlled by insecticides in newly established turf, but in thatchy turf insecticides are bound in the organic layer and may not reach the target insect in the soil.

Disease activity is also greater in thatchy turf since the environment is ideal for disease organisms to develop. As the thatch layer is intermittently wet and dried, sugars and other carbohydrates in plant tissue are released and provide the energy source needed for microorganisms to develop. Temperatures and humidity are also favorable in the thatch layer for disease organisms to develop.

Cultivation practices that reduce thatch or maintain thatch at an optimum level significantly reduce pest problems. Topdressing, for example, is an important cultural control for preventing centipede decline. All of the cultivation operations are important for disease control on intensively maintained turf such as golf greens.

However, the positive contributions of a thatch layer should not be overlooked. Thatch has a moderating influence on soil temperature. During extremely cold temperatures a thatch layer could provide the difference between survival and winterkill. Thatch also increases the wear tolerance of turf on golf greens and athletic fields. And, perhaps most important, the thatch layer acts as a filter for harmful air pollutants and inactivates, or binds, chemicals that might otherwise appear in runoff or groundwater. A dense turf with a moderate thatch layer provides an attractive and highly effective control for environmental contamination from air pollutants. In fact, such a turf prevents contamination of our groundwater and greatly reduces urban runoff.

RECORD KEEPING

Historical records of environmental conditions of maintenance practices and pest activity provide the information needed to predict insect, disease, and weed problems. Many pest problems can be predicted from temperature and moisture conditions. Reviewing past records suggests that brownpatch will develop on Saint Augustine grass lawns in the fall, when nighttime temperatures are in the 60s and rainfall or irrigation is excessive. Likewise, white grubs become a problem on all turfgrass species 6 to 8 weeks after the last major flight of adult beetles each spring. Various species of beetles can be seen either feeding on foliage or flying around lights at night.

Such predictions allow the turfgrass manager to make timely preventive applications of chemicals. All pest problems—insects, diseases, and weeds—are most effectively controlled when diagnosis is made at an early stage of development of the pest. In the case of annual weeds and some disease problems, preventative applications of chemicals can be made based on historical records. Annual bluegrass and crabgrass are most effectively controlled by preemerge herbicides applied prior to their germination. The timing of those applications is based on historical dates of emergence.

Detailed and accurate records on turf maintenance practices may also provide key information needed to diagnose a problem. Fertilizer records may eliminate nutrition as a cause of weak, chlorotic turf. Irrigation and rainfall records might also rule out drought as a cause. Thus, the turfgrass manager might suspect nematodes, diseases, or other conditions as the cause of the problem. Without detailed and accurate records, critical time is lost in the process of diagnosing a problem, and ineffective or potentially detrimental applications of chemicals may be made.

MONITORING PEST POPULATIONS

The turfgrass manager must make the decision to apply a chemical control or to manage the problem with cultural practices. For all pests a critical population exists above which chemical treatment is required. This critical population will vary with pests, grass species, turf use, and environmental conditions. For example, a bermudagrass lawn, athletic field, or golf course fairway could tolerate 4 to 6 white grubs per square foot without chemical treatment. The turf may require more frequent irrigation and additional fertilization, but chemical control is not necessary. However, the same grass on a golf green will require chemical control because of the reduced root system on a golf green and the demand for high quality turf.

A Saint Augustine grass lawn with 25 or more chinch bugs per square foot may need a chemical control if environmental conditions are hot and dry. But the same population of insects during rainy periods may not require treatment. Natural populations of bacteria and predators that kill chinch bugs often develop under wet conditions.

Similarly, brownpatch developing on a Saint Augustine grass lawn in the fall should be treated, but the same conditions in spring will improve without chemical treatment when hot, dry conditions develop.

Weeds also have a critical population above which treatment is required. A single dandelion in a bluegrass lawn does not require a chemical application, but 5 or more per 1,000 square feet may need treatment. Likewise, annual bluegrass populations may determine whether or not a bentgrass golf green needs complete renovations or just continued management.

TARGETING CHEMICAL APPLICATIONS

Monitoring pest populations and scouting turfgrass areas for pest activity allows the turfgrass manager to make timely chemical applications to specific areas and for specific pests. Broad-spectrum chemical applications to the entire property are not always required for pest control when the turf manager takes the time or designates a trained applicator to scout and monitor the property. Where this practice has been implemented, the use of chemicals was significantly reduced, and pest control was improved.

Chinch bugs provide an example of the effectiveness of targeting chemical applications. Adult chinch bugs can be found year-round in Saint Augustine grass lawns, yet chemical controls are not always needed. Experience suggests that when chinch bug populations reach 25 per square foot, damage is likely to occur if left untreated. Observations also suggest that chinch bug populations are quite sporadic, and the entire lawn or turf facility may not need to be treated. Also, as previously mentioned, wet conditions or natural predators may reduce populations to acceptable levels without chemical controls. Only when populations of chinch bugs are above critical levels and visual symptoms indicate damage is occurring should chemical applications be made, and then only infested areas of the lawn require treatment. In the case of chinch bugs, shaded areas of the lawn rarely, if ever, require treatment. Such a procedure requires continued scouting of the lawn as populations may redevelop in the same areas or develop in other areas of the lawn. However, reinfestation can occur even when the entire lawn is treated.

White grub and brownpatch provide other examples of the effectiveness of targeting chemical applications. White grub populations, like chinch bugs, are quite sporadic, but timing of applications is more critical for white grubs. Chemical controls are most effective for white grubs when larvae are small, immature, and near the soil surface. Timing chemical applications to correspond to those conditions provides the greatest control.

Brownpatch control also requires timely chemical applications for effective control. When environmental conditions favor disease development and the first symptoms are visible, applications are needed. If applications are delayed beyond this period, control is very difficult.

BIOLOGICAL CONTROL OF PESTS

The use of biological controls for turfgrass pests is not new, but the concept is gaining in popularity and use. One of the most successful biological controls of a turfgrass insect was the introduction of a parasite, *Neodusmetia sangwani,* for the control of Rhodesgrass scale in Texas. The scale attacked numerous turfgrasses and was a serious pest in South Texas lawns and golf courses in the 1950s and 60s. Chemical control of the insect was generally ineffective because of the habitat and complex life cycle of the pest. Today, some twenty years after introduction of the parasite, Rhodesgrass scale has been effectively controlled.

Other biological insect controls include the milky spore disease for control of Japanese beetle larvae and *Bacillus thuringiensis* for control of armyworms, sod worms, and other larvae.

Another biological control is the use of turfgrass varieties with resistance to specific pests. Floralawn Saint Augustine grass is an excellent example of the value of resistant varieties. Floralawn is resistant to both chinch bugs and Saint Augustine Decline.

In time more biological controls for turfgrass pests will be available to the turfgrass manager to reduce his dependence on chemicals for control. Healthy turfgrass is attractive and valuable. Preserving the soil and water underneath turfgrass areas is also important. Applying all of the principles of IPM—adapted varieties, cultural practices, record keeping, monitoring populations, scouting turf areas, targeting applications, and maintaining biological controls—can provide effective pest control, minimize the use of chemical controls, and preserve and protect your turf and environment.

Turfgrass Maintenance Programs 11

Tradition claims that the art of greens maintenance may have been passed from one generation to the next by greenskeepers of chiefly Scottish descent. In fact, most of the first greenskeepers in the United States were Scottish. Perhaps the Scots earned this reputation since golf originated in Scotland, where most golf courses were found prior to the twentieth century.

Greens Maintenance

Today, the golf course superintendent has replaced the greenskeeper, and science is rapidly replacing art in the profession of greens maintenance. Yet, there still may be more art than science involved in greens maintenance. For example, science tells us of the need to fertilize greens, which nutrients to apply, and what ratio of nutrients are needed to maintain a healthy turf on greens. But science tells us little about the playability of the greens—the speed, uniformity, texture, graininess, and trueness. Playability of greens depends more on the skill of the superintendent to judge when to apply fertilizer, how much to apply, and what material to use. Too often textbook fertilization practices produce thatchy greens, excessive grain, and disease problems, all of which lead to poor playing surfaces. A superintendent who relies more on experience and observation to develop a fertilizer program usually has very good playing greens.

Similarly, greens irrigated by automatic systems programmed to apply water at specific times and amounts are often too wet to play golf. Whereas, greens watered by a superintendent based on his own experience and frequent observation are usually drier, less weedy, and better playing surfaces.

Topdressing is another practice that requires more art than science. The scientific approach to topdressing, using particle size distribution, percolation, and moisture retention, can provide helpful information but tells the superintendent little about putting quality, ball holding, or compatibility with existing greens mixtures. The superintendent must develop a topdressing material with all of these criteria in mind. Even after developing a topdressing material, the superintendent must also decide when to topdress, how much to apply, and how to work the topdressing into the turf. These decisions on topdressing, watering, and fertilization are part of the art of greens maintenance.

Rather than playing down the contributions science has made to greens maintenance, these points emphasize the importance of experience and observation to the maintenance of fine playing surfaces. Without the skills acquired by experience and observation, even the best educated managers fail in the development of fine playing greens.

The superintendent must keep in mind that practices which work for one golf course may not work for another. Greens construction, grass species, location, and maintenance programs all determine the response to specific practices. Also, superintendents must recognize that the difference between success and failure is often in the timing of maintenance practices. Cultural practices, equipment, and staff required for greens maintenance cannot be put together in a haphazard order. Timing of each operation can be as important as performing the operation. Delays in carrying out operations only result from poor planning. Maintenance programs must be flexible to allow for unusual conditions and unscheduled activities.

MOWING PRACTICES DETERMINE PUTTING QUALITY

Regardless of other practices, proper mowing is required for good putting greens. Proper mowing includes daily mowing, daily changing of mowing patterns, mowing at the correct height, precise adjustment of mowers, daily cleaning and sharpening of mowers, training of mower operators, and visual inspection of results. Mowing is the single most important practice in greens maintenance.

Mowing height is the only variable in the requirements for proper mowing. Mowing height is dependent on grass species, environmental conditions, and desired speed of greens. Tifdwarf bermudagrass and bentgrass greens can be mowed as short as $1/8$ inch, but Tifgreen bermudagrass should not be mowed below $5/32$ inch. During midsummer heat stress bentgrass greens should be raised to $3/16$- or $1/4$-inch mowing heights. Overseeded bermudagrass greens may be mowed as high as $1/4$ inch during establishment but should be lowered to $3/16$ inch within 4 weeks after planting and $5/32$ inch or less in early spring.

If fast greens are desired for tournament play, mowing heights can be lowered below the recommended minimums for a short period. However, other practices such as brushing, verticutting, and topdressing are as important to putting speed as mowing height.

Daily mowing at recommended heights produces dense, fine-textured putting greens without shocking the turf. Less frequent mowing results in the removal of an excessive amount of leaf tissue at each mowing and puts the turf under stress. Removal of half of the leaf tissue at a single mowing can result in severely reduced root growth for several days.

Changing mowing patterns at each mowing helps to eliminate graininess, to reduce wheel or mower wear and compaction, and to establish a target by setting the green apart from the apron or collar. Where triplex greens mowers are used, the final cut around the perimeter of the green should be moved in and out at least the width of a wheel each day or should only be mowed on alternate days. Some superintendents make this perimeter cut with a walking greens mower to reduce wear and compaction.

Proper mower adjustment and sharpening is essential to produce a clean, uniform cut on putting greens. Immediately after use, each mower should be thoroughly cleaned, height and cut adjustments checked, reels lapped in, and other maintenance performed as needed to have the mower ready for service the next day. If this routine is followed, equipment failures can be prevented or corrected before the next use. However, standby mowers should always be available in case a mower is taken out of service for several days.

Not everyone can mow a golf green. Even with training some people do not have the physical or mental dexterity to mow greens. Greens mowing is a skill acquired only by experience and observation. Training people to mow greens requires instilling an appreciation for a uniform, smoothly cut green in addition to artful techniques. Just going through the physical exercise of mowing a green is not enough; the operator must appreciate the finished product.

Finally, the golf course superintendent must inspect greens frequently to be sure they are properly mowed. Perhaps this is best accomplished by playing the course.

GREENS OFTEN OVERWATERED

Watering practices have nearly as much effect on playability of greens as mowing practices. Wet greens provide poor playing conditions and lead to heavy infestations of weeds. Ball marks and footprints are also problems on wet greens. But dry greens are usually very hard and do not hold a well-played golf shot.

Watering practices must be based on soil properties (greens construction), grass species, environmental conditions, and other maintenance practices. Watering schedules are critical on greens with poor drainage or on greens with excessively high infiltration rates. Properly constructed greens allow a much wider margin for error in watering schedules.

Greens with poor drainage must be watered slowly, or at frequent intervals, to wet the soil 4 to 6 inches deep. On poorly drained greens, if water is applied at rates above 0.5 inch per hour, water runs off the green faster than it moves into the soil. Thus, the collar and apron get wet before the putting surface is adequately watered. Automatic systems should be cycled so that water is applied intermittently to such greens. Intermittent watering allows water to penetrate several inches into the soil before excessive runoff occurs. Then, with the exception of spot watering, greens should hold up several days without watering.

Sand greens with very high infiltration rates require light and frequent applications of water. Again, the collar and apron of these greens are often wet while the putting surface appears dry. Careful design of the irrigation system may be required to maintain the putting surface without keeping the surrounding area wet.

Environmental conditions have more influence on watering than any other factor. Water use rates may vary from 0.05 to 0.3 inches of water per day depending on temperature, wind, humidity, and sunlight. In drier climates during summer months, water use rates will approach 0.3 inches of water per day. Under these conditions frequent watering is almost a necessity. During cooler months water use rates are less than 0.1 inch of water per day, and weekly watering may be adequate. Watering schedules must be adjusted according to fluctuations in water use rates. For lack of a more accurate measure of water use rate, daily evaporation readings available from meteorological stations may be used to estimate water use rates. In most southern climates daily water use rates are about three-quarters of the daily evaporation rate reported by the weather bureau.

Management practices such as dethatching and aeration also influence watering practices. Thatch restricts water penetration and leads to shallow-rooted turf. Thus, light and frequent applications of water are required on thatchy greens. Vertical mowing, aeration, and topdressing aids thatch removal and decomposition and improves water penetration. Spiking and coring also help to alleviate crusts and surface compaction. Thus, these cultivation practices improve moisture conditions on greens and allow for longer intervals between irrigations.

AVOID EXCESS NITROGEN

Fertilization practices affect growth rate, density, color, drought tolerance, disease activity, and putting quality of golf greens. Ideally, nutrients should be available to the grass in amounts needed to maintain growth and color without increasing susceptibility to drought and disease and without increasing grain and thatch. Realistically, the superintendent should maintain adequate levels of phosphorous, potassium, and minor nutrients in the soils and provide nitrogen and iron as the grass requires.

Soil test and plant tissue analyses help the superintendent monitor the amount and availability of phosphorus, potassium, and minor nutrients. However, visual observations of color and density and clipping removal are essential for estimating nitrogen needs. Soil tests and tissue analyses alone are not enough to determine nitrogen needs on putting greens.

Considerable expertise is required of the superintendent to maintain healthy, dense turf, and good color without developing lush growth. Although grass species, environmental conditions, greens construction, and cultural practices influence the nitrogen requirements of putting green turf, the superintendent must evaluate all of these factors to maintain the required level of nitrogen.

Bermudagrass greens require approximately 0.05 pounds of nitrogen per 1,000 square feet per day during the growing season; bentgrass greens require much less. The only means the superintendent has of meeting that requirement is to apply nitrogen daily through fertigation. If a superintendent applies only 0.5 pounds of soluble nitrogen per 1,000 square feet in a single application, the daily requirement of bermudagrass is exceeded tenfold for the next several days. Thus, there would be a short period of luxury consumption of nitrogen resulting in lush growth.

Organic and slow-release nitrogen sources should be used to provide small amounts of soluble nitrogen over a longer time period. For maintenance soluble nitrogen should not be applied at rates greater than 0.5 pounds per 1,000 square feet on bermudagrass and 0.3 pound on bentgrass. Slow-release products such as sulfur-coated urea, IBDU, and urea-formaldehyde can be applied in combination with soluble nitrogen sources to extend the period of nitrogen availability.

Potassium's importance as a major fertilizer nutrient is often overlooked on putting greens. Researchers consistently show grass responses to potassium to include root growth, drought tolerance, disease resistance, wear tolerance, and color on putting green turf (Goss 1969; Gilbert and Davis 1971; Beard 1973). These responses to applications of potassium are observed even where soil levels of potassium are adequate. Other researchers have shown that potassium applications may reduce the requirements of bentgrass for nitrogen (Markland and Roberts 1967). Thus, some of the desired responses to fertilization such as root growth, color, and disease tolerance can be produced without the excess growth associated with nitrogen applications.

Since potassium losses on greens are similar to those of nitrogen, light and frequent applications of potassium are required to maintain its availability to the grass. On golf greens, potassium should be applied at about the same rate and frequency as nitrogen.

Relative to nitrogen and potassium, lower levels of phosphorus are required for greens maintenance. Also, phosphorus accumulates in the soil, whereas nitrogen and potassium are readily leached below the root zone of grasses. Under most conditions, two or three applications of phosphorus per year are adequate for either bermudagrass or bentgrass greens.

Since iron is readily tied up in alkaline soils and not available to the grass, light and frequent applications of iron are required to maintain its availability on most greens. Monthly applications of iron sulfate or iron chelate at 1 to 2 ounces per 1,000 square feet are required under conditions where iron is not readily available to the grass.

CULTIVATION IMPROVES PUTTING GREENS

Cultivation practices including spiking, coring, brushing, verticutting, and topdressing affect putting quality more than they affect turf quality. Most of these practices are unique to putting green maintenance since they affect ball roll and ball holding. Spiking, coring, and topdressing help soften the green and improve ball holding. Brushing, verticutting, and topdressing reduce graininess and thatch accumulation and improve the uniformity, trueness, and speed of greens.

Again, there is more art than science involved in determining how often to perform these operations, how severely to verticut, how much topdressing to apply, and what materials to use for topdressing. Ideally, all of these operations are performed often enough to avoid disrupting the putting quality of greens.

Brushing can be done in conjunction with mowing to reduce graininess. During spring and fall on bentgrass and summer on bermudagrass, greens can be brushed lightly every day. Brushing can be accomplished by attaching a stiff-bristled brush to the front of the mowing unit so that the bristles barely touch the surface of the grass. Frequent brushing can reduce the need for vertical mowing, but vertical mowing is required to help control grain and thatch, to increase the speed of greens, and to prepare bermudagrass for overseeding. As with brushing, light and frequent vertical mowing is required during the growing season. Bermudagrass greens should be verticut weekly during summer months. And with the new grooming mowers, greens can be lightly vertical mowed on a daily basis.

Spiking and coring are important to aeration (root growth), water penetration, thatch, and ball holding. Spiking improves conditions caused by surface crusts and surface compaction. Greens can be spiked frequently with little disruption to play. Coring provides more effective aeration and thatch control but causes greater disruption of play than spiking. Coring also improves the ball holding ability of greens more effectively than spiking. Depending on the severity of problems, greens should be cored two to three times each year and spiked often as needed to maintain water infiltration rate, break surface crusts, and hold properly played golf shots.

Topdressing is one of the most important, yet most neglected, practices in greens maintenance. There was a time when topdressing was the greenskeeper's most effective tool. Topdressing was used for fertilization, disease control, thatch control, and improving putting quality. The art of topdressing seems to have been lost since the widespread use of commercial fertilizers, pesticides, and mechanical aerifiers. The high cost of labor, equipment, and materials has also contributed to the reduced emphasis on topdressing as a cultural practice.

For best results topdressing materials should be screened, sterilized, and composted prior to use on greens. Materials used for topdressing should be evaluated by a laboratory to avoid the addition of excess silt or clay which could seal drainage on a green or the addition of fine gravel which interferes with play and mowing equipment. Topdressing materials should be prepared during the off season, if such a time exists, so that they can be composted and available when needed.

As with all cultivation practices, light and frequent topdressing is more effective and more desirable than occasional applications of a heavy top-dressing. Heavy topdressings are disruptive to play and tend to produce layers that interfere with water movement and root development. For most management programs, four or five applications of topdressing, properly timed, are adequate for bermudagrass or bentgrass greens. Topdressing should follow aeration in late spring and fall and at least twice between those applications to maintain putting quality and ball holding ability of greens throughout the summer.

PEST MANAGEMENT—INSECTS, DISEASES, AND WEEDS

These cultural practices are intended to develop fine putting greens as well as to reduce pest-related problems. Practices that promote healthy, dense turf also help prevent many pest problems. Proper mowing, fertilization, and watering practices help resist invasions of weeds and reduce outbreaks of some diseases. However, even when recommended cultural practices are routinely followed, problems occur when environmental conditions are favorable for insect, disease, or weed development.

Preventative applications of pesticides are recommended on golf greens when environmental conditions favor pest development. For example, fungicides should be applied under humid conditions in the spring and fall for brownpatch. Similarly, preemergence herbicides may be applied in the fall to prevent annual bluegrass infestations. Pest problems such as brownpatch, annual bluegrass, and others that have a history of developing each year should be controlled on a preventative schedule.

Other pest problems that are less predictable should be controlled on a curative or as-needed basis. Repeated use of some pesticides can lead to problems such as pest resistance, thatch accumulation, or injury to turfgrass. Therefore, only those applications that are needed to prevent damage to greens should be made.

Spring Transition in Bermudagrass

Bermudagrass, *Cynodon dactylon* (L.) Pers., is a warm-season perennial grass with a creeping growth habit. Bermudagrass spreads both by stolons and rhizomes which readily root and tiller at the nodes. Common, Sahara, Cheyenne, and Sonesta are seeded varieties of bermudagrass. Other varieties, including Tifgreen, Tifway, Tifdwarf, Texturf-10, Santa Ana, and Midiron, must be established from vegetative stock, sprigs, or sod.

All varieties of bermudagrass turn straw-colored and become dormant during winter months. During late fall soluble sugars are converted to starch granules and stored in the stolons, roots, and rhizomes during winter months. Where winter temperatures frequently drop below 10° F, bermudagrass is subject to significant winterkill. Midiron bermudagrass is significantly more cold tolerant than others.

Green-up and recovery of bermudagrass begin when nighttime temperatures remain above 60° F for several days in the spring and soil temperature reaches 64° F at the 4-inch depth. The grass makes rapid recovery in the spring by producing new shoots from the nodes of previously dormant stolons and rhizomes. Research conducted at Texas A&M University (DiPaola, Beard, and Brausand 1982) suggests that early spring green-up of bermudagrass is accompanied by a rapid dieback of old roots and production of new roots. This phenomenon of new shoot production, root dieback, and new root production describes spring transition in bermudagrass and accounts for the vulnerability of the grass to low temperatures, herbicides, and competition from winter grasses during the transition period.

The date of occurrence for each phase of growth—spring green-up, rapid growth, fall hardening, and winter dormancy—may vary several weeks depending on the dates of the first and last killing frosts. Thus, the length of the growing season may range from five to eight or nine months, depending on the length of the frost-free period. Obviously, in some areas of the country, bermudagrass may stay green year-round.

In the Transition Zone of the U.S. between cool-season and warm-season grasses, bermudagrass is subject to severe loss of stand (winterkill) during the dormant period. Winterkill may be the result of direct low temperature

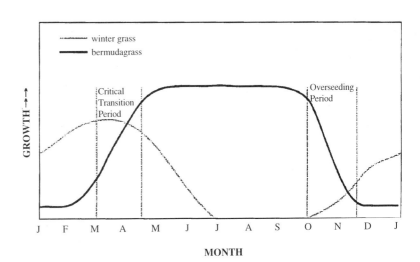

Bermudagrass growth curve
(Houston, Texas)

kill, desiccation, disease, traffic, competition with cool-season grasses, or a combination of these factors. Where winterkill is a major concern, management practices during the critical fall and spring periods can have a significant impact on the amount of winterkill incurred.

In addition to the cyclic patterns of shoot and root growth in bermudagrass, energy reserves show a definite cyclic pattern. Energy reserves accumulate during the fall when photosynthetic activity is high and shoot growth is greatly reduced. Energy reserves, principally starch, are gradually depleted during winter months. In the spring energy reserves are rapidly depleted during the spring green-up and root dieback period. During summer months energy reserves accumulate very little, since they are repeatedly used for regrowth following mowing. Again, management practices can have a significant influence on the reserve energy status of bermudagrass throughout the year.

New shoot production, root dieback with subsequent root production, and depletion of energy reserves put bermudagrass in a vulnerable condition during spring green-up. A significant change in temperature, untimely applications of fertilizers or herbicides, or competition from cool-season grasses could result in a significant loss of bermudagrass turf during the spring transition period.

ENVIRONMENTAL FACTORS AFFECTING SPRING TRANSITION

Temperature, shade, moisture, soil conditions, competition, and traffic are the major environmental factors affecting bermudagrass recovery in the spring. Temperature has both direct and indirect effects on spring recovery. Low-temperature kill of bermudagrass occurs somewhere below 10° F, depending on the variety of bermudagrass. Low-temperature kill likely occurs during winter months and should not be considered a part of the spring transition phenomenon, although it would certainly affect spring recovery.

Bermudagrass begins to green-up in the spring when nighttime temperatures exceed 60° for several days (soil temperature at 64° or above at the 4-inch depth). When these conditions occur lateral buds (tillers) found at the nodes of bermudagrass stolons and rhizomes break dormancy, carbohydrate reserves are converted to soluble sugars, and the first new leaves appear. About this time some of the old roots of bermudagrass begin to deteriorate, and new roots are produced at the node.

As long as the temperature remains favorable during this transition period, recovery progresses until complete green-up of the turf occurs. Depending on the temperature, complete green-up may require two to six weeks (the higher the temperature, the faster the process is completed). However, if periods of favorable temperatures are interrupted by occasional freezing temperatures, green leaves may be killed and new leaves must be produced. These intermittent freezes delay spring recovery and place a greater demand on the reserve carbohydrates in the stolons and rhizomes of bermudagrass. If, for some reason, these reserves are low at the beginning of spring green-up, energy reserves may be transported from one tiller to support leaf production on another. When this occurs to a significant extent, some tillers die and a thin turf develops. Then surviving tillers must grow and spread to fill in where other tillers died. This is a common occurrence in many areas where bermudagrass is grown and 20 to 80 percent of tillers may be killed. Rate of recovery is, of course, directly related to the percent loss of tillers.

Indirectly, temperature affects spring transition in bermudagrass through its influence on nutrient availability and on disease activity (and nematodes). The effects of these organisms on plant growth are well known and will not be discussed at this point. Fungicides and nematicides can be used in the spring to reduce their effect on spring recovery of bermudagrass.

Shade affects spring transition in bermudagrass by weakening the plant (reducing energy reserves) and increasing its susceptibility to winterkill. Bermudagrass growing in partial shade does not accumulate as high a level of energy reserves as that growing in full sunlight. Thus, the grass is slower to recover in the spring.

Shade also has the effect of prolonging exposure of the grass to low temperatures, snow cover, and other extreme environmental conditions. Increased exposure to low temperatures increases winterkill in bermudagrass and delays spring recovery.

Where shade is a factor, management should be adjusted to enhance bermudagrass recovery in the spring. Fertilizer rates should be lower in bermudagrass growing in shade to reduce depletion of energy reserves. Also, mowing heights should be higher in shade to increase total energy reserves and to increase insulation or protection of the stolons during winter months.

Moisture, either too little or too much, also has an effect on spring transition in bermudagrass. During dry periods in late winter and spring, significant losses of lateral buds or tillers, can occur through desiccation. Thus, as in the case of low temperature kill, complete recovery of bermudagrass is delayed until the surviving tillers fill in the dead areas.

Dry spring conditions also slow the mobilization and transport of soluble carbohydrates to lateral buds. Thus, leaf production is delayed until moisture becomes available. Timely irrigations will overcome the delay in the spring recovery associated with dry conditions.

Perhaps more serious than dry conditions which can be overcome by irrigation, wet soil conditions also delay spring recovery in bermudagrass. Under wet soil conditions in spring, the conversion of energy reserves in the plant to soluble sugars is very inefficient. Where bermudagrass is exposed to prolonged wet conditions in the spring, energy reserves are depleted with little new growth produced to support the plant. Thus, some tillers are killed and a weak, thin turf develops. The solution to wet soil conditions is to provide for effective surface drainage, and, in some situations, install underground tile drains.

Compacted soil conditions delay spring recovery by restricting oxygen availability to the root system. This has the same effect on grass as wet soil conditions. Soil compaction can be alleviated in early spring by core aeration. Core aeration should be delayed until dangers of hard freezes are past.

Competition from winter weeds, particularly annual bluegrass, can also retard recovery of bermudagrass in the spring. A dense stand of winter weeds shades bermudagrass and competes with bermudagrass for moisture and nutrients. Furthermore, when annual weeds die in spring, the turf is weak and susceptible to invasion by crabgrass. Thus, weeds should be controlled to reduce competition with bermudagrass and speed its recovery in spring.

Traffic not only increases soil compaction but increases wear on dormant bermudagrass turf. Heavy traffic removes much of the dormant bermuda cover and exposes the stolons and crowns to greater temperature and moisture stress, increasing winterkill due to low temperature and desiccation. The effect traffic has on compaction further compounds its effect on spring transition.

Obviously, when all environmental factors that affect spring transition (temperature, moisture, shade, compaction, competition, and traffic) are combined the effect can be striking in terms of bermudagrass recovery. The winters of 1983–84 and 1989–90 produced severe losses of bermudagrass in the Transition Zone. All of these environmental factors were involved in those losses. Losses of bermudagrass were most pronounced where northern exposures, shade, and traffic were involved.

CULTURAL EFFECTS ON SPRING TRANSITION

In addition to environmental factors that affect spring transition, cultural practices also have a significant influence on spring transition in bermudagrass. Practices such as fertilization, irrigation, and mowing that promote leaf growth enhance recovery of bermudagrass in the spring. Fertilization practices have been shown to have striking effects on spring recovery.

High rates of soluble nitrogen can be detrimental to spring recovery of bermudagrass. Timing of the spring application of nitrogen is important. The application should be after the danger of a severe freeze is past, but before complete recovery of bermudagrass. Generally, nitrogen should be applied after 20 to 30 percent green-up of bermudagrass. Nitrogen applied at that time will promote leaf growth, which in turf stimulates stolon and root development. Very early applications of soluble nitrogen increase the risk of injury from a late spring freeze.

In addition to the effect of nitrogen on spring recovery, potassium has been shown to reduce winterkill and promote early spring recovery. High potassium levels in bermudagrass increase carbohydrate storage in stolons and rhizomes and reduce its susceptibility to low temperature kill and to desiccation. Potassium also promotes root development in the fall and early spring. In addition to the level of potassium in the grass tissue, the ratio of potassium to phosphorus in the plant can have an effect on spring recovery. A high potassium-to-phosphorus ratio promotes early spring recovery, but a high phosphorus-to-potassium ratio has been shown to increase winterkill and delay spring recovery in bermudagrass. Potassium should be applied with nitrogen in late fall and early spring in a one-to-one ratio.

Iron deficiency can also cause a delay in spring recovery in bermudagrass. Iron deficiencies are most pronounced in the early spring when soil temperatures are low. Soils with a high pH, high phosphorus level, or high moisture level are particularly prone to show iron deficiencies in the spring. Soil compaction also contributes to iron deficiencies. Where these conditions occur foliar applications of iron at the time grass begins to green-up in the spring can promote recovery of bermudagrass. All of these soil conditions are common to bermudagrass turf situations on golf courses, sports fields, and lawns.

Other nutrient deficiencies such as sulfur or magnesium that may occur in turfgrass should be corrected through fertilization. Since bermudagrass has been shown to have a restricted root system in early spring, soil nutrient deficiencies at that time have a pronounced effect on spring recovery of bermudagrass.

Irrigation practices through the winter and spring affect spring recovery of bermudagrass. Even though top growth is dormant during the winter, the roots continue to take up water to keep the crown and stolons alive. Desiccation of bermuda during winter months is a major cause of slow recovery in spring. During extended dry periods, dormant bermudagrass should be occasionally irrigated to maintain moisture in the root zone. Soils should not be kept wet, however.

In the spring when bermudagrass begins to break dormancy, even short dry periods can have a detrimental effect on recovery. The soil should not be allowed to become dry during the spring transition period if rapid green-up and recovery is desired. Although moisture stress has been shown to promote deep rooting during summer months, moisture stress during the critical transition period would cause a significant delay in spring recovery.

Mowing practices that promote leaf growth also reduce the time required for complete recovery of bermudagrass in the spring. Where bermudagrass is mowed close, such as on golf courses, raising the mowing height as little as $\frac{1}{16}$ inch could make a significant improvement in spring transition. However, where bermudagrass is overseeded with ryegrass, close mowing in the spring reduces competition by the ryegrass and increases sunlight exposure to bermudagrass. Very close mowing of overseeded golf greens during the spring will improve the recovery of bermudagrass.

Vertical mowing to reduce thatch should be done before bermudagrass greens-up in the spring, but after the danger of a prolonged cold period is past. Otherwise, vertical mowing should be delayed until bermudagrass has completely recovered.

OVERSEEDING EFFECTS ON SPRING RECOVERY

Overseeding bermudagrass with cool-season grasses is a common practice on golf courses, sports fields, and lawns. The cool-season grasses provide color and increase wear tolerance of bermudagrass turf during winter months. However, cool-season grasses also compete with bermudagrass during spring transition and significantly delay recovery of bermudagrass.

During early spring when bermuda is beginning to green up, cool-season grasses are at their peak growth period. Cool-season grass tillers that may have been initiated in the fall and winter develop very rapidly in the spring and produce a dense turf cover. In contrast, bermudagrass is just beginning to break dormancy and produce new shoots from stolons and rhizomes near the soil surface. Consequently, cool-season grasses absorb much of the sunlight, and very little reaches new bermudagrass leaves. Likewise, the root system of cool-season grasses is very active compared to bermudagrass in early spring. Thus, bermudagrass recovery is significantly delayed by competition from cool-season grasses.

Until environmental factors, particularly temperature, change to favor bermudagrass, cool-season grasses remain dominant. Where this change occurs in late spring, turfgrass managers should use cultural practices (vertical mowing, aeration, fertilization, topdressing, close mowing, etc.) to suppress cool-season grasses and promote bermudagrass. Otherwise, the change from cool-season grasses to bermudagrass occurs too abruptly and results in a poor transition.

Where suppression of cool-season grass is desirable, turf should be aerated in early spring (March) with a coring-type aerator. The turf should also be vertically mowed throughout the transition period to reduce the leaf surface of cool-season grasses. Initially (March), turf should be vertical mowed weekly to thin the cool-season grasses and increase the exposure of bermudagrass to sunlight. During the following several months (April and May), twice monthly vertical mowing should be adequate to thin the cool-season grasses and reduce competition with bermudagrass.

Fertilization practices during the transition period are also critical to bermuda recovery. As long as temperatures favor growth of cool-season grasses, nitrogen rates should be kept at a minimum to maintain acceptable color. When temperatures increase to favor bermudagrass (60° F nights and 75° F or higher daytime temperatures), nitrogen rates should be increased to promote bermudagrass recovery. Applications of nitrogen every 2 weeks at a rate of 1 pound per 1,000 square feet should be made through the transition period, or until bermudagrass has completely recovered.

If cool-season grasses continue to dominate bermudagrass through April, greens should be aerated and lightly topdressed in early May. Light, frequent vertical mowing should also continue until bermudagrass becomes the dominant grass. Close mowing ($\frac{5}{32}$ inch or lower) during the transition period will also weaken the more competitive cool-season grasses, such as perennial ryegrass. After significant bermudagrass recovery has been observed, raise the mowing height to $\frac{3}{16}$ inch or higher until bermudagrass completely recovers.

Watering practices during the transition period are critical on overseeded sites. Daily applications of water that wet only the top 2 inches of soil should be avoided after temperatures favor bermudagrass recovery. Light, frequent applications of water favor cool-season grasses and extend their period of dominance over bermudagrass. On the other hand, thoroughly wetting the soil 6 to 8 inches deep and allowing the cool-season grasses to show signs of moisture stress before applying additional water will give bermudagrass a competitive edge over cool-season grasses.

DISEASE PREVENTS BERMUDAGRASS RECOVERY

Turfgrass diseases such as *Pythium,* brownpatch, dollar spot, leaf spots, and nematodes can cause significant losses of bermudagrass in the spring. Bermudagrass turf should be observed closely during spring transition for symptoms of these diseases. Also, preventative applications of fungicides should be made to critical turf areas such as golf greens.

In areas where spring dead spot has been a problem, turf management practices that reduce the severity of the disease should be followed. Dethatching bermudagrass turf, keeping nitrogen application rates to a minimum, and applying fungicides in the fall have been shown to reduce spring dead spot severity.

Nematodes interact with turf diseases to produce significant losses of bermudagrass during winter and early spring. Nematodes weaken the grass and increase its susceptibility to disease infestations. The combination of nematodes attacking roots and disease organisms attacking leaves, stems, and crowns can produce losses of turf in irregular patterns. On golf greens and other critical turf sites, treatments should be made in fall and spring to reduce nematode population.

Sports Field Maintenance

Coaches are often more concerned with injuries, personnel problems, and opponents than with the condition of the turf on their field. Winning is always more important than looking good, but it is possible to do both.

A quick look at the growing list of injuries across the country provides further incentive to condition the field as well as the players. From a playing standpoint, a good turf should be tough, wear-resistant, and not easily torn by cleats. It should be soft enough to prevent abrasions when players fall, yet firm enough to permit good footing.

Surveys conducted by proponents of artificial turf show that as many as half of the serious knee and ankle injuries are related to poor field conditions—hard field surfaces, thin grass cover, rough surfaces or slick, muddy conditions. Significantly fewer injuries occur on properly conditioned fields. Thus, say the manufacturers of artificial turf, a uniform, consistent artificial playing surface will reduce serious knee and ankle injuries. Certainly they are right. But a properly conditioned natural grass field will reduce those and other injuries even more. Whether natural or artificial turf is better is not the concern here. Rather, the steps required to keep the fields in good playing condition is.

Few school systems have an experienced groundskeeper, much less an adequate budget, to keep a field in good condition. Most schools have little problem growing grass on a football field during the summer when it is not in use. But under playing conditions, wear and tear on the grass together with soil compaction make it difficult for even the most experienced groundskeeper to maintain a field.

TIMELY MOWING INCREASES TURF DENSITY

Bermudagrass responds to close mowing by initiating new shoots. When mowed at the proper height and frequency, a weak, thin turf can be converted to a much thicker and more wear-resistant turf. Common and Texturf-10 bermudagrass sports fields should be mowed twice weekly at a height of 1 to 1½ inches. Hybrid bermudagrass such as Tifway should be mowed every 2 or 3 days at a height of ½ to ¾ inch. Bermudagrasses form a thicker and more wear-resistant turf that remains green longer in the fall when mowed frequently at shorter heights. There are no substitutes for close, frequent mowing. A fine sports field requires strict adherence to these recommended schedules.

FERTILIZATION PROMOTES GRASS RECOVERY

Several aspects of fertilization are critical to the development of a healthy turf on a playing field. Nitrogen is required to produce a good turf, but it should be available to the grass at low and uniform rates. A single application of fertilizer should not provide more than 1 pound of soluble nitrogen per 1,000 square feet. On a newly planted field this amount of nitrogen should be applied at 2- to 3-week intervals. For maintenance fertilization, 4 to 5 week intervals are satisfactory.

On a sports field that receives frequent use, potassium is as important as nitrogen to the survival of the turf. High potassium levels in grass tissue greatly increase the wear tolerance of grass. Potassium should be applied at nearly the same rate as nitrogen.

Phosphorus is important during the establishment of turf on a new field and for the recovery of turf worn by game use. On a new field a 1-to-1 ratio of phosphorus to nitrogen would be adequate. Under maintenance conditions a 1-to-3 or 1-to-4 ratio of phosphorus to nitrogen should be used. Thus, a 3-1-2 or 4-1-3 ratio of N-P-K would be ideal for maintenance of sports fields.

Timing of fertilizer applications is just as important to the vigor of the turf as the rate and analysis of fertilizer applied. Applications should be made in the early spring and continued until a satisfactory turf cover develops. A complete fertilizer such as a 12-4-8 or 16-6-12 should be applied in early spring and summer.

Midsummer applications of fertilizer should be avoided unless the grass has not completely covered the field. Excess growth during the summer does not contribute to the durability or quality of the turf during the playing season but only increases maintenance requirements. If nitrogen is applied during summer months rates should not exceed ½ pound of N per 1,000 square feet per month.

Fall applications of fertilizer enhance turf color and promote grass recovery. Although the grass may not appear to respond to late-season fertilization, grass roots do respond to late-season fertilization, and root growth helps to strengthen the turf. Also, where intense use has thinned the turf, a late-season application of a complete fertilizer will hasten turf recovery. A complete fertilizer should be applied in the fall at a rate of 1 pound of N per 1,000 square feet. Even where the grass appears healthy, late fall fertilization will strengthen the turf. Do not apply high rates of a soluble nitrogen fertilizer in the late fall. Such an application promotes succulent growth and increases the risk of winterkill.

AERATION IMPROVES THE PLAYING SURFACE

Aerate fields when the soil is moist (not wet) to get maximum penetration of the spoons. Multiple passes over the field with the aerator increase the effectiveness of aeration. Following aeration, a heavy mat should be dragged over the field to break up soil cores and smooth the surface. Aeration can be done in early spring, summer, and even during periods that the field is in use. Frequency of aeration is dependent on the level of use of the field.

WATER ONLY WHEN NEEDED

Wet conditions add to the deterioration of turf on a sports field. Coordinate watering practices with the scheduled use of the playing field to minimize problems. The surface must be dry when the field is in use. When supplemental watering is required, schedule it at least 12 hours prior to using the field. As water is needed, wet the soil to a depth of 4 to 6 inches on a weekly basis and follow with light watering as necessary. When fields are wet because of rainfall, reschedule the use of the fields when possible to reduce damage to the turf.

RENOVATION KEEPS A FIELD IN PLAY

If the field resembled a parking lot more than a playing area at the end of last season, renovation is in order. School and community pride are at stake with respect to the condition of its sports fields, not to mention the team's performance and the players' safety.

Renovation of extensively used football fields is an annual requirement involving aeration, topdressing, weed control, fertilization, and, in extreme cases, replanting.

The first step in renovation involves correcting the conditions that caused the field to deteriorate. Poor drainage, soil compaction, weeds, and excessive use or lack of a maintenance program could all lead to the deterioration of turf. Renovation followed with a good maintenance program can change a poor field into a well-turfed field in a single season.

A good playing field must be firm, resilient, and uniform from a players standpoint and attractive from a spectator's standpoint. The physical condition of the soil is just as important as the turf to a firm, resilient, and uniform surface. A hard, compacted soil or a wet, poorly drained soil cannot provide a good playing surface, regardless of the amount of grass on the field. With or without good turf, a firm, uniform, and resilient playing surface should be mandatory on all football fields.

Some fields cannot be satisfactorily improved without replacing the soil. Such fields are characterized by thin turf, very hard surfaces when dry, waterlogged and slick surfaces when wet, and an excessive number of playing injuries.

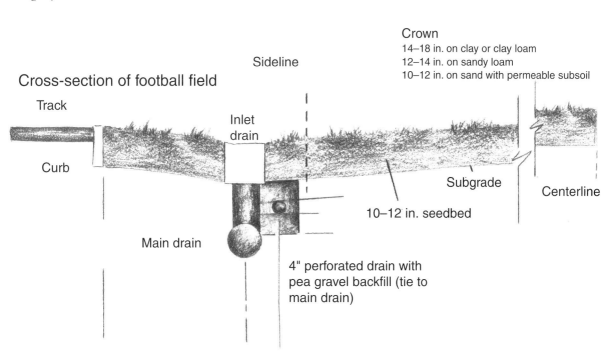

Cross-section of football field

Track

Curb

Sideline

Inlet drain

Crown
14–18 in. on clay or clay loam
12–14 in. on sandy loam
10–12 in. on sand with permeable subsoil

Subgrade

Centerline

Main drain

10–12 in. seedbed

4" perforated drain with pea gravel backfill (tie to main drain)

Short of replacing the existing soil with a good topsoil, providing adequate surface drainage, aeration and topdressing improve the physical condition of the field. A field constructed with a clay or clay loam soil should have an 18-inch crown to provide surface runoff together with outlets along the sidelines to remove excess water from the field. If these conditions are not met, then improving drainage would be the first step in renovation.

A soil similar in texture to that on the field should be used to build up the crown. Prior to adding the topsoil, aerate the field with a coring-type aerator by running the unit over the field in 3 or 4 directions. Distribute the required topsoil down the center of the field and level with a grader. The final surface may be smoothed with a heavy steel mat or other drag to eliminate any ridges or depressions. If the crown needs to be raised more than 2 inches, the field should be disked 4 to 5 inches deep and topsoil added prior to grading.

Where perennial weeds (dallisgrass, knotweed, nutgrass) are a problem, they should be eliminated with herbicides prior to mechanical renovation.

If improved hybrid bermudagrass is to be planted in place of common bermudagrass, or if weeds are so numerous that little desirable grass can be found, complete vegetation control can be obtained with a herbicide such as Roundup. For Roundup to be effective the weeds and grasses must be actively growing. Where Roundup is used for weed and grass control, the field can be replanted about 2 weeks after treatment (the time required for the herbicide to kill existing vegetation). Prior to replanting cultivate the field with a disk or tiller to alleviate soil compaction and to produce a finely pulverized seedbed for grass establishment.

Replanting should be completed by June 1 to have a complete turf cover by the season opener. A good maintenance program can produce a dense turf cover in 8 to 10 weeks on a football field. In fact, between June 1 and September 1, 1956, Texas A&M's Kyle Field was transformed from bare ground to excellent turf cover. Records indicate that sprigging at a rate of 300 bushels per acre, watering as needed to keep the grass growing, fertilizing at a rate equivalent to 1 pound of N per 1,000 square feet every 2 weeks, and selective weed control provided the only magic needed in 1956 (Potts and Irvin 1957). The same magic can be performed on any sports field.

Bermudagrass provides an attractive, resilient playing surface for about seven months out of a year—April through October. All bermudagrasses cease growth and become dormant during the winter months. Where the field is used extensively between January and April, as it is in collegiate and high school baseball, bermudagrass should be overseeded with one or more of the improved perennial ryegrasses to provide color, uniform surface conditions, and wear tolerance during the dormant period. The ryegrasses remain through the spring season and are gradually replaced by bermudagrass as it recovers in late spring. The transition from ryegrass to bermudagrass is smooth and essentially unnoticed by the players and fans. The color, texture, density, and playing conditions of the two grasses are very similar.

OVERSEEDING IN LATE FALL

A successful overseeding program requires four to six weeks in the fall when the field is not in use. When a field is used exclusively for baseball, the overseeding operation does not interfere with the use of the field. The cost of overseeding is small compared to the benefits it produces, considering that the high school and college season is played during the time the ryegrasses are at their best and bermudagrass at its worst. The lush, dark green turf produced by the ryegrasses adds to the interest and excitement of the players and fans.

In preparation for overseeding, bermudagrass turf should be thinned with a flail mower or dethatching mower. Grass clippings and thatch can be removed after mowing by sweeping or vacuuming the field. Where common bermudagrass is the permanent turf, close mowing may be the only operation required to develop a good seedbed for perennial ryegrass.

Seeding rates for perennial ryegrass range from 6 to 8 pounds of seed per 1,000 square feet on the outfield to 25 pounds per 1,000 square feet on the infield. In each of these areas, a drop-type distributor can be used to seed a 4-foot wide border around each area to keep the seed off the dirt areas of the infield and the warning track. The area inside of the 4-foot border can be planted with a cyclone-type distributor. The outfield and sideline areas are seeded in 2 directions at right angles to each other. The infield should be seeded in 4 to 5 directions to ensure uniform seed distribution.

After seeding topdress the infield with a sandy loam soil to smooth the surface and to help hold the seed in place. The topsoil may be dragged with a carpet drag to smooth the playing surface. After planting apply a starter fertilizer to the entire field at a rate of 50 pounds of nitrogen per acre.

After seeding and fertilizing, water lightly 3 or 4 times a day for 10 to 14 days. As the seedlings emerge watering frequency should be gradually reduced to daily watering, then eventually to an as-needed basis. It is very important to keep the soil surface moist, but not wet, during the establishment period.

Ryegrasses should be mowed about 2 weeks after planting at a height of ½ inch on the infield and ¾ inch on the sideline and outfield areas. During late fall and winter weekly mowing is satisfactory to maintain the ryegrasses. During spring months the ryegrasses require mowing at 2- to 3-day intervals at these heights. The infield can be mowed with a walking-type greens mower every other day during the playing season to produce a fast, uniform playing surface.

MAINTENANCE OF SKINNED AREAS

The nongrass (skinned) areas of the baseball field are just as important to the playability and appearance of the field as the grass areas. Most ball field managers would agree that the skinned areas require more time to maintain than the grass areas. The first requirement for the maintenance of the skinned areas is that they meet specifications for whatever league the field is being used.

The composition of the skinned areas must be such that it provides firm footing but also remains resilient. The dirt surface should be loose and firm and readily absorb moisture. Skinned areas should be sloped toward the sidelines or outfield to provide surface drainage. Soils suitable for the skinned areas range from a sandy loam to a sandy clay loam. Sand and calcined clay (Turface) may be worked into the skinned areas throughout the season to maintain the loose, firm, and resilient nature of the playing surface. Topsoil, sand, and calcined clay should be stockpiled and covered before the season begins so that they remain dry and available when needed.

Prior to the season opening, scarify the skinned areas to loosen the soil several inches deep. Work sand or calcined clay into the top inch or two of soil by hand raking or dragging with a nail drag. Also, trim the grass edges of the infield with a mechanical edger and lift the sod by hand to keep the edges sharp. Repeat the procedure several times during the season to keep the edges sharp and to prevent soil buildup along the grass edge.

After each practice session or game, routine maintenance is required to keep the infield area in good playing condition. First, sweep the grass edge of the infield with a stiff broom to remove soil buildup along the grass edge of the infield. Next, hand rake the areas around the bases to replace soil that was moved by players sliding into bases. Then drag the skinned area with a nail drag followed by a carpet drag to smooth the surface. Regular maintenance of these areas keeps the field in top playing condition and helps avoid major reworking of the skinned areas during the season.

PITCHER'S MOUND AND HOME PLATE AREA

Just as the skinned area of the infield requires regular maintenance, a few minutes each day repairing the pitcher's mound and home plate area keeps them in good playing condition. Sweep the mound with a stiff broom after each use to remove any loose material. Then moisten the worn area and add moist clay to fill the hole. The fresh clay is tamped by hand to pack the mound. Clay or clay loam soil used to build the mound should be stockpiled and kept moist for regular repair of the worn part of the mound. After repairing the mound rake the entire area by hand and drag with a steel mat or carpet drag. If the clay sticks to the equipment or to cleats, add sand or calcined clay to the surface to prevent sticking. Check the height and slope of the mound regularly to be sure they meet specifications.

The same procedure is followed on the home plate area—batter's box and catcher's box. The boxes are swept after each use, fresh clay is added and tamped, the area is raked by hand, dragged, topdressed with sand and calcined clay, and smoothed with a carpet drag. If rain is forecast, cover the entire infield with a tarp to keep the skinned areas dry.

FOUL LINES AND CHALKED AREAS
Straight, sharp lines help define and dress up the field. Cut lines 2¾ inches wide and mark them with marble dust. Re-mark all of the lines before each game day. A properly lined and marked field is essential to the playability and appearance of the field.

Commercial Lawns

Commercial property managers desire attractive landscapes to present a welcome mat to potential clients and customers. Often, the landscape provides the first impression a customer has of a business. Neat, attractive and well-maintained landscapes provide a positive and lasting impression. Poorly maintained properties provide a negative impression that may be difficult to overcome.

Lawn qualities that managers desire include a uniform appearance, a dark green color, high density, and year-round green color. Of course, the property manager expects these qualities at a minimum cost.

To meet the demands of property managers, lawn management contractors must develop a maintenance program based on the needs of the grasses present on the site. Mowing schedules, watering practices, fertilization, weed control, pest management, cultivation, and overseeding must all be based on the needs of specific grasses growing under the conditions existing at the site. Finally, the lawn management contractor must justify each of these operators and establish a competitive and reasonable price. The successful bidder for maintenance of a commercial property is too frequently the low bidder. Although the low bidder often gets the initial maintenance contract, he or she just as often loses it because the product does not meet the demands of the client. Experience has shown that a competitive bid must provide adequate funds for maintenance and a reasonable profit. Failure to meet either of those needs leads to problems for the lawn management contractor after acquiring the contract.

Developing a program specific for each site that meets the client's demands is the first responsibility of the lawn management contractor. Developing such a program is the concern of this chapter, but pricing is equally important to the success of the commercial lawn management contractor.

MOWING PRACTICES
Without question, mowing practices have the greatest effect on turf quality of any single operation. They also have the largest effect of any single operation on the cost of the program. Thus, mowing practices must be the first concern.

Grass variety, environmental conditions, irrigation practices, and fertilization all influence mowing requirements on a particular site. Hybrid bermudagrasses, common on many new projects, have, by far, the highest mowing requirements of all southern turfgrasses. Buffalograss and bahiagrass have the lowest mowing requirements of the commonly used turfgrasses.

When considering the quality of the lawn and the cost of the program, mowing frequency is the first concern. A ten-day mowing schedule is minimal for lawns, and, then, only for low maintenance grasses such as Buffalograss and bahiagrass. Generally, weekly mowing is required for maintaining acceptable quality for lawns on commercial properties. For hybrid bermudagrass and Emerald zoysia lawns, five-day mowing intervals are required during the summer months. Less frequent mowing intervals with these grasses results in unsightly scalping and slow recovery. Such conditions are unacceptable on highly visible properties. To prevent scalping, mowing height is often raised several times during the growing season. But Emerald zoysia and the hybrid bermudagrass develop serious thatch problems at taller mowing heights. Then, late season renovation is required. There is no substitute for frequent mowing.

Proper mowing heights are also important to maintaining turf quality. Bermudagrass and Emerald zoysia turf become thin and spindly at mowing heights above 1½ inches. Likewise, other grasses lose density at taller mowing heights. Even tall fescue and Saint Augustine grasses lose density and become thatchy at taller mowing heights, but they will provide acceptable turf at heights of 2½ to 3 inches.

Since mowing frequency is inversely related to mowing heights, the taller heights allow for less frequent mowing. For example, raising the mowing height from 1½ to 2 inches might reduce the mowing frequency from 5 days to 7 days. Such a reduction might mean a 25 to 30 percent savings to the client. However, the client must understand that the quality of the turf will not be as good as with the more frequent mowing schedule (table 11-1).

The type of mower used can also have a significant effect on the quality of turf produced. At mowing heights of 1 inch or less, a reel-type mower produces the finest quality of cut. At heights of 1½ inches or more, a rotary-type mower might be more practical. Generally, rotary motors are more maneuverable and faster than reel-type mowers in tight areas with numerous trees, landscape plantings, and structures. Thus, taller mowing heights which allow rotary mowers might mean less time on the site per mowing as well as fewer mowings per season.

Clipping removal is another factor to consider when planning mowing practices. If the client insists on removing grass clippings at each mowing, then the time scheduled for mowing may increase 30 percent or more. There is little doubt that clipping removal improves the appearance of the turf immediately after mowing, but clippings can contribute nutrients to the lawn.

At mowing frequencies of 7 to 10 days, clipping removal is usually man-

Table 11-1. Mowing Practices for Commercial Lawns

Grass	Mowing Height (inches)	Mowing Frequency (days)
Bahia, buffalograss	3	7–10
Tall fescue, bluegrass, Saint Augustine	2–3	5–7
Common bermudagrass, Meyer zoysia, centipede	1½	5–7
Emerald zoysia, hybrid bermudagrass	1	5

datory because of the amount of clippings produced. At a mowing frequency of 5 to 7 days, clipping removal is optional. Thus, it may be desirable to increase mowing frequency to 5-day intervals and leave the clippings in place for Saint Augustine or bluegrass turf, rather than remove the clippings on a 7-day mowing schedule.

Grass clippings contribute very little to thatch accumulation. Research has shown that leaving grass clippings in place increased thatch only 3 to 5 percent. However, those same clippings make a significant contribution to the nutrient content of the turf. As much as 3 pounds of N per 1,000 square feet are recycled through the turf by leaving the clippings in place. This recycled N may reduce N fertilization needs by 30 percent and extend the response period to an application of N by several weeks.

For these reasons it may be advantageous to the client to increase mowing frequency and leave the clippings on the lawn. Mowing the lawn when the grass is dry and using a mulching mower will improve the appearance of a lawn where clippings are not removed.

WATERING PRACTICES

Watering practices are critical to the success of any lawn management program. When the client is responsible for watering, properly scheduled irrigations can supplement the lawn management program. But when irrigation is inadequate or excessive, it detracts from the success of the program and often interferes with scheduled operations.

Where the contractor has watering responsibilities, thorough and infrequent watering is ideal. When soils are uniform and at least six to eight inches deep, thorough and infrequent watering is not only ideal but also practical. However, those conditions are often not met. More commonly, sites vary in soil type and depth, making irrigation a challenge. In such situations, the entire site is irrigated to meet the needs of the most droughty areas. Consequently, light and frequent applications of water are required.

Approximately ½ inch of water should be applied at 2- to 5-day intervals depending on environmental conditions. During spring and fall, 5-day intervals may be adequate. During midsummer, ½ inch of water may be required every other day. Irrigation should be scheduled only when needed during winter months. Such an irrigation schedule will meet the needs of the droughty areas and will not interfere with other maintenance operations. If possible, schedule irrigations to occur 24 hours prior to mowing so that the grass is in good condition and the leaf surface is dry for mowing operations.

Whoever has responsibility for watering must avoid excessive application of water. Experience has shown that acceptable turf can be maintained with timely applications that total only 50 to 60 percent of annual evapotranspiration rates. In southern states that means about 30 inches of irrigation water per acre per year are adequate. Unfortunately, most commercial properties receive over 50 inches of supplemental water per year.

Excessive water not only interferes with maintenance operations but contributes to pest problems, leaches valuable nutrients, and promotes excess growth. All of these consequences increase the cost of lawn management and reduce turf quality. If a lawn receives 50 inches of water when 30 inches is adequate, over 500,000 gallons of water per acre are wasted. At a cost of $1.50 per 1,000 gallons, $750 per acre are wasted. Added to the cost of water would be the additional cost for fertilizer, pest control, and mowing required to compensate for the excess water.

Warm-season turfgrasses provide better quality turf under moderately dry conditions than under wet conditions. Monitoring irrigation to keep it at 1 to 1½ inches of water per week during the growing season is an effective means of reducing maintenance costs and improving turf quality.

FERTILIZATION

Fertilization produces the color of lawns that property managers demand. In addition to color, fertilization promotes growth and increases turf density. As with watering, excessive fertilization leads to increased maintenance costs and deteriorated turfgrass quality. Mowing, water use, and pest management all increase with increasing rates of fertilization. The key to maintaining satisfactory color without significantly increasing maintenance costs is matching fertilizer application to specific needs for a site. Grass variety, environmental conditions, irrigation practices, and mowing practices all affect fertilizer requirements for a specific site.

Grasses have a significant effect on the amount of nitrogen fertilizer needed for southern lawns. Although 2 pounds of N per 1,000 square feet per year may be adequate on centipedegrass lawns, 8 pounds may be needed on a bermudagrass lawn overseeded with ryegrass. Applications of N should not exceed 1 pound of soluble nitrogen per 1,000 square feet. When slow-release nitrogen sources are used, application rates may be 1.5 to 2 pounds N. Higher rates of soluble N produce excessive growth for a short period, but the residual response is of short duration. Slow-release sources, however,

Table 11-2. Nitrogen Needs of Commercial Lawns

Grasses	Nitrogen Needs (lbs./1,000 sq. ft./year)
Bahia, centipedegrass, buffalograss	1–2
Saint Augustine, zoysia, tall fescue, bluegrass	3–4
Common bermudagrass	4–5
Hybrid bermudagrass	5–6

produce a more uniform response for a long period of time. During summer months slow-release sources should be used (table 11-2).

Late fall applications of N are needed on commercial sites to maintain color into late season. Fall fertilization also reduces weed problems and promotes early spring recovery of lawns. Fall applications of fertilizer should include N and K at rates of 1 to 1.5 pounds per 1,000 square feet about 6 weeks prior to the average first frost date. Follow soil test recommendations for phosphorus, lime, and other fertilizer needs.

Environmental conditions, irrigation practices, and mowing practices need to be considered when developing fertilization practices. Soil conditions and shade are common environmental variables that affect fertilization practices. Sandy-textured soils generally need more frequent applications of fertilizer than clay or clay loam soils. Slow-release nitrogen sources maintain turf color for a much longer period on sandy-textured soils.

Light intensity (shade) has a significant effect on nitrogen requirements. Moderate shade might reduce nitrogen needs by 20 percent, but heavy shade might reduce nitrogen needs by 50 percent. Turfgrasses growing in shade cannot utilize the level of nutrients needed in full sunlight, and heavy fertilization under shaded conditions increases disease occurrence.

Irrigation practices also affect the response of lawns to nitrogen fertilization. Excessive application of water significantly increases leaching of fertilizer nutrients, N and K in particular. Overwatering results in less efficient use of fertilizer nutrients. Consequently, overwatering, a common occurrence on commercial properties, leads to higher fertilizer requirements.

Mowing practices also impact fertilizer requirements on commercial lawns. Where the property manger insists on removing grass clippings after each mowing, fertilizer requirements increase by about 30 percent.

Considering the effects of fertilization on turfgrass color, vigor, and growth, the professional lawn management contractor must establish a fertilization program based on grass variety, site conditions, watering practices, and mowing practices. For example, compare a bermudagrass lawns growing on a sandy soil where grass clippings are removed at each mowing to a bermudagrass lawn on a clay loam soil where clippings are recycled. Assuming both sites are properly watered, the lawn on the sandy soil with clippings removed may require a pound of N every three weeks to maintain the same color and density as the other lawn fertilized with a pound of N every five to six weeks. It may be the same grass under similar watering and mowing practices, yet one lawn requires twice as much nitrogen. Thus, the contractor must develop individual fertilization programs for each property the company maintains.

CULTIVATION PRACTICES

Aeration and vertical mowing may be routine maintenance practices on some properties, but other properties may not require either cultivation practice. Heavily thatched properties require vertical mowing (dethatching) to prevent scalping each time the lawn is mowed. Aeration also helps water management of heavily thatched lawns.

On sloping sites aeration may be a routine practice to improve water infiltration and reduce water runoff, even though the lawn management contractor may not be concerned about the more uniform appearance produced by aeration.

Cultivation practices, like other maintenance practices, must be developed according to individual site conditions. Since cultivation practices are expensive, the benefits must be evaluated in terms of their costs to the client. A heavily thatched lawn may cost a client more for additional water and pest management than for the dethatching operation. Likewise, aeration can be cost effective where water use, thatch, and nutrient and pesticide losses are reduced by aeration.

It is the responsibility of the contractor to determine the need for and value of dethatching and aeration. Compacted soils, excessive thatch, steep slopes, and poorly drained sites are characteristics of lawns that need cultivation. The frequency and intensity of cultivation practices depend on the severity of the above conditions.

Compacted sites are characteristically hard and droughty and have a poor turfgrass cover. Such sites respond to aeration by going longer between irrigations and by improving turfgrass color and density. Aeration may be needed at monthly intervals until turf color and density are restored to acceptable standards.

Excessive thatch might be defined as more than ¼ inch of a thatch layer in a bermudagrass or bluegrass lawn or 1 inch of thatch in Saint Augustine, centipedegrass, or tall fescue. Excess thatch leads to scalping after mowing, shorter intervals between watering, increased nitrogen needs, reduced effectiveness of weed control and pest management, and increased susceptibility to winterkill. Thatch reduction may require two or more vertical mowings per year; monthly aeration; and adjustments in mowing, watering, and fertilization practices. Mowing height should be gradually reduced and mowing frequency increased, frequency of watering reduced, and nitrogen applications reduced until thatch is reduced to an acceptable level.

Steep slopes may need regularly scheduled aeration to increase water retention on the slope and maintain a turf cover. Core aeration is the most effective method of increasing water retention on slopes. On heavy textured soils with very slow infiltration rates, monthly aerations may be needed.

Poorly drained sites also respond to aeration. Standing water and saturated soils are indicative of overwatering, low infiltration rates, layered soil profile, inadequate slope, or other problems. Such problems are temporarily improved by frequent aeration, but long-term solutions to the drainage problem should be suggested to property management.

WEED CONTROL

Weed control is an essential component of any commercial lawn management program. Cultural practices to promote healthy turf are an important part of the weed control program, but herbicides are frequently needed to control persistent weed problems.

On properties for which there are no records of weed problems, a fall preemerge application should be scheduled on nonoverseeded properties. Many annual winter grasses and broadleaved weeds can be prevented with the application.

Winter weeds that escape the preemerge application can be controlled in dormant bermudagrass with glyphosate (Roundup). In other grasses, a hormone-type product can be used for broadleaved weeds. Both postemerge products should be applied when weeds are immature and temperatures are above 50° F.

Summer annual grasses and broadleaved weeds require a spring application of a preemerge product. Crabgrass, grassburs, barnyardgrass, and other annual grasses are effectively controlled by timely preemerge products. To reduce injury to turfgrass, preemerge products should be applied after greenup of the turfgrass.

In bermudagrass turf MSMA plus a hormone-type product can be used to control most weeds that escape the preemerge application. In other grasses a hormone-type product can be used for broadleaved weeds. The hormone-type products should not be applied when temperatures are consistently above 85° F.

Perennial weeds such as dallisgrass and bahiagrass can be controlled by spot treatment with Roundup. In centipedegrass turf, bahiagrass, and bermudagrass can be selectively controlled by Poast, a postemerge product for grassy weeds.

PEST MANAGEMENT

Pest management is assumed to be part of the lawn management program by property managers. In fact, property managers do not want to see pest problems develop—they expect pest problems to be prevented.

Prevention of pest problems is the basis of any good lawn management program. Cultural practices including mowing, watering, and fertilizing help keep pest problems to a minimum. Frequent observation and monitoring of the turf help identify problems at an early stage of development, when they are most susceptible to chemical control. Finally, accurate diagnosis and corrective action controls most pest problems.

Occurrences of pest problems should be recorded so that predictions can be made about their development. Major pest problems, including brownpatch, chinch bugs, and white grubs, can be predicted with accuracy. Observing and monitoring pest populations during the critical period will help target chemical applications when they can be most effective.

An effective pest management program includes a calendar schedule of major pest problems for a specific site. Grass varieties, environmental conditions, and management practices need to be considered. For example, brownpatch would be expected in late fall on Saint Augustine grass lawns. Irrigation might be reduced to a minimum, high rates of soluble N fertilizers should be avoided, and grass clippings should be removed during fall months when brownpatch activity is highest. Preventative applications of fungicides might also be made during this period.

Likewise, chinch bug populations should be monitored during summer months on Saint Augustine grass lawns to make timely applications of insecticides. Adult chinch bugs can be found at most times in susceptible varieties of Saint Augustine grass. Insecticide treatments do not need to be made unless the immature stages are found in high numbers, twenty-five or more per square foot.

White grub populations also need to be monitored from midsummer through fall. On all grasses except bermudagrass, treatments for grubs are needed when counts are above four to five grubs per square foot. Bermudagrass lawns can tolerate higher populations of these insects, and needless and expensive applications of insecticides can be prevented.

When biological controls are available for insect problems, they should be the first choice of the lawn care operator. For example, milky spore disease is effective against the larvae (white grub) of the Japanese beetle. Also *Bacillus thuringiensis* is an effective biological control for armyworms, cutworms, and sod webworms.

Calibrating Equipment for Chemical and Fertilizer Applications to Turfgrass

Today's concern with the preservation of our environment, with the conservation of our resources, and with the cost of chemicals and fertilizers makes precise calibration of equipment a requirement for chemical and fertilizer applications. When excessive application of nitrogen fertilizers contaminates groundwater, wastes natural resources, and costs millions of dollars, precise calibration of equipment should be our concern. When excessive application of chemicals leads to the destruction of wildlife, a further waste of resources, and millions of wasted dollars, precise calibration must be our major concern. When excessive application of chemicals and fertilizers leads to damaged turf and ornamental plants in addition to wasted resources and dollars, there is no choice but to take the time to precisely calibrate equipment. Yet, homeowners, and even professional turf managers, often guess at a spreader setting or estimate the weight or volume of product to add to a sprayer. Guessing, estimating, and carelessness must be eliminated from chemical and fertilizer applications to turfgrass.

Today more than ever, the rate of application and the uniformity of application are as important as the chemical or fertilizer selected for use. Errors in rate or uniformity of applications lead to all of the problems associated with excessive applications—wasted resources, wasted dollars, injury to plants and wildlife, and damage to the environment—or with insufficient applications—ineffective response and wasted dollars.

Precise calibration of equipment is essential for accurate and efficient applications of chemicals and fertilizers. Calibration of applicators takes a little time and requires knowledge of a few principles, but the effort put into calibration is returned many fold.

The objective of precise calibration of equipment is accurate and efficient distribution of chemicals and fertilizers. Today, it is a violation of federal laws to apply chemicals at rates other than those specified on the product label. Not only are applicators subject to fines, but they may be held liable for damage to plants or to the environment for misapplication of chemicals.

GRANULAR APPLICATORS

Granular applicators are used for the distribution of dry fertilizer materials and granular formulations of chemicals—herbicides, fungicides, and insecticides. Granular applicators may be drop-type (or gravity flow) spreaders or centrifugal-type spreaders.

DROP-TYPE. Drop-type spreaders distribute materials between the wheels of the spreader as it is pushed or pulled across the turf. Drop-type spreaders operate by gravity flow of the material through the spreader opening. The rate of application is controlled by the width of the opening on the spreader and the speed of the applicator.

To calibrate a drop-type spreader the operator weighs the amount of material dispersed per unit area at a specific spreader setting and constant speed. The person who will make the actual application should be pushing the spreader or driving the tractor so that the speed during the actual application will be the same as the speed used during the calibration.

Some drop spreaders have a calibration tray that attaches beneath the spreader discharge. In this case, the operator makes a pass over a given distance, weighs the product collected in the tray, and calculates the rate of application per 1,000 square feet or per acre. In the absence of a calibration tray, the operator must either collect the material over plastic or concrete to obtain a weight or determine the loss of weight from the spreader when making a pass over a given area.

Calibration is a trial-and-error process. If the first spreader opening (setting) applies too much material, the opening should be reduced; if the first setting applies too little material, the opening should be increased. This process is repeated until the setting is found that distributes the targeted amount of material.

Measurements required to calibrate a drop-type spreader include the distance the operator covers and the weight of material applied. Obviously, a scale or balance of some type is required to determine weight. For small units a postage scale calibrated in ounces may be used.

Calculations should be kept simple to reduce the chance for errors. If the target application rate is in units per 1,000 square feet, measure the required distance to cover 100 or 200 square feet. For example, if you are using a 3-foot wide spreader, measure 33 feet or 66 feet for 100 or 200 square feet, respectively. Refer to table 11-3 to determine the appropriate distance to measure for a given spreader width.

After several passes over the distance to establish a consistent and practical speed, load the spreader and make a pass over the starting and ending lines that mark the distance. Be certain to travel at a consistent speed when crossing the starting and ending lines. Do not begin walking at the starting point or stop at the finish point. Collect the material from the calibration tray or from the surface between the two lines. Weigh the material in ounces or pounds. (If you have a scale that weighs in grams, convert the weight to ounces for the calculation using the relationship of 1 ounce equals 28.4 grams.)

Using one of the following equations, calculate the application rate and compare that figure to the target rate.

$$\frac{\text{ozs. product collected per 100 sq. ft. x 10}}{16} = \text{lbs. product per 1,000 sq. ft.}$$

$$\frac{\text{ozs. product collected per 200 sq. ft. x 5}}{16} = \text{lbs. product per 1,000 sq. ft.}$$

$$\frac{\text{lbs. product collected per 1/100 sq. ft. x 100}}{} = \text{lbs. product per acre}$$

For example, a lawn care operator wants to apply a 15-5-9 fertilizer at 10 pounds per 1,000 square feet using a 3-foot drop-type spreader. The operator measures a distance of 33 feet and marks the starting and ending points with stakes. After establishing a consistent walking speed, the operator loads the spreader, moves the spreader setting to 5, attaches the calibration tray provided with the spreader, and prepares to make a pass across the distance. The operator begins walking several feet before passing the starting stake so

Table 11-3. Distance to Measure to Cover 100 sq. ft. or 1/100 Acre of Turf

Width of Spreader	DISTANCE TO MEASURE (IN FEET) TO COVER SPECIFIED AREA	
	100 Sq. Ft.	1/100 Acre
2	50	—
3	33⅓	—
4	25	—
6	16⅔	72½
8	—	54½
10	—	43½
12	—	36⅓

that he is up to speed when he opens the spreader. The operator closes the spreader at the ending stake, but takes several steps past the stake so that his speed remains constant.

The operator dumps the fertilizer collected over the 33-foot distance into a plastic bag and weighs the contents. The operator finds that 12 ounces of the 15-5-9 fertilizer were collected. Using the first equation, the operator calculates that 7.5 pounds of product were applied per 1,000 square feet:

$$\frac{12 \text{ ozs. product collected per 100 sq. ft.} \times 10}{16} = \begin{array}{l} 7.5 \text{ lbs. product} \\ \text{per 1,000 sq. ft.} \end{array}$$

Therefore, the operator increases the spreader setting to 6.5 and makes another pass across the trial path. This time 16 ozs. of product are collected which is the operator's target rate:

$$\frac{12 \text{ ozs. product collected per 100 sq. ft.} \times 10}{16} = \begin{array}{l} 10 \text{ lbs. product} \\ \text{per 1,000 sq. ft.} \end{array}$$

It is important to recognize that the operator must calibrate the spreader for each formulation or brand of 15-5-9 fertilizer. A different brand of a 15-5-9 fertilizer may have granules of different size or density, thus requiring a different spreader setting.

CENTRIFUGAL SPREADERS

The same procedure is followed for centrifugal-type or cyclone spreaders; however, it may be more convenient to weigh the material remaining in the spreader instead of trying to collect the widely dispersed material. Thus, the operator would weigh the product put into the spreader and subtract the product remaining in the spreader after a trial run to determine the amount applied.

With cyclone spreaders the swath (width) that the spreader covers in a single pass must be measured for each product to be applied since it will vary according to the size and density of individual particles. Also, since the spreader covers a relatively large area, a 250- to 500-square foot trial area may be used instead of the 100 square feet recommended for small drop-type spreaders.

Use table 11-4 to determine the distance to travel to calibrate a cyclone spreader.

To calculate the amount of product applied per 1,000 square feet or per acre, use one of the following equations:

$$\frac{\text{oz. product applied per 250 sq. ft.} \times 4}{16} = \text{lbs. product per 1,000 sq. ft.}$$

$$\frac{\text{oz. product applied per 500 sq. ft.} \times 2}{16} = \text{lbs. product per 1,000}$$

$$\frac{\text{oz. product applied per 500 sq. ft.} \times 87}{16} = \text{lbs. product applied per acre}$$

For example, an operator has a spreader that covers a 6-foot wide swath when applying a granular fungicide. Desiring to apply the product at 7.5 pounds per 1,000 square feet of lawn, the operator measures a trial swath 42 feet long, puts 5 pounds of product into the spreader, and makes a pass across the trial path. After making a pass across the trial path, the operator weighs the material remaining in the spreader and finds it to be 3.9 pounds. Using the first equation for centrifugal, or cyclone, spreaders, he makes the following calculation:

$$\frac{(5.0 \text{ lbs.} - 3.9 \text{ lbs.}) \text{ per 250 sq. ft.} \times 4}{} = \text{lbs. product applied per 1,000 sq. ft.}$$

$$\frac{1.1 \text{ lbs. per 250 sq. ft.} \times 4}{} = 4.4 \text{ lbs. product per 1,000 sq. ft.}$$

Thus, at the setting used for the trial, the operator applies 4.4 pounds of fungicide per 1,000 square feet. Since the target rate is 7.5 pounds, the operator has the option of lowering the setting slightly and making twice as many passes over the area or increasing the setting significantly and making a single pass over the area. In either case, he must adjust the setting and make trial runs until the correct setting is found.

To avoid skips or overlaps at the full rate of product, calibrate the spreader to apply one-half the recommended rate of application and make two passes across the turf at right angles to one another or parallel to one another at intervals of one-half of the swath width. In this example, it would require applying 3.75 pounds (7.5 lbs. x ½) of product per 1,000 square feet per pass at intervals of 3 feet (6 ft. x ½).

LIQUID APPLICATORS
Hand-held backpack sprayers, hose-end sprayers, and boom-type sprayers

Table 11-4. Distance to Measure to Cover 250 sq. ft. or 500 sq. ft. of Turf

| Width of Spreader | DISTANCE TO MEASURE (IN FEET) TO COVER SPECIFIED AREA | |
	250 Sq. Ft.	*500 Ft.*
5	50	—
6	42	
7	35½	—
8	31	—
9	28	—
10	25	50
12	—	42
14	—	35½
16	—	31
18	—	28
20	—	25

Table 11-5. Length of Calibration Course for Hand-Held Nozzle Based on the Effective Spray Swath

Effective Swath Width (feet)	Length of Calibration Course (feet)
2	62½
3	42
4	31
5	25
6	21
7	18
8	15½
10	12½

are all used to apply wettable powders, dispersable granules, and liquid materials to turfgrass. All of these sprayers must be calibrated prior to making a chemical application to turf.

BACKPACK SPRAYERS. Two- to three-gallon backpack sprayers with a single hand-held nozzle are generally used to spray ornamental plants with fungicides and insecticides, to spot treat weeds, or to chemically edge along fences and buildings. Recommendations for mixing and spraying these products with a backpack sprayer usually suggest adding a specific weight or volume of product per gallon of water and spraying foliage to the point of runoff. Such sprayers work well for that type of chemical application.

Broadcast applications to turf with the backpack sprayer are not recommended without a pressure regulator to maintain a constant pressure. In combination with a compressed air or CO_2 cylinder and a pressure regulator, the backpack sprayer can be used for broadcast applications of chemicals.

To calibrate a backpack sprayer for broadcast applications, the operator must determine the volume of water per 1,000 square feet that the sprayer applies at a given pressure and pace. For example, an operator determines that at 30 psi he can cover 200 square feet with a quart of water walking or moving at a comfortable pace. Thus, he will be applying 5 quarts per 1,000 square feet. He may want to decrease the pressure slightly, walk or move at a slightly faster pace, or change nozzles so that he will be applying 1 gallon of water per 1,000 square feet. Then, if he has a 2-gallon sprayer, he adds enough product to cover 2,000 square feet and fills the sprayer to the 2-gallon mark.

Another procedure to calibrate a hand-held backpack sprayer is to determine the effective swath (width) the operator makes from left to right as he walks with the sprayer and use the following procedure to calculate the volume of water applied per 1,000 square feet.

Step 1. Measure the effective spray swath in feet, that is, the width the spray covers as the operator moves the nozzle from left to right. This is most effectively measured on concrete where the spray pattern is clearly visible.

Step 2. Refer to table 11-5 to determine the length of the calibration course.

Step 3. Record the time required to walk the calibration course spraying from left to right as during the actual application.

Step 4. Maintaining operating pressure, catch the water for a time equal to that required to walk the calibration course.

Step 5. Measure the volume of water caught in pints. The pints of water caught equals the gallons of water applied per 1,000 square feet. To adjust the volume of water applied, the operator may change nozzle size, operating pressure, or walking pace.

For example, an operator using a hand-held nozzle attached to a backpack sprayer covers a swath 4 feet wide while walking at a pace that allows time to uniformly wet the turf (or concrete). Using information in table 11-5, the operator measures a 31-foot long calibration course. The operator times a trial pass over the calibration course. After determining it required 60 seconds, the operator then measures the volume of water the sprayer applies in 60 seconds. He collects 12 ounces of water in 60 seconds. To convert to pints he divides by 16 (16 ounces equals 1 pint). Thus, he collected .75 pints ($^{12}/_{16}$) over the calibration course, an amount equivalent to 0.75 gallons of water per 1,000 square feet. When he sprays his lawn with this sprayer at the same pressure, he puts in enough product to spray 1,000 square feet for each 3 quarts (.75 gallons) of spray solution.

HOSE-END SPRAYERS. Hose-end sprayers are used to apply fungicides, insecticides, herbicides, and liquid fertilizers to turf. Since hose-end sprayers operate from water pressure, they need to be calibrated at the water outlet from which they will be operated. Hose-end sprayers should be calibrated on concrete where the spray pattern is clearly visible. Also, you can better judge how fast to move to thoroughly wet the turf (concrete) without puddling water.

Add a pint or quart of water to the reservoir of the hose-end sprayer, open the water outlet, and spray the concrete uniformly until the reservoir is empty. Calculate the area wet by the sprayer by multiplying the width times the length of the wet surface. Then, add enough product to cover the area wet by a quart of water, fill the reservoir to one quart, and make the application.

For example, a homeowner wants to apply Ortho's Chickweed and Clover Control to her lawn with a hose-end sprayer. She determines that 1 pint of water covers 300 square feet at her pace. The product label recommends 4 ounces of product per 600 square feet. Thus, she adds 2 ounces of product and fills to 1 quart (2 pints) with water (2 x 300 sq. ft. equals 600 sq. ft.). Each quart of her reservoir should cover 600 square feet of lawn.

BOOM SPRAYERS. Boom sprayers are used for broadcast applications of chemicals and fertilizer to large turf areas. Boom sprayers can be precisely calibrated to apply materials uniformly at a recommended rate. As with other sprayers, operating pressure, nozzle size and spacing, and operating speed determine the volume of water applied per 1,000 square feet or per acre. For most products, 1 to 2 gallons of water per 1,000 square feet is a desirable application rate. For some herbicides, however, only 0.5 gallon of water per 1,000 square feet is the target application rate. Remember also that the higher the volume of water applied, the more frequently the tank must be refilled. When spraying large acreage, applicators prefer lower volumes of water.

To calibrate a boom sprayer the operator must determine the volume of water per 1,000 square feet or per acre that the sprayer applies at a given pressure and speed. There are several methods to measure this volume. The following procedure simplifies the operation and can be used for most boom sprayers.

Step 1. Measure the distance (in inches) between nozzles on the boom.

Step 2. Refer to table 11-6 for the length of the calibration course.

Step 3. Measure the calibration course.

Step 4. Record the time required to drive or walk the calibration course at a practical speed or pace.

Step 5. While the sprayer is stationary, collect the water from one nozzle for the time equal to that needed to drive or walk the calibration course. The sprayer must be maintained at the operating pressure to be used for the application.

Step 6. Measure the volume (in ounces) of water caught. The number of ounces equals the gallons of water applied per acre.

Step 7. Adjust the pressure, speed, or nozzle size to achieve the desired volume. Repeat the procedure until you are close to the desired volume.

Step 8. Check the volume of several nozzles. The volumes from different nozzles should be within 10 percent of each other.

Table 11-6. Length of Calibration Course for Boom Sprayers Based on Nozzle Spacings

Nozzle Spacing (inches)	Length of Calibration Course (feet)
12	340
14	291
16	255
18	227
20	204
25	163
30	136
40	102

CALIBRATION EXAMPLES

An operator wants to apply MSMA to a football field to control dallisgrass. The operator purchases Daconate 6 which contains 6 pounds MSMA per gallon. The label recommends applying 3 pounds MSMA per acre in 50 gallons of water. The operator has a 12-foot boom (nozzles spaced 18 inches apart) sprayer with a 50-gallon tank. Using table 11-6 he marks off a 227-foot calibration course, adjusts the pressure to 20 psi, and drives the calibration course. He records 65 seconds to travel the 227 feet. He parks the tractor or other vehicle used to pull the sprayer and collects the water from one nozzle for 65 seconds. He measures the volume and finds it to be 35 ounces, or 35 gallons of water per acre. Thus, he increases the operating pressure to 25 and measures the output for 65 seconds from the same nozzle. This time the operator records 48 ounces, or 48 gallons per acre. He measures the output from 3 other nozzles and gets 46, 51, and 53 gallons per acre. All of these are within 10 percent of the average and are very close to the desired rate of 50 gallons per acre.

The operator then adds 2 quarts of Daconate 6 (3 pounds of MSMA) to the tank and fills it to 50 gallons. His tank should cover one acre.

Another operator has a small hand-held boom sprayer with nozzles 12 inches apart. Using information in table 11-6 he measures a course of 170 feet (340/2) and times a trial pass over the course. He required 45 seconds to walk the 170 feet. Thus, he collects the spray from one nozzle for 90 seconds (2 x 45 secs.) He measures the volume at 60 ounces, which is equivalent to 60 gallons of water per acre. Since he only needs to spray small areas, he converts gallons per acre to gallons per 1,000 square feet by dividing by 43.56 (43,560 sq. ft. per acre). Thus, the sprayer applies 1.38 gallons of water per 1,000 square feet. If he has a 50-gallon spray tank, he can cover 50/1.38 or 36,000 square feet of lawn with each tank. Then, the operator adds enough product to the tank to cover 36,000 square feet of lawn. In the case of Daconate, he adds 0.5 gallons times 36,000/43,560, or .41 gallons (52 ounces).

References

Anslow, R. C. 1965. The rate of appearance of leaves on tillers of the gramineae. *Herb. Abs.* 36 (36):149–55.

Aspelin, A. L. 1994. Pesticide sales and usage. *1992 and 1993 Market Estimates*. U.S. Environmental Protection Agency, Washington, D.C. 33 pp.

Barrios, E. P.; F. J. Sundstrom; D. Babcock; and L. Leger. 1986. Quality and yield response of four warm-season grasses to shade. *Agro. J.* 78:270–73.

Beard, J. B. 1965. Factors in the adaptation of turfgrasses to shade. *Agro. J.* 57:457–59.

————. *Turfgrass Science and Culture*. Englewood Cliffs, N.J.: Prentice-Hall Inc.

Beard, J. B., and R. L. Green. 1994. The role of turfgrasses in environmental protection and their benefits to humans. *Journal of Environmental Quality* 23:452–68.

Bingaman, D. E., and H. Kohnke. 1970. Evaluating sands for athletic turf. *Agro. J.* 62:464–67.

Biran, I.; B. Bravdo; I. Bushkin-Haran; and E. Rawitz. 1981. Water consumption and growth rate of 11 turfgrasses as affected by mowing height, irrigation frequency, and soil moisture. *Agro. J.* 73:85–90.

Bonnett, O. T. 1961. *The Plant: Its Histology and Development*. Bulletin 672. Univ. of Ill. Agri. Exp. Sta. 112 pp.

Booysen, P. V.; M. M. Tainton; and J. D. Scott. 1963. Shoot apex development in grasses and its importance in grassland management. *Herb. Ab.* 33 (4):209–13.

Brown, K. W., and R. L. Duble. 1975. Physical characteristics of soil mixtures for golf green construction. *Agro. J.* 67:647–52.

Burton, G. W. 1943. A comparison of the first year's root production of seven warm season grasses. *Agro. J.* 35:192–96.

————. 1951. The adaptability and breeding of suitable grasses for the south. *Adv. Agro.* 3:197–241.

Burton, G. W.; E. H. DaVane; and R. L. Carter. 1954. Root distribution and activity in southern grasses. *Agro. J.* 46:229–33.

Burton, G. W.; G. M. Prine; and J. E. Jackson. 1957. Drought tolerance and water use of several southern grasses. *Agro. J.* 49:498–503.

Callahan, L. M. 1977. *Performance of Kentucky bluegrass under lawn conditions*. Rpt. 104. Univ. of Tenn. Farm and Home Science.

Carrow, R. N.; B. J. Johnson; and G. W. Landry. 1988. Centipedegrass response to foliar applications of iron and nitrogen. *Agro. J.* 84:746–50.

Childers, N. F., and D. G. White. 1947. *Manila Grass for Lawns.* USDA Circular 26. Meyaguay, Puerto Rico. 16 pp.

Cooper, J. P. 1958. Pattern of bud development of the shoot apex and its ecological significance. *J. of Ecology* 39:228–78.

Cooper, J. P., and N. M. Tainton. 1968. Light and temperature requirements for the growth of tropical and temperate grasses. *Herb. Abs.* 38 (3):167–76.

Craig, R. M. 1974. Coastal dune vegetation. *Proc. Fla. State Hortic. Soc.* 87:548–52.

Crews, D. E., and W. B. Gilbert. 1974. Manganese toxicity to pencross bentgrass. Master's thesis. North Carolina State University, Raleigh.

Davis, W. B. 1973. Sands and their place on the golf course. *Southern Golf Course Operations* 4 (4):9–10.

Davis, W. B.; J. L. Paul; J. H. Madison; and L. Y. George. 1970. *A Guide to Evaluating Sands and Amendments Used for High Trafficked Turfgrass.* Univ. of Calif. Agri. Ext. AKT-n113. 93 pp.

Dean, H. A.; M. F. Schuster; J. C. Boling; and P. T. Riherd. 1979. Complete biological control of *Antonina graminis* in Texas with *Neodusmatia sangwani. Bulletin of the Entomological Society of America* 25 (4):262–67.

Dickens, R., and J. Pedersen. 1985. *AU Centennial: A New Centipedegrass.* Circular 281. Alabama Agri. Exp. Sta. 6 pp.

DiPaola, J. M.; J. B. Beard; and H. Brausand. 1982. Seasonal root growth of bermudagrass and Saint Augustine grass. *Hort. Science* 17 (5):829–31.

Dittmer, H. J. 1938. A quantitative study of the subterranean members of three grasses. *Amer. J. Bot.* 25:654–57.

Duble, R. L. 1987. Herbicide injury symptoms on selected trees and shrubs. *Southern Turfgrass* 22 (2):14–15.

Dobie, Mrs. Frank J. 1972. The pleasure Frank Dobie took in grass. Speech presented at Texas A&M University, College Station.

Dudeck, A. E., and H. C. Peacock. 1985. Effects of salinity on seashore paspalum. *Agro. J.* 77:47–50.

Evans, M. W. 1940. Developmental morphology of the growing point in grasses. *J. Agri. Res.* 61 (7):481–520.

————. 1949. *Vegetative Growth, Development, and Reproduction in Kentucky Bluegrass.* Bulletin 681. Ohio Agri. Exp. Sta. 39 pp.

Esau, K. 1943. Ontogeny of the vascular bundle in *Zea mays. Hilgardia* 15 (3):327–68.

Fitts, O. B. 1925. Preliminary studies on fine grasses under turf conditions. *USGA Green Section Bulletin* 5 (3):58–62.

Forbes, I.; B. P. Robinson; and J. M. Latham. 1955. Emerald zoysia: An improved hybrid lawn grass for the South. *Golf Course Report* 23 (2):22.

Frolik, E. F., and F. D. Keim. 1940. *Buffalograss for Lawns.* Circular 63. Nebraska Agri. Exp. Sta. 8 pp.

Frost, K. R., and H. C. Schwalen. 1955. Sprinkler evaporation losses. *Agri. Engineering.* 36:526–28.

Gibeault, V. A. 1985. *Turfgrass Water Conservation.* Publication No. 21405. Cooperative Extension, University of California, Division of Agriculture and Natural Resources.

Gibeault, V. A.; R. Austio; S. Spaulding; and V. B. Youngner. 1980. *Calif. Turfgrass Culture* 30:9–11.

Gilbert, W. B., and D. L. Davis. 1971. Influence of fertilizer ratios on winter hardiness of bermudagrass. *Agro. J.* 63:591–93.

Goss, R. L. 1970. Some interrelationships between nutrition and turfgrass diseases. In: *Proceedings First International Turfgrass Research Conference*, Bingley, England. pp. 351–61.

Grau, F. V., and A. M. Radko. 1951. Meyer zoysia. *USGA J. and Turf Management* 4 (6):30–31.

Hall, M. H. 1995. Root responses of bermudagrass to mowing height and frequency. Master's thesis, Texas A&M University, College Station. Forthcoming.

Hansen, M. C. 1962. Physical properties of calcined clays and their utilization for root zones. Master's thesis, Purdue University, West Lafayette, Ind.

Hanson, A. A.; F. V. Juska; and G. W. Burton. 1969. *Turfgrass Science*. Madison, Wis.: Amer. Soc. of Agro. 715 pp.

Hanson, A. A., and F. V. Juska. 1961. Winter root activity in Kentucky bluegrass. *Agro. J.* 53:372–74.

Harlan, J. R.; J. M. DeWet; W. W. Huffine; and J. R. Deakin. 1970. *A Guide to the Species of* Cynodon. Bulletin 673. Oklahoma Agri. Exp. Sta. 37 pp.

Harrison, C. M. 1934. Responses of Kentucky bluegrass to variations in temperature, light, cutting, and fertilization. *Plant Phys.* 9:83–106.

Hooper, B. 1970. The real change has just begun. *Life.* 68 (1):102–106.

Hoveland, C. S. 1961. *Bahiagrass for Forage in Alabama*. Circular 140. Auburn University Agri. Exp. Sta. 19 pp.

Hummel, N. W. 1993. USGA recommendations for a method of putting green construction. *USGA Green Section Record*. March/April, 1–21.

Hyder, D. N. 1972. Defoliation in relation to vegetative growth. In: *The Biology and Utilization of Grasses*. Edited by V. B. Youngner and C. M. McKell, pp. 304–17. New York: Academic Press.

Johns, D., Jr. 1976. Physical properties of various soil mixtures used for golf green construction. Master's thesis, Texas A&M University, College Station.

Juska, F. V., and A. A. Hanson. 1964. *Bermudagrass Varieties for General Purpose Turf*. USDA Handbook 270. Washington, D.C.

Kaempffe, G. C., and O. R. Lung. 1967. Availability of various fractions of urea-formaldehyde. *J. Agri. Food Chem.* 15 (6):967–71.

Kaplan, R., and S. Kaplan. 1989. *The Experience of Nature*. New York: Cambridge University Press.

Klein, M. G. 1982. Biological suppression of turf insects. In: *Advances in Turfgrass Entomology*. Edited by H. D. Niemczyk and B. G. Joyner, pp. 91–95. Columbus, Ohio: ChemLawn Corp.

Kleinig, C. R. 1966. *Mats of unincorporated organic matter underirrigated pasture*. *Aust. J. Agri. Res.* 17:327–33.

Kneebone, W. R. 1979. *Kentucky Bluegrass Lawns in Arizona*. Bulletin Q390. Univ. of Arizona Cooperative Ext. Ser. 2 pp.

Krans, J. V., and J. B. Beard. 1985. Effect of clipping on growth of Marion Kentucky bluegrass. *Crop Sci.* 25:17–20.

Kurtz, K. W. 1975. The selection and management of turf for shaded areas. *California Turfgrass Culture* 25 (3):17–21.

Ledeboer, F. B., and C. R. Skogley. 1967. Investigations into the nature of thatch and methods of its decomposition. *Agro. J.* 59:320–23.

Letey, J.; W. C. Morgan; S. J. Richards; and N. Valoras. 1966. Effect of oxygen diffusion rate on root growth. *Agro. J.* 58:531–35.

Leopold, A. C. 1949. The control of tillering in grasses by Auxin. *J. of Botany* 36:437–40.

Liu, Z. W.; R. L. Jarret; R. R. Duncan; and S. Kresovich. 1994. Genetic relationships and variation of ecotypes of seashore paspalum (*Paspalum vaginatum*). *Genome* 37:1011–17.

Long, J. A., and E. C. Bashaw. 1961. Microsporogenesis and chromosome numbers in Saint Augustinegrass. *Crop Sci.* 1:42–43.

Longenecker, D. E., and P. J. Lyerly. 1974. Control of Soluble Salts in Farming and Gardening. Texas Agri. Exp. Sta. B-876. 36 pp.

McBee, G. G., and E. C. Holt. 1966. Shade tolerance studies on bermudagrass and other turfgrasses. *Agro. J.* 58:523–25.

Maas, E. V. 1986. Salt tolerance of plants. *Applied Agri. Res.* 1 (1):12–26.

Madison, J. H. 1971. *Practical Turfgrass Management.* New York : Van Nostrand Reinhold Co.

Madison, J. H.; J. L. Paul; and W. B. Davis. 1974. Alternative method of greens management. *Proceedings of Second International Turfgrass Research Conference.* Madison, Wis. 431–37.

Markland, R. E., and E. C. Roberts. 1965. Influence of varying nitrogen and potassium levels on growth of bentgrass. *Agron Abstr.* p. 46.

Meinhold, V. H.; R. L. Duble; R. W. Weaver; and E. C. Holt. 1973. Thatch accumulation in bermudagrass turf. *Agro. J.* 65:833–35.

Menn, W. G., and G. G. McBee. 1970. A study of nutritional requirements for Tifgreen bermudagrass. *Agro. J.* 62:192–94.

Moser, L. E.; S. R. Anderson; and R. W. Miller. 1968. Rhizome and tiller development of bluegrass as influenced by photoperiod, cold treatment, and variety. *Agro. J.* 60:632–35.

Niemczyk, H. D., and H. R. Krueger. 1982. Binding of insecticides on turfgrass thatch. In: *Advances in Turfgrass Entomology.* Edited by H. D. Niemczyk and B. G. Joyner, pp. 61–69. Columbus, Ohio: ChemLawn Corp.

Nutter, G. C. 1955. Characteristics and production of centipedegrass turf. *Bulletin of Florida Turf Assoc.* 2 (3):6–8.

Oswalt, D. L.; A. R. Bertrand; and M. R. Teel. 1959. Influence of nitrogen fertilization and clipping on grass roots. *Soil Sci. Soc. Proc.* 23:228–30.

Potts, R. C., and Barlow Irwin. 1957. Kyle Field gets a new turf. Press release. Texas A&M University.

Powell, A. J.; R. E. Blaser; and R. E. Schmidt. 1967a. Effect of nitrogen on winter root growth of bentgrass. *Agro. J.* 59:529–30.

———. 1967b. Physiological aspects of turfgrass with fall and winter nitrogen. *Agro. J.* 59:303–307.

Ralston, D. C., and W. H. Daniel. 1973. Effect of porous rootzone materials underlined with plastic on the growth of creeping bentgrass. *Agro. J.* 65:229–32.

Reinert, J. A. 1982. A review of host resistance in turfgrasses to insects with emphasis on the southern chinch bug. In: *Advances in Turfgrass Entomology.* Edited by H. D. Niemczyk and B. G. Joyner, pp. 3–12. Columbus, Ohio: ChemLawn Corp.

Reinert, J. A., and H. D. Niemczyk. 1982. Southern chinch bug resistance to organophosphates in Florida. In: *Advances in Turfgrass Entomology.* Edited by H. D. Niemczyk and B. G. Joyner, pp. 77–81. Columbus, Ohio: ChemLawn Corp.

Reeves, S. A.; G. G. McBee; and M. E. Bloodworth. 1970. Effect of N, P, and K tissue levels and late fall fertilization on cold hardiness in bermudagrass. *Agro. J.* 62:659–62.

Reeves, S. A., and G. G. McBee. 1972. Nutritional influences on cold hardiness of St. Augustine grass. *Agro. J.* 64:447–50.

Roberts, E. C., and E. J. Bredakis. 1960. Turfgrass root development. *Golf Course Reporter.* 28 (8):12–24.

Roser, C. H. 1931. Golf course costruction practices. *American Landscape Architect,* September.

Sauer, J. D. 1972. Revision of *Stenotaphrum* with attention to its historical geography. *Brittonia* 24:202–22.

————. Letter to author, May 22, 1971.

Scott, J. M. 1920. Bahiagrass. *Agro. J.* 12:112–14.

Seginer, Ido. 1967. Net losses in sprinkler irrigation. *Agro. Meteorol.* 4:281–91.

Sellers, W. D. 1965. *Physical Climatology.* Chicago: University of Chicago Press.

Sharman, B. C. 1945. Leaf and bud initiation in the graminae. *Botanical Gazette* 106:269–89.

Shih, S. F., and G. H. Snyder. 1985. Water-table effects on pasture yield and evaporation. *Transactions of the Amer. Soc. of Agri. Eng.* 28 (5):1573–77.

Sifers, S. I.; J. B. Beard; and M. H. Hall. 1990. Cutting height requirements of seashore paspalum (Adalayd). Prog. Rpt. 4764. Tex. Agri. Exp. Sta. 1 p.

Stuckey. I. H. 1941. Seasonal growth of grass roots. *Amer. J. of Bot.* 28:436–91.

————. 1942. Some effects of photoperiod on leaf growth. *Amer. J. Bot.* 29:92–97.

Tashiro, H. 1982. The incidence of insecticide resistance in soil-inhabiting turfgrass insects. In: *Advances in Turfgrass Entomology.* Edited by H. D. Niemczyk and B. G. Joyner, pp. 81–84. Columbus, Ohio: ChemLawn Corp.

Taylor, T. H., and W. C. Templeton, Jr. 1966. Tiller and leaf behavior in orchardgrass. *Agro. J.* 58:189–92.

Thomas, J. C. 1994. Soil and tissue testing for turf management. *Texas Turfgrass* 47 (3):17–22.

Toler, R. L. 1972. *Floratam: A New Disease-Resistant St. Augustinegrass.* Bulletin L-1146. Texas Agri. Exp. Sta.

Turgeon, A. J. 1980. *Turgrass Management.* Reston, Va.: Reston Publishing Co.

Ulrich, R. S. 1986. Human responses to vegetation and landscapes. *Landscape Urban Planning* 13:29–44.

USGA Staff. 1993. USGA recommendations for a method of putting green construction. *USGA Green Section Record.* March–April, pp. 1–33.

Waddington, D. V.; T. L. Zimmerman; G. J. Shoop; L. T. Kardes; and J. M. Duich. 1974. *Physical Properties of Physically Amended Soils.* Pennsylvania Agri. Exp. Sta. Prog. Rept. 337. 96 pp.

Waddington, D. V.; E. L. Moberger; J. M. Duich; and T. L. Watschke. 1976. Long-term evaluation of slow-release nitrogen sources on turfgrass. *J. Amer. Soil Sci. Soc.* 40 (4):593–97.

Waddington, D. V.; J. M. Duich; and T. R. Turner. 1977. Turfgrass fertilization with IBDU and ureaform. *Proceedings of the Controlled Release Pesticide Symposium,* Corvallis, Oreg. 319–34.

Walker, T. J., and D. A. Nickle. 1981. Introduction and spread of pest mole crickets. *J. Ann. Entomological Soc.* 74:158–63.

Ward, C. Y., and R. E. Blaser. 1961. Carbohydrate reserves and leaf area in regrowth of orchardgrass. *Crop Sci.* 1:366–70.

Weaver, J. E., and E. Zink. 1946. Length of life of roots of ten species of perennial grasses. *Plant Physiol.* 21:201–17.

Weaver, R. W.; E. P. Dunigan; and J. F. Parr. 1974. The effects of two soil activators on soil microorganisms and crop yields in the southern U.S. Bulletin 189. Southern Cooperative Series. 24 pp.

Weinbrenn, C. 1948. Investigations into the germination of C. *dactylon* seed. In: *Experiments with* C. dactylon *species.* 76–85. Ladybrand, South Africa: South African Turf Research Station, Norco Printing Co.

Weinmann, H., and E. P. Goldsmith. 1948. Underground reserves of C. *dactylon.* In: *Experiments with* C. dactylon *at the South African Turf Research Center.* 56–75. Ladybrand, South Africa: Norco Printing Co.

Whitcomb, C. D. 1972. Influence of tree root competition on growth of four cool-season turfgrasses. *Agro. J.* 64:355–58.

Wilkinson, J. F. 1977. Understanding slow-release nitrogen. *Weeds, Trees, and Turf* June:12–18.

Wilkinson, J. F., and D. T. Duff. 1972. Effects of fall fertilization on cold tolerance, color, and growth of Kentucky bluegrass. *Agro. J.* 64:345–48.

Wilkinson, J. F., and J. B. Beard. 1974. Morphological responses of *Poa pratensis* and *Festuce rubra* to reduced light. *Proceedings Second International Turfgrass Research Conference. Amer. Soc. of Agro.,* Blacksburg, Va. 231–40.

Wilson, F. L. 1961. *St. Augustine Lawn Grasses.* University of Florida Agri. Circular 217. 15 pp.

Winstead, C. W., and C. Y. Ward. 1974. Persistence of southern turfgrasses in a shade environment. *Proceedings Second International Turfgrass Research Conference,* Amer. Soc. of Agro., Blacksburg, Va. 221–30.

Youngner, V. B. 1969. Physiology of growth and development. *Turfgrass Science, Agronomy Monograph* 14:187–216.

———. 1980. Zoysiagrasses in California. *Calif. Turfgrass Culture* 30 (1):1–2.

Youngner, V. B.; V. A. Gibeault; and J. R. Breece. 1972. Turf bermudagrasses. *California Turfgrass Culture* 22 (1):1–3.

Youngner, V. B., and C. M. McKell, eds. 1972. *The Biology and Utilization of Grasses.* New York: Academic Press.

Youngner, V. B.; F. Nudge; and R. Ackerson. 1976. Growth of bluegrass leaves and tillers with and without defoliation. *Crop Sci.* 16:110–13.

Index

ISBN 1-58544-161-9

90000